James Chrystal

A History of the Modes of Christian Baptism

James Chrystal

A History of the Modes of Christian Baptism

ISBN/EAN: 9783337226442

Printed in Europe, USA, Canada, Australia, Japan

Cover: Foto ©Lupo / pixelio.de

More available books at **www.hansebooks.com**

A HISTORY OF THE MODES OF CHRISTIAN BAPTISM

FROM

HOLY SCRIPTURE, THE COUNCILS ECUMENICAL AND PROVINCIAL, THE FATHERS, THE SCHOOLMEN, AND THE RUBRICS OF THE WHOLE CHURCH EAST AND WEST,

IN

ILLUSTRATION AND VINDICATION OF THE RUBRICS OF THE CHURCH OF ENGLAND SINCE THE REFORMATION, AND THOSE OF THE AMERICAN CHURCH.

BY

REV. JAMES CHRYSTAL, A.M.,
A PRESBYTER OF THE PROTESTANT EPISCOPAL CHURCH.

———

PHILADELPHIA:
LINDSAY AND BLAKISTON.
1861.

PREFACE.

A WORD in explanation of the objects of this work. It is an apology for the belief of the early Church, that Christ enjoined trine immersion. Its aim is to show that the preference expressed by the present rubric of the Church of England and the other British Churches is one well founded in Scripture and in Christian antiquity, and the mistaken, though it is charitably presumed well meant endeavors of those who excuse its violation. The task is one which becomes every year more difficult, as the landmarks set up by the hand of sound theological learning are gradually disappearing before ignorance and prejudice. A late style of interpretation not only opposes the mode enjoined in the rubric, but spurns the testimony and wishes of our older and more erudite divines. In so defending the teaching of the rubric and the primitive Church, the author deems that he acts in accordance with the letter and spirit of his ordination vow, to give his "faithful diligence always so to minister the doctrine and *sacraments*, and the discipline of Christ, as the Lord hath commanded and as this Church hath received the same according to the commandments of God."

As the subject of the modes of Christian baptism is generally treated of not thoroughly and impartially, but wholly in a partisan spirit, he has undertaken at much expense of time and labor to examine and to translate the original records to which appeal is made, to give them as near as might be in their own words: strange as it may seem this had not been fully done. The subject of the modes of baptism has been in our own part of Christendom so mixed up with that of the subjects of baptism, that many are led to believe that there is a necessary connection between opposition to infant baptism and opposition to dipping and the contrary, than which nothing can be more unfounded, as the case of the Eastern Catholic or Orthodox Communion on the one side, and the Mennonites on the other, clearly shows. The modes are ordinarily treated as a sort of adjunct to the question of infant baptism in works written on that subject. Infant baptism presents a field of controversy almost exhausted by the profound Dr. Wall and those who have followed him. But it is a striking fact that the subject of the modes has been almost untouched, the late books, or rather parts of books, being little more than a rehash of what had preceded, with the addition only of some new blunder.

This it has been his endeavor to correct. In the execution of his task he has treated necessarily of the mode in the early Church and especially in the British Churches. These sources will throw light upon the American rubric.

On the other hand, while dealing with this subject, it naturally fell in with his purpose to glance at the origin of those Antipædobaptist sects who use immersion as the only mode, and who deem it invariably necessary, and to show by the confessions of their own founders and their early followers that all the baptismal succession which they claimed was what comes from men, on the Antipædobaptist theory unbaptized, mutually baptizing each other, and which began in the first half of the seventeenth century. These facts are so clear that no man who thoroughly investigates them in the pages of the earlier immersing Antipædobaptists and their opponents can doubt them.

This work will doubtless be found to possess many defects. He craves for it therefore at the hands of an intelligent religious public an impartial perusal, and the pointing out of all faults, that he may correct them.

WILMINGTON, DEL., June 11, 1861.

CONTENTS.

	PAGE
PREFACE, ...	xv
CHAP. I. Purpose of the Work, ...	25
II. Traces of Baptism before or contemporary with Christ. Proselyte Baptism, ...	31
III. Principles of Interpretation, ...	33
IV. Of the Mode as commanded by Christ, . . .	36
V. The Ancient Versions, ...	54
VI. Of the Mode practised by the Church during the early Centuries, and how far any Mode was enjoined by the Church; and of the Penalties of Violating or Changing the Mode.	
Sect. 1. The Fathers, ...	57
2. The Ecumenical Councils and Church Law,	88
3. The Greek Provincial Synods, . . .	97
4. The Latin Provincial Synods, . . .	99
5. Rubrics of different parts of the Western Church, regarding the Mode, . . .	108
6. Baptismal Offices of the Catholic Church of the East, or Orthodox Church, . .	119
7. Rubrics of Eastern Errorists, . . .	121
VII. Of Changes in the Mode, and of the Contests between the Greek and Latin Churches, . . .	143
VIII. The Trine Immersion, ...	155

CONTENTS.

	PAGE
CHAP. IX. Of admitting the Compends as Valid Baptism,	163
X. Of the Mode in the Church of England,	174
XI. Anglican Theologians who favor the Primitive Mode, or its restoration in practice,	188
XII. The American Rubrics,	205
XIII. The Remedy,	211
XIV. Baptisteries: Ancient Baptismal Rites,	218
XV. Testimony of the Greek Church,	220
XVI. Writers of the Latin Communion,	231
XVII. Writers of the Lutheran and Reformed Communions,	234
XVIII. The Antipædobaptist Sects and their Weak Points,	237
XIX. Conclusion,	265

APPENDIX.

A. Passages of Holy Writ relating to Baptism disputed among later authors,	273
B. Total Immersion in Baptism,	285
C. The Apostolical Constitutions,	285
D. Council of Nice,	286
E. Canon VII of the Second Ecumenical Council,	286
F. Ancient Pictures of Baptism,	287
G. Fonts,	289
H. Intrusion into other men's Dioceses,	290
I. Menno on the Mode,	294
J. Whence did Menno and the Mennonites derive their Baptism?	300
K. Rise of the Baptists in England,	302
L. Blount's Mission,	305

		PAGE
M.	The Baptism of the first Immersing Antipædobaptist congregation in England,	307
N.	Date of the adoption among English Antipædobaptists of the idea that Immersion is essential,	311
O.	Baptismal succession among the Tunkers or Dunkers,	312
P.	Whence the Antipædobaptists derive their Baptism?	313

ERRATA.

Page 76, "Century IV" should be placed before "Athanasius," on p. 69.
" 86, "Segin" should be "Segni."
" 96, line 40, "previous to" should be "at."
" 108, line 20, insert "Western" before "Church regarding the Mode."
" 119, omit "Division I" in line 30.
" 168, line 21, for "The Eastern patriarchates would," read "Would the Eastern patriarchates do," &c.
" 170, line 42, "Anabaptists" should be "Antipædobaptists."
" 171, line 3, Do. do. do.
" 172, line 35, after "$\beta a\pi\tau\iota\sigma\mu o\varsigma$" add "$\beta\acute{a}\pi\tau\iota\sigma\mu a$."
" 215, line 24, "who" should be "which."
" 215, line 26, "restitution" should be "restoration."

ON THE

MODES OF BAPTISM.

CHAPTER I.

PURPOSE OF THE WORK.

IN writing a history of the modes of baptism, we have deemed it best to range the facts in accordance with particular rubrics, first, because not only have they fallen into neglect, but because the reasons for them are almost forgotten among the mass, and because, naturally, the contents of such a work cluster about such centres of theory and practice. But the author has endeavored by presenting historical truth, as near as might be in the words of the actors themselves, to make it not without its value to impartial men of all creeds. He has endeavored to state every event, not so as to make it fit a preconceived theory of his own, but as it is. The citations from original authorities, from the Latins who flourished from Tertullian to Innocent the Third; that is, from the end of the second century to the thirteenth; and those from the Greeks, beginning with the Apostolic Fathers, and ending with Andreas Cretensis of the eighth century, he has labored to make more complete than now exist elsewhere. Of the former, there are in Migne's Cursus Completus 217 volumes; of the latter 98.

Every rubric which could be found of the whole church, East and West, with many of those of heretical bodies, will be found translated, with the references. Those passages of the Fathers which are often so quoted as to give an imperfect and false view, he has tried to correct by fuller references to their works. The view of the Greek Church he has given in the words of Greeks and Russians themselves, and from their own acknowledged formularies.

To the Churchman, the history of the mode in the English, and in the early church, with the statements of the Fathers, and the more learned Anglican and American divines, may not be uninteresting.

The present rubric of the Church of England for the "Public Baptism of Infants," reads as follows: "And then naming it after them (if they shall certify him that the child may well endure it), he (the priest) SHALL DIP it in the water discreetly and warily, saying, N., I baptize thee," etc. "*But if they certify that the child is weak, it shall suffice to pour water upon it.*"

In the office for the "Private Baptism of Infants," which is to be used only when need compels, the words are: "Then let the priest baptize it in the form before appointed for public baptism of infants; saving, that at the dipping of the child in the font, he shall use this form of words: 'If thou art not already baptized, N., I baptize thee,'" &c.

In the office for the Public Baptism of such as are of riper years, the dipping is mentioned first.

From the first two rubrics, which are all that relate to the baptism of infants, the following truths are evident:

1. That the Church of England teaches the doctrine of infant baptism.

2. That she nowhere enjoins or authorizes sprinkling in her rubrics.

3. That for healthy children, afflicted with no weakness, her uniform rule, from which any deviation is irregular and unauthorized, is immersion.

4. That she allows pouring only when they certify that the child is weak, and that this is allowed at no other time.

Ecclesiastical history makes clear still another fact, which we will number 5: that the whole church, since the days of St. Cyprian, has ever deemed either sprinkling or pouring as valid in case of necessity, when alone these rubrics admit it.

For proof of these statements, see below, in the chapters relating to the Church of England, the sentiments of her divines, and the rubrics of the church since the Reformation, including the present, all which are there given.

The rubric of the American Church, although changed, still places immersion first, leaving undecided the number of immersions, whether single or trine. The allusions of the office to mode point to dipping and nothing else, and the two bishops who alone constituted the upper house at the time of the revision, both thought, as their own writings show, that this mode was "the general practice of the primitive church," so that the object of the alteration was not a desire on their part to favor other modes at the expense of dipping. Indeed, Bishop Seabury states clearly "that the original mode of Christian baptism was . . . . by washing or immersing the whole body in water." He adds: "This, too, seems most congruous to the general expressions of Holy Scripture."* And Bishop White uses language which shows both solemnity of feeling and sound learning. He says: "Whether baptism ought to be by immersion, or by affusion, I dare not deny or conceal, that in the Gospel age, and for some ages afterwards, the former was the usual mode."†

He pleads for the restoration of immersion, and describes "the present general practice as a deviation from what it was originally, which it is desirable to restore to the standard of the rubrics, as they were framed in the Church of England; and as they continue to this day in the liturgy of that and of the American Church, although fallen by universal custom into neglect."‡ So far were these venerable men from condemning this preference of the rubric of the English church in favor of dipping.

To enforce more particularly the points above stated under 2, 3, 4, and 5, will be the object of the present work. The question of the subjects of baptism has been set at rest by the universal custom of the church in all ages in admitting infants through the door of baptism into the fold of Christ, and to a share of covenant blessings, which custom is enjoined in the words of baptism *as these words were understood by the Apostles and their immediate successors.*§

---

* v. his Sermons, vol. i, Disc. iii.
† v. On the Catech., Lect. v.
‡ v. Id. Diss. vii.
§ Consult, on the whole subject of the baptism of infants, the masterly and almost exhaustive work of Wall,—History of Infant Baptism. "Jerram and Wall," though brief, is still excellent in its way. v. also Hodges.

We deal only, or at least mainly, with the question of the mode.

And, with respect to this, we propose to show from Holy Scripture, Councils, Fathers, and the Baptismal Offices of the whole church, and from the most learned divines of all creeds, and particularly those of our own church, that this preference of the rubric is based upon the unanimous authority of the primitive and Apostolic church, and that this immersion was trine, not single, and that while the church has admitted other modes than this as valid, yet that such modes were regarded as "divine compends," and were resorted to only as such, and in cases of necessity alone. This will correspond with the teaching of the rubric.

The importance of a careful and candid consideration of this whole subject of the mode will be seen at once. It is a matter for unceasing controversy in every part of the church, unreformed and reformed. In the East and Western Europe, we find the Greek Church branding the affusion of the Latins and of all Westerns as irregular, and as defective in mode, though, most of them say, not in validity; while, in its Patriarchates, it insists on trine immersion, except in necessity, as essential to the validity of the sacrament. In Western Europe, and more especially in the United States and British America, large and zealous bodies of professing Christians are equally tenacious of immersion as the sole mode, though, unlike the Eastern Church, they do not require it to be trine. Now to make peace and secure unity, even in this one respect, would do much for the cause of Christ and the spread of his doctrine on earth. There is no safer or more reasonable way than to ascertain what was the earliest and usual custom, and to follow this; and this, the united learning of the world being witness, was by trine immersion. Were this mode the rule again in the West, the objections of the Easterns would be obviated, and in the West various bodies of Antipædobaptists would be drawn back into the pale of our reformed Church, for it would be impossible, for their sad error as to the subjects of baptism, to maintain itself in the estimation of candid and intelligent men, if that were their only distinctive tenet.

At the outset, an obstinate class of prejudices present themselves. It is a shameful thing to confess, though it is nevertheless true, that the rubric on the mode is constantly violated in the case of healthy children, where no necessity exists; and not only is this the case, but there are also many among our own people who do not actually seem to know that the English branch of our church expressly requires the immersion as the rule; and indeed it would be well if the prevalent ignorance and carelessness were ascribable to the people alone.

The causes of this state of things are ignorance or regardlessness—

1. Of the present rubrics of the English Church, and of the "consensus" of its most learned theologians.

2. Of the fact, that until after the Reformation, the ordinary as well as enjoined practice was to immerse three times, and that this was ever enjoined in the Use of Salisbury, the ordinary use in England prior to the Reformation, and that this was also enjoined after the Reformation, in the First Book of Edward VI.

3. Of the use and the rubrics of Christian antiquity, so far back as any notice of mode exists, and of Church Law on this subject.

4. The idea that there is some connection between a fondness for immersion, and a dislike of infant baptism, than which nothing can be more unfounded, as the example of Christian antiquity which enjoined the baptism of infants, and the rule of trine immersion, the Church of England in her rubric, and the present Greek Church amply attest.

May these humble pages be instrumental in recalling the facts and in removing prejudice. The subject is one which, whatever may be its own intrinsic merits, deserves consideration at this moment, when causeless schism is rife, and many, very many, are among our foes who, were we truer to our own rubrics, might be with us; for not every Baptist is such because he rejects infant baptism, so much as because he doubts whether any other mode than immersion is valid. If we paid more attention to mode, we should have fewer to contend with on the point of the subjects. Still another consideration should move those who have put on the white robe of the ministry. When they were ordained to the priesthood, the bishop asked them—

"Will you then give your faithful diligence always so to minister the doctrine and sacraments, and the discipline of Christ, as the Lord hath commanded, and as this Church hath received the same, according to the commandments of God;

so that you may teach the people of your cure, and charge with all diligence to keep and observe the same?"

And every one answered:

"I will so do, by the help of the Lord." Now here is a solemn vow, before God and man, regarding the ministration of baptism. What the whole church in the earliest ages deemed Christ's commandment to be, and how the English Church understood and practised it, will be shown.

CHAPTER II.

TRACES OF BAPTISM BEFORE OR CONTEMPORARY WITH CHRIST—PROSELYTE BAPTISM.

The question of the antiquity and origin of Proselyte Baptism need not occupy much of our attention. One thing is certain, whatever be the date of its rise, that the only mode by which it was administered was by total immersion. This is all that is to our purpose. The following statements, with the original references which accompany them in Lightfoot and Wall, will amply demonstrate this:

Rev. Dr. John Lightfoot, in "Horæ Hebraicæ," ed. London, 1684, vol. 2, p. 119: "They baptize a proselyte in such a confluence of waters as was fit for the washing of a menstruous woman. Of such a confluence of waters the lawyers have these words: A man that hath the gonorrhœa is cleansed nowhere but in a fountain; but a menstruous woman, as also all unclean persons, were washed in some confluence of waters, in which so much water ought to be as may serve to wash the whole body at one dipping. Our wise men have esteemed this proportion to be a cubit square, and three cubits depth, and this measure contains forty seahs of water."

Dr. Lightfoot, Horæ Heb., same, p. 120: "As soon as he grows whole of the wound of circumcision, they bring him to baptism, and being placed in the water, they again instruct him in some weightier, and in some lighter commands of the law," which being heard, "he plungeth himself, and comes up, and behold, he is an Israelite in all things. The women place a woman in the waters up to the neck, and two disciples of the wise men, standing without, instruct her about some lighter precepts of the law, and some weightier, while she in the meantime stands in the waters. And then she plungeth herself; and they, turning away their faces, go out, while she comes up out of the water."

In the baptizing of a proselyte, this is not to be passed over; but let it be observed, namely, that "others baptized him," and that "he baptized himself," or dipped, or plunged himself in the waters. Now what that plunging was, you may understand from those things which Maimonides speaks in *Mikvaoth*, in the place before cited: " Every person baptized (or dipped, whether he were washed from pollution, or baptized into proselytism) must dip his whole body, now stripped and made naked, at one dipping. And wheresoever in the Law, washing of the body or garments is mentioned, it means nothing else than the washing of the whole body. For if any wash himself all over, except the very tip of his little finger, he is still in his uncleanness. And if any hath much hair, he must wash all the hair of his head, for that also was reckoned for the body. But if any should enter into the water with their clothes on, yet their washing holds good, because the water would pass through their clothes, and their garments would not hinder it."*

We have cited a few out of many testimonies. Whatever may be the disagreements among the learned as to the time of the origin of proselyte baptism, the author, after much and patient investigation, has failed to find any with regard to the mode. They all agree that it was by dipping the whole person in water. So that, if Christian baptism be derived from this, it would seem most reasonable to suppose that, like it, it must have been at the beginning performed by immersion. See Stackhouse, Hist. of Bible, b. viii, chap. i, pp. 1234, 1235, note; and Bp. Seabury's Serm. Disc. iii, vol. i, p. 94.

---

* To the same effect as the foregoing, see Dr. Wall, Hist. of Inf. Bapt., Introd. 1, 2; Brown's "Jewish Antiq.," vol. ii, p. 85; "Lewis's Hebrew Republic," vol. ii, p. 460; "Jennings's Jewish Antiq.," p. 65.

CHAPTER III.

PRINCIPLES OF INTERPRETATION.

We commence with the testimony of Holy Scripture. This is the source of doctrine. But it should ever be interpreted by the historical witness of the earliest ages of the church. In other words, in case a doubt should arise regarding the proper interpretation of a passage relating to a certain doctrine or rite, we should not despise the voice of the early successors of the Apostles. It is a principle of common sense, as well as sound criticism, that the *historical witness* of the Christians who lived the nearest the Apostolic age, is of the greatest importance as an aid in determining the meaning of obscure or disputed passages of the New Testament. This is so patent that he who would dispute it could be convinced by no argument. Every such man in practice, if not in theory, has adopted the principle that ignorance is the mother of sound and reliable criticism.

The *mere opinions* of the early Christians are to be treated as their opinions, not binding upon us, unless they have been ratified by some decision of a council truly œcumenical in representing what has been held always, everywhere, and by all.

There is comparatively little, either of doctrine or rite, that can claim such a distinction. The great mass of theological squabbles are regarding things upon which the whole church has never spoken, and never will. Fathers may, and undoubtedly do, sometimes lean to fanciful interpretations of Scripture. As interpreters, where they differ from each other, or where they do not represent the Catholic consent of all ages, they are to be received or rejected as they deserve. The Catholic Church is not responsible for the opinions of any of her sons who go beyond her voice as uttered in the Nicæno-Constantinopolitan Symbol, and in the six Ecumenical Councils, any more than she is for those which make against those documents. In the former case, persons, or *part* of the church, speaks where the *whole* church should speak, and are therefore guilty of mischievous arrogance, by usurping the authority of the whole church. In the latter, they resist her authority. There is much less reason for quarrel in doctrine than men usually imagine. When a man recites the Nicæno-Constantinopolitan Symbol, he recites the sole creed of the Catholic or Ecumenical Church. When he reads over the decisions of the six councils, which justly claims to represent the "quod semper, quod ubique, quod ab omnibus," he has read all that can claim his assent on the score of ecumenicity. The remaining squabbles are hardly deserving of attention. They are to be classed with private opinions.

Should, however, the Fathers be found to testify from Apostolic times to a *fact* in rite, or discipline, or doctrine, as held from the beginning, the considerations which should induce us to reject their testimony, and alter a venerable rite, ought certainly to be of the most urgent character. Their testimony in such a case forms a Catholic consent, which justly claims our attention and obedience.*

The imprimatur of an ecumenical council stamps rite, and discipline, and doctrine with ecumenicity. But the church, in the only places where she has ever spoken, in the six Ecumenical Councils, has always acted on the principles which she established at Nicæa, in Canon 6: "Let the ancient customs be maintained;" in other words, her decisions in rite and in doctrine witness to what has been held "quod semper, quod ubique, quod ab omnibus," always, everywhere, and by all.

What the ancient customs were in baptism, we shall soon see.

The above train of remark is designed to meet that pernicious mode of criticism which rejects all aids from the testimony of the primitive Christians for the right interpretation of the Scriptures, and which verifies the profane remark of a Latin cardinal, that Scripture is a "nasus cereus"—a nose of wax—which this mode and its votaries twists hither and thither, as best suits their whims and prejudices.

* Even Daillé, On the Fathers, bk. ii, chap. vi, pp. 363, 403, 407, ed. Phila., differs not so widely from this principle. What he says of the use of the Fathers would not be approved by all his brethren.

In understanding Homer or Cicero, we wisely avail ourselves of every means which antiquity affords for understanding the customs referred to, the meaning of words, &c.; but some are so unwise as to throw away this principle where it applies with tenfold effect and advantage. It is as fatal to the pretensions of Rome and to her heresies as it is to Unitarianism. For any and all of her errors, tried by this touchstone, are found utterly wanting. We find in the early ages, and in the six Ecumenical Councils, no idolatry in giving relative worship and honor to images, no worship of the Virgin and saints, no worship in a tongue not understood by the people, no toleration of the novelty that a Roman Pontiff, or a part of the church, may decide either against or beyond the whole in ecumenical council assembled.

In accordance with this principle, instead of spending time in giving our own opinions as to the meaning of the following passages, we refer the reader to the Fathers, the councils, and the rubrics, which plainly point to immersion, and which will be found under their proper heads.

CHAPTER IV.

OF THE MODE AS COMMANDED BY CHRIST.

The Holy Scriptures are the sole *source* of faith. When a dispute has arisen the whole church has interpreted them, and given her definitions in accordance with that construction which always, everywhere, and by all has been put upon them from the beginning. And this was the only reasonable and safe course. But, in so doing, the church has *not set up another source of authority*. She has determined only the *means of interpretation* and all sound criticism. All satisfactory and final decision must rest upon these principles. Any departure from them has always been attended with evil.

We are to examine, in accordance with these principles, whether there be in the New Testament sufficient grounds for the rubric of the Church of England which requires immersion in the case of every healthy infant.

So much has been said upon this subject that we propose to give only a brief epitome of the reasons for the mode.

I. That immersion was the mode enjoined and practised, is evident from the use of the term $Βαπτίζω$.

The point is not what the word in *one* or *two* instances may mean, but what is its *general signification*, what would the Apostles understand by it. Now the word $Βαπτίζω$, in the time of the Apostles, as well as before and after that time, ordinarily meant immersion or dipping. No clear instance seems to be adduced where sprinkling or pouring is necessarily the meaning. The Apostles, therefore, would understand the word in its usual meaning as a command to dip; and that they did so understand it, both the usage of the New Testament and of the ages nearest the Apostolic abundantly demonstrate.

It is sometimes objected that the word immerse sometimes means to steep, to drench, to wet; but all these ideas are naturally derivable from that of immersion. Besides, whoever supposed that Christ said, "Go ye, steeping all nations, or drenching all nations, or wetting all nations."

Moreover our English verb "dip," if used as a command, would surely not be misunderstood. And yet Worcester, in his Dictionary, gives, among its meanings,

1. To moisten, to damp, to wet.

"And though not mortal, yet a cold, shuddering dew, dips me all o'er."—MILTON.

2. To engage in any affair.

"He was . . . dipt in the rebellion of the commons."—DRYDEN.

3. To mortgage, to pledge.

"Live on the use, and never dip thy lands."—DRYDEN.

4. To take out with a ladle, or other small vessel, as "to dip water with a cup." (v. "dip" in Webster.)

But what should we think of a man who, when told to go and dip an object, should pour or sprinkle water upon it, under the plea that "dip" does not *always* mean to immerse. But such a man's course would not be more strange than that of a Churchman, who, when his own church bids him dip a child, pours or sprinkles water upon it, when no necessity demands, against the *prevalent* sense of the word, with the usage of the Apostles and the primitive Church to enforce that sense.

Three specific and one generic term express the idea of the application of water.

$Χέω$, ... to pour.
$Ῥαντίζω$, ... to sprinkle.
$Βαπτίζω$, ... to immerse.
$Λούω$, ... to bathe or wash—the whole body.
Add, $Νίπτω$, ... to wash—some part of the body.

If the bare idea of washing alone were to be expressed, we should expect $Λούω$. If mode specifically, one of the first three. But $Βαπτίζω$, a word on all hands admitted to be ordinarily modal, is used to denote the command. All, except the first, are used in the New Testament and in their ordinary sense.

The ingenious, but late and baseless theory of a noted Congregationalist, makes $Βαπτίζω$ mean to purify, but $Καθαρίζω$ is the proper term for this.

Our Saviour's command was understood by the primitive

Christians, who knew the meaning of the word, to be modal. Mr. Beecher will hardly improve upon them much by starting a new notion. Καθαρίζω is used in its common acceptation in the New Testament repeatedly, but not of baptism. The Fathers do indeed speak of baptism as a purification, as regeneration, as an enlightening, a charisma, a sanctification. (See Macaire, Theol. Dogmat. Orth. t. 2, p. 376.) But these terms do not relate to mode; they relate to the blessing to which the sacrament is related.

The Import of Βαπτίζω.

The Fathers, and even later writers, although admitting the baptism of clinics, seem always, where they touch upon the command to baptize, to understand it as a command to immerse. The use of this mode itself, so much more difficult than any other, is an evidence of this. But they show this by word as well as deed. See Tert. adv. Prax. cap. 26. De Bapt. cap. 13. St. Cyprian, Ep. 25 and Ep. 63. St. Basil, De Spirit. Sanct. cap. 15. St. Jerome on Matt. 28 : 19. St. Chrysostom, Hom. de Fide. Theodoret, Bp. of Cyrus, Hæret. Fab. lib. 4, c. 3. Pope Pelagius, Ep. ad Gaudent. Pope Gregory the Great, Moral. lib. 18, cap. 27, and in Job, p. 91, ed. Migne. Gennadius of Marseilles, de Eccl. Dogmat. cap. 52. Leidrad, Bp. of Lyons, de Sac. Bapt. cap. 6. Rabanus Maurus, de Cleric. Instit. lib. 1, cap. 25. Paschasius Radbert on Matt. lib. 9, cap. 20. Alcuin, Ep. 90, ad Frat. Lugdun. Bruno, Bp. of Segni, v. Tract 3, de Sacr. Eccl. "quid in circuitu eundo significet." Peter Lombard. Sentent. lib. 4, dist. 3, 1. Some of the earlier of these passages are mentioned by Bingham as setting forth a belief in the divine origin of the mode of trine immersion. Bk. xi, chap. xi, sect. 7. But concerning others of them, it may be doubted whether they express this idea, because tingo, tinguo, tinctio, or intinctio, is used. These terms often possess the signification of dyeing, &c., but such dyeing was by dipping. Their use in these writers will explain itself in favor of dipping. Grotius on Matt. 3 : 6, remarks, "That the ancient Latins used 'tingere' for 'baptizare' should excite no wonder, for 'tingo' properly and generally signifies the same as 'mersare.'" ("Quod autem *tingere* pro *baptizare* usurpant Latini veteres mirum videri non debet, cum Latine *tingendi* vox et proprie et plerumque idem valeat quod *mersare*.") Rigaltius on cap. 8, de Poenitentia, of Tert., utters a sentiment not dissimilar. Writing of Tertullian, he states, that "wherever he (Tertullian) speaks of baptism, he uses the words lavacrum, tingere, intingere, ablui, mergitari, and immersio, which by no means signify aspersion." "Nam ubicunque de baptismo sermonem facit, lavacrum dicit, et tingere, et intingere, et ablui, et mergitari, et immersionem, quae adspersionem minime significant." Between the significations of dipping and dyeing, as the use of these words in Latin shows, there is a very close connection. The reader may glance at the Latin of the quotations from the Fathers, and Latin writers of the later ages which follow. Indeed, the remarks of Grotius and Regaltius are borne out by Rabanus Maurus, a writer of the 9th century, who states (v. ref. above) that βάπτισμα is translated into Latin by tinctio, and that the immersion of a man in water is called *tinctio*. Dr. Towerson (Anglican) uses similar language: "The words of Christ are, that they should baptize or dip those whom they made disciples to him, for so, no doubt, the word βαπτίζειν signifies." On the Sacraments, p. 20; v. id. p. 18. So Bishop Jeremy Taylor, vol. xiv. p. 62, Heber's ed. But it would be idle to suppose that, because a word sometimes departs from its general meaning, that therefore it has no general meaning. On this principle, "mergo" and dip would have none, for there are instances of as clear exception to their usual signification as can be found for that of βαπτίζω.

Cardinal Bellarmine, the great champion of Latinism, asserts that "βάπτισμα properly signifies immersion." So Maldonatus, on St. Luke, 12:50. The Greek, Alexander de Stourdza, as quoted hereafter, says that βαπτίζω always signifies to plunge. Calvin and Luther taught similarly.* Yet all these, following St. Cyprian and the custom of the whole church, deemed baptism by sprinkling or pouring, in case of necessity, to be valid. Some of them wrote at a time, and in parts of Christendom, when it had become the general custom to use these instead of immersion.

LUTHER.

(On the Sacrament of Baptism.)

"First, the noun *baptism* is Greek; in Latin, it can be rendered immersion, when we immerse anything into water, that it may be all covered with water; and although that custom has grown out of use with most persons (for they do not wholly submerge the children, but only pour on a little water), yet they ought to be entirely immersed, and immediately drawn out. For this the etymology of the noun seems to demand." De Sacramento Baptismi, init (Op. Lutheri, 1564, vol. 1, fol. 319.) "Primo, nomen baptismus Graecum est; Latine potest verti mersio, cum immergimus aliquid in aquam, ut totum tegatur aqua. Et quamvis ille mos jam aboleverit apud plerosque (neque enim totos demergunt pueros, sed tantum paucula aqua perfundunt) debebant tamen prorsus immergi, et statim retrahi, Id enim etymologia nominis postulare videtur."

* v. below.

CALVIN.

(Institutes of the Christian Religion, bk. iv, chap. 15; on Baptism, 19, at the end.)

The word baptize, itself, signifies immerse, and it is certain that the rite of immersing was observed by the ancient church. Calvini, Instit. Christ. Relig. lib. iv, cap. 15, de Bapt. 19. (Genevæ, 1612, p. 470.) Ipsum baptizandi verbum mergere significat, et mergendi ritum veteri ecclesiæ observatum fuisse constat.

For these and many other references to the opinions of distinguished writers of different communions, v. Dr. Conant's Meaning and Use of Baptizein, sect. viii.

POLI.

(Synopsis Critic. in Matt. 3 : 6.)

"Et baptizabantur," &c., *i. e.*, Immergebantur in aquas. Differunt enim haec tria, ἐπιπολάζειν (leviter tingere); δύνειν, quod est, fundum petere cum sua pernicie; et βαπτίζειν, quod est, immergere; non ergo abs re disputatum est de toto corpore immergendo in ceremonia baptismi. A βάπτω, tingo, est βαπτίζω, quod sign. in aquas immergo. . . . Mersatione, non perfusione, agi solitum hunc ritum, indicant et vocis proprietas, et loca ad cum ritum delecta. John 3 : 23; Acts 8 : 38. Et allusiones multæ apostolorum quæ ad adspersionem referri non possunt. Rom. 6 : 3, 4. Colos. 2 : 12.

Dr. Barrow: "What the action itself enjoined is, and what the manner and form thereof, is apparent by the words of our Lord's institution: *going forth*, saith he, *teach* or disciple *all nations, baptizing them*. The action is baptizing or immersing *in* water."

ST. AUGUSTINE.

(In Aurea Catena, on St. John, 4 : 1–6.)

"Jesus both baptized, and baptized not. He baptized in that he cleansed, He baptized not in that He dipped not."

To those of the clergy who, like Wall, think βαπτίζω equivalent in Christ's command to λούω, and who would therefore translate, "Go ye therefore and teach all nations, *washing* them," &c., his language in his Defence will be found especially useful. (V. id. pp. 458–462.) Had this illustrious man turned his attention to the modes as thoroughly as to the subjects of baptism, he would with his eminent truthfulness have modified some of his statements so as not to differ so much as in them he does from the councils and early Fathers, whose testimony he so much revered, and whose doctrines he has set forth against Antipædobaptist error. Compare his statement, vol. ii, p. 419, that the ancients did not ground trine immersion on a "command in Scripture," with the passages hereafter quoted from them, and Bingham, bk. xi, chap. xi, 7, which will serve to correct it. His statement, vol. iv, p. 423, as to the light in which the Catholics viewed the trine immersion, should not have been so general. It was true (in part) of Gregory the Great, but not of the ancient Catholics generally, as they will show.

II. Another reason why we should justify the Church of England in her *preference* for immersion as the rule is derived from the places of baptism.

St. Matt. 3 : 5, 6. Then went out to him Jerusalem, and all Judea, and all the region round about Jordan, and were baptized of him in Jordan.. ἐν τῷ Ἰορδάνῃ.

St. Mark 1 : 4, 5. John did baptize in the wilderness, and preach the baptism of repentance for the remission of sins. And there went out unto him all the land of Judea, and they of Jerusalem, and were all baptized of him in the river of Jordan. ἐν τῷ Ἰορδάνῃ ποταμῷ.

Mark 1 : 9. Jesus came from Nazareth of Galilee, and was baptized of John in Jordan. εἰς τὸν Ἰορδάνην.

St. John 3 : 23. And John also was baptizing at Ænon, near to Salim, because there was much water there. ὅτι ὕδατα πολλὰ ἦν ἐκεῖ.

III. A third reason for the rubric are the *circumstances* connected with the baptisms of the New Testament.

Praying the candid reader to ponder well, we here give them.

St. Matt. 3 : 13–16. Then cometh Jesus from Galilee to Jordan unto John, to be baptized of him. But John forbad him, saying, I have need to be baptized of thee, and comest thou to me? And Jesus, answering, said unto him, Suffer it to be so, now : for thus it becometh us to fulfil all righteousness. Then he suffered him : and Jesus, when he was baptized, went up straightway out of the water.

St. Mark 1 : 9, 10. And it came to pass in those days, that Jesus came from Nazareth of Galilee, and was baptized of John in Jordan.

And straightway *coming up out of the water* he saw the heavens opened, and the Spirit like a dove descending upon Him.

Acts 8 : 35. Then Philip opened his mouth and began at the same scripture, and preached unto him Jesus.

36. And as they went on their way, they came unto a cer-

tain water: and the eunuch said, See, *here is* water; what doth hinder me to be baptized?

37. And Philip said, If thou believest with all thine heart, thou mayest. And he answered, and said, I believe that Jesus Christ is the Son of God.

38. And he commanded the chariot to stand still; and they went down both into the water, both Philip and the eunuch; and he baptized him.

39. And when they were come up out of the water, the Spirit of the Lord caught away Philip, and the eunuch saw him no more: and he went on his way rejoicing.

Romans 6 : 3, 4, 5. Know ye not, that so many of us as were baptized into Jesus Christ were baptized into his death? Therefore, we are buried with him by baptism into death, that like as Christ was raised up from the dead by the glory of the Father, even so we also should walk in newness of life. For if we have been planted together in the likeness of his death, we shall be also in the likeness of his resurrection.

Colossians 2 : 12. *Buried with him in baptism, wherein* also ye are *risen* with him through the faith of the operation of God, who hath raised him from the dead.

CHRIST'S BAPTISM.

The universal Church of Christ, in the ancient liturgies which she has handed down, constantly refers to Christ's baptism *in* the Jordan, to his *ascent*, and to his *descent*. He who wishes to scan them will find them adverting to the baptism of our Lord. The fullest exhibition of them is in Asseman's Codex Liturgicus, but the author of Oxford Tract 67, translates parts of some of them, among which may be found references to the mode. V. id. N. Y. ed. p. 226, seq. The Gelasian, Gregorian, Roman, that of Chelle, unite in representing Christ as "baptized in Jordan." The Armenian speaks of his "descending into Jordan." So the Coptic, "descending into Jordan," in two places. So the Maronite, "Christ went down and was baptized therein," "in Jordan," "in the river Jordan." Malabar, "in the river Jordan." Apostolic revised, and Apostolic by Severus: "John mingled the waters of baptism, and Christ sanctified them, and descended, and was baptized in them. When He ascended out of the waters," &c.

Apostolic of James of Edessa: "Thou who wert baptized and ascendedst out of the waters." "Who went down and was baptized of John in Jordan." "The church saw Christ in the river Jordan." "Who was baptized in Jordan."

Jerusalem: "The creator of all creatures was baptized, and ascended out of the waters."

Jerusalem: "He . . . typified to us in His baptism the mystery of His death and resurrection."

Jerusalem: "The Son of God was washed, and ascended from the waters."

Apostolic by Severus: "By thy holy baptism; by thy descent into the waters, thou turnedst the people from the error of idols." "Who in the river Jordan wert baptized by John."

ORIGEN.

(In Aurea Catena, on John 1 : 24–28.)

"As the serpent lies hid in the Egyptian river, so doth God in this (the Jordan); for the Father is in the Son."

AUGUSTINE.

(In Aurea Catena, on St. Matt. 3 : 16.)

"Christ, after He had been once born among men, is born a second time in the sacraments; that as we adore Him then born of a pure mother, so we may now receive Him immersed in pure water. His mother brought forth her Son, and is yet virgin; the wave washed Christ and is holy. Lastly, that Holy Spirit which was present to Him in the womb, now shone round Him in the water."

AUGUSTINE.

(In Aurea Catena, on St. Matt. 3 : 13–15.)

"The Saviour willed to be baptized, not that He might Himself be cleansed, but to cleanse the water for us. From the time that *Himself was dipped in the water*, from that time has He washed away all our sins in water. . . . Thus the blessing, which like a spiritual river flows on from the Saviour's baptism, hath filled the basins of all pools, and the courses of all fountains."

RABANUS.

(In Aurea Catena, on St. Matt. 3 : 16.)

"As by the immersion of His body He dedicated the laver of baptism, He has shown that to us also, after baptism received, the entrance to heaven is open, and the Holy Spirit is given, as it follows, *and the heavens were opened.*"

M. POLI.

(Synopsis Criticorum, in St. Matt. 3 : 13–16.)

"Ascendit autem, nempe, in terram; ergo descenderat, et in flumine baptizatus fuit."

Rev. Dr. Featley.

(In his "Clavis Mystica," Lond. 1636, p. 213.)

"This 'ΙΧΘΥΣ or mystical Fish is taken by John in the river Jordan, and that Head before which the cherubims and seraphims, and all principalities in heaven bow, is bowed by John on earth, and dipped under the water in the river Jordan; this the particle εἰς intimateth, 'εβαπτίσθη εἰς 'Ιορδάνην, that is, word for word, He was baptized into the river Jordan."

Bishop Beveridge.

(Works, ed. Oxford, 1846, vol. viii, p. 337.)

"When Jesus was baptized, . . . had we been present at this time with Jesus at Jordan, . . . we should have seen One coming out of Jordan; who was that but 'God the Son?' . . . 'God the Son' was seen *ascending out of the water*."

Bishop Lancelot Andrews.

(Sermons, Oxford, 1841, vol. iii, p. 244.)

Speaking of Christ's baptism, he says: "Indeed, I must needs say, great humility there was in it; as at His circumcision, to take on Him the brand of a malefactor, so here to submit Himself to the washing proper to sinners only. . . . And where? Not in a basin by Himself, but even in the *common river*. With the rest of the many. . . . 'The waters were baptized by Him, they baptized Him not;' *He went into them*," &c.

Bishop Jeremy Taylor.

"The custom of the ancient churches was not sprinkling, but immersion, in pursuance of the *sense of the word in the commandment*, and the *example of our blessed Saviour*."—Doctor Dubitantium, bk. iii, chap. iv, rule xv, 3. Bishop Heber's ed. vol. xiv. p. 62.

Dr. Lightfoot.

(In "Horæ Hebraicæ," vol. ii, p. 121.)

"That the baptism of *John* was by plunging the body (after the same manner as the washing of unclean persons, and the baptism of proselytes, was) seems to appear from those things which are related of him; namely, that he *baptized in Jordan;* that he baptized in *Enon, because there was much water there;* and that Christ being baptized *came up out of the water:* to which that seems to be parallel. Acts 8 : 38. *Philip and the eunuch went down into the water*," &c.

BLOOMFIELD.
(On Mark 1 : 9.)

"Εἰς is *not* here for ἐν, as most commentators imagine, who adduce examples which are quite inapposite. The sense of ἐβαπτ εἰς is, '*was dipped*' or *plunged into*. Or we may suppose, that, as in the phrase λούεσθαι εἰς βαλανεῖον, there is a *significatio prægnans*, for, 'to be washed (by being plunged) into a bath;' so the sense here may be, 'He underwent the rite of baptism (by being plunged) into the water.'"

KUINOEL.
(In Marc. 1 : 4, 5.)

"Cohortabatur homines, ut se immergi in aquam paterentur."

(In Johan. 1 : 31.)

"Jam Johannes Baptista volebat exprimere sententiam hanc, mihi persuasissimum erat, a Deo admonitus eram, me eo ipso tempore quo Judæos flumini immergerem, Messiam esse cogniturum et Jesum, cum a me immergeretur flumini, Messiam esse cognovi." V. id. in Marc. 1 : 8, 9.

MACKNIGHT.
(On Matt. 3 : 13–16.)

"He (Christ) submitted to be baptized; that is, to be buried under the water by John, and to be raised out of it again, as an emblem of his future death and resurrection. In like manner, the baptism of believers is emblematical of their own death, burial, and resurrection. . . . Perhaps, also, it is a commemoration of Christ's baptism."

BAPTISM OF THE EUNUCH.
(Acts 8 : 38, 39.)

WHITBY.
(In loc.)

"Baptism was here performed by a κατάβασις, or descent of the baptized person in the water."

BURKITT.
(In loc.)

"Observe, 5. The manner of the administration of baptism to the eunuch; he went down into the water and was baptized by Philip: in those hot countries it was usual so to do, and we do not oppose the lawfulness of dipping in some cases, but the necessity of dipping in all cases."

ST. JOHN 3 : 23.

CALVIN.

"From these words (John 3 : 23) it may be inferred, that baptism was administered by John and Christ, by plunging the whole body under water. . . . Here we perceive how baptism was administered among the ancients; for they immersed the whole body in water." In Johan 3 : 23; Act. 8 : 38.

M. POLI.

(Synopsis Criticorum, in John 3 : 23.)

"Intellige. vel : 1, rivos multos : vel potius ; 2, simpliciter aquæ copiam ; tantam scilicet in qua facile corpus humanum mersaretur, quo tum more baptismus peragebatur; plerumque scilicet, non autem semper," &c.

CORNELIUS A. LAPIDE.

(Comment. in loc.)

"Baptizabat Christus," ait Cyrillus, "per discipulos suos, Joannes quoque ipse non per alios, sed manibus suis, nec in eisdem fontibus, in quibus Christus, sed juxta salim, et in fonte quodam certo atque vicino, quia aquæ multæ erant illic." Unde colligas Joannem ita baptizasse, ut non solum caput (ad hoc enim modica aqua erat opus) sed et corpus aquis ablueret."

"ὕδατα πολλὰ, 'many streams,' *i.e.* from the adjunct, much water. A sense (perhaps proceeding from Hebraism) often occurring in the Apocalypse."—Bloomfield, *Greek Test.*, *in loc.*

"'ὅτι ὕδατα πολλὰ ἦν ἐκεῖ,' *quoniam aquæ ibi copia erat*, tanta scilicet, ut Grotius ad h. l. notavit, in qua facile corpus humanum immergeretur, quotum more baptismus peragebatur. ὕδατα non *rivos* denotat, sed *aquæ copiam*," ut Apoc. i, 15, al.

"Because there was much water there." So much, as *Grotius* has remarked on this place, as would easily suffice for the immersion of a man's body, in which mode baptism was then administered. ὕδατα does not mean *streams*, but *much water*.

Kuinoel in loc.; v. also id. on v. 26, which he explains: "Qui tecum versatus, et a te flumine immersus est."

IV. Still another reason for the preference for immersion is, that it alone expresses the Scriptural symbolism and deep meaning of the sacrament as a burial with Christ and a resurrection with Him.

The Apostle Paul refers to this in the oft-quoted passages, Romans 6 : 3–5, and Colossians 2 : 12.

The Fathers often mention immersion as setting forth Christ's death, burial, and resurrection.* The councils allude to it. The Baptismal Offices of the ancient church are full of it.† The English and American Offices for Baptism and the Homily of the Resurrection contain the same reference.‡ It is, therefore, still the authoritative interpretation of the English and American churches. All doubt as to the meaning of the passages in the Offices and in the Homily will be removed by the fact that they were designed at a time when trine immersion was the usual practice, to call attention to this emblematic signification; for they date far beyond the rise of the present violations of the rubric, by using modes which it does not enjoin, but which it by implication condemns as irregular, except in necessity. With the primitive understanding of St. Paul's language, above referred to, the great bulk of our divines, as well as the Greeks, Latins, and the Reformed of all communions, have agreed.

Romans 6 : 3, 5.

The Fathers of the church understood this passage of baptism. Moreover it is in the present English Baptismal Office, in the Gallican, the Greek, the Syriac, the Jerusalem, and the Antioch Liturgies, and in that of Severus; and it occurs as a baptismal lesson in the Syriac Liturgy revised by Severus, and in those of Jerusalem and Milan. V. Oxf. Tracts, No. 67, N. Y. ed., 1839, p. 78, and last note on it, where the references are given. This whole tract is valuable as to the mode. See, among others, the quotations on this passage from the author, under the name of Athanasius, St. Cyril of Jerusalem, St. Ambrose, and St. Chrysostom. They will all be found to agree in understanding the Apostle's allusion to be to immersion and emersion in baptism. The reader who is desirous of more will find them in Greek and English in Conant's " Meaning and Use of βαπτίζω," sect. 5, N. Y., 1860. This work gives more examples

---

* v. in chapter vi, sect. i.
† v. in J. A. Asseman, Codex. Liturg. tom. ii, passim.
‡ v. last prayer, in both Off. Inf. Bapt., and in Hom. above, p. 392.

of the Greek terms relating to baptism than can be found elsewhere. Most of his quotations refer to the symbolism of the rite, while the former references are directly explanatory of the part of Scripture above.

Romans 6 : 3–5, is interpreted of immersion in baptism by the following writers on it: Dr. Wall, Hist. of Inf. Bapt., Oxf. ed., 1844, vol. iv, p. 153; Dr. Bloomfield, Gr. Test. in loc.; Bingham, Orig. Eccl. bk. xi, chap. xi, sect. iv; Arbp. Secker, in D'Oyly and Mant in loc.; Dean Stanhope in loc.; Dr. Hammond in loc. Sir Norton Knatchbull, Annot. on N. T., Camb., 1693, p. 300, has a learned and copious comment on this, giving quotations from Fathers, schoolmen, &c.* Burkitt in loc.; Bp. Jeremy Taylor's Works, London, 1828, vol. ii, p. 394, and p. 253; Wells, rector of Catesbach, in Leicestershire, in loc.; Arbp. Tillotson's Works, ed. 1707, vol. i, Serm. vii, p. 82; Wm. Tyndale, 1536, A.D., Doct. Treat., ed. Camb., 1848, in "Obedience of a Christian Man" on Baptism, p. 253; Bp. Nicholson on the Catechism, pp. 158, 161, ed. Oxf., 1842; Poli, Synop. Critic, in loc.; Mori, Prælect. in Rom. 6 : 4; John Locke in loc.; Bp. Tomline, art. 27, in loc. (in Elem. of Theol.); Olshausen in loc.; Suicer's Thesaurus, "'Αναδύω;" Chalmers and Macknight in loc.

Prof. Stuart, the Congregationalist, who opposes, yet frankly admits, that most writers interpret this passage of immersion. His view is a late one, and against the unanimous consent, so far as expressed, of the earlier centuries, and indeed against the views of many of the most distinguished Protestant theologians.

Cranmer's Catechism, 1548, A.D.

Baptisme and the dippyng into the water doth betoken that the old Adam, with al his sinne and evel lustes, ought to be drowned and killed by daily contrition and repentance: and that, by renewynge of the Holy Gost, we ought to rise with Christ from the death of sinne, and to walke in a new lyfe, that our new man may lyve everlastyngly in righteousness and truthe before God, as Saincte Paule teacheth, saying, "Al we that are baptised in Christe Jesu are baptised in hys death. For we are buried with him by baptisme into deth," &c.

V. in Fallow's "Order of Baptism," London, 1838, p. 81; v. also id. p. 82, as follows: "Yf a man aske you, what doth the baptisynge in the water betoken? Answer ye, it betokeneth that olde Adam, with all his synnes and euel desyers, ought daylye to be killed in us, by trewe contricion and repentaunce; that he may arise againe from death, and, after he is risen with Christ, may be a new man, a new creature, and may live everlastyngly in God and before God, in righteousness and holynes, as Saincte Paule wryteth, saying, 'Al we that are baptised are buried with Christe into death; that as

---

* v. p. 49.

Christe rose agayne, by the glorie of his Father, so we also should walk in newness of life.'"

Catechism of Edward VI.

"Baptism is also a figure of our burial in Christ, and that we shall be raised up again with him in a new life."

Sir Norton Knatchbull.

Annot. on New Testament, Cambridge, 1693, p. 300, speaking of the doctrine of the resurrection, he remarks: "There was need of some significant type or figure which might make so impenetrable a notion familiar and perceptible to the sense of man, to which purpose nothing seemed more fit and easy, in the wisdom of God, than the burying of our bodies in water by baptism, from whence they receive an immediate resurrection. So that, in conclusion, we may positively affirm *that baptism is properly and solely a type of the resurrection;* and to this truth do give their suffrage the Apostles, Fathers, Schoolmen, almost all interpreters, ancient and modern, and even our English Church itself, its judgment being manifest in the rubric of the Common Prayer, which enjoins the dipping of infants in baptism, allowing in some cases the liberty of sprinkling or perfusion. The thing of itself is so manifest that there is no need of testimonies to confirm it; but because there be not few who teach otherwise, led thereunto by example and vulgar error, it will not be amiss if but to free myself from the imputation of too much confidence, out of innumerable testimonies, to cite some few; and we first begin with the Apostle Paul" (then after quoting Rom. 6 : 3, 4, &c.; Col. 2 : 12; 1 Cor. 15 : 29): "As much as if he had said, in vain doth the Church use the sign of baptism if there be no resurrection. You have it abundantly proved also in the primitive and later writers. For example, that believing on his death, διὰ τοῦ Βαπτίσματος αὐτοῦ κοινωνοὶ τῆς ἀναστάσεως αὐτοῦ—by his baptism ye were made partakers of his resurrection: Ignat. Ep. ad Trall. Βάπτισμα εἰς τὸν θάνατον τοῦ Κυρίου διδόμενον—baptism was given to set forth the death of the Lord: Ep. ad Philadel., in the name of Ignatius. 'The death of Christ:' Const. Apost. Τοῦ πάθους καὶ τῆς ἀναστάσεως αὐτοῦ ἐν τῷ Βαπτίσματι τελοῦμεν τὰ σύμβολα—in baptism we perform the signs of his passion and resurrection: Just. Mar. We know one saving baptism, since there is but one death for the world and one resurrection, ὧν τύπος ἐστι τὸ Βάπτισμα, whereof baptism is the type, &c.: Basil. Mag. Hear what St. Paul saith: 'They were all baptized in the cloud and in the sea' Βάπτισμα καλεῖ τὴν θαλάσσης ὁδον 'He calleth their passage through the sea baptism, for it was an escape from death,' &c.: Basil, Selenc. Ὅταν μέλλωμεν Βαπτίζειν, when we go about to baptize, we bid to say, I believe in the resurrection of the dead, and in this faith are we baptized: Chrysost. Baptismus resurrectionis pignus, et imago, Baptism is a pledge and figure of the resurrection: Ambr. Baptismus arrhabo resurrectionis, Baptism is an earnest of the resurrection: Lactant. Aquarum elemento sepelimur, We are buried in the element of water: Anselm. Mersio mortis et sepulturæ formam gerit, Immersion bears the form of death and burial: Bernard. Laudabilius, et communius, Baptism is performed more laudably, more safely, and more commonly by dipping; for, by dipping, the figure of Christ's burial is represented: Thos. Aquin. Ipsum baptizandi verbum mergere significat, &c., The word baptism doth signify dipping under; and it is evident the ancient Church used the ceremony of dipping: Calvin. Baptismus Græca vox est, &c., Baptism is a Greek word, and signifies properly immersion into the water; and this signification doth properly agree with our baptism, and hath analogy to the thing signified; for by baptism we are buried together, and, as it were, drowned with Christ, being dead to sin, &c: Zanch. I could add to these an innumerable heap of testimonies, but these, I think, are enough to prove two irrefragable doctrines. First, *that baptism is properly and solely the type of the death and resurrection of Jesus Christ*, by faith wherein we are assured of the humanity and Godhead of our Saviour, the very foundation of our Christian faith. And secondly of the resurrection of all true Christians, &c.

"I shall only add the judgment of an ingenuous and learned man (Estius), whose testimony in this matter is not to be suspected or refused. His words are these: 'Porro quamvis immersionis cærimonia et olim fuit communior,' &c., Though the ceremony of immersion was anciently more common, as appears by the unanimous discourse of the Fathers, when they speak of this matter, and doth more lively represent the death, burial, and resurrection of the Lord and us, which are mystically done in baptism. The which signification of immerging the Fathers do often urge," &c.

Bishop Trower.

(On this passage, in his remarks on the Epistle for the sixth Sunday after Trinity.)

"The Apostle's reasoning, and the symbolical meaning of holy baptism, must have been better understood (as was observed on considering the Epistle for Easter day) when baptism was performed by immersion; that is, when the person to be baptized was wholly dipped or buried in the water, *as is still the rule of our Church*, though from various circumstances the alternative which is allowed, of pouring water on the candidate for baptism, is now generally adopted. The symbolical meaning, however, of this sacrament is ever the same. It represents a death, and burial, and resurrection. And to understand the Apostle's language, we should remember, that sin is compared in holy Scripture to a body, and our sinful nature is called 'the old man,' as our renewed and holy nature is called 'the new man.' The death, then, and burial, which are symbolized in baptism, are the death and burial of 'the old man,' which is also here said to be 'crucified' with Christ, 'that the body of sin might be destroyed, that henceforth we should not serve sin.' The resurrection symbolized by the reappearance of the baptized person from the water, is the 'newness of life,' in which he is henceforth pledged to 'walk.'"

Dr. Whitby.
(In loc.)

"It being so expressly declared here, and Col. 2 : 12, that 'we are buried with Christ in baptism,' by being buried under water; and the argument to oblige us to a conformity to his death, by dying to sin, being taken hence, and this immersion being religiously observed by all Christians for thirteen centuries, and approved by our Church, and the change of it into sprinkling, even without any allowance from the author of this institution, or any license from any council of the Church, being that which the Romanist still urgeth to justify his refusal of the cup to the laity, it were to be wished that that custom might be again of general use, and aspersion only permitted as of old, in case of the *clinici*, or in present danger of death."

It should be observed that the references to the symbolism of the sacrament in the early Christian writers are to trine, not single immersion, which they expressly condemned. So some later writers are as specific.*

The sacrament of the Lord's Supper sets forth Christ's death in a manner peculiar to itself. But it should not be forgotten that there is a deep significance in baptism, in shadowing forth the same truth in connection with the burying of the baptized in the liquid grave.

In the early Church, its symbolism better expressed that idea than is now done:

1. By the anointing of the candidate's body as for burial.
2. By the total immersion itself.
3. By the number of the immersions—three—to represent the abode of Christ in the grave, and his resurrection thence after three days.
4. By the times of baptism, Easter, Pentecost, and Epiphany. v. Bingham, bk. xi, chapters 1 : 6–11. Bp. Kaye's Clem. of Alex. p. 441. Justini Martyri, Quæst. et Respons. ad Orthodox. Quæst. 137, c. Respons.

To restore the ancient rites would tend to draw in Latins and others, who justify themselves now by our defects, although they

---

* See W. Palmer, farther on. On Col 2 : 12, v. Whitby, Pierce, Valpy, and Macknight.

cannot claim to follow closely primitive usage either in this rite or the Eucharist, and to bind all our people in the strong bonds of our already primitive doctrine then joined with primitive rite.* The ancient immersion differs from pouring in possessing a *divine* symbolism.

V. A fifth reason for the Church's dipping as the rule is, that she should be tenacious of that which was in the beginning, since all change is dangerous and productive of divisions, for in every part of the Church there are many who are ever fond of the old. This principle was embodied by the Nicene Church in the words, "Let the ancient customs be maintained." Departure from it was a chief means of separating the Catholic Church into two distinct parts, in the year 1054. There never can be unity until it is enforced in the West, with regard to the ecumenical mode. It bears the stamp of the quod semper, quod ubique, quod ab omnibus, and it is the only mode that does.

There are a certain class of objections urged against these points, but inasmuch as they are without foundation in the first 1200 years, and since indeed they run counter to them, it hardly comes within our province to discuss them now. In the Appendix, the principal of them will be found with answers. The body of the work will contain the views of the Early Church, as expressed in the language of Fathers, of Rubrics, and of Church Law. All these will be found far the most valuable. We give much of what is in the Appendix for what it is worth, without becoming responsible for it.

As during the first 1200 years the use of sprinkling and pouring was not defended from the New Testament, except so far as necessity is concerned, we shall not go beyond this course, but leave them in their proper place with what will be found, in the estimation of candid and impartial men, the sufficient and universally received grounds of their practice. Of the later opinions for their use, many of which are now current, we shall speak in their order. It is not our purpose

---

* The Anglican communion should restore every Christian rite and custom of the first five hundred years, and with the *primitive sense and use*. It is duty. It would do much for orthodox unity. Some of them which were in 1 Bk. Edw. VI, were by Puritan influence wrongly and injuriously laid aside. The *abuse* of a thing is not sufficient reason for departure from the *use*. *All* the early rites are innocent and edifying *when understood*.

either to affirm or to deny regarding them. Some of them would never have existed, were it not that it has been ignorantly and falsely supposed that they were necessary, in order to oppose the Baptists and other denominations, whose baptism, even on their own principles, must be deemed invalid, as will be seen hereafter. There is no necessary connection between an approval of the primitive interpretation of these texts and countenancing their errors. Indeed, as Wall remarks, it was the disuse of the early mode, and the introduction of sprinkling, which led to the rise of the Antipædobaptist sects in England. (See Hist. of Inf. Bapt. ed. Oxf. 1844, vol. ii, p. 413, and vol. iv, p. 458.) The general sentiment of Anglican divines has coincided, as quotations will prove, with the sense of immersion in the passages above.

CHAPTER V.

THE ANCIENT VERSIONS.

In all these the term $\beta\alpha\pi\tau i\zeta\omega$ is either transferred, translated by some word not specifying any particular mode, or translated by a term signifying immersion.

The Fathers frequently use words signifying to dip as synonymous with $\beta\alpha\pi\tau i\zeta\omega$. The De Baptismo of Tertullian, the first of the Latin writers, abounds with this use.

Gotch, formerly of Trinity College, Dublin, has collected the testimony of the ancient versions into a brief space. It is well to remember, however, in considering his work, that it is written by a Baptist, and in their interest, and that in all its parts it may not be reliable. We give it, because it is the best thing that we can find. The author may have fallen into error, in attempting to make the rendering in some cases specific as to mode where it is general. He states finally: "We have now gone through all the ancient versions which have been published, and noticed many modern ones, in the course of our examination."

The conclusions to which the investigation leads us, are:

I. With regard to the ancient versions, in all of them, with three exceptions (viz., the Latin from the third century, and the Sahidic and Basmuric), the word $\beta\alpha\pi\tau i\zeta\omega$ is *translated* by words purely native; and the three excepted versions adopted the Greek word, not by way of transference, but in consequence of the term having become current in the languages.

Of native words employed, the Syriac, Arabic, Ethiopic, Coptic, Armenian, Gothic, and earliest Latin, all signify to *immerse;* the Anglo-Saxon, both to *immerse* and to *cleanse;* the Persic, to *wash;* and the Slavonic to *cross.* The meaning of the word adopted from the Greek, in Sahidic, Basmuric, and Latin, being also to *immerse.*

II. With regard to the modern versions examined, the Eastern generally adhere to the ancient Eastern versions, and translate by words signifying to *immerse.* Most of the Gothic dialects, viz., the German, Swedish, Dutch, Danish, &c., employ altered forms of the Gothic word signifying to *dip.* The

Icelandic uses a word meaning *cleanse*. The Slavic dialects follow the ancient Slavonic; and the languages formed from the Latin, including the English, adopt the word *baptizo*; though, with respect to the English, the words *wash* and *christen* were formerly used, as well as *baptize*.

It may, perhaps, be acceptable to place these results together in a tabular form, as follows :*

VERSION.	DATE.	WORD EMPLOYED.	MEANING.
SYRIAC:			
Peshito	2d cent.	خٓڡ݂ܡ	*immerse.*
Philoxenian	6th cent.		"
ARABIC:			
Polyglott:	7th cent. (?)	مبغ ،عمّد	*immerse.*
Propaganda	1671		"
Sabat	1816		"
PERSIC:	8th cent. (?)	شوبیدن شستن	*wash.*
Modern (Martyn)	185	غسل	*ablution.*
ETHIOPIC:	4th cent.	ጠምቀ፡	*immerse.*
Amharic	1822		"
EGYPTIAN:			*immerse.*
Coptic	3d cent.	ⲱⲙⲥ, }	*plunge.*
Sahidic	2d cent.	} Ⲃⲁⲡⲧⲓⲍⲉ	
Basmuric	3d cent.		
ARMENIAN	5th cent.	Մկրտել	*immerse.*
SLAVONIC:	9th cent.	крестити	*cross.*
Russian	1519	}	
Polish	1585		
Bohemian	1593	} *the same root.*	"
Lithuanian	1660		
Livonian, or Lettish	1685		
Dorpat Esthonian, &c. &c.	1727	}	
GOTHIC:	4th cent.	*daupjan.*	*dip.*
German	1522	*taufen*	"
Danish	1524	*dobe*	"
Swedish	1534	*dopa*	"
Dutch &c. &c.	1560	*doopen*	"
Icelandic	1584	*skira*	*cleanse.*
ANGLO-SAXON	8th cent.	*dyppan, fullian*	*dip, cleanse.*
LATIN:			
The Early Fathers	2d cent.	*tingo*	*immerse.*
Ante Hieronymian	3d cent.	*baptizo*	
Vulgate	4th cent.	"	
French	1535	*baptiser*	
Spanish	1556	*bautizar*	
Italian &c. &c.	1562	*battezzare*	
English: Wicklif	1380	{ *wash, christen, baptize*	
Tindal	1526	*baptize*	
Welsh	1567	*bedyddio*	*bathe.*
Irish	1602	*baisdim*	
Gaelic	1767	*baisdeam*	

* v. also W. Judd's Remains.

Now, whatever be the judgment of the learned as to the propriety of using "immerse" instead of "baptize," as a translation of some of these renderings, it cannot be doubted,

1. That in ancient and in modern versions, and in the writings of the Fathers, $\beta\alpha\pi\tau\iota\zeta\omega$ is translated by a word signifying to dip or to immerse.

2. And that in these versions no other *mode* is ever specifically mentioned: every translation may be classed under one of two heads :

1. Either it does not specify mode ;
2. Or it specifies immersion.

As will be shown hereafter, the Fathers often use terms expressive of one mode, that is immersion, as of synonymous meaning with $\beta\alpha\pi\tau\iota\zeta\omega$. The *usus loquendi*, as well as the *usus scribendi* of the early centuries, was but in conformity with the idea which they entertained, that the mode of trine immersion was enjoined in the commission to baptize, or that it was a tradition from the Apostles.

CHAPTER VI.

OF THE MODE PRACTISED BY THE CHURCH DURING THE EARLY CENTURIES, AND HOW FAR ANY MODE WAS ENJOINED BY THE CHURCH, AND OF THE PENALTIES OF VIOLATING OR CHANGING THE MODE.

Criteria by which to judge:

    I. The Fathers.
    II. The Councils, œcumenical and provincial.
    III. The Baptismal Offices of the Church.

SECTION I.

THE FATHERS.

The Fathers first claim our attention, since they are the earliest witnesses. Their testimony, as we shall find, reaches up in the case of Justin Martyr to within forty or fifty years of the death of St. John,* when many who had seen the Apostles were still living, and while his words and precepts, as well as those of the other Apostles, were still fresh in their memories. Whether we admit those remains of the apostolic Fathers which bear upon our subject as genuine or not, will make but little difference. *All* the remains of the age immediately succeeding the apostolic speak in favor of dipping as the mode, or describe baptism in such a way as evidently, or most naturally, implies it. Barnabas and Hermas only add their testimony where proof is already overwhelming.

The most complete and the fairest way in which to ascertain the mode of baptism among the disciples and the immediate

---

* v. Murdock's Mosheim, vol. i, p. 118.

successors of the Apostles, is to let them speak, and this it is purposed to do.

CENTURY I.

BARNABAS, A. D. 50.

(Epistle, chap. xi.)

"Consider how He has joined both the cross and the water together. For this He saith, 'Blessed are they, who, putting their trust in the cross, *descend into the water;* for they shall have their reward in due time.' . . . And what follows?

"'And there was a river running on the right hand, and beautiful trees grew up by it; and he that shall eat of them shall live forever.' The signification of which is this: That *we go down into the water* full of sins and pollutions, but *come up again,* bringing forth fruit; having in our hearts the fear and hope which is in Jesus by the Spirit."—*Archbishop Wake's Trans.**

HERMAS, A. D. 75.

(Commands, iv, 3.)

"And I said unto him, 'I have even now heard from certain teachers that there is no other repentance besides that of baptism; when *we go down into the water* and receive the forgiveness of our sins.'"†—*Archbishop Wake's Trans.*

THE SAME.

(Similitude, ix, 16.)‡

"Before a man receives the name of the Son of God, he is ordained unto death; but when he receives that seal, he is

---

* Barnab. ep. cap. xi : Ἡμεῖς μὲν καταβαίνομεν εἰς τὸ ὕδωρ. . . . καὶ ἀναβαίνομεν.

† Herm. lib. 2. Mandat. iv. cap. 3. Cum in aquam descendimus et accipimus remissionem peccatorum nostrorum.

‡ The learned reader will do well to notice the expression and context of the last passage. "Necesse est, inquit, ut *per* aquam habeant ascendere," &c. Of course, the notion of Hermas regarding baptizing the dead is one thing, his view of baptism another. The passage is referred to not as a proof of mode, but that the reader's attention may let nothing escape.

freed from death, and assigned unto life. *Now that seal is the water of baptism, into which men go down under the obligation unto death, but* come up appointed unto life."*—*Archbishop Wake's Trans.* (v. id. below, for another reference to immersion.)

OLD WRITING ASCRIBED TO ST. DIONYSIUS THE AREOPAGITE.

"And attentively consider the intimate relationship which exists between sacraments and their outward symbols. For since death is not, as some think, the negation of being, but the separation of parts conjoined, which separation consigns the soul into the unseen; for, by being deprived of the body, it loses the power of being recognized; and since the body, to human appearance, disappears, the total hiding or covering by means of water is fitly taken for an image of the death and burial. The symbolic teaching, therefore, mystically instructs him who is baptized according to sacred rite, to imitate, by *the three immersions in the water*, the death and the burial for three days and nights of Jesus the Life-giver, for it is conceded to men to imitate Him."†

See also id. De Eccl. Hierarch., cap. ii, 2, vii, p. 395, where he speaks of trine immersion again.

CENTURY II.

JUSTIN MARTYR.

(Chevallier's Trans., 1 Apol. 79 and 80.)

"We will state in what manner we are created anew by Christ, and have dedicated ourselves to God; that we may not, by omitting this, appear to dissemble anything in our explanation. As many as are persuaded and believe that the things which we teach and declare are true, and promise that they are determined to live accordingly, are taught to pray and to beseech God with fasting to grant them remission of their past sins,

---

* Herm. lib. 3. Simil. ix, cap. 16: Illud autem sigillum aqua est, in quam descendunt morti obligati, ascendunt vero vitæ assignati.

† S. Dionys. Areopag. de Eccl. Hierarch., cap. 2 : 3, 7, p. 403, ed. Migne. "Τὸν οὖν ἱερῶς βαπτιζόμενον ἡ συμβολικὴ διδασκαλία μυσταγωγεῖ ταῖς ἐν τῷ ὕδατι τρισὶ καταδύσεσι τὸν θεαρχικὸν τῆς τριημεροννύκτου ταφῆς Ἰησοῦ τοῦ ζωοδότου μιμεῖσθαι θάνατον, ὡς ἐφικτὸν ἀνδράσι τὸ θεομίμητον."

while we also pray and fast with them. *We then lead* them to a place where there is water, and there they are regenerated, as we also were; for they are then washed *in that water* (ἐν τῷ ὕδατι τότε λουτρὸν ποιοῦνται) in the name of God, the Father and Lord of the universe, and of our Saviour Jesus Christ, and of the Holy Spirit. . . . . The Apostles have also taught us for what reason this is, since at our first birth we were born without our knowledge or consent, by the ordinary natural means, and were brought up in bad habits and evil instructions, in order that we may no longer remain the children of necessity or of ignorance, but may become the children of choice and judgment, and may obtain *in the water* (ἐν τῷ ὕδατι) remission of the sins which we have before committed, the name of God, the Father and Lord of the universe, is pronounced over him who is willing to be born again, and hath repented of his sins; he who leads him to be washed *in the laver of baptism* (τοῦτον λουσόμενον ἄγοντες ἐπὶ τὸ λουτρόν), saying this only over him," &c. Below Justin says, that the baptized person (λούεται) "is washed."

On this passage see Wall, and Reeves in his Apologies in loc. See also Prof. Stuart, Bib. Repos., Jan.–Apr., 1833, p. 356. He says, "I am persuaded that this passage, as a whole, most naturally refers to immersion; for why, on any other ground, should the convert who is to be initiated go out to the place where there is water? There could be no need of this if mere sprinkling or partial affusion only was customary in the time of Justin."

TERTULLIAN.

"We, following the example (or command) of our Lord and Saviour Jesus Christ, are born in the water." De Bapt., cap. i.*

"The law of immersion has been imposed, and the form has been prescribed. 'Go,' said He, 'teach the nations, immersing them in the name of the Father, and of the Son, and of the Holy Ghost.' (Matt. 28 : 19.) Comparing with this law the limitation, 'Except a man be born of water and of the Spirit,

---

* v. ut supra. Sed nos pisciculi secundum ΙΧΘΥΝ nostrum Jesum Christum in aqua nascimur, nec aliter quam in aqua permanendo salvi sumus. v. not. in ed. Migne in loc.

he cannot enter into the kingdom of God,' we are forced to believe in the necessity of baptism.

"*Therefore all who believed, after these words were uttered, were immersed.* Then, also, when Paul believed he was immersed. (Acts 9 : 6.) And this is that which the Lord commanded when he deprived him of sight : 'Arise,' said He, 'and go into Damascus, and there it shall be told thee what thou must do' (ibid.), that is, to be immersed, which was the only thing wanting to him. For he had already learned and believed that the Nazarene is the Lord, the Son of God."* De Bapt., cap. xiii.

No man who desires to have a clear view of the historical testimony of the early Church, as well as its opinion, in regard to the mode, should fail of reading the whole of " De Baptismo" in the original.

"To begin with baptism : when we are about to come to the water, ... we do in the Church testify, under the hand of a chief minister, that we renounce the Devil, and his pomp, and his angels. Then are we thrice dipped, pledging ourselves to something more than the Lord hath prescribed in the Gospel." De Corona, cap. iii, Oxf. trans.†

The expression, "pledging ourselves to something more than the Lord hath prescribed in the Gospel," refers (Dean Waterland thinks) to the answers made in the baptismal creed, which had been, in Tertullian's day, on account of the rise of heresies, considerably enlarged beyond what we find in the Gospel. This must be the correct opinion, as will be seen by the next quotation, v. his works, vol. ii, p. 186, n. "x."

" He (Christ) gave, as His last command, that they should immerse into the Father, and the Son, and the Holy Ghost, not into one person. For we are immersed not once, but

---

* Ut supr. "Lex enim tinguendi imposita est, et forma præscripta. Ite, inquit, *docete nationes, tinguentes eas in nomine Patris et Filii et spiritus sancti* (Matt. 28 : 19). Huic legi collata definitio illa : *nisi quis renatus fuerit ex aqua et spiritu, non intrabit in regnum cœlorum* (Joan. 3 : 5), obstrinxit fidem ad Baptismi. Itaque omnes exinde credentes tinguebantur. Tunc et Paulus ubi credidit, tinctus est (Act. 9 : 6). Et hoc est quod Dominus in illa plaga orbationis præceperat : *exsurge*, dicens, *et introi Damascum* (ibidem), *illic tibi demonstrabitur quid debeas agere*, scilicet tingui, quod solum ei derent."

† Ut supra. Denique, ut a baptismate ingrediar, aquam adituri, ibidem, sed et aliquanto prius in ecclesia sub antistitis manu contestamur nos renuntiare diabolo, et pompæ, et angelis ejus: dehinc ter mergitamur amplius aliquid respondentes, quam Dominus in Evangelio determinavit.

thrice, at the naming of every person of the Trinity."* Adv. Praxeam, cap. xxviii, 30. De Bapt., cap. xiv †

Tertullian, in mentioning the places of baptism, always implies immersion; thus De Baptismo, cap. iv: "There is no difference whether one is washed in a sea or in a pool, in a river or in a fountain, in a lake or in a canal; nor is there any difference between those whom John dipped in the Jordan, and those whom Peter dipped in the Tiber." (Nulla distinctio est, mari quis an stagno, flumine an fonte, lacu an alveo diluatur, nec quidquam refert inter eos quos Joannes in Jordane, et quos Petrus in Tiberi tinxit.)

The above show:

1. That Tertullian believed that all the baptisms of the New Testament performed after the words of the commission were uttered, were performed by trine immersion.

2. That he believed that Christ enjoined this mode.

In addition, it should be remarked that, in the first five hundred years, the great bulk of orthodox testimony, so far as expressed, is in favor of both these views. The practice of the Church for a thousand years coincides with them.

CENTURY III.

HIPPOLYTUS.

(Discourse on the Holy Theophany, ii.)

"For thou hast heard how Jesus came to John, and was baptized by him in the Jordan. O wonderful transactions! How was the boundless river that makes glad the city of God, bathed in a little water; the incomprehensible fountain that sends forth life to all men, and has no end, covered (ἐκαλύπτετο) by scanty and transitory waters!"

The same Discourse on the Holy Theophany, x. After

---

* Ut supra. Et post resurrectionem spondens missurum se discipulis promissionem Patris: et novissime mandans ut tinguerent in Patrem et Filium et Spiritum Sanctum, non in unum. Nam nec semel, sed ter, ad singula nomina in personas singulas tinguimur.

† Ut supra. v. also De Bapt., c. 14, where he says, "Sed de ipso Apostolo revolvunt, quod dixerit: *non enim me ad tinguendum Christus misit* (1 Cor. 1 : 17), quasi hoc argumento Baptismus adimatur. Cur enim tinxit Gaium et Crispum et Stephanæ domum (ibidem)? Quanquam etsi non eum miserat Christus ad tinguendum, tamen aliis Apostolis præceperat tinguere."

quoting Is. 1 : 16–19, he says : "Thou sawest, beloved, how the prophet foretold the cleansing of holy baptism. For he who goes down with faith into the bath of regeneration, is arrayed against the evil one, and on the side of Christ; he denies the enemy, and confesses Christ to be God; he puts off bondage, and puts on sonship; he comes up from baptism, bright as the sun, flashing forth the rays of righteousness; but greatest of all, he comes up a son of God, and a fellow heir with Christ."

These are given (slightly altered) as in Conant's "Meaning and Use of Baptizein," sect. v, exam. 203, 226, where they will be found with the Greek.

St. Cyprian, A. D.

We come now to an important epoch in the history of baptism, and one regarding which blunder upon blunder is heaped. It is customary to represent Cyprian as asserting that the mode is a matter of indifference. No author is misquoted so constantly for the present irregularities in using sprinkling and pouring, in cases where no necessity requires, and none so unjustly, as will be seen on examination. There are certain stereotyped mistakes in the generality of histories which are copied without careful examination from one writer to another through successive centuries, and such has been the fate of the original mistakes concerning the testimony of Cyprian.

Let us glance in a spirit of candor at the facts. All the testimony which has preceded points clearly to immersion as the mode, and where it is stated most fully that immersion was not single but trine. But the primitive mode seems an impossibility in cases of necessity, and sprinkling is used instead. For the early Christians deemed baptism necessary to salvation, and therefore used this last mode when the regular one *could not* be used. Cyprian states the case thus:

"You have inquired also, dearest son, what I think of those who in sickness and debility obtain the grace of God, whether they are to be accounted legitimate Christians, in that they are sprinkled, not washed, with the saving water. *Wherein diffidence and modesty forbid me to prejudge any that he think not as he deems right, and act as he thinks.* I, as far as my poor ability conceiveth, account that the Divine blessings can in no respect be mutilated and weakened, nor any less gift be imparted, where what is drawn from the Divine bounty is accepted with the full and entire faith both of the giver and receiver. For in the saving Sacrament the contagion of sin is not so washed away, as, in the ordinary washing of flesh, is the filth of the skin and body, so that there should be need of saltpetre and other appliances, and a bath and pool, in which the poor body may be washed and cleansed. Far otherwise is the breast of the believer washed, otherwise is the mind of man cleansed by the worthiness of faith. *In the saving sacraments, when need compels and God vouchsafes His mercy, His compendious methods confer the whole benefit on believers.* Nor should it disturb any one that the sick seem only to be sprinkled or affused with water, when they attain the grace of the Lord, since holy Scripture speaks by the prophet Ezekiel, and says: ' *Then will I sprinkle clean water upon you, and ye shall be cleansed from all your filthiness; and from all your idols will I cleanse you; a new heart will I give you, and a new spirit will I put within you.*' (Ezek 36 : 25, 26.) Likewise in Numbers: ' *The man that shall be unclean until the even, shall be purified on the third day and on the seventh day, and shall be clean. But if he shall not be purified on the third day and on the seventh day, he shall not be clean; and that soul shall be cut off from Israel, because the water of sprinkling hath not been sprinkled upon him*' (Numbers 19 : 7 and 19 : 20.) And again: ' *And the Lord spake unto Moses, saying, Take the Levites from among the children of Israel, and cleanse them: and thus shalt thou do unto them to cleanse them; thou shalt sprinkle water of purifying upon them.*' (Numb. 8 : 5–7.) And again: ' *The water of sprinkling is a purification.*' (Numb. 19 : 9.) Whence it is apparent that the sprinkling also of water has like force with the saving washing, and that when this is done in the Church, where the faith both of the giver and receiver is entire, all holds good, and is consummated and perfected by the power of the Lord and the truth of faith," &c. Ep. 69 (ad Magnum) Oxf. Trans.

Now let us examine this passage, and what follows it.

And first, and chiefly, it is to be noted that the question is not, whether in the case of a well or healthy infant or adult, sprinkling or pouring may be used. The question, as stated by Cyprian himself, is, whether " Those *who in sickness and debility* obtain the grace of God are to be accounted legitimate Christians, in that they are sprinkled, not washed, with the saving water." What can be clearer than this? and yet how often is this very passage quoted as though Cyprian meant to countenance the irregularity of using other modes than immersion in any other case than that of *necessity*. He says distinctly as his conclusion: "In sacramentis salutaribus, *necessitate cogente, et Deo indulgentiam suam largiente*, totum credentibus conferunt divina compendia." "In the saving sacraments, when necessity compels, and God grants the indulgence, DIVINE COMPENDS confer the whole benefits on believers."

He did not himself deem pouring or sprinkling a full administration as to *mode*, though he did in case of necessity as to *validity*, for he expressly classes it among "divine compends," and the CONDITIONS *of its use* are stated as "when *necessity compels* and *God grants the indulgence*." Again, in the last part of this famous epistle, he again alludes to this lawfulness of using a divine compend in case of necessity: "We do in very deed experience, that those who on *pressure of necessity* have been baptized in sickness, and have received grace, are freed from the unclean spirit whereby they were before moved, live in the Church in praise and honor, and daily advance more and more, through the increase of faith, to the full growth of heavenly grace; and contrariwise, some frequently of those baptized in good health, if afterwards they begin to sin, are shaken by the return of the unclean spirit." Cyprian states, towards the end of this epistle: "Therefore, as far as it is given me by faith to conceive and judge, my judgment is this: that whosoever shall in the Church have obtained the Divine grace by the law and rule of faith, be deemed a legitimate Christian. Or, if any think that they have obtained nothing, in that they have only been affused with saving water, but are still empty and void, they must not be deceived, and so, if they escape the ills of their sickness and recover, be they baptized. But if they cannot be baptized who have been already sanctified by the baptism of the Church, why lay a stumbling block as to their own faith or the mercy of the Lord?"

It is well to remember that the immersion of a person who had been affused in sickness, was advised by Cyprian, not because he deemed affusion in such circumstances invalid, but in order that the person who had received such compendious baptism might be freed from the pain of thinking and feeling that he was still unbaptized, and consequently, out of the covenant of mercy. Such baptism was wholly, in Cyprian's esteem, unnecessary, and indeed inadmissible, except for this reason.

A large part of the Church uses conditional baptism in cases where *doubt* exists for *any* cause.

But Cyprian may mean that it was not usual, even conditionally, to repeat such baptism as was administered by the compends to clinics,* and the language of canon 47 of Laodicea certainly implies that it is perfectly valid, as he thought, for the words convey no limitation as to mode.

We have seen no evidence, during the first 1600 years, to convince us that such baptism *must* be repeated, whatever Cyprian may have deemed allowable conditionally, when a clinic was dissatisfied or in distress of doubt.

This, then, is the position of Cyprian. He deems pouring and sprinkling compends of the sacrament of baptism, but compends prophesied of in the passages of Holy Writ, to which he refers in the part just cited; and he deems that these divine compends may be used when necessity compels, and when God grants his indulgence. This is precisely the position of the Church of England. She, too, in common with the whole Church, since Cyprian's days, deems a compend of the sacrament of baptism better than no administration at all, and as allowable in case of necessity. But neither Cyprian, nor the Ecumenical Church, nor the particular Church of England, has authorized it at any other time. Cyprian deemed not only necessity a prerequisite to the administration of the abbreviated forms, but also the "indulgence" (indulgentiam) of God. A careful reading of the whole part of this epistle which relates to the baptism of clinics, will do away with the idea that he authorizes it by his advice at any other time. If it be said that he quotes texts which, if one receives his interpretation, would seem to apply generally, yet it should be remembered that this part of the epistle should be taken in connection with those portions of it in which he distinctly calls them not the full sacrament, but divine compends of the sacrament, and states that they may be used when necessity

---

* v. Marshall's St. Cyprian in loc. v. quot. farther on in this vol. from "Orth. et Papisme." v. another view in the quot. from Macaire. We have found no one until the rise of the immersing Antipædobaptists who positively asserted that sprinkling and pouring in necessity is *invalid*. But a part of the Greeks (Orthodox) deem it *doubtful*. The Russians admit it. We have not found an instance of its repetition anywhere, though such may be found among the later Constantinopolitan Greeks.

compels, and God grants his indulgence. Moreover, it should be remembered that this is a private interpretation of Cyprian's, regarding the import of the passages from Ezekiel and Numbers; and moreover, and what is most important, no ecumenical council of the Church has ever adopted it.* *So far then as bringing these passages* in support of what he deems a compend, all must rest upon his single opinion, *but so far as the adoption of the principle, that a compend of a sacrament may be used instead of the full administration*, his view has been *universally received;* and without receiving it, it would be indeed difficult to prove that any church exists on earth. For the Church has applied this principle of necessity to many things besides the imperfect administration of baptism. But let it be remembered that Cyprian's authority can be cited for sprinkling only where the Anglican rubric can, that is, in necessity, and that on catholic principles his unsupported interpretation is not to be taken for catholic doctrine, but as private opinion: for nothing becomes catholic doctrine except by bearing the test of having been held "always, everywhere, and by all," and having been so proclaimed by one of the six ecumenical councils, whose decisions we profess our willingness to hold every time we repeat, "I believe one Catholic and Apostolic Church." When a man goes either AGAINST or BEYOND the ecumenical Church, whatever his station or rank in the Church, he must stand or fall by himself, and it is so with those private ideas of Cyprian, though he expresses them with moderation and modesty, as both the beginning and conclusion of this epistle show. The Church in ecumenical council assembled is the only tribunal of the ecumenical Church. To that the individual opinions of even her noblest and best sons must be brought as to a test. One of the opinions of Cyprian has already passed that test. The Church, in the seventh canon of the Second General Council, decided that the baptism of some heretics is valid, thereby

---

* As to St. Cyprian's application of these passages the reader will judge. The *opinion* of a Father is very widely different from his *historical* testimony. As to the quotation from Isaiah, the Septuagint renders it, "shall be astonished." Gesenius thinks shall sprinkle is wrong. v. Campbell on Baptism, n. p. 173.

The learned are not wholly agreed as to the rendering, and hence not in regard to its being a prophecy regarding a "divine compend," as St. Cyprian deemed it of the fuller administration. But this does not affect the fact, that nearly, if not all Christian orders are derived through men baptized by compends, and whose baptism, if we deny, we deny, so far as nearly or quite all of Christendom is concerned, the existence of a church.

condemning by implication his view, that *all* heretical baptism is invalid.* See Poole's St. Cyprian.

But his views regarding using the compend of a sacrament in case of necessity, has acquired the force of ecumenical and catholic custom. And in giving it this place, the Church seems only to have acted upon the same plea of necessity to which our Lord refers in the case of David's eating the show-bread, and which must, from the constant presence of the law of necessity in the Church, ever prevail as an *exceptional custom*, but not as the rule. The great principle of necessity is best illustrated by the case which the Saviour himself adduces of the eating of the show-bread by David, and "them that were with him," and "which," he adds, "it is not lawful to eat, but for the priests alone" (Matt. 12 : 3, 4, and Luke 6 : 3, 4), and which was to be eaten "by Aaron and his sons" in the holy place, and of which it is recorded in the pages of inspiration, that it was "most holy unto him of the offerings of the Lord made by fire by a perpetual statute." (Lev. 24 : 9.) Now here is a ceremonial observance, as baptism is, commanded by God to be done in a certain way; and yet, in a case of necessity, that usage is departed from; and so the Church has acted when urgent necessity has compelled. It is not the regular way for a layman to baptize, and yet so universal has it been in cases of necessity, and that, too, from the earliest times, that unless we admit it as valid we shall place in doubt the baptism and consequent claim to covenant mercy of vast multitudes of our predecessors in the faith, and shall, besides, place in the same doubt the validity of the orders received, and of the orders conferred by all who received no other baptism. But one instance out of many has been given. But it would be easy to add to the list. Canonicity is essential to regularity, but, in all parts of the Church, the canons have been more or less departed from, and hence there has been a lack of regularity. Nevertheless, the whole Church has never established the principle that in every case regularity is essential to validity.

Necessity admits no law. The principle advocated, then, in

---

* This Council also condemned, by implication, the opinion of Pope Stephen, S. Cyprian's opponent on this question. Another ecumenical council anathematized Pope Honorius as a heretic. Every Latin, therefore, who follows the decisions of a Roman Pontiff in points not decided upon by one of the six ecumenical councils follows a fallible as well as an unauthorized (*i. e.* to decide doctrine) guide, which may lead him to perdition, as it has many.

this epistle of Cyprian has been approved in the practice of this Church, namely, that a compend of a sacrament in case of necessity is valid. But this does not authorize the use of a compend at any other time.

St. Cyprian was so far from believing that, in ordinary cases, the mode is indifferent, that he expressly states his belief that Christ commanded immersion.

Epistle 25:* The Lord, after his resurrection, when sending forth his Apostles, commanded and said: "All power is given unto me in heaven and in earth. Go ye, therefore, and teach all nations, *immersing* them in the name of the Father, and of the Son, and of the Holy Ghost; teaching them to observe all things whatsoever I have commanded you."

The above command of Christ, Cyprian implies, the Apostles obeyed.

Epistle 63:† For, if the Apostle lies not, when he says, "As many of you as were immersed into Christ have put on Christ, then truly he who was then baptized into Christ has put on Christ."

The Author of the Questions upon the Scripture, under the Name of Athanasius.

(On the Epistles of Paul, Rom. 6:5, Prop. 92.)

"We have been planted together; that is, made fellow heirs. For as the body of the Lord when buried in the earth gave life to the world, so our bodies also buried in baptism guarantee our justification. But the similitude consists in this: as Christ died, and rose again on the third day, so we also dying in baptism rise again. For the plunging of the child three times into the bath, and the raising him out of it again, symbolize the death, and the resurrection of Christ on the third day."

Cyril of Jerusalem.

"You made the saving confession, and descended thrice into the water, and again ascended, thus shadowing forth by

---

* Ep. 25, ed. S. Mauri, p. 82: "Dominus post resurrectionem mittens apostolos mandat et dixit. *Data est mihi omnis potestas in cœlo et in terra. Ite ergo et docete gentes omnes, tingentes eos in nomine Patris et Filii et Spiritus Sancti, docentes eos observare omnia quæcunque præcepi vobis.*"

† Ep. 75 (p. 306): "Nam si non mentitur apostolus dicens, *quotquot in Christo tincti estis, Christum induistis;* utique qui illic in Christo baptizatus est, induit Christum."

means of a symbol the three days' burial of Christ." Catech. v. Mystag. ii, n. iv.*

The same. Catechetical Lectures of St. Cyril: Oxford Trans. 1838. Introductory Lecture, chap. ii : "Even Simon Magus once came to the laver of baptism; he was baptized, but not enlightened. His body he dipped in water, but admitted not the Spirit to illuminate his heart. His body went down and came up; but his soul was not buried together with Christ, nor with him raised."

The same. Lecture iii : "Whereas, then, He (Christ) was to crush the *heads of the dragon*, He descended, and in the waters bound the mighty one, that we might receive power to tread upon serpents and scorpions."

(The reference in "heads of the dragon" is to Job 40 : 23, in Sept.)

The same. Lecture iii, 12: "Thou descendest into the water bearing sins, but the invocation of grace having sealed thy soul, allows not that thou shouldest henceforth be swallowed up by the fearful dragon. Dead in sins thou wentest down, quickened in righteousness thou comest up; *for if thou wert planted together in the likeness of the Saviour's death, thou shalt be counted worthy of His resurrection also.* For as Jesus took on Him the world's sins, and died, that having been the death of sin, He might raise thee up in righteousness; so thou also, by descending into the water, and in some sense being in the waters buried, as He was in the rock, art raised again, to walk in newness of life."

The same. Lecture xx, myst. ii, chap. iv : "After these things, ye were led to the holy pool of Divine baptism, as Christ was carried from the cross to the sepulchre which is before our eyes. And each of you was asked, whether he believed in the name of the Father, and of the Son, and of the Holy Ghost, and ye made that saving confession, and descended three times into the water, and ascended again; here also covertly pointing by a figure at the three-days' burial of Christ. For, as our Saviour passed three days and three nights in the heart of the earth, so you also, in your first ascent out of the water, represented the first day of Christ in the earth, and by your descent, the night; for as he who is in the night sees no more, but he who is in the day remains in the light, so in descend-

* Ὁμολογήσατε τὴν σωτήριον ὁμολογίαν, καὶ κατεδύετε τρίτον εἰς τὸ ὕδωρ, καὶ πάλιν ἀνεδύετε καὶ ἐνταῦθα διὰ συμβόλου τὴν τριήμερον τοῦ Χριστοῦ αἰνιττόμενοι ταφήν.

ing, ye saw nothing as in the night, but in ascending again, ye were as in the day. And at the selfsame moment ye died and were born; and that water of salvation was at once your grave and your mother."

St. Basil.
(De Spirit. Sanct. cap. xv.)*

"There is but one death for the world and one resurrection from the dead, of both which baptism (or immersion) is a type.

"Therefore has *the Lord, the dispenser of life, established the rite of baptism* (or immersion) *for us, that it might afford a figure of death and of life, the water fulfilling the image of death,* but the Spirit giving the pledge of life. So that from this, that which we seek, viz., why the water is joined to the Spirit, becomes evident.

"For there being in baptism two ends to be attained, the first to abolish the body of sin, that it may no longer bear fruit unto death; and, secondly, to live to the Spirit and to bear fruit unto holiness: the water affords the image of that death, by receiving the body as in a grave, but the Spirit imparts its life-giving power, by renewing our souls from the death of sin to the pristine life. This, then, is what is meant by being born of water and of the Spirit; death being brought to pass in the water, but life being wrought in us through the Spirit. In three immersions, therefore, and in the same number of invocations, the great mystery of baptism is finished, so that both the figure of death is exhibited and the souls of the baptized are illuminated by the transmission (or gift) of the knowledge of God."

See also De Spirit. Sanct. c. xxvii, where he speaks of the trine immersion as derived *through* tradition. In the first part of the quotation above, he implies that it, or at least immersion, was *established* by the Lord. The expressions, then, contain no contradiction. Tradition was the means, the command of God the source of the transmission.

Ambrose.
(On the Sacraments, chap. vii.)

"Thou wast asked, 'Dost thou believe in God, the Father

---

* Ἐν τρισὶν οὖν καταδύσεσι, καὶ ἰσαρίθμοις ταῖς ἐπικλήσεσι, τὸ μέγα τοῦ βαπτίσματος τελειοῦται, ἵνα καὶ ὁ τοῦ θανάτου τύπος ἐξεικονίσθῃ, καὶ τῇ παραδόσει τῆς θεογνωσίας τὰς ψυχὰς φωτισθῶσιν οἱ βαπτιζόμενοι. In this chap. xv, St. Basil teaches that the *divine* symbolism is effected by immersion. He thought immersion referred to in Rom. 6, and Col. 2. But a part is quoted above; v. the whole.

Almighty?' and thou repliedst, 'I believe,' and wast dipped, that is, buried. A second demand was made, 'Dost thou believe in Jesus Christ, our Lord, and in his cross?' thou answeredst again, 'I believe,' and wast dipped. Therefore thou wast buried with Christ; for he that is buried with Christ rises again with Christ. A third time the question was repeated, 'Dost thou believe in the Holy Ghost?' and thy answer was, 'I believe,' then thou wast dipped a third time; that thy triple confession might absolve thee from the various offences of thy former life."*

"The Apostle then teaches, as you have heard in the present lesson, 'so many of us as were baptized into Jesus Christ, were baptized into his death.' (Rom. 6 : 3, &c.) What is the meaning of 'into his death?' As Christ died, so dost thou taste death. As Christ died to sin, and lived to God, so thou also, by the sacrament of baptism, didst die to the snares of former sins, and thou didst rise by Christ's grace. A death there is, therefore, but not in reality a death of the body, but only in a similitude. For when thou wast dipped thou didst undergo the similitude both of a death and burial."†

St. Ambrose, tom. ii, part ii, uses tinguo as a synonym for baptizo. Again and again he refers to baptism as a type of death and resurrection. v. "Baptismus," in the index of his works. v. De Sacram., cap. vi and vii.

St. Jerome.

(On Ephesians 4 : 5, 6.)

"We are thrice dipped in water, that the mystery of the Trinity may appear to be but one; and therefore, though we

---

* Ambros. de Sacram., lib. 2, c. 7. Interrogatus es, "credis in Deum, Patrem Omnipotentem?" Dixixti, "credo" et mersisti, hoc est, sepultus es. Iterum interrogatus es, "credis in Dominum nostrum Jesum Christum?" Dixisti, "credo," et mersisti. Ideo et Christo es consepultus. Qui enim Christo consepelitur, cum Christo resurgit. Tertio interrogatus es, "Credis et in Spiritum Sanctum?" Dixisti, "credo." Tertio mersisti, ut multiplicem lapsum superioris aetatis absolveret trina confessio.

† S. Ambros. De Sacr , cap. 7, clamat ergo Apostolus, sicut audistis in lectione præsenti: "Quoniam quicunque baptizatur, in morte Jesu baptizatur. (Rom. 6 : 3, et seq.) Quid est in morte ? Ut quomodo Christus mortuus est, sic et tu mortem degustes, quomodo Christus mortuus est peccato. Deo vivit ; ita et tu superioribus illecebris peccatorum mortuus sis per baptismatis sacramentum, et surrexeris per gratiam Christi. Mors ergo est, sed non in mortis corporalis veritate, sed in similitudine ; cum enim mergis, mortis suscipis et sepulturæ similitudinem." See more in the same place. v. Curs. Comp., S. Hieron, t. i, p. 421, ed. Migne.

be thrice put under water, to represent the mystery of the Trinity, yet it is reputed but one baptism."* Bingham's Trans.

(Adv. Lucif., cap. iv.)

"Many other things which are observed by tradition in the churches have acquired the authority of written law, as, for instance, to immerse the head thrice in the laver, &c."†

(On Matt. 28 : 19.)

"At first they teach all nations, then, when taught, they immerse them in water."‡

St. Jerome seemed to think that the number of immersions had come down by tradition. But it is not so clear that he, or any of the Fathers who speak of trine immersion as de-

---

* S. Hieron. in Ephes., cap. 4 : 5, 6. Et ter mergimur, ut Trinitatis unum appareat sacramentum . . . . . Potest unum baptisma et ita dici, quod licet ter baptizemur, propter mysterium Trinitatis : tamen unum baptisma reputetur.

† Adv. Lucifer, c. iv. We give the whole passage, to show what the patristic idea of tradition was, and how it differs from, and in some things how entirely it is ignored by Rome; and yet what follow are things mentioned by many of the early Fathers as traditions universally held by the Church, and which had descended from the Apostles, and which no man might break.

Au nescis etiam ecclesiarum hunc esse morem, ut baptizatis postea manus imponantur, et ita invocetur spiritus sanctus? Exigis ubi scriptum est? In Actibus Apostolorum. Etiam si Scripturæ auctoritas non subesset, totius orbis in hanc partem consensus instar præcepti obtineret. Nam et multa alia, quæ per traditionem in Ecclesiis observatur, auctoritatem sibi scriptæ legis usurpaverunt, *velut in lavacro ter caput mergitare*, deinde egressos, lactis et mellis prægustare concordiam ad infantiæ significationem, die Dominica, et omni Pentecoste, nec de geniculis adorare, et jejunium solvere, multaque alia scripta non sunt, quæ rationabilis sibi observatio vindicarit. Ex quo animadvertis nos ecclesiæ consuetudinem sequi, licet ante advocationem spiritus constet aliquem baptizatum. v. also Tert. de Corona, cap. iii, and St. Basil, cap. xxvii.

If, at the present time, we were to restore the ancient rites mentioned by these authors, the step would be a wise one. This handle would be taken from the Latin with the ignorant, as it now is with those who know the wide abyss between the few ancient customs known as traditions, most of which the Roman Church has laid aside, and her own private and Western traditions, which do not reach back to primitive times, and which lack the quod semper, quod ubique, quod ab omnibus, of Catholic testimony. The great trouble now is, that the ignorant are so apt to confound Latinism with Catholicity, whereas, in some points, they are utterly opposed to each other.

‡ In Matt. 28 : 19. Primum docent omnes gentes, deinde doctas intingunt aqua.

scending by tradition, mean also that immersion itself did. Their statements do not necessarily militate against the opinion that the mode of dipping was enjoined by God.

If the reader will glance at what St. Jerome says regarding tradition, in our second quotation, he will find little cause to disagree with him. The context of the first passage answers an objection to trine immersion. The points for which Jerome pleads tradition are:

1. Trine immersion.
2. Tasting milk and honey, after coming out of the waters of baptism.
3. To stand while praying on the Lord's day, and during all the time of Pentecost; and during all these periods to abstain from fasting. (V. with reference to this, which is *now* a law of the whole Church, canon 20 of the Ecumenical Council of Nice, with Hammond's note on it.)

The reader who would see what ceremonies are mentioned, as attested by *tradition*, will do well to consult Tertullian, De Corona, cap. iii, and St. Basil, De Spirit. Sanct., cap. xxvii. The ancient and modern sense of it is often widely different, and especially among Latins the late notion is diametrically against the earlier. The Greeks err also in this respect, though less than the Latins. Perfect orthodoxy is not only compatible with the due observance of ancient rites, but is most consonant with them. The only trouble might be that the weak might be injured, owing to prevalent ignorance, or to the idea, foolish and wrong indeed, but nevertheless widely spread, that these rites, or some of them, have some connection with later errors in doctrine. It would have been a good movement if they had been restored, or (where they still existed) retained, so far as they were primitive, at the Reformation; and if the Nicæno-Constantinopolitan symbol had been restored to the form in which the Church left it, and if all the canons of the six Ecumenical Councils were enforced. In time these things may be done.

Old Writings, under the Name of St. Augustine.

"After you made profession of your faith, we plunged your heads three times in the sacred font,—which order of baptism is used for the twofold signification of the mystery (or sacrament). For rightly were you thrice dipped who have received baptism in the name of the Trinity. Rightly were you thrice dipped who have received baptism in the name of Jesus Christ, who rose from the dead on the third day. For that trine immersion is a symbol of the Lord's burial, by which you have been buried with Christ in baptism, and have risen with Christ in faith. So that, washed from your sins, you may live by imitating Christ in holiness and virtue. Wherefore a blessed Apostle says, 'Know ye not that so many of us as were baptized into Jesus Christ were baptized into his death? Therefore we are buried with him by baptism into death; that like as Christ was raised up from the dead by the glory of the Father, even so we also should walk in newness of life. For if we have been planted together in the likeness of his death, we shall be also in the likeness of his resurrection,'" &c., to end of v. 6 in Eng. vers.*

See to the same purport his works, ed. Venetiis, 1731, "De Vera et falsa penitentia, lib. 1, 7, p. 233. See also tom. 6, Appendix, p. 290, Sermo de Myst. Bapt. ad Neoph. He mentions the trine immersion, tom. 5, Appendix, Sermo 24. De via trium dierum 1, p. 50; and in Sermo 40, de Elia 4, p. 79.

But candor obliges us to state that, whatever be the value of these references, it is very doubtful whether some, perhaps any of them, is a genuine production of St. Augustine, although they are often quoted as such. We do not, therefore, bring them as proofs; and the same remark will apply to Dionysius the Areopagite, and to Athanasius, as already given. The proof is sufficient and even abundant without any of these. But, nevertheless, these quotations and the writings from

---

* S. Augustin, Opera. ed. Venet., 1731, lib. 1, 7, p. 233, Appendix. De vera et falsa pœnitentia. "Qui enim baptizatur, mortem crucis et sepulturam Christi repræsentat in immersione sua: in signo enim crucis quisque in aqua submergitur, et submersus sepultus ostenditur." V. id. t. 6, Appendix, p. 290, Sermo de Mysterio Baptismatis ad Neophytos.

"Postquam vos credere promisistis, tertio capita vestra in sacro fonte demersimus. Qui ordo baptismatis duplici mysterii significatione celebratur. Recte enim tertio mersi estis, qui accepistis baptismum in nomine Jesu Christi, qui tertio die resurrexit a mortuis. Illa enim tertio repetita demersio typum dominicæ exprimit sepulturæ; per quam Christo consepulti estis in baptismo, et cum Christo resurrexistis in fide, ut peccatis abluti in sanctitate virtutum Christum imitando vivatis. Unde beatus Apostolus ait, an ignoratis quoniam quicunque baptizati sumus in Christo Jesu, in morto ipsius baptizati sumus? Consepulti enim sumus cum illo," &c.

which they are taken, are not wholly without *historical* value, for they are early.

CENTURY IV.
GREGORY NYSSEN.
(On Christ's Baptism.)

"We, who receive baptism, in imitation of our Lord, and Teacher, and Guide, are not buried in the earth, for this covers the entirely lifeless body, and enwraps the weakness and corruption of our nature; . . . but coming to the water, the element cognate to the earth, we hide ourselves in it, as the Saviour hid himself in the earth; and this we do three times, to represent the grace of His resurrection performed after three days."*

ZENO, BISHOP OF VERONA.

In favor of immersion. v. Opera, ed. Migne, pp. 480, 481.

CHRYSOSTOM.

"In baptism are fulfilled the pledges of our covenant with God: burial and death, resurrection and life; and these take place all at once. For when we immerse our heads in the water, the old man is buried as in a tomb below, and *wholly sunk* forever; then as we raise them again, the new man rises in its stead. As it is easy for us to dip and to lift our heads again, so it is easy for God to bury the old man, and to show forth the new. And this is done thrice, that you may learn that the power of the Father, the Son, and the Holy Ghost fulfilleth all this. To show that what we say is no conjecture, hear Paul saying, '*We are buried with Him by baptism into death.*' And again, '*Our old man is crucified with Him.*' And again, '*We have been planted together in the likeness of His death.*' And not only is baptism called a 'cross,' but the 'cross' is called 'baptism.' *With the baptism*, saith Christ, *that I am baptized withal shall ye be baptized;* and, *I have*

---

* Greg. Nyss. de Bapt. Christi, ed. Migne, 1858, p. 585. Ἡμεῖς δὲ τὸ βάπτισμα παραλαμβάνοντες, εἰς μίμησιν τοῦ Κυρίου καὶ διδασκάλου καὶ καθηγεμόνος ἡμῶν, εἰς γῆν μὲν οὐ θαπτόμεθα, ... ἐπὶ δὲ τὸ συγγενὲς τῆς γῆς στοιχεῖον, τὸ ὕδωρ, ἐρχόμενοι, ἐκείνῳ ἑαυτοὺς ἐγκρύπτομεν, ὡς ὁ Σωτήρ τῇ γῇ καὶ τρίτον τοῦτο ποιήσαντες, τὴν τριήμερον ἑαυτοὺς τῆς ἀναστάσεως χάριν ἐξεικονίζομεν.

a baptism to be baptized with (which ye know not); for as we easily dip and lift our heads again, so He also easily died and rose again when He willed, or rather much more easily, though he tarried the three days for the dispensation of a certain mystery."* Oxford Trans.

(Hom. xl, on 1 Cor.)

"After the enunciation of these mystical and fearful words, and the awful rules of the doctrines which have come down from heaven, this also we add at the end, when we are about to baptize, bidding them say, 'I believe in the resurrection of the dead,' and upon this faith we are baptized. I say, after we have confessed this together with the rest, *then at last are we let down into the fountain of those sacred streams.* This, therefore, Paul recalling to their minds, said, 'If there be no resurrection, why art thou then baptized for the dead?' i. e., the dead bodies. For, in fact, with a view to this art thou baptized, affirming a resurrection of thy dead body, that it no longer remains dead. And thou indeed in the words makest mention of a resurrection of the dead; but the priest, as in a kind of image, signifies to thee by very deed, the things which thou hast believed and confessed in the appointed words. When without a sign thou believest, then he gives thee the sign also; when thou hast done thine own part, then also doth God fully assure thee. How, and in what manner? By the water. For the being baptized and immersed, and then emerging, is a symbol of the descent into hell, and the return thence. Wherefore also Paul calls baptism a burial, saying, 'Therefore we are buried with him by baptism into death.'"† Oxf. Trans.

(Hom. de Fide.)

"Christ delivered to his disciples one baptism in three immersions of the body, when he said to them, 'Go, teach all nations, baptizing them in the name of the Father, and of the Son, and of the Holy Ghost.'"‡ Bingham's Trans.

---

* St. Chryost. in Joan. iii, 5. Hom. xxv. Καθάπερ ἔν τινι τάφῳ, τῷ ὕδατι καταδυόντων ἡμῶν τὰς κεφαλὰς, ὁ παλαιὸς ἄνθρωπος θάπτεται, καὶ καταδὺς κάτω κρύπτεται ὅλος καθάπαξ εἶτα ἀνανευόντων ἡμῶν, ὁ καινὸς ἄνεισι πάλιν.

† Chrysostom. Hom. xl (40), in 1 Cor. p. 689 (p. 452, d. edit. Francof.) Τὸ γὰρ βαπτίζεσθαι καὶ καταδύεσθαι, εἶτα ἀνανεύειν, τῆς εἰς ᾅδου καταβάσεώς ἐστι σύμβολον, καὶ τῆς ἐκεῖθεν ἀνόδου διὸ καὶ τάφον τὸ βάπτισμα ὁ Παῦλος καλεῖ λέγων, Συνετάφημεν οὖν αὐτῷ διὰ τοῦ βαπτίσματος εἰς τὸν θάνατον.

‡ Chrysostom. Hom. de Fide, tom. vii, p. 290, edit. Savil. Ἐν τρισὶ καταδύσεσι τοῦ σώματος ἓν βάπτισμα τοῖς ἑαυτοῦ μαθηταῖς παρέδωκε, κ.τ.λ.

CENTURY V.

Theodoret, Bishop of Cyrus.

"He (Eunomius) subverted the law of holy baptism, which had been handed down from the beginning from the Lord and the apostles, and made a contrary law, asserting that it is not necessary to immerse the candidate for baptism thrice, nor to mention the names of the Trinity, but to immerse once only into the death of Christ."* On Eunomius, v. Socrates, Eccl. Hist. bk. iv, c. vii, and bk. v, c. xxiv, and Sozomen under "Eunomius," in the index.

Sozomen, the Church Historian.

(Eccl. Hist. book vi, chap. 26.)

Some say that this Eunomius was the first who dared to bring forward the notion, that the divine baptism ought to be administered by a single immersion; and to corrupt the tradition which has been handed down from apostles, and which is still observed by all (or among all). . . . But whether it was Eunomius, or any other person, who first introduced heretical opinions concerning baptism, it seems to me that such innovators, whoever they may have been, were alone in danger, according to their own representation, of quitting this life without having received the rite of holy baptism; for if, after having received baptism according to the ancient mode of the Church (*i. e.*, by trine immersion), they found it impossible to reconfer it on themselves, it must be admitted that they introduced a practice to which they had not themselves submitted, and thus undertook to administer to others what had never been administered to themselves (*i. e.*, single immersion into the death of Christ). The absurdity of this assumption is manifest from their own confession; for they admit that those who have not received the rite of baptism have not the power of administering it. Now, according to their opinion, those who have not received the rite of baptism in conformity with

---

* Theodoret. Hæret. Fabul. lib. iv, c. iii, p. 236 (Hal. 1772, iv, 356).
Αὐτὸς καὶ τοῦ ἁγίου βαπτίσματος ἀνέτρεψε τὸν ἄνεκαθεν παρὰ τοῦ Κυρίου καὶ ἀποστόλων παραδοθέντα θεσμόν, καὶ ἄντικρυς ἀντενομοθέτησε. μὴ χρῆναι λέγων τρὶς καταδύειν τὸν βαπτιζόμενον. μηδὲ ποιεῖσθαι τὴν τῆς Τριάδος ἐπίκλησιν· ἀλλ' ἅπαξ βαπτίζειν εἰς τὸν θάνατον τοῦ Χριστοῦ.

their mode of administration (*i. e.*, single immersion) are unbaptized; and they confirm this opinion by their practice, inasmuch as they rebaptize (*i. e.*, by single immersion) all those who join their sect, although previously baptized (*i. e.*, by trine immersion) by the Catholic Church.* There is a mistake in Bohn's trans., in the fifth and sixth lines of this chapter, p. 282. See the Greek.

Leo I, Bishop of Rome.

This writer will be found in the chapter on the Councils below. V. also Opera, ed Migne, t. i, ser. vii, p. 382.

St. Peter Chrysologus.

(V. Opera, ed. Migne, Paris, 1846. Sermo cxiii, p. 511.)

He mentions the trine immersion as the usual custom of his day. He was Archbishop of Ravenna.

St. Maximus, of Turin.

(Ed. Migne, Paris, 1847, p. 778.)

See also id. p. 775, which shows that the immersion was total.†

"Before we immersed your whole body in this font, we asked: Dost thou believe in God the Father Almighty? Thou answeredst, I believe," &c.

Gennadius, of Marseilles.

(De Eccl. Dogmatibus, lib. cap. 52.)

Speaking of heretics, he uses language which might imply that Christ commanded not only baptism in the name of the Trinity, but also immersion: "It is not to be believed that those are baptized who have not been immersed in the name of the Father, and of the Son, and of the Holy Ghost, according to the rule established by the Lord."‡

---

* Sozom. lib. vi, c. xxvi. (Cant. p. 252.) Φασὶ δέ τινες, πρῶτον τοῦτον Εὐνόμιον τολμῆσαι εἰσηγήσασθαι, ἐν μιᾷ καταδύσει χρῆναι ἐπιτελεῖν τὴν θείαν βάπτισιν, καὶ παραχαράξαι τὴν ἀπὸ τῶν ἀποστόλων εἰσέτι νυν ἐν πᾶσι φυλαττομένην παράδοσιν.

† St. Maximus Taurin. ed. sup. p. 775. "In hoc ergo fonte antequam vos toto corpore *tingeremus*, interrogavimus: credis in Deum Patrem omnipotentem?" &c. Gennad. Massil.

‡ Gennad. Massil. ut sup. Neque enim credendum est eos fuisse bap-

CENTURY VI.

Pelagius, Bishop of Rome.

"There are many who say that they baptize in the name of Christ alone, and by a single immersion. But the Gospel command, which was given by God himself, and our Lord and Saviour Jesus Christ, reminds us that we should administer holy baptism to every one, in the name of the Trinity and by trine immersion, for our Lord said to his disciples, 'Go, baptize all nations in the name of the Father, and of the Son, and of the Holy Ghost.'"*

St. Gregory, Presbyter of Antioch.

In De Baptismo Christi, Sermo i, he represents Christ as saying to St. John the Baptist: "Cover me in the floods of the Jordan, as she who bore me wrapped me in the clothes of infancy."†

Pope Vigilius also favors trine immersion (v. S. Isadori op. ed. Migne, t. viii, p. 831).

---

tizatos, qui non in nomine Patris et Filii et Spiritus sancti juxta regulam a Domino positam tincti sunt. He refers, it is true, to "form," but in tincti specifies mode. By "form," is meant the words of invocation, I baptize thee, in the name of the Father, &c.,—by mode, the way of administering the rite by water. But v. Gennad. Massil. De Eccl. Dogmat., cap. 74, where he says, "Ille post confessionem vel aspergitur aqua, vel intingitur, martyr vero vel aspergitur sanguine, vel contingatur igne." v. Wall, vol. ii, p. 390. There is nothing to show that "aspergitur," which is the reading of the manuscript which Migne follows, and of others besides, refers to any case but that of necessity. Migne in loc. does not say what other readings there are. The remark of Wall, that Gennadius makes the mode indifferent, needs therefore to be modified. This passage should be taken in connection with the preceding quotation and contemporary writings.

* Pelag. Epist. ad. Gaudent. ap. Gratianum, distinct. 4, c. 82: Multi sunt, qui in nomine solummodo Christi una etiam mersione se adserunt baptizare. Evangelicum vero præceptum, ipso Deo et Domino salvatore nostro Jesu Christo tradente, nos admonet, in nomine Trinitatis, trina etiam mersione sanctum baptisma unicuique tribuere, dicente Domino discipulis suis, "Ite, baptizate omnes gentes in nomine Patris, Filii, et Spiritus Sancti."

† Greg. Presb. Antioch. ut sup. Demerge me Iordanicis fluentis his, quemadmodum quæ me genuit infantilibus involvit panis. V. ed Migne. tom. 88. Curs. Comp. p. 1870.

Pope Gregory the Great.

We come now to a writer of whom we shall speak again.

He is the first orthodox writer who deemed that the trine immersion might be changed to the single for convenience. Yet he states, that the custom at Rome, in his day, was the trine. And it is evident that he thought immersion itself of Divine origin. He explains thus: "Our very descent into the water is called baptism, that is, immersion." V. Moralium, lib. xviii, cap. xxvii. Job, p. 91, ed. Migne.*

CENTURY VII.

See Council IV of Toledo. In this century an innovation was made in Spain, alone, however, in substituting single for trine immersion. But in other parts of the Church the ancient mode remained. As to the Spanish custom, and the light in which it was viewed in other parts of the Church, see Alcuin's testimony hereafter.

CENTURY VIII.

John Damascene.

(On the Orthodox Faith, bk. iv, chap. ix, ed. Migne, p. 1117.)

"Baptism exhibits Christ's death. Therefore we are buried with the Lord by baptism, as says the holy Apostle."

On p. 1120: "The rite of baptism is a type of Christ's death; for, by the three immersions, baptism portrays the three days of the Lord's burial."

It should be remembered that this writer stands pre-eminent among the Easterns for the influence which he has exercised upon them for good or ill. In what is quoted above, he only follows the earlier Fathers and St. Paul.†

---

* V. Greg. Magn. Ep. 41, ad Leand. Nos . . . tertio mergimus, etc. and Moral. ut sup. Unde etiam baptisma, id est tinctio dicitur ipsa nostra in aquam descensio. Tingimur quippe, etc. On baptisteries, v. ref. in index of Gregory's works, t. 3, "Baptisteria." For a learned note on Can. vii, Constantin. 1, and the mode, v. t. iv, p. 343. V. farther on for more of Gregory's language.

† Joann. Damascen. de Fide Orth. lib. iv, cap. ix, de fide et bapt., ed. Migne, t. i, p. 1117. Τὸ γὰρ βάπτισμα τὸν τοῦ κυρίου θάνατον δηλοῖ Συνθαπτόμεθα γοῦν τῷ Κυρίῳ διὰ τοῦ βαπτίσματος, ὥς φησιν ὁ θεῖος Ἀπόστολος. And p. 1120: Τυπος τοῦ θανάτου τοῦ χριστοῦ ἐστι τὸ βάπτισμα. Διὰ γὰρ τῶν τριῶν καταδύσεων, τὰς τρεῖς ἡμέρας τῆς τοῦ κυρίου ταφῆς σημαίνει τὸ βάπτισμα.

Germanus, Patriarch of Constantinople.

"We have been baptized with reference to (or in imitation of) the death and resurrection of Christ himself. For by the descent into the water and the ascent, and by the three submersions, we symbolize and confess the three days' burial and the resurrection of Christ himself. And still further, also, because he was baptized in the Jordan by John," etc. v. id. Rerum Eccl. Contemplatio, ed. Migne, Paris, 1860, p. 385.

Alcuin.

Epistola xc, ad fratres Lugdun., vol. i, p. 289, seq., ed. Migne, Paris, 1851, contends strongly against single immersion and for the trine. He calls the latter the universal custom of the Holy Church of God. His language is very strong and his references to the Fathers apposite. He deduces the trine immersion from Scripture. But the passage is too long to quote.

So also ep. cxiii, ad Paulinum Patriarcham: He is very severe against all who used single immersion, even with the due invocation of the Trinity. See in chapter on the change of mode.

Writing to Paulinus, he speaks of some "who assert that there ought to be but one immersion, and who neglect to imitate in baptism the three days' burial of our Saviour, even when an Apostle says 'you have been buried with Christ in baptism.' (Rom. 6 : 4 ; Col. 2 : 12.) But there are others, who are willing to use the trine immersion, but to invoke the whole Trinity at every immersion; thus they study to name all the three persons thrice; but the truth itself teaches, 'Go ye, therefore, and teach all nations, baptizing them in the name of the Father, and of the Son, and of the Holy Ghost.' (Matt. 28 : 19.) What need of thrice repeating the whole Trinity, if once suffices."*

---

* Alcuin, ep. cxiii, ad Paulinum: "Unam asserentes mersionem fieri debere, triduanamque nostri salvatoris sepulturam in baptismo negligentes, cum apostolus disceret: Consepulti enim estis cum Christo in baptismo. (Rom. 6 : 4 ; Col. 2 : 12.) Alii vero trinam volentes facere mersionem et in unaquaque mersione invocationem Sanctæ Trinitatis: ac per hoc totas tres personas ter nominare studentes, dum ipsa veritas præciperet. Ite, docete omnes gentes, baptizantes eas in nomine Patris et Filii et Spiritus Sancti. (Matt. 28 : 19.) Quid opus est tertio replicare, quod semel dictum sufficit?"

Leidradus, Bishop of Lyons.

(Lib. de Sac. Bapt. cap. vi.)

He explains the term in the original, which signifies baptism as immersion. "Baptismus Græce, Latine tinctio interpretatur."

He quotes Gregory the Great as to the single and trine immersion *seemingly* in approval. But see,

Theodulphus.

(Aureliensis Episcopi. lib. de Ordine Baptismi, cap. xiii.)

His testimony is strongly for trine immersion. He mentions it as the custom of his age.

CENTURY IX.

Rabanus Maurus, Archbishop of Mentz.

(De Cleric. Instit. lib. i, cap. xxv.)*

"*Baptism*, in Greek βάπτισμα, is translated into Latin by immersion (tinctio). And it is called immersion (tinctio), not only because man is immersed in water, but because by the Spirit of Grace he is changed for the better, and made far another being than he was before." So lib. de Sac. Ord. cap. v, cap. xiii. He testifies in id. cap. xiv, to the trine immersion as the custom of his age: "It behooves, therefore, that baptism be performed by trine immersion, with an invocation of the Holy Trinity." (V. also id. cap. xiv; v. Homilia cxiii; Hebdomada vii, post Pentecosten.)

Walafrid Strabo informs us that even in his day trine immersion was still the Roman custom, and indeed the universal use. He condemns the opinion of Gregory the Great in favor of dispensing with trine immersion in the case of the Spaniards. Yet his view of the mode is not inconsistent with the English rubric, for he teaches that in case of *necessity* pouring may be

---

* Rabani Mauri, Decleric. Instit. ut sup. Baptismum βάπτισμα Græco, Latine tinctio interpretatur, quæ non tamen ob hoc quod homo in aquam mergitur tinctio dicitur, sed quia Spiritu gratiæ ibi in melius immutetur, et longe aliud quam erat efficitur.

used: "It ought to be noted, that many have been baptized, not only by immersion, but by pouring, and so it can still be performed if there be necessity, as we read in the passion of St. Laurentius, that one was baptized from a pitcher which had been brought in. This even usually happens when the large size of the bodies of the more mature, and the small size of the vessel which serves as a font, renders it impossible that they should be immersed." V. De Rebus Eccl. cap. xxvi.*

Haymo, Bishop of Halberstadt.

On Romans 6 : 4, he witnesses to the trine immersion as the custom of his age.

Paschasius Radbert, Abbot of Corby.

This man expresses the opinion of others when he translates βάπτισμα by tinctio, and from the context shows that he means immersion. V. in Matt. lib. ix, cap. xx.†

Hincmar, Archbishop of Rheims.

This noted prelate shows clearly that trine immersion was the custom, and that its primitive symbolical meaning was even still further extended. V. De Una et non trina Deitate, cap. x. (See in the chapter on the Councils in this work.)

Regino, Abbot of Prum.

Of similar purport. V. De Eccl. Discip. Appendix I, 63, p. 388, ed. Migne.

John, the Deacon.

Ep. ad Senarium Paulani Nolani Episcopi, ep. xxxii, p. 330.

---

* Walafrid Strabo. V. ut sup. farther on in this work.
† Paschas. Radbert. in Matt, lib. ix, cap. xx. Dicitur autem βάπτισμα Græce, Latine vero tinctio, secundem similitudinem lanæ tinctæ ut puta naturalem habens colorem cum *tingitur* et vertitur in purpuram, vel alicujus coloris accipiens dignitatem ; sic et cum homo cum Christo in mortem venerit, etsi fuerit aliquo infectus colore peccati vel corruptionis, totus ad Christum transit mundus et innovatus, jam spiritalis effectus, sicut ait Apostolus. 1 Cor. 15 : 43, 44.

CENTURY X.
Atto, Bishop of Vercelli.

He uses strong language in favor of immersion. v. Expos. in Rom. 6 : 4.*

CENTURY XI.
Anselm, Bishop of Lucca,

Testifies to the trine immersion and its symbolism as still maintained. V. Collectio Canonica, lib. ix, cap. xvii.†

Lanfranc, Archbishop of Canterbury.

This writer, holding the chief see in the English Church, will serve to strengthen other testimony as to its mode of administration. He says, on Philipp. 3 : 10, *configuratus morte ejus.* "In baptism, for as Christ lay for three days in the sepulchre, so let there be a trine immersion in baptism.‡"

Ivo, Bishop of Chartres.

In Panormiam, cap. 58, lib. 1, this writer embodies canon 50 of the Apostles; but in id., cap. 59, lib. 1, the single immersion is declared sufficient. V. also Sermo 1, de Sacr. Neoph., hab. in Sanct. Synod. He followed Gregory the Great's opinion as to the number of immersions, which receives

---

* Atto, Vercell. Epis. in Rom. 6 : 4. In morte ergo ipsius baptizati sumus, quoniam sicut ille mortuus est, ita et nos, cum abrenuntiamus diabolo et operibus ejus, sæculo et pompis ejus, quodammodo morimur, dum aquis immergimur. Et quia dixerat mortem ejus nostram significasse mortem, ut ostenderet quia sepultura illius nostram significavit sepulturam adjecit: *consepulti enim sumus cum illo per baptismum in mortem.* Quæsi enim Christo consepelimur dum SUB AQUIS LATEMUS: et velut cum ipse resurgimus, cum ex aquis renascimur, ut mortui vitiis, Deo virtutibus vivere incipiamus. Et sciendum quia sacramenta *quamdam similitudinem* habent earum verum, quarum sunt sacramenta; *quod si non haberent sacramenta non essent.*

† Anselmi Lucensis Epis. ut supra. "Quod dum tertio baptizatus mergitur, triduanæ sepulturæ sacramentum signatur."

‡ Lanfranc in Epist. ad Philipp. 3 : 20 (Eng. vers. 3 : 10). *Configuratus morte ejus.* In baptismo, ut enim tribus diebus jacuit Christus in sepulcro, sic in baptismate trina sit immersio.

more favor hereafter. He deemed the waters of aspersion in the Old Testament prefigurative of baptism, which was by immersion.

Bruno, Bishop of Segni.

This prelate derives trine immersion from the words of the commission, Matt. 28 : 19. V. Tractatus 3, de Sacr. Eccl. "Quid in circuitu eundo significet."

CENTURY XII.

Hildebert of Le Mans.

He exhibits the truth that even in century 12 the immersion was still total. Tract. Theol., cap. xl, de Sacr.

Hugo of St. Victor.

Although a Latin, it is worthy of being noted that this author so far differs from Gregory the Great as to deem the trine, not the single immersion, the preferable mode. Unless, as perhaps may be said with truth, that was Gregory's opinion. V. Op. Pars. 2, Dogm. Tract. 5, cap. 4.

In this century, whatever may have been thought by individuals, we have clear information from two writers that the trine immersion was still retained as the general practice. V. Herveus Burgidolensis Monach. in Rom. 6 : 4, and Bernard of Clairvaux, Sermo in Cœna Domini. Cf. Odonis de Soliaco Parisiensis Episcopi. Synod. Constit., cap. iii, 1.

Robert Pulleyn, or Pullus,

An English theologian of this period, deserves notice for the view which he gives, that the trine immersion, although not absolutely necessary, like the form of words, is nevertheless of such importance that, when not used, the administration lies under the fault of negligence. V. Sentent., lib. 5, cap. 17, and lib. 5, cap. 14.*

---

* Rob. Pullus, ut sup. "Negligentia autem culpam habet."

Peter Lombard

Defines thus: "Baptism is called a dipping in (intinctio), that is, a washing of the surface of the body." As to the immersion, he thinks, "it may be once or thrice, according to the various usage of the Church." V. Sentent., lib. 4, Dist. 3, 1, and lib. 4, Dist. 4, 9, to the same purport. V. Magistri Blandini, Sentent., lib. 4, de Eccl. Sac., Dist. 4. This opinion afterwards became embodied in the later ideas and practice of the Latins, and still continues.*

It will be well to notice, in this connection, a mistake sometimes made by persons inexperienced in the language of the early writers. Some of the Fathers speak of the ancient Jewish and heathen purifications as *typical* of baptism. Some say, that as these purifications were often by sprinkling, that therefore the early writers deemed these modes comprehended in the term to baptize. But the slightest knowledge will refute this. For to say of a thing that it is *typical* or figurative of another, and that it is exactly the *same*, are two very different things. It is not essential that the figure and that of which it is a figure should be in all respects alike. It is enough that there be likeness in a single point. When, therefore, the Fathers speak of heathen lustrations, or Jewish sprinklings, as figurative of baptism, we must not so understand them as to make them contradict their repeated statement that βαπτίζω is expressive of mode. The point usually aimed at by them is, that as both these are symbolical of expiation, of cleansing and of purifying, in this respect they are figurative or typical of that divine baptism which washes away sins. (Acts 22 : 16.) That which prefigures baptism may be a rite in which no water is used. St. Augustine asks, "Who that is even moderately versed in the Scriptures, can be ignorant that the sacrament of circumcision in figure preceded that of baptism." St. August. Cont. Julianum Pelagianum, cap. 6, 18, ed. Venet., 1733, "Quod sacramentum circumcisionis in figura praecessisse baptismatis, quis vel mediocriter sacris litteris eruditus ignoret." This tendency to find a figure, wherever there is even a slight similarity, is a characteristic of much that is said by even the earlier Fathers.

* Pet. Lom. ut supra. Baptismus dicitur intinctio, id est ablutio corporis exterior.

SECTION II.

THE ECUMENICAL COUNCILS AND CHURCH LAW.

A council which truly represents the whole Church in all ages is rightly named ecumenical. Christ has commanded us to hear the Church; and *the Church, i. e.* the whole Church, speaks as such, *i. e. defines* or decrees only in ecumenical council. The great curse of Christendom has been that *portions* of the Church have taken upon themselves to represent the whole; and they have claimed, for the private opinions of their bishops, in some representation of a part of the Church, the authority of the whole Church. This is the great evil which underlies the present schisms and disorders of Christendom. The Greek Church, the Latin Church, and indeed almost every other part of the Church, claims for its own local opinions or interpretations the homage of ecumenical doctrine,—of doctrine held always, everywhere, and *by all;* and hence the disputes are endless. *The* Church has never spoken except in ecumenical councils, and on most of the present disputes in Christendom has uttered no special and particular decision. In forbidding, under severe penalties, in Canon vii of the third Ecumenical Council, any other creed than that of Nicæa to be composed, exhibited, or produced as *the* Church creed, she has stated that to be sufficient, and has condemned not only what is spoken *against* but *beyond* it. Quarrels among Christian people would be done away if this were heeded.

Of course in saying that an ecumenical council is the highest, and indeed *the sole* tribunal of the whole Church, we do not assert that it is infallible. The promises to the Christian Church are perhaps no stronger than those to the Jewish, and yet it fell into idolatry as did the Christian Church. But it may be doubted whether, for this idolatry, any ecumenical council was ever responsible. The second of Nicæa did not represent the quod semper, quod ubique, quod ab omnibus, of Catholic testimony, nor was it universally received when held; and it can hardly be doubted that the council, in all its acts and canons, has never been received by the whole West, nor is it now even by the See of Rome, in *all* its enactments.

Six councils and the Nicæno-Constantinopolitan Symbol would then be left as entitled to the claim of œcumenicity. Of course no reflecting man, devoid of prejudices, would ever look upon the Latin Synods, which claim to represent the whole Church, and therefore to be œcumenical, as being anything more than provincial or local. Their claim to represent the whole Church is simply absurd, arrogant, and impious.

The œcumenical councils were all held before the period when any considerable innovations had been made in the mode. All Christian antiquity concurred in the exclusive use of trine immersion as the rule.

Gregory the Great, indeed, deemed the single immersion preferable in a peculiar locality (Spain), and under the peculiar circumstances of a certain case; but his own custom, that of Rome, was to dip three times, as he informs us. Moreover, his view operated, even in Spain, no further than the period of danger from Arianism, and there the trine immersion was afterwards restored. So that it could hardly be said that the Church needed any buttressing up of the ancient mode by any special enactment. And we must not expect, therefore, to find the whole Church speaking with reference to our present irregularities, for they did not exist; and *the* Church has never defined where no necessity existed; and yet it is worth noticing, that the only method referred to in the Church's decisions as the rule, is the trine immersion. *If* certain canons do possess œcumenical authority, and if, as seems true, they do approve any compendious mode, yet it must be remembered that the case referred to in both is clinic baptism, that is, baptism in case of *necessity*, and therefore these cannot with fairness be quoted in favor of continuing such compendious modes when there is no necessity; the more especially, as we have already seen that the Fathers, wherever they speak on this subject at all, speak of trine immersion as the ordinary and universal mode.

The first fifty canons of the Apostles, whatever may have been thought of their origin, seem to have been held as authoritative and universally binding from very early, perhaps the earliest times, by the whole Church, east and west, although not decided upon by an œcumenical council.

Canon 50 declares: "If any bishop or presbyter do not perform three immersions of one initiation, but one immersion which is given into the death of Christ, let him be deposed;

for the Lord did not say, 'Baptize into my death;' but, 'Go ye and make disciples of all nations, baptizing them into the name of the Father, and of the Son, and of the Holy Ghost.' Do ye, therefore, O bishops, immerse thrice into one Father, and Son, and Holy Ghost, according to the will of Christ by the Spirit."

It is to be observed, first, as to the *object* of the penalties of this canon:

1. That it condemns and deposes those who baptize *with one immersion into the death of Christ.*

2. It does not absolutely condemn those who baptize with one immersion into the Father, the Son, and the Holy Ghost.

3. *But it does enjoin it as a duty upon every bishop and presbyter, to baptize by trine immersion; and this trine immersion it grounds upon the authority of Christ, and of His Apostles.*

Conclusion. This canon then being received by the whole Church, expresses the ecumenical belief that trine immersion is the *duty of* every bishop and presbyter, and that it is grounded upon the authority of the Apostles, and upon the words of the commission given by Christ to his Apostles: "Baptizing (that is, immersing) them in the name of the Father, and of the Son, and of the Holy Ghost." In other words, it is an expression of the belief of the whole ancient Church in the *Divine origin and obligation* of trine immersion.*

---

* "Beveridge's Συνοδικόν, sive Pandectæ Canononum SS. Apostolorum et Conciliorum ab Ecclesia Græca receptorum." Oxonii, 1672.

Annotations on Canon 50 of the Holy Apostles. v. Συνοδικόν, or Pand. Can. tom. i, p. 33.

Balsamon: "This canon also is of the same import (as Can. 49 of the Apos.), for it decides that the sacrament (or mystery) of Holy Baptism ought to be administered by three immersions, in the name of the Father, and of the Son, and of the Holy Ghost; and that we ought to baptize once on account of the unity of the Godhead and the Trinity of Persons, or on account of the death of Christ upon the cross, and on account of his resurrection after three days. For, says the Apostle, also, 'We are baptized into his death.' But the 'βαπτίσματα' here, it seems to me, are to be taken for 'submersions' (τὰ δὲ βαπτίσματα 'ἐνταῦθα ἀντὶ καταδύσεων ὑποληπτέον μοι), he therefore who baptizes by one immersion into the deaths of the Lord, the canon says, shall be deposed as one who acts contrary to the doctrine of the Lord, and who is openly impious."

Zonaras: "Here, by τρία βαπτίσματα, the canon signifies three immersions in one initiation, that is, in one baptism. So that at every immersion the baptizer adds one name of the Holy Trinity. For, to immerse once only the person to be baptized in the holy laver, and to celebrate one immersion only into the death of the Lord, is impious, and the one who so baptizes, shall be deposed."

We have already seen the opinions of Chrysostom, Theodoret, and Pope Pelagius, who derived this mode immediately

Aristenus: "Let him who initiates not by three immersions, but by one into the death of the Lord (which the Lord said not) be deposed from the priesthood."

"The Lord commanding to baptize into the name of the Father, the Son, and the Holy Ghost. If any bishop or presbyter acts contrary to the Lord's command, and baptizes by one immersion only, on the ground that baptism sets forth the death of the Lord, let him be deposed."

"Matthæi Monachi sive Blastaris Syntagma Alphabeticum," p. 38, t. 2. Pan. Can. Oxon. 1672.

"Canon autem 49 tria unius mysterii baptismata perficere *jubet* (tres nempe immersiones in uno baptismo, et ad unamquamque immersionem, unum S. Trinitatis nomen pronunciare)," &c.

Bishop Beveridge, in his annotations on this canon in the "Συνοδικον," tom. ii, p. 30, states: "Postea in edita ejusdem Johannis collectione alius sub canones 51, nomine hisce verbis exprimitur . . . ὑμεῖς οὖν, ὦ ποθινότατοι, εἰς ἕνα πατέρα καὶ υἱὸν καὶ ἅγιον πνεῦμα τρίτον βαπτίζετε."

Bishop Beveridge, id. t. i, proleg. p. 4, states that in the first three centuries councils were held for the adjudication of ecclesiastical cases; that these councils enacted the Apostolical canons, and that these were collected into the code of canons of the primitive Church, at the end of the second century, or at least at the beginning of the third. The objection that canon 50 points to the fourth century, and to Eunomius as the occasion of its enactment, he refutes by showing from Sozomen's testimony, Eccl. Hist., bk. vi, chap. xxvi, that the trine immersion was long before Eunomius, and ("quod longe ante Eunomium, Monarchiani, Praxeani, aliique complures hæretici Trinitatem denegarent: qui autem Trinitatem negant, trinam in baptismo mersionem admittere non possunt; quippe quæ tres distinctas in divina natura personas supponit, in quas singulas baptizatur;") that, long before Eunomius, the Monarchians, the Praxeans, and many other heretics, denied the doctrine of the Trinity, and that they, on account of this denial, did not baptize into all the persons of the Trinity, since this would have seemed to teach the doctrines; nor did they use the trine immersion for the same reason, but they immersed once only, and that into the death of Christ. He adds: "Quinetiam Tertullianus Praxean in Trinitatem non baptizasse, ac proinde nec trinam adhibuisse mersionem, haud obscure indicat, ubi de Christo adversus Praxean loquens, ait, 'et novissime mandans ut tingerent in Patrem, et Filium, et Spiritum Sanctum, non in unum.' Tertul. adv. Prax. cap. 26. Neque enim video quare ista verba, 'et non in unum,' adderet, nisi vel Praxeas ipse, vel alius saltem aliquis hæreticus, non in Trinitatem, sed 'in unum,' Christum scilicet, vel ejus mortem baptizandum esse contenderit." He then adds, after referring to early authorities: "Certissimum est, trinam in baptismo mersionem diu ante Eunomium ab Ecclesia Catholica usitatum fuisse, usque adeo ut ab ipsis etiam Apostolis manasse visum fuerit." He thinks, however, that trine immersion is not prescribed in the Holy Scriptures; nevertheless, he thinks it nearest the truth to conclude that "Talem ritum in ipsum baptismatis sacramentum aliter introductum fuisse, quam ab aliqua Apostolicorum saltem virorum synodo, ut qui soli eum instituendi potestatem habuerint," &c. On the whole subject of the Apostolical Canons v. Bp. Beveridge's Annot. in Can. Apos. Pan. Can. t. ii.

These canons were also received and confirmed (*i. e.* the whole 85) in the Quinisext or Trullan Council, v. id. Conc. Can. ii. Beveridge further thinks that they were *collected* by Clement of Alexandria.

from the words, Matt. 28 : 19, "baptizing (*i. e.* immersing them) in the name of the Father, *and* (immersing them in the

Canon 50 is in the translation of Dionysius, which was in the old code of the Roman Church, as will be seen by the following; it was probably (since 50 are mentioned) approved in a Roman Synod :
"Decretum Synodale Stephani Papæ iv, ex concilio Lateranensi, A. D. 769, &c.
"Quinquaginta Canones Apostolorum suscipiendos."
Item : "Non amplius suscipiantur Apostolorum canonum prolata per sanctum Clementem, nisi quinquaginta capita, quæ suscipit sancta Dei catholica Romana ecclesia." V. Hardouin. Conc. tom. iii, p. 2018.
This Canon is even in a stronger form as the 45th, in the "Epitome Canonum quam Hadrianus summus Pontifex hoc nomine primus Carolo Magno Romæ obtulit, A. D. 774." Thus
Canon 45 : "Si quis episcopus vel presbyter non per trinam mersionem baptizaverit, deponatur." V. Hardouin. Conc. t. iii, p. 2033.
Two of the canons are cited by Pope John the Second. V. Hardouin. t. ii, p. 1155. V. also Can. 29, cited in what the Greeks and Latins regard as the 7th Ecumenical (2d of Nicea). v. Hardouin. Conc. t. iv, p. 514.
Notæ Severinus Binii (ap. Mansi. Conc. t. i, p. 57 : " *Canones Apostolorum.*) Canones hos auctoritate Apostolorum conditos, eorumque traditione nobis traditos, Clemens Romanus S. Petri discipulus Græce conscripsit : Dionysius autem Romanus abbas, cognomento Exiquus, Græcarum literarum peritissimus, tempore Justini. Imperatoris scriptor celeberrimus, eosdem Latine, quam potuit accuratissime et fidelissime, transtulit. Horum 50, priores tantum, quorum ultimus de trina in baptismate mersione, præter Apostolicam et orthodoxam doctrinam, ab antiquis pontificibis, conciliis et Patribus approbatam, nihil continentes, velut authentici recipiuntur, cap. 3, dist. 16, et juxta vulgatam SS. Patrum regulam, quoniam auctor eorum alius ignoratur, Apostolica traditione ad nos dimanasse, recta creduntur, reliqui posteriores a Gelasio Pontifice canon. sancta. dist. 15, inter apocrypha recensentur." Benius states, however, of the remaining 35, with the exception of the 65th and the last, "that they are found to have been confirmed and approved either by the authority of the Roman Pontiffs, or by the decrees of councils, or by the opinions of certain Fathers," and finally concludes that "it is manifest, so much so that it may not be lightly or rashly doubted, but that all these (with the two exceptions above mentioned), received by Pontiffs, by Councils, and by Fathers, or rather translated in accordance with their opinions, may be, and ought to be received as authentic."
Binius on Can. 50 of the Apos. states (v. Mansi Conc. t. i, p. 63) : "In hoc canone directe damnatur error eorum qui baptizabant in nomine Christi mortui pro nobis, et ad hunc ritum magis introducendum utebantur una mersione tantum. Contra hos ergo docetur, invocandum esse Trinitatem, et additur ter esse mergendum tum propter consuetudinem illius temporis, tum in detestationem illius erroris." He then states that the intention of the canon can be ascertained from its conclusion, and adds : "Et quamquam fortasse hinc et ex cap. 'Multi sunt,' de consecr. dist. 4, trina mersio necessitate sacramenti, ad baptismum requiri videatur, ideoque Sancti Patres . . . hanc trinam mersionem ex Apostolica traditione ortam scribant, et quod maximum est in concilio Constant. primo can. 7, error Eunomii docentis, ut testatur Theod. lib. 4, hæret. fabular, non oportere baptizandum ter immergere, damnatus sit; tamen,

name) of the Son, *and* (immersing them in the name) of the Holy Ghost." This interpretation is certainly approved by

etc. . . . Ex auctoribus supra commemoratis nihil aliud probatur, quam quod illo tempore ritus baptizandi per trinam mersionem consuetudine vulgari receptus fuerit. Eunomius per concilium Constantinop. damnatus fuit, quoniam hæretico Spiritu, et ad introducendos falsos errores, illam cœremoniam auferebat."

In the margin in the ed. of Binius, Colon. 1606, A. D., after stating that trine immersion is not of necessity to the sacrament, he adds: "Tamen ex ecclesiæ præcepto et consuetudine usurpari debuit," *i. e.* trine immersion. This canon 50 is contained in the Codex Canonum vetus Ecclesiæ Romanæ, v. ed. Paris, 1678.

Pope Julius wished the Church to "be ruled according to the canons of the Apostles." "Optarem ecclesias non in dissensione esse, sed secundum canones Apostolorum regi," this was according to Hardouin in A. D. 342. V. Hardouin. Conc. t. i, p. 626.

Pope Zephyrinus enumerates sixty of them. A. D. 215. V. Hardouin, t. i, Conc. p. 106.

Pope Urban II says in Hardouin Conc. t. vi, parte, ii, initio, p. 1648, that "the Oriental, and part of the Roman Church, used the authority of the canons of the Apostles."

Pope Stephen asserts that the first fifty only are to be received. v. Hardouin, tom. iv, p. 19; but Pope John VIII, v. Hardouin Conc. t. iv, p. 19, decreed that all of them should be admitted. They were frequently cited in the councils, and were appealed to as possessing authority. v. in indice Hardouin Conc. V. also Hammond (Canons of the Church) on the Apos. Canons, p. 188.

The language which follows of the great annalist of the Latins, is especially strong in favor of these canons. He includes in his praise the canon which enjoins trine immersion. Pity it is that the sadly erring body to the defence of whose private whims and fancies, as though they were ecumenical doctrines, he prostituted his mind, and whose errors and innovations he was too complaisant to support, should not pay more attention to the implied censure which the following contains on her course in departing from the primitive and catholic mode.

Would to God that she and all the West would, to-morrow, restore the Nicene creed to its simple integrity, and restore primitive rites in baptism, the Eucharist, and all things else, and would that the East might display the same spirit of a disposition neither to go *against*, nor beyond the few, but amply sufficient decisions of the whole Church. Then would the Church be one.

Baronius Annales, ed. Venetiis, A.D. 1706, t. ii, p. 13: "Quinquaginta tantum canones, eosdemque a Dionysio in Latinum translatos, novit antiquitas, qui in nova editione quadraginta novem numero continentur, ita ut ultimus habeatur ille quo agitur de trina in baptismate mersione."

Again, id. p. 14, Baronius continues: "Ilis igitur de auctoritate et numero canonum Apostolicorum discussis; illi tantum nobis ex Apostolicis fontibus canones fluxisse jure videri possunt, qui vel a Patribus inter alios sacros conciliorum canones sunt recepti, vel Romanorum Pontificum auctoritate firmati, aut in communem usum Ecclesiasticæ disciplinæ transisse noscuntur. Quæ enim ab Apostolis tradita essent, et ad posteros temporum successione dilapsa, ea summorum Pontificum auctoritate, conciliorum decretis, et universalis Ecclesiæ consuetudine roborata ac penitus stabilita esse, ut nefas sit his adversari, quis poterit dubitare? His

this canon. And this passage may, doubtless, from the construction of the Greek as naturally admit the sense of trine as single immersion. In fact, until the time of Eunomius, we find no trace of the single immersion among the early Christians. They sometimes speak of baptizing or immersing without mentioning the number of the immersions. But the single immersion cannot be found approved among orthodox Christians until Gregory the Great's day, and then only under the circumstances before mentioned, for a time, in one locality. But we shall treat of this subject farther on.

The other canon bearing upon the administration of this sacrament, where the mode is distinctly defined, is the somewhat doubtful Canon 7 of the second Ecumenical Council. It is as follows:

"As regards those heretics who come over to the orthodox faith, and the part of those who are saved, we receive them according to the following order and custom: We receive the Arians, and Macedonians, and Sabbatians, and Novatians, who call themselves Cathari and Aristeri, and the Quartodecimans or Tetradites, and the Apollinarians, upon their giving in a written renunciation of their errors, and anathematizing every heresy which does not agree in opinion with the Holy Catholic and Apostolic Church of God: and having first sealed them, or anointed them with the holy ointment upon the forehead, and eyes, and nostrils, and ears, we say: The seal of the gift of the Holy Spirit.

"But the Eunomians who baptize with *one immersion* . . .

includi quinquaginta illa capitula a Dionysio e Græco translata, certissimum est. Alia superaddita, duobus illis exceptis, sic aliis in locis posita esse noscuntur, ut in dubium æque revocari possit, an inde accepta fuerint, vel in ea translata. Sed utcumque acciderit: quod sancta Ecclesia ea probasse noscatur, sive quod ab Apostolis fuerint instituta, sive quod conciliorum, decretis fuerint confirmata merito jureque authentica habeantur."

Bishop Beveridge, in his Codex Canonum Eccl. Prim. Vindic. ac Illust., ed. Lond. A. D. 1678, p. 248, speaking of canon 50 of the Apostles, and the trine immersion, says of this last custom: "Aliquo tamen modo id ab Apostolis traditum, negare non ausi sumus, utpote quod a S. Patribus, nec semel assertum legimus;" then, after quoting Tert. de Cor. Milit., cap. iii, to show the antiquity of trine immersion, he adds, p. 249, "Cum vero exiguum adeo temporis spatium inter sanctos Apostolos et Tertullianum effluxerit, vix dubitari potest, quin ritus Ecclesiastici tunc temporis passim in Ecclesia usitati ab Apostolica traditione manarint."

On the whole subject of the Apos. canons, v. the Codex Canonum Eccl. Prim. of Bishop Beveridge: it is masterly. V. also Turrianus and Daille, for different views from each other, and from Bishop Beveridge.

if they wish to be joined to the orthodox faith, we receive as heathens, and on the first day we make them Christians; on the second, catechumens; then on the third, we exorcise them with blowing three times in their faces and ears; and then we instruct them, and oblige them to remain some time in the church and hear the Scriptures, and then we *baptize* them." Hammond's Trans.*

It is to be noted that, by this canon, the Arians, who retained the Catholic custom of trine immersion into the Trinity, were to be received as baptized, while the Eunomians, who were also Arians, but of a very radical type, and who had departed from the *form* of words, *i. e.* into Father, Son, and Holy Ghost, and the *mode* by trine immersion, were to be received as unbaptized.

Here, again, it must be observed that the Eunomians were probably condemned for both these errors, and not for one only. Although it is true that the canon mentions only the error as to mode. For the passages already adduced from Theodoret and Sozomen plainly show the mind of the age against these innovations. This, however, may be said with truth, that the

---

* Canon vii, 1 Constantinople (Ap. Mansi. Conc. t. iii, 364), Gentiano Herveto Interprete.

Εὐνομιανοὺς μέντοι, τοὺς εἰς μίαν κατάδυσιν βαπτιζομένους . . . ὡς Ἕλληνας δεχόμεθα . . . καὶ τότε αὐτοὺς βαπτίζομεν.

"Non est hic canon (*i. e.* Can. vii, Constantinop. 1), in Arabica parafrasi, nec in collectione canonum Joannis Antioch. qui et scholasticus dictus est, Patriarcha C. P. Nec in epitome canonum Symeonis magistri, uterque enim sex tantum priores canones hujus concilii. Est totidem verbis canon xiv, Synodi Trullanæ. Vide etiam epistolam ad Martyrium Antioch. apud. Leunclavium in jure Græco Rom., pag. 290, unde hic canon descriptus videri potest." Mansi, Conc. t. iii, p. 363.

Below, he states, "Quod in Niceno concilio supra præstitimus, expunctam in Romana, Biniana G. L. et regia collectionibus. Herveti interpretationem restituimus, et veterum suo loco post Dionysianam collocavimus, ut omnia ex amissim respondeant." Id. Conc. t. iii, p. 558.

But the canons of this council, "Ex interpretatione Dionysii Exigui," are only three in number, which read differently from the seven as generally given, and are not so full. V. Mansi Conc. t. iii, p. 565.

"Ex interpretatione veteri, quæ legitur in compilatione Isadori Mercatoris;" they are seven in number, but read differently from the same in Gent. Herveto interp.

The "Synopsis Canonum Conc. Constantinop. ex collectione vetustissima canonum breviatorum in MS. Codice Lucensi," numbers but five in all, and every one of them is quite brief.

The "Paraphrasis Arabica" numbers only four.

Canon vii is in the "Συνοδικόν," which is received by the Eastern Church. In this work the canon contains the clause regarding the "Eunomians, who baptize with one immersion," and directs to receive them as heathen.

single immersion of the Eunomians is condemned, and, up to this time, we find no mention even of its existence among the Christians of the second, third, and fourth centuries. It first appears among the bitter foes of Christ's divinity, and was introduced by them in conjunction with a change in the form of words, and was then condemned. Whether the single immersion has a better or worse claim than the trine to the sanction of New Testament usage may be examined hereafter. It certainly can claim no distinct mention in the period between the death of St. John and the rise of the Eunomian heresy. If it should be concluded that this canon is not really an enactment of this council, nevertheless it should be remembered that it is to be found in Canon 95 of the Trullan Synod, so that if not ecumenical, it can at least claim the sanction of the whole Greek or "Orthodox" Church since that period. This church also receives Canon 50 of the Apostles.

The conclusion then from these canons is, that they plainly teach the duty of trine immersion. If they be rejected as not being of ecumenical authority, then it must be concluded that the whole Church has never made a clear enactment as to the mode. But in that case the unanimous testimony of all the Fathers to the trine immersion as the divine or ecumenical mode, the voices of so many provincial councils, and of every rubric of the Church, East and West, absolutely enjoining this mode, in case of every well person, for over a thousand years after Christ, should leave us in no doubt as to the past teachings of Christ's Church, and as to what, acting upon the principle of the quod semper, &c., its decision will be, if any is ever given. While, on the other hand, nothing can be found in favor of using any of the compendious modes of pouring or sprinkling in the case of a well person, in the Fathers of the first six hundred years, nor in the rubrics or councils, ecumenical or provincial, for at least 1200 years after Christ.

To sum up all briefly: all the testimony as to the mode, from all the ecumenical councils, is in favor of trine immersion, and absolutely nothing against it or in favor of single immersion, sprinkling, or pouring, except, of course, the case of necessity.

Two other canons remain to be considered. It is claimed that, previous to the Council of Chalcedon, the canons of the Provincial Synods of Ancyra, Neocæsarea, Gangra, Antioch, and Laodicea, were received into the code of the whole Church, and possess ecumenical authority.

Whatever be the truth with regard to this, these canons have reference, not to the healthy, but to the sick. They are:

Canon 12 of Neocæsarea: "If any man has been baptized in sickness, he must not be promoted to be a presbyter, for his faith was not of his own free choice, but of necessity. Unless, perhaps, an exception is made on account of his subsequent diligence and faith, or on account of a scarcity of men." Hammond's Trans.

Canon 47 of Laodicea: "Those who have received baptism in sickness and then have recovered, must learn the creed, and be made to know that they have been vouchsafed the Divine grace." Hammond's Trans.

These canons affect *only* the case of necessity. Clinic baptism is all that is contemplated by them, and even in this case a clinic was, unless in unusual cases, debarred from orders. Nevertheless, such baptism is not required to be repeated, but the latter canon expressly states that such must "be made to know that they have been vouchsafed the Divine grace." No mode is stated, though it is clear that many clinics were baptized by the "compends," when the full administration was not possible. Hence it may be asserted, since the Church decides absolutely and without exception, that she has determined the validity of the compends, *when administered to clinics*. Such a conclusion agrees not only with the language of the canons, but also with the constant practice of the Church.

SECTION III.

THE GREEK PROVINCIAL SYNODS.

Canons 12 of Neocæsarea and 47 of Laodicea, in favor of clinic baptism, and Canon 50 of the Apostles (embodied in the Greek code in the Trullan Synod), and 7 of 1 Constantinople, in favor of trine immersion, are received by the Easterns.

We have elsewhere stated, that between Michael Cerularius and the Synod of Florence, they varied in their practice, now receiving and now rejecting all baptisms not performed by trine immersion. The records of their local synods are difficult to be found. The Latin editions of the councils contain little besides the records of the first six general councils, and the representations of the whole or of provinces of that part of Christendom.

But four documents, or extracts from them, will be found translated in Palmer's "Dissertations on the Orthodox Communion."

The first three, and a local synod at Constantinople, in A.D. 1484, decide for the validity of Latin, Lutheran, and Calvinistic baptism, when administered by the compends. The last, which is not received by the Russians, is that of Constantinople, in 1756, which decides against that validity, and indeed against the Latins or any other Westerns being in the Church at all. It is very bitter. But it represents only the extreme Eastern view. The Synod of Moscow, in 1666–1667, and the Letter of Jeremiah III, Patriarch of Constantinople, admit baptism by affusion. The former deals with the Latins as does the first document above-mentioned: the Letter of Jeremiah with the Lutherans and Calvinists.

These express the Russian view,—about four-fifths of the whole Eastern Church.

It should be remarked, however, that they did not vouch for its *regularity;* on the contrary, their whole tenor strongly favors trine immersion—they only decide for the bare *validity* of the other modes. Yet they do not limit their decision regarding *validity* to the case of necessity, but it is extended to all baptisms performed by sprinkling or pouring, even without necessity.

The reader who wishes to see most on this subject, and the translation of parts of original documents, will consult Palmer's work. Allusions to other synods will be found there. Greek synods seem to have been held between A.D. 1260 and in 1484, which admitted Latin baptism, although performed by the compends. The Synod of Moscow, in 1666–1667, simply "followed and confirmed" them, while it at the same time "not only abrogated the custom of rebaptizing Latins, which had been decreed by a previous local synod held under the Patriarch Philaret Niketich, grandfather of the reigning sovereign Alexis, but gave reasons and precedents to satisfy the scruples of Alexis, showing that the erroneous decrees of a local council might be so corrected and abrogated by another greater and more general council." The decision of Jeremiah III was based upon the decree of a synod held at Constantinople, early in the eighteenth century, which admitted, like him, Lutheran and Calvinistic baptism. v. Palmer, pp. 108, 174, 202.

SECTION IV.

LATIN PROVINCIAL SYNODS.

These differ from the œcumenical in being expressions of the teaching of parts of the Church, not the whole. Nevertheless, their *witness* is valuable, although their *authority*, from the fact of their being provincial, cannot claim universal sanction. They serve to mark, historically, the gradual departure in the Western part of the Church, in this as in other things, from primitive views and practice, until finally the views of even the earlier Roman bishops, Leo the Great and Pelagius, are supplanted by modern notions of an entirely contradictory nature. What these prelates derived from the immediate command of God is now treated as matter of indifference, to be determined by local custom, with the bishop's approval. v. end of this chapter, Carlo Borromeo, &c.

COUNCIL OF CARTHAGE, A.D. 348, UNDER ST. GRATUS.

"The same Bishop Gratus said, 'Let us consider the first title, of rebaptizing. Wherefore, I ask this sacred assembly to express their opinions whether, when a man has descended into the water, and has been questioned as to his belief in the Trinity, according to the faith of the Gospel and the doctrine of the Apostles, and has made a good confession, concerning the resurrection of Jesus Christ, he ought to be again questioned concerning the same faith, and again *immersed* in water?' All the bishops answered, 'Far be it! Far be it!' "*

POPE LEO I.

(In Hardouin's "Councils," *i.e.*, those received by Latins.)

"Pope Leo to all the Bishops throughout Sicily sends greeting in the Lord." "Although, therefore, both those things which pertain to the humiliation and to the glory of Christ

---

* Conc. Carthag. A.D. 348. An descendentem in aquam . . . . liceat iterum interrogari in eadem fide et in aqua iterum *intingi?* v. in Hardouin Conc. t. i, p. 685, can. i.

find their fulfilment in one and the same person, and everything which he possessed of divine power and human infirmity tends to our restoration as its result, nevertheless in a special manner, by the death of the crucified and by his resurrection from the dead, the power of baptism forms a new creature from the old: so that in those who are regenerate or baptized, both the death and the resurrection of Christ are operated. For the Apostle Paul says, 'Know ye not, that so many of us as were baptized into Jesus Christ were baptized into his death? Therefore, we are buried with him by baptism into death: that like as Christ was raised up from the dead by the glory of the Father, even so we also should walk in newness of life. For if we have been planted together in the likeness of his death, we shall be also in the likeness of his resurrection.' And the teacher of the Gentiles stated this idea in other and fuller language, when he wished to recommend the sacrament of baptism. So that it appears from the spirit of his doctrine, that that day and that time has been chosen for baptizing the sons of men, and for making them the sons of God, in which, by a likeness and by the mode of administering the sacrament, those things which are performed upon the members may correspond to those which have been performed upon the Head; for while, in accordance with the rule of baptism, death intervenes by the dying unto sin, and while 'the trine immersion is an imitation of the three days' burial, the rising again out of the water is an image of Christ rising from the grave.' "*

The Fourth Council of Toledo enjoined, in accordance with the opinion of the Roman Bishop, Gregory the Great, the single immersion in the limits of its own jurisdiction; while Gregory, however, testified that *the mode at Rome was still the ancient trine immersion.* This is the first clear appearance of the single immersion, either in the Fathers or councils of the Church, as a mode allowed among the orthodox. (v. chap. "On Changes of the Mode.")

Pope Zacharias speaks of the immersion in such a way as

---

* Leo ad Episc. Siculos. "Appareret ex hujus doctrinæ spiritu regenerandis filiis hominum, et in Dei filios adoptandis illum diem esse, et illud templum electum, in quo per similitudinem, formamque mysterii, ea quae geruntur in membris, his quae in ipso sunt capite gesta congruere: dum in baptismate regula, et mors intervenit interfectione peccati; et sepulturam triduanum imitatur trina demersio; et ab aquis elevatio, resurgentis ad instar est de sepulchro." v. Hardouin, t. i, p. 1757.

to imply that it was the general custom, not only in the Church, but even among heretics.*

Pope Stephen II was consulted, in A.D. 754, regarding the validity of baptism administered *in necessity* by pouring. Stephen's answer was, that in such case it was valid. This, it will be seen, was nothing more than a restatement of St. Cyprian's principle, "Necessitate cogente et Deo indulgentiam largiente." (v. also Hardouin Conc., t. iii, p. 1987.)

Hinemar of Rheims, A.D. 858.

Describing baptism, he speaks thus to his presbyters: "He is baptized by trine immersion in the name of the Father, and of the Son, and of the Holy Ghost, that just as the inner man, which is made after the image of the Holy Trinity, through invocation of the Holy Trinity, is restored to the same image; and as that which fell under subjection to death by three grades of transgression, being thrice raised out of the font rises by grace to life, and as the inner man in the faith of the Holy Trinity is to be created anew after the image of its Creator, so also the exterior man ought to be washed by trine immersion. So that what the Spirit works invisibly in the soul, this the priest should imitate visibly in the water. For the original transgression was committed by three circumstances, by delight, by consent, and by the act. And so every sin is effected either by thought, word, or deed. Wherefore the trine ablution seems to answer to the three classes of sins. Or, if you choose, it should be used on account of original sin, which, in infants, avails to their destruction; or on account of those sins which, in the case of men of more advanced age, are added by the will, word, or deed. And because, according to the Holy Scriptures, there is one God, one faith, and one baptism, the candidate for baptism is thrice immersed in the name of the Father, and of the Son, and of the Holy Ghost: that the mystery of the Trinity may appear to be but one; and he is not baptized into the names of Father, Son, and Holy Ghost,

---

* Zachar. ad Boniface, Hard., t. iii, p. 1910. He mentions the candidate as "Mersus in fonte baptismatis;" and again, "Quicunque mersus esset in nomine Patris." He speaks even of errorists, "Qui sine invocatione Trinitatis mergunt in fonte baptismatis," and adds, "Fraternitati turae notum est, quod de illis sacrorum canonum series Continet, quod et tenere te firmiter hortamur."

This looks like a reference to canons 49 and 50 of the Apostles, and canon 7 of 1 Constantinople.

but into one name, which is God, according to an Apostle. One Lord, one faith, one baptism."*

Council of Worms, A.D. 868.

Canon 5, in Hardouin Conc., p. 738, tom. v, is almost word for word the same as Canon 5 of the fourth Council of Toledo, and it quotes Gregory the Great as did that, and also favors the single immersion in the same words. The reason given for the enactment of this canon by both these synods is the same.† "While some priests baptized with three immersions, and the others with but one, a schism was raised endangering the unity of the faith." But it is worthy of notice that immersion was the ordinary mode, and indeed the only one referred to by these canons. Gregory the Great also, in the reply which he made to Leander, Bishop of Sevil, and which forms, in a great measure, the ground why these canons in favor of single immersion were established in the provinces represented by these assemblies, expressly states that the Roman method was by trine immersion.‡

Council of Tribur, A.D. 895.

The trine immersion is referred to in this synod almost in the words of Pope Leo the Great.§ "The trine immersion is an imitation of the three days' burial, and the rising again out of the water is an image of Christ rising from the grave."|| We shall soon see how well the requirements of the rubrics of this period agree with this mode.

---

* Hincmar. ad Presbyteros de Bapt. in Hardouin. Conc., t. v, p. 418. The passage is long. We give the conclusion: "Ter baptizandus mergitur in nomine Patris et Filii et Spiritus Sancti, ut Trinitas (Trinitatis?) unum appareat sacramentum; et non baptizatur in nominibus Patris et Filii et Spiritus Sancti, sed in uno nomine, quod intelligitur Deus, juxta Apostolum. Igitur unus Deus, una fides, unum baptisma."

† "Dum quidam sacerdotes in quibusdam partibus terrae trinam, quidam simplam mersionem faciunt, a nonnullis schisma esse conspicitur et unitas fidei scindi videtur," so Conc. Toletanum 4, can. 5.

‡ Greg., lib. i, Eph. 41, ad Leand. "Nos autem quod tertio mergimus," &c.

§ Leo, quoted above, where see.

|| Concilium Triburense, A.D. 895. (v. Hardouin. Conc., t. vi, p. 443.) "Trina namque in baptismate immersio triduanam imitatur sepulturam: et ab aquis elevatio, instar est resurgentis de sepulchro."

Synod of Clermont, A.D. 1268.

This synod decreed that, if in case of necessity a child had been baptized by a layman, the priest was to make diligent inquiry as to whether the baptism had been rightly performed, and, if it had been, he was to supply only the parts which were wanting, thus: "At the font everything which is usually done shall be performed, the immersion only excepted. But if it is doubtful under what form of words the child has been baptized, then let the priest baptize him, but while he immerses him let him say, 'If thou art not already baptized, I baptize thee in the name of the Father, and of the Son, and of the Holy Ghost. Amen.'"*

Synod of Cologne, A.D. 1280.

Even at this late period we find immersion referred to as the mode, but in a certain necessity, when this was utterly impossible, we find pouring allowed.† Nevertheless were there doubt concerning the form of the words, the child might be again baptized. The words of the council follow:

"We decree that baptism be celebrated in a worthy manner, with proper distinction of the words, in the repetition of which the salvation of the baptized depends; and that he who baptizes (cum immergit baptizandum in aqua), when he immerses the candidate in water, shall neither add to the words, nor take from them, nor change them, but shall say, 'Peter, or John, I baptize thee in the name of the Father, and of the Son, and of the Holy Ghost. Amen.'"‡

---

* Syn. Claromontan. v. Hard. Conc., t. vii, p. 591. "Super fontes autem fiant omnia quæ solent fieri, sola immersione excepta. Si vero dubium fuerit, sub qua forma verborum puer fuerit baptizatus; tunc sacerdos eum baptizet, dum tamen cum immergens dicat: 'Si tu non es baptizatus, ego baptizo te in nomine Patris et Filii et Spiritus Sancti. Amen.'" .... "Ad elevandum vero puerum de sacro fonte non plures quam tres patrini recipiantur."

† Item, si timeatur de morte infantis antequam nascatur, et caput ejusdem infantis appareat extra uterum, infundat aquam quæ adfuerit, super caput nascentis, dicens: "Ego te baptizo," &c.

‡ Synod. Colon. v. Hard. Conc., t. vii, p. 822. Si timeatur de morte infantis, antequam nascatur, et caput ejusdem infantis appareat extra uterum, infundat aquam quæ adfuerit, super caput nascentis dicens: Ego te baptizo, &c.

The case here contemplated often occurs. But in case of doubt regarding this "form," the infant, if it survived, was to receive conditional baptism. v. in loc.

This seems to be the first canon of a council which mentions distinctly any other mode than immersion. Canon 12 of Neocæsarea, and Canon 47 of Laodicea, refer to the case of those who have been "baptized in sickness," but do not mention any mode, although they imply probably the compends as well as dipping. In this case (Cologne) pouring is directed only in absolute necessity, *i. e.* in danger of death.

Synod of Nismes, A.D. 1284.

In this council also the method of pouring is mentioned, but only in case of necessity.

"We admonish, therefore, that, so soon as an infant is born, if it is in imminent danger of death, and if it cannot be brought to a presbyter, it shall be baptized by the males present, in warm or in cold water, but not in any other liquid, and in a clean vessel of wood, stone, or some other material. But if a vessel cannot be had, let water be poured upon its head, and let the due form of words be used." . . . . Again below: "But let it be so done that the baptizer, while he thrice immerses the infant in water, shall say, 'Peter, or Martin, I baptize thee in the name of the Father, and of the Son, and of the Holy Ghost. Amen.' Notwithstanding if but one immersion has been performed, the child will nevertheless be baptized. . . . . But if a sufficient quantity of water cannot be had for wholly immersing the infant, let a certain quantity of water be poured upon its head."*

Council of Ravenna, A.D. 1311.†

In this synod, for the first time in the history of baptism, and more than thirteen hundred years after the birth of Christ,

---

* Synod. Nemausensis. v. Hard., t. vii, p. 904. "Vel si vas haberi non possit, fundatur aqua super caput baptizandi. . . . . Sed ut infantem ter immergendo (injungendo) in aqua baptizans dicat sic: Petre, vel Martene, ego baptizo te in nomine Patris, et Filii, et Spiritus Sancti. Amen. Si tamen una tantum immersio facta fuerit, erat nihilominus baptizatus. . . . Si tamen tanta copia aquæ haberi non possit, ut infans in ea totaliter mergi possit: cum scutella, vel scypho, vel alio vase, aliqua quantitas aquæ super infantem effundatur a baptizante, et effundendo dicat baptizans: ego baptizo te in nomine Patris, et Filii, et Spiritus Sancti. Et erit infans baptizatus."

In another case of necessity mentioned just afterwards (similar to the one in last reference), a midwife is allowed to baptize by pouring.

† v. Hard. Conc., tom. vii, p. 1366; v. also Augusti, Denkwurd. vol. vii, p. 234, for reference between A.D. 1284–1311.

we find trine aspersion and trine immersion *seemingly* put on the same footing. The synod, of course, is not of much authority, being provincial only, and acting against the uniform testimony of all the preceding synods, which required immersion as the rule, deviating from it only in cases of necessity. "Baptism is to be administered by trine aspersion *or* immersion." (Sub trina aspersione, vel immersione.)

It should be remembered, that this council last cited represented the opinion, not of the whole Church, East and West, but that of a province only in the West. The East, amid all its idolatry and fearful corruption, still adhered firmly to the ancient mode. Whatever may have been its faults, it must be said, to its praise, that its stand for ancient rite and ancient doctrine was noble. Its firmness, among other things, against a mutilated eucharist, against the Latin notion of purgatory, against the unauthorized injection of the "filioque" into the symbol or creed of the whole Church, against the Roman supremacy, and the subversion by the Roman Pontiffs of the canons of the Catholic Church, and the Latin position that a part of the Church might usurp the prerogative of the whole, and claim for its own provincial acts the majesty of ecumenical sanction, and also its manly stand for the ancient trine immersion of the whole Church, must in time meet with universal approval. The impartial and intelligent Christian, who scans the history of the long struggle between the Roman Pontiffs and Western Europe on the one hand, and the Apostolic Sees of the East and Eastern Europe on the other, will find in both parties much ignorance and much superstition, with fearful idolatry; in other words, the position of the Christian Church, from the last half of the eighth century onward, was almost identical with that of the Jewish and Israelitish apostasy, yet, upon a candid examination of the principles of the Easterns, and a fair survey of the facts, he is forced to confess that the verdict in most of the questions controverted must be in favor of the East, and condemnatory of the course of the Roman bishops.

And yet it must not be supposed that all Westerns were thoroughly imbued with the lax notions of the synod which has just been cited. On the contrary, we have proof of the reverse at Florence. At that council, A.D. 1439, a passage at arms occurred between Mark of Ephesus on the side of the Greeks, and Gregory the monk and Protosyncellus on that of the Latins. Mark laid to the charge of the latter that they had "two baptisms, one administered by trine immersion, and the other by pouring water upon the top of the head." To which Gregory replies, "That there are two baptisms, no one ever asserted, for holy baptism is one," &c.; "and that the trine immersion is necessary is evident, for thus has it been handed down by the saints, to signify the three days' burial of the Lord. So, indeed, it has been handed down, and so the rituals of the Latins teach that it shall be observed."

Yet just below he defends, by the reason subjoined, this mingling of immersion and affusion:

"But we by no means immerse the infants' heads; for we *cannot* teach them to hold the breath, nor can we prevent the water from going through their ears, nor can we close their mouths. But we so put them into the font as to omit nothing which is really necessary for the carrying out of the tradition. The laver being a sort of image of the womb, and by this image of the womb setting forth the regeneration. And lest the head, in which is the seat of all the senses, and the vehicle of the soul, may be without holy baptism, we take up water in the hollow of the hand out of the sacred font and pour it over it, &c. For when a tyrant charged it upon Saint Apollonius as a reproach that he had not been washed in baptism, and that, therefore, he was not a Christian, God, in kindness, heard the saint's prayers, and satisfied his desires. For a cloud being sent down from above bathed his head in dew. If, therefore, pouring upon the head be not baptism, it would not have been so done, but in some other way."*

It will be noticed that Gregory puts forth a strong view as to the value of the trine immersion, and that his plea for pouring is based upon necessity, or something akin to it.

So far as the application of his argument to the case of healthy infants is concerned, Mark might have replied, that the whole Church found no necessity, during more than a

---

* v. Hardouin, Conc., t. ix, p. 620. ″Ότι μὲν ἀναγκαῖον ἐστι καὶ τὸ διὰ τριῶν καταδύσεων φανερόν· ὅυτω γὰρ ὑπὸ τῶν ἁγίων παρεδόθη. As this pouring had probably become a quite common mode in Italy and other countries, while in other parts of the West, and especially in England, the trine immersion still remained as the general mode, the point of the defence is to make out a case for a mode of which we hear now, which was a transition from the three total immersions to one partial immersion with trine affusion. v. Augusti Denkwurd. vol. vii, p. 234. His reference in A.D. 1287, is the first mention of it that we have seen.

thousand years, for departing from the full administration by trine and total immersion, and infants were the same in his day as before. The present Latin mode, in ordinary use, is so far removed from any immersion that a part of Gregory's words would not apply in its defence.

The Latin Synod of Trent, A.D. 1545–1563, seems to have determined nothing further as to mode. But the "Catechism," put forth by its authority, and edited by command of Pope Pius the Fifth, directs that "pastors . . . must briefly explain that, by the common custom and practice of the Church, there are three ways of administering baptism. For those who ought to be initiated with this sacrament are either immersed into the water, or have the water poured upon them, or are sprinkled with the water. And whichsoever of these rites be observed, we must believe that baptism is rightly administered; for in baptism water is used to signify the spiritual ablution which it accomplishes. Hence, baptism is called by the apostle *a laver* (Tit. 3 : 5; Eph. 5 : 26); but ablution is not more really accomplished by the *immersion* of any one in water, *which was long observed from the earliest times of the Church*, than by the effusion thereof, which we now perceive to be the general practice, or aspersion, the manner in which there is reason to believe Peter administered baptism, when on one day he converted and baptized three thousand persons. (Acts 2 : 41.) But whether the ablution be performed once or thrice must be held to make no difference; for that baptism was formerly, and may still be, validly administered in the Church in either way, is sufficiently evident from the Epistle of Gregory the Great to Leander. The rite, however, which each individual finds observed in his own Church is to be retained by the faithful." (Catech. Pt. ii, chap. ii, Quest. 17 and 18, Buckley's Trans.)

These views, in some points, differ widely from the belief and apostolic tradition which prevailed during the first 500 years of the Church. Two Roman bishops even, Leo and Pelagius, add their strong and marked condemnation of them. For the word difference is not strong enough to express the discrepancy between the Tridentine unauthorized notions and the belief of the whole primitive Church. The latter *condemns* the former.

Carlo Borromeo, Arbp. of Milan, A.D. 1576.

This prelate directs: "Let the rite of baptism be carefully observed, but let there be no confusion. Let baptism be so administered, as the custom of the Church approved by the bishop demands, whether it be by pouring or by immersion."*

Council of Bourges, A.D. 1584.

This synod ordered baptism to be by "trine immersion or affusion." (Conc. Bituricense, tit. xix, can. iii. v. in Hard. Conc. t. x, p. 1474.) "Observent baptizantes trinam immersionem seu effusionem."

Council of Aix, A.D. 1585.

The decree respecting baptism is exactly the same in sense as that of Carlo Borromeo just cited, and in almost the same words. It looks like a copy from it.

The modern Roman custom is well epitomized in these words of Carlo Borromeo. The criteria seem to be "the custom of the (particular) church, approved by the bishop;" as these change, it differs.

SECTION V.

RUBRICS OF DIFFERENT PARTS OF THE CHURCH REGARDING THE MODE.

Tertullian, and Cyril of Jerusalem, especially, are very valuable witnesses as to all the Christian rites of their day. St. Cyril is, in the Oxford Translation, within the reach of all. His descriptions, on account of their fulness, may serve in bearing out the primitive character of many parts in various rubrics, which are sometimes thought otherwise.

The most complete collection of rubrics is to be found in the work of Asseman, cited below. But wherever we could find one which he has omitted, we have inserted it. In some

---

* Carlo Borromeo, Arbp. of Milan. v. Concilium Mediolanense, iv, A.D. 1576. Constitutionum Pars. ii, 2. v. in Hardouin, Conc., t. x, p. 841. "Baptizandi ritus accurate servetur: nec vero ullo modo confundatur; ita scilicet, ut pro ecclesiæ usu, per episcopum probato, vel aquæ infusione, vel immersione baptismus ministretur."

few instances, we have been indebted for fuller recensions than he has given to writers who will be mentioned in their proper place.

RUBRICS REGARDING THE MODE OF BAPTISM. FROM THE "CODEX LITURGICUS" OF JOSEPH ALOYSIUS ASSEMAN. EDIT. ROMAE, 1749.

DIVISION I.

OFFICES FOR CELEBRATING BAPTISM IN THE ROMAN CHURCH, FROM THE "BOOK OF THE SACRAMENTS" OF POPE GELASIUS.

Office I.

"Then thou shalt immerse him thrice in the water."*

Office II.

"Thou shalt thrice immerse him in the water.
"Afterwards, when the infant has ascended from the font," &c.†

Office III.

"Then thou shalt immerse him thrice in the water."‡

Office IV.

"Then let the priest baptize by trine immersion alone, invoking but once the Holy Trinity, and saying thus: And I baptize thee in the name of the Father, and let him immerse once, And of the Son, and let him immerse a second time, And of the Holy Ghost, and let him immerse a third time."§

The Latin of this office is word for word the same as the office in the Sacramentary of Gregory the Great. v. Muratori, Liturg. Rom. vet. t. ii; Augusti Denkwurd, vol. vii, p. 218; Assem. Cod. Lit. t. ii, p. 9–11.

---

* v. Asseman. Cod. Lit. t. ii, p. 5. "Deinde per singulas vices mergis eum tertio in aqua."

† v. id. t. ii, p. 7. "Et cum interrogas, per singulas vices mergis eum tertio in aqua. Postea cum ascenderit a fonte infans," &c.

‡ Like Ordo 1, above.

§ v. id. t. ii, p. 9. "*Deinde Baptizet Sacerdos sub trina mersione tantum*, Sanctam Trinitatem semel in vocans, ita dicendo: Et ego te baptizo in nomine Patris; et mergat semel; et Filii; et mergat iterum; et Spiritus Sancti; et mergat tertio ut autem surrexerit Fonte," &c.

OFFICE V.

Nothing is said of the mode except "Baptizas." This office, from the prayers used in it, seems designed "ad baptizandum infirmum," "for baptizing a weak infant or person." The custom of the Church has ever been to admit the compends in such cases. They are cases of necessity. The *rule*, the *normal* method, cannot be used. It is only in this case that the ancient rubrics do not enjoin trine immersion. They do not, however, specify any other even then. In *some* cases of sickness the rule might possibly be followed. In some, pouring or sprinkling was necessitated by the circumstances. The clergyman's judgment would determine. Hence the seeming indefiniteness of the rubric.

DIVISION II.

BAPTISMAL OFFICES FORMERLY USED IN THE GALLICAN CHURCH.

OFFICE I.

(From a Gothic Missal.)

In this office the mode is not stated, but may be inferred from the prayers; thus, p. 34, "Let us pray . . . that all who shall descend into this font," &c., and p. 35, "Sanctify, oh Lord, the waves of this flood, as Thou didst sanctify the floods of the Jordan, that he who descends into this font," &c. And again, "Give place to the Holy Spirit, that to every one who descends into this font, it may be made a laver of the baptism of regeneration, for the remission of all their sins."*

OFFICE II.

(From an Ancient Gallican Missal.)

Mode not stated, but may be inferred from the office itself. Thus, on p. 37, there is a prayer that guilt may be abolished "under the waves" (sub undis), and sinners are spoken of as being buried with Christ by baptism, and below (p. 38) occurs the prayer that God may "pour out His Holy Spirit upon the

---

* v. id. t. ii, p. 34–35. "Oremus . . . ut omnes qui descenderint in hanc fontem," &c. . . . "Sanctifica, Domine, hujus laticis undas, sicut sanctificasti fluenta Jordanis: ut qui in hanc fontem descenderint." . . . "Da locum Spiritum Sanctum ut omnes qui descenderint in hanc fontem, fiat eis lavacrum Baptismi regenerationis in remissione omnium peccatorum."

life-giving laver, that the people buried in the laver with their Redeemer in the likeness of the sacred and divine mystery, as they die to Him by baptism they may rise with Him in His kingdom;" and again, p. 38, "Bless, oh Lord, this water, that it may be a fountain of life-giving water to those who are to be baptized *in* it."*

Office III.
(From an ancient Gallican Sacramentary.)

Nothing is mentioned as to the mode, but what it was may be easily gathered from the office itself; thus, p. 40, there is a prayer "that the water may be to all who are about to descend into it a fountain of life-giving water, that every one who is baptized in it may be made a temple of the living God."†

DIVISION III. (v. p. 52 Asseman, Cod. Lit.)
VARIOUS OFFICES OF CERTAIN CHURCHES IN THE WEST.

[There is a slight mistake in Asseman's numbering of the sections. We have generally followed his arrangements.]

Office I.
(From an ancient book of the Sacraments of the Monastery of Gellone.)

"And having received the infants from their parents, let them baptize them by trine immersion alone, invoking but once the Holy Trinity, saying thus: 'I baptize thee in the name of the Father,' and he is to immerse once; 'and of the Son,' and he is to immerse a second time; 'and of the Holy Ghost,' and he is to immerse a third time."‡

---

* v. id. t. ii, p. 37, 38. "Exoremus ... ut sub undis fecibus transfectione secreta chirographum pristinum evacueretur: et debitoribus cum Christo per Baptismum consepultis, ita hic agitur mortis imitatio; ut," &c. ... "Infundat vitali lavacro spiritum suum Sanctum ut populus ... consepultus in lavacro Redemptori suo, in similitudinem sacri divinique mysterii, cui commoritur per Baptismum; eidem couresurgat in Regno ... Benedic, Domine, hanc aquam ... ut sit eis, qui in ea baptizandi sunt, fons aquae salutaris."

† v. id. p. 40. "Ex antiq. Sacram. Gallic. quod in MS. Bobiense, annorum mille vulgavit Mabillonius." "Exorcidio te ... ut (aqua) sit omnibus, qui in eam descensuri sunt, fons aquae salutaris in vitam aeternam: ut cum baptizatus in ea quisquis fuerit, fiat templum Dei vivi in remissione peccatorum."

‡ v. id. p. 54, Ordo i. Ex MS. libro Sacramentorum Gellonensis monasterii. "Et acceptis infantibus de parentis, baptizant eos sub trina mersione tantum sanctum Trinitatem semel invocantes, ita dicendum: Baptizo te in nomine Patris, *et mergit semel;* et Filii, *et mergit iterum;* et Spiritus sancti, *et mergit tertio.*"

Office II.

(From the same manuscript, "Codice Gellonensi." Office for baptizing a sick or weak person.)

"And he is to take him in his hands and baptize him by trine immersion, once only invoking the Trinity, saying thus: 'I baptize thee in the name of the Father,' and he is to immerse him once; 'and of the Son,' and he is to immerse him a second time; 'and of the Holy Ghost,' and he is to immerse him a third time: or he shall pour water upon him with a shell (conca). He is to raise him from the font."*

Office III.

(From an ancient manuscript, Codex of Saint Remigius, of Rheims.)

"The presbyters, or deacons, or, if it is necessary, even the acolytes, are to enter barefooted. They are to clothe themselves in clean garments, and they are to go within, to the fonts, and into the water, and they are to receive them (the children) from their parents. The males are to be baptized first, and then the females, by trine immersion, the officiators invoking the Holy Trinity but once, saying thus, 'I baptize thee in the name of the Father,' and he is to immerse once; 'and of the Son,' and he is to immerse a second time; 'and of the Holy Ghost,' and he is to immerse a third time."†

Office IV.

(From an ancient Pontifical of the Church of Poictiers.)

Mode not specified, "baptizatur" only being used, but from the hymn in the same the mode may be inferred. All the expressions plainly point to immersion.‡

---

* Ordo ii, p. 55, ed. Ex eodem MS. Codice Gellonensi (Gellone). "Ordo ad infirmum caticuminum faciendum sive baptizandum."
"Et excepit eum in manus suas, et baptizat eum sub trinam mersionem, tantum sanctam Trinitatem semel invocans, ita dicendo: Baptizo te in nomine Patris, et mergit semel. Et Filii, et mergit iterum. Et Spiritus sancti, et mergit tertio: aut conca perfundit. Levat eum a fonte," &c.

† Ordo iii. Ex MS. Codice S. Remigii Remensis ante annos 900, exarato. "Et ingrediuntur presbyteri aut diaconi, etiam se necesse fuerit acolythi discalceati, induentes se aliis vestibus mundis, et ingrediuntur ad fontes intro in aqua, et accipientes eos a parentibus suis baptizantur primi masculi, deinde feminæ sub trina mersione, tantum sanctam Trinitatem semel invocantes, ita dicendo; Baptizo te in nomine Patris, et mergis semel. Et Filii, et mergis iterum. Et Spiritus sancti, et mergis tertio. Cum autem surrexerint a fonte," &c.

‡ Ordo iv, id. p. 61. Ex MS. Pontificale ecclesiæ Pictaviensis annorum 800.

Office V.

(From an ancient manuscript of the Diocese of Paris.)

"Then the priest is to baptize by trine immersion, invoking once only the Holy Trinity, saying thus: 'I baptize thee in the name of the Father,' and let him immerse once; 'and of the Son,' and let him immerse a second time; 'and of the Holy Ghost,' and let him immerse a third time."*

Office VI.

(Of S. Germain des Pres.)

"Then let the priest baptize by trine immersion only, invoking the Holy Trinity, and saying thus: 'And I baptize thee in the name of the Father,' and let him immerse once; 'and of the Son,' and let him immerse a second time; 'and of the Holy Ghost,' and let him immerse the third time."†

"Accedite ergo digni
Ad gratiam lavacri;
Quo fonte recreati
Refulgeatis agni.
  Tibi laus.

"Hic gurges est fideles
Purgans liquore mentes,
Dum rore corpus fudat,
Peccata tergit unda.
  Tibi laus.

"Gaudete candidati,
Electa vasa regni,
In morte consepulti
Christi fide renati.
  Tibi laus."

---

* Ordo v, id. p. 61. Ex MS. codice Parthenonis B. M. Calensis in dioecesi Parisiensi, annorum circiter 800.

"*Deinde baptizet sacerdos sub trina mersione, tantum sanctam Trinitatem semel invocans ita dicendo:* Ego te baptizo in nomine Patris, *et mergat semel.* Et Filii, *et mergat iterum.* Et Spiritus Sancti, *et mergat tertio.*

"*Ut autem surrexerint a fonte,*" &c.

† Ordo vi, id. p. 63. Ex MS. Colbertinæ n. 1027. Qui fuit olim monasterii S. Germani a Pratis, estque annorum circiter 800. v. Martene tom. i, p. 189; Rotomagi, 1700 A.D.

"*Deinde baptizet sacerdos sub trina mersione, tantum, sanctam Trinitatem invocans, ita dicendo:* Et Ego te baptizo in nomine Patris, *et mergat semel.* Et Filii, *et mergat iterum.* Et Spiritus sancti, *et mergat tertio.*

"Ut autem surrexerit a fonte," &c. (The last part in Martene, as above.)

Office VII.

(From an old Sacramentary of Moisae.)

"Then let the priest baptize by trine immersion, once only invoking the Holy Trinity, and saying thus : 'I baptize thee in the name of the Father,' and let him immerse once ; 'and of the Son,' and let him immerse a second time ; 'and of the Holy Ghost,' and let him immerse a third time."

This is the *rule*, but this rubric is one of the first which provides for the case of *necessity*.

"But if a weak infant should come to baptism . . . before wetting him with water, question him as to the words of the Creed, and say, 'Dost thou believe in God?' then shalt thou immerse him in the water; but after the infant has ascended from the font," &c.

Here the reader will observe the immersion in the case even of the weak infant, and the lack of mention of any other mode.*

Office VIII.

(Ex. MS. Gemmiticensi.)

"Then let the priest baptize him by trine immersion, once only invoking the Holy Trinity, and saying thus : 'And I baptize thee in the name of the Father,' and let him immerse once ; 'and of the Son,' and let him immerse a second time ; 'and of the Holy Ghost,' and let him immerse a third time."*

---

* Ordo vii, id. p. 66. Ex MS. libro sacramentorum Monasterii Moisacencis nunc Bibliothecæ Colbertinæ, n. 428, annorum circiter 800.

"*Deinde baptizet sacerdos sub trina mersione, tantum sanctam Trinitatem semel invocans ita dicendo :* Baptizo te in nomine Patris, *et mergat semel.* Et Filii, *et mergat iterum.* Et Spiritus Sancti, *et mergat tertio.*

"Ut autem surrexerint a fonte," &c.

"*Sin autem infirmus infans venerit ad baptizandum . . . ante quam perfundas eum aqua, interroga eum verba symboli, et dic.* credis in Deum, &c. *Deinde mergis eum in aqua, postea vero cum ascenderit a fonte infans,*" &c.

† Ordo viii, p. 70. Ex MS. Gemmiticensi tempore Theoderici Abbatis, qui obiit anno. 1032, descripto. Apud Martene De Antiquis Eccl. Ritibus, Rotomagi, 1700. Cap. i, art. xviii, ordo xiii. v. the latter, as it contains this rubric.

"*Deinde baptizat eum sacerdos sub trina mersione tantum sanctam Trinitatem semel invocans, ita dicendo :* Et te baptizo in nomine Patris, *et mergat semel.* Et Filii, *et mergat iterum.* Et Spiritus Sancti, *et mergat tertio. Ut autem surrexit a fonte,*" &c.

Office IX.

(From a Codex of the Monastery of Gladbach, in the Diocese of Cologne.)

"Let the presbyter receive the infants from their parents as is meet, and they having made the demand for baptism, let him baptize by trine immersion, first the males, then the females, at the same time naming them, and saying these words: 'I baptize thee in the name of the Father, and of the Son, and of the Holy Ghost,' and let him perform this baptism, dipping in the form of a cross, first towards the east, the second time towards the right hand, which is the south; the third time towards the left, that is the north. But when the infants have been lifted out of the font," &c.*

Office X.

(From a Syrian Pontifical. Church of Apamea.)

"Then he is to baptize him by trine immersion, once only invoking the Holy Trinity, thus: 'And I baptize thee in the name of the Father,' and let him immerse once; 'and of the Son,' and let him immerse a second time; 'and of the Holy Ghost,' and let him immerse a third time. That thou mayest have eternal life. Amen."†

Office XI.

(Of Lodi, in Italy.)

"Then shall the priest baptize him by trine immersion, saying thus: 'John or Mary, I baptize thee in the name of the

---

* Ordo ix, id. ii, 72. Ex MS. Codice Gladbacensis Monasterii in Dioecisi Coloniensis.

"Presbyter accipiens infantes a parentibus eorum, sicut justum est, et ab eis rogatus sub trina mersione primum masculos, et postmodum feminas nominando baptizet his verbis: Baptizo te in nomine Patris, Et Filii, Et Spiritus Sancti.

"Sed et hoc in modum crucis facere memento: primum vero in orientalem plagam, secundum in dexteram, quod est australem plagam, tertio in sinistram, hoc est in aquilonarem partem.

"Cum autem infantes elevati fuerint a fonte, compater singulorum accipiens eos, habeat intra cubam, pedibus infantis adhuc in aquam consistentibus," &c.

† Ordo x: Ass. Cod. Lit., tom. ii, p. 74. Ex MS. Pontificali insignis ecclesiæ Apamiensis in Syria, annorum circiter 500. "*Tunc baptizat eum sub trina mersione Sanctam Trinitatem semel tantum invocando sic:* Et ego te baptizo in nomine Patris, *et mergitur semel.* Et Filii, *et mergitur iterum.* Et Spiritus Sancti, *et mergitur tertio.* Ut habeas vitam æternam. Amen."

Father,' and let him immerse once; 'and of the Son,' and let him immerse a second time; 'and of the Holy Ghost,' and let him immerse a third time."*

Office XII.

(Of the Church of Vienne in Gaul.)

"Then let the Archbishop baptize him by trine immersion, once only invoking the Holy Trinity, and saying thus: ' And I baptize thee in the name of the Father,' and let him immerse once in the water; 'and of the Son,' and let him immerse a second time; ' and of the Holy Ghost,' and let him immerse the third time."†

Office XIII.

(From an old Ritual of the Church of Limoges.)

To this office no date is assigned. It admits lay baptism, and a compend "*in imminent danger of death*" (periculum mortis imminere), "And let him (*i. e.* the layman) baptize him (*i. e.* the infant), sprinkling three times upon the head of the child, and repeating this form: ' Peter or Petronilla, or creature of God, I baptize thee in the name of the Father,' † the first aspersion; ' and of † the Son,' the second aspersion; 'and of the Holy Ghost,' † third aspersion. Amen."

Trine aspersion is mentioned again in other places, and what is unusual, trine affusion in the same office, though both, perhaps, in case of necessity, only.

On page 87 there is a passage which points to trine immersion: "Then shall the presbyter say, ' Has any one done anything to this child with the intention of baptizing it?' If the reply is, ' No;' then shall the presbyter say to the child, 'And

---

* Ordo xi, Ass. Cod. Lit., tom. ii; p. 77. Ex MS. codice bibliothecæ S. Genovesæ Parisiensis annorum circiter 200, in quo nonnulli ritus Ecclesiæ Laudensis in Italia continentur.

"*Deinde sacerdos baptizat eum sub trina immersione, sic dicendo*, Johannes, vel Maria, Ego baptizo te, in nomine Patris, *et mergat semel.* Et Filii, *et mergat secundo.* Et Spiritus Sancti, *et mergat tertio. Ut autem surrexerint a fonte, portetur infans ad altare,*" &c.

† Ordo xii: Ass. Cod. Lit., p. 78. Ex MS. Codice Ecclesiæ Viennensis in Gallia, annorum circiter 200.

"Deinde baptizet archiepiscopus eum sub trina mersione tantum sanctam Trinitatem semel invocans, ita dicendo. Et ego te baptizo in Patris, *et mergat semel in aqua.* Et Filii, *et mergat iterum.* Et Spiritus Sancti, *et mergat tertio. Ut autem surrexerit a fonte.*"

I baptize thee in the name of the Father,' let him pour water at the same time once upon its head; 'and of the † Son,' let him pour water a second time; 'and of the Holy † Ghost. Amen;' at the same time pouring a third time. But let the quantity of water poured be moderate, lest, on account of its coldness, the tenderness of the child suffer damage.

"But if, in reply to the presbyter's question, the answer is, 'Something has been done with the intention of baptizing it on account of the fear of death,' then shall the presbyter say:

"'If thou art not yet baptized, I baptize thee in the name of the Father,' &c. And let him do this by immersing thrice, as above." As there is no mention of immersion until the last, it seems likely that some ancient rubric requiring trine immersion had been altered to trine affusion. The lack of date and discrepancies of this character render the authority of this manuscript of little worth. It seems a mixture of earlier and later rubrics; although, even in this, the trine immersion seems the rule, and the "compends" the exceptions. In danger of death, Cyprian's rule "necessitate cogente" would certainly apply. The exception is similar to the one in the present English rubric, the principle of necessity, according to the opinion of Cyprian, justifying in both the use of the "compend" instead of the full administration.

It scarcely need be said that if any part of this rubric seem to allow the use of the compends in any other case than that of necessity, there is not only discrepancy between it and the primitive Church belief as already exhibited, but positive opposition. There can be no doubt which to follow.*

---

* Ordo xiii: Ass. Cod. Lit., p. 81, tom. ii. Ex antiquo Rituali Ecclesiæ Lemoricensis.

"In primis notandum est quod sacerdotes debent monere frequenter, et etiam instruere plebem suam, in forma ipsius baptismi, in lingua laica et Romana, ne propter imperitiam laicorum aliquando infans absque forma per sanctam Ecclesiam statuta baptizetur, videlicet si videant in puerum periculum mortis imminere, statim, si adsit et possit haberi masculus, accipiat aquam frigidam vel calidam, non alium liquorem cum scutella vel cipho, vel alio vase, vel cum manu: Et baptizet cum faciendo tres aspersiones super caput ejusdem pueri, et dicendo sic formam: Petre, vel Petronilla, vel creatura Dei, Ego baptizo te. In nomine Patris, † *prima aspersio*. Et † Filii, *secunda aspersio*. Et Spiritus Sancti, † *tertia aspersio*. Amen." . . . "Tunc presbyter dicit; a-t-on rien fait a cet enfant pour le vouloir baptizer? Si dicatur non. Dicit presbyter puero Et ego baptizo te. In nomine † Patris, *Infundendo simul aquam supra caput ejus.* Et † Filii, *simul*. Et Spiritus † Sancti. Amen. *Simul et tertio. Infusio tamen illa sit modesta, ne aquæ frigiditate teneritas in-*

Office XIV.
(Old Roman Missal, altered.)

"Then let him baptize by trine immersion, with a single invocation of the Holy Trinity, thus: 'I baptize thee in the name of the Father,' and let him immerse him once; 'and of the Son,' and let him immerse him a second time; 'and of the Holy Ghost,' and let him immerse him a third time; 'that you may have eternal life. Amen.'"*

Office XV.
(Ex Rituali Cadomi.)

"Then let the priest baptize the infant by trine immersion, invoking the Holy Trinity, and saying: 'And I baptize thee in the name of the Father,' and let him immerse him once; 'and of the Son,' and let him immerse him the second time; 'and of the Holy Ghost,' and let him immerse him the third time."†

DIVISION IV.
ORDER OF BAPTISM FROM A ROMAN RITUAL.
(Ex Rituali Romano Sanctorii Cardinalis S. Severinæ Nuncupati.)

This rubric speaks the modern Roman custom. On page 103, t ii. Asseman, the Order of Solemn Baptism reads: "Let the priest pour thrice on the head of the candidate, or infant, in the form of the cross, and let him baptize him once only, and, at the same time, once only invoking the Holy Trinity,

---

fantis gravetur, sed si dicat: On y a fait aucune chose pour doute de mort. *Tunc dicit presbyter.* Si baptizatus es, non te baptizo. Sed si nondum baptizatus es, ego baptizo te. In nomine Patris. Et immergendo ter ut supra."

* Ordo xiv: Ass. Cod. Lit., t. ii. p. 89. Ex veteri Missali Romano ad usum fratrum minorum accommodato annorum circiter 200.

"Tunc baptizetur sub trina mersione sancta Trinitatem semel tantum invocando sic: Ego te baptizo in nomine Patris, *et mergat semel.* Et Filii, *et mergat secundo.* Et Spiritus Sancti, *et mergat tertio,* ut habeas vitam æternam. Amen." (Ver. Aug. 6, '60.)

† Ordo xv: "Ex Rituali Cadomi, anno 1614, edito." Asseman. Cod. Lit., p. 91, t. ii; more fully in Martene De Antiq. Eccl. Ritib., tom. i, cap. i, art. xviii, ordo xix, p. 212, ubi v.

"Deinde baptizet sacerdos infantem sub trina immersione, sanctam Trinitatem semel invocans et dicens: Et ego te baptizo in nomine Patris, † *et mergat semel.* Et Fi†lii, *et mergat iterum.* Et Spiritus † Sancti, *et mergat tertio. Ut autum surrexerit a fonte,*" etc.

and let him say: 'And I baptize thee,'" &c. But on page 104, in the same Order of Solemn Baptism, "But if the baptism is performed by immersion . . . let him baptize by trine immersion, once only invoking the Holy Trinity, and saying: 'And I baptize thee,' &c. And an adult, or a large infant, let him take by the arms near the shoulders, the person to be baptized having the upper part of his person naked, but the rest modestly clad; and then let the priest baptize him as above, by immersing him thrice, or his head thrice, in the water, and by lifting him out of it the same number of times.

"But let him take an infant in his hands, and let him immerse him gently and cautiously, or a part of his head thrice with like gentleness and caution in water, and let him lift him out thrice as above," &c. On page 105, in the same Order: "Then let him baptize him by trine immersion, once only invoking the Holy Trinity, and saying thus: 'And I baptize thee,'" &c.

In the "Ordo Baptismi Adultorum extra Sabbatum Paschæ et Pentecostes," at p. 112, occurs this passage: "And the candidate is led to the baptizing, &c., as far as to the trine immersion."

"But when the candidate has risen from the font." On p. 119, "Infusionem sive intinctionem," as well as "mersionem," are mentioned. On pp. 120 and 123, the rubrics, which specially apply to the case of the weak and to danger of death, direct the use of the compendious modes.

SECTION VI.

BAPTISMAL OFFICES OF THE CATHOLIC CHURCH OF THE EAST, OR "ORTHODOX" CHURCH.

DIVISION I.

BAPTISMAL OFFICES OF THE CHURCH OF CONSTANTINOPLE, AND OF THE "ORTHODOX" GREEKS, FROM THE EUCHOLOGIUM.

OFFICE I.

Order of Holy Baptism.

"Let the priest baptize him, holding him erect, and looking towards the east, and let the priest say: 'The servant of God, N., is baptized into the name of the Father, and of the Son, and of the Holy Ghost, now and forever.' And let the priest plunge him and then raise him out at the naming of every person."*

Office II.

On p. 146: "An office for administering baptism to a child at the point of death." Modes not mentioned farther than in the words, "Then he is to baptize him, saying, 'The servant of God is baptized,'" &c.†

Office II.

DIFFERENT FORM.

P. 148. The same office in a different form in Arabic, mode not stated, except in the Latin translation, Ac baptizabis, "And thou shalt baptize," &c.‡

Office III.

Office of the "Orthodox Church" in Russia.
(From King's Greek Church in Russia.)

"The priest baptizes him, holding him upright and turning his face towards the east, saying: 'N., the servant of God, is baptized in the name of the Father. Amen (first immersion). In the name of the Son. Amen (second immersion). In the name of the Holy Ghost. Amen (third immersion). Now and forever, even unto ages of ages. Amen.'"

Office 10 of Apamea, in Syria, may belong to the Eastern Church; but v. Asseman.

---

* Ἀκολουθία Τοῦ Ἁγίου Βαπτίσματος. Βαπτίζει αὐτὸν ὁ Ἱερεὺς, ὄρθιον αὐτὸν κατέχων. Καὶ βλέποντα κατὰ ἀνατολὰς, λέγων· Βαπτίζεται ὁ δοῦλος τοῦ Θεοῦ. Ὁ δεῖνα, Εἰς τὸ ὄνομα τοῦ Πατρὸς, καὶ τοῦ Υἱοῦ, καὶ τοῦ Ἁγίου Πνεύματος, νῦν καὶ ἀεὶ, καὶ εἰς τοὺς αἰῶνας τῶν αἰώνων. Ἀμήν.

Ἑκάστῃ προσρήσει, κατάγων αὐτὸν, καὶ ἀνάγων.

† Ordo Sancti Baptismi celebrandi Puero Morti Proximo. (Ass. Cod. Lit., t. ii, p. 146.)

Ex. MSS. Georgii Corresi Chiensis.

Mode not mentioned farther than in the words. "Εἶτα βαπτίζει λέγων· Βαπτίζεται ὁ δοῦλος τοῦ Θεοῦ." κτλ.

‡ "Idem officium alia ratione compositum legitur in Cod. Vaticano Arabico 43, ad usum Græcorum Melchitarum." (Ass. Cod. Lit., t. ii, p. 148.)

SECTION VII.

RUBRICS OF EASTERN ERRORISTS.

Monophysite and Nestorian Offices.

DIVISION I.

ORDER OF BAPTISM OF THE CHURCH OF ALEXANDRIA (COPTIC) AND OF THE ETHIOPIANS.

Pp. 167, 180, 185 : "Lo, John the Baptist bears testimony, saying: I have baptized my Saviour in the waters of the Jordan."

"And let the deacon lead the person to be baptized from the west to the east, to the left hand of the priest, who shall ask his name, and shall immerse him thrice. After every immersion the priest shall raise him up and shall blow in his face, and at the first immersion he shall say: I baptize thee, N., in the name of the Father. Amen. At the second, I baptize thee, N., in the name of the Son. Amen. †. At the third, I baptize thee, N., in the name of the Holy Ghost. Amen."

But on p. 191, under "Nota," "Afterwards the priest shall immerse every one of them separately in that water, saying: I baptize thee, N., in the name of the Father, and of the Son, and of the Holy Ghost. And if any child of this number be weak, he shall sprinkle water over the whole of his body. But when they ascend out of the water the priest shall put his hands on their heads," &c.*

---

* Caput 3. Ordo Baptismi Ecclesiæ Alexandrinæ Coptitarum, et Æthiopum, nunc primum Coptice, et Latine evulgatur e MSS. Codd. Vaticanis, et Ecclesiæ S. Stephani Æthiopum de Urbe. (Ass. Cod. Lit., t. ii, 167, 180, and 185.) "*En Joannes Baptista testimonium perhibuit dicens.* Ego equidem in Jordanis aquis meum salvatorem baptizari." Id. p. 180. "Et diaconus baptizandum ab occidente ad orientem Jordanis deducet ad sinistram sacerdotis, qui nomen ejus petit, et illum ter immergit, post singulas immersiones eum erigat, et in faciem ejus insufflet, et dicat in prima immersione.

"Ego te baptizo N. in nomine Patris. Amen. *In secunda.* Ego te baptizo N. in nomine Filii. Amen. †. *Tertia.* Ego te baptizo N. in nomine Spiritus Sancti. Amen."

But on p. 191 id., under "Nota," "*Postea Sacerdos unumquemque eorum seperatim immerget in aqua illa dicens:* 'Ego te baptizo N. in nomine Patris, et Filii, et Spiritus Sancti:' et si puer aliquis ex eis sit infirmus, aquam aspergct super totum corpus ejus. Singulis autem ascendentibus ex aqua imponat manus sacerdos in capite," &c.

DIVISION II.

OFFICE OF HOLY BAPTISM OF THE CHURCH OF THE ARMENIANS, FROM THEIR RITUAL.

"Then he is to place the infant in the font, and is to apply some of the same water with his hand upon its head, and is to say thrice, 'N. is baptized in the name of the Father, and of the Son, and of the Holy Ghost. Redeemed by the blood of Christ, the child attains the freedom of the adoption which belongs to the sons of our heavenly Father, so that he may be a joint-heir with Christ, and a temple of the Holy Ghost, now and forever.' But, while saying these words, the priest shall thrice immerse the candidate, burying thrice in the water the guilt of original sin. He signifies also the three days' burial of Christ and His resurrection."*

(The same, p. 202.)

"And sprinkles water upon his head thrice, and says: 'This name is baptized in the name of the Father, and of the Son, and of the Holy Ghost. He is redeemed by Christ's blood, and receives freedom from our heavenly Father, that he may be made a joint-heir with Christ, and a temple of the Holy Ghost.' This the officiator says thrice, and thrice immerses the candidate, burying the guilt of his past sins, and symbolizing the burial of Christ. And he shall wash the whole of the candidate's body, and shall say, 'As many of you as have been baptized into Christ have put on Christ.'"†

---

* Caput 4. Officium Sancti Baptismi Ecclesiæ Armenorum ex Rituali eorundem libro, nunc primum Armeno-Latine publica luce donatur.

"*Deinde deponit parvulum in fonte, et de ipsa aqua inmittit manu supra caput illius, dicens ter:* 'N. Baptizatur in nomine Patris, et Filii et Spiritus Sancti. Redemptus sanguine Christi a servitute peccatorum, consequitur libertatem adoptionis filiorum patris cœlestis, ut fiat cohæres Christi, et templum Spiritus Sancti, nunc, et semper, et in sæcula sæculorum.'"

Hæc autem dicens ter mergit oblatum, ter in aqua sepeliendo peccata vetustatis. Significat quoque triduanam Christi sepulturam et resurectionem.

† Idem Officium Baptismi ex MS. quodam Collegii de Propag. Fide, quod . . . . Latine tantum habuemus.

Ass. Cod. Lit., t. ii, p. 202. *Et aspergit caput ter, et dicit.* Hoc nomen baptizatur in nomine Patris, et Filii et Spiritus Sancti, redemptus sanguine Christi, et recipit libertatatem Patris Cœlestis ut fiat cohæres Christi, et templum Spiritus Sancti: *hoc dicit ter, et ter immergit sepeliens peccata veterana, et significat triduanam* sepulturam Christi: et lavans totum corpus dicit: qui in Christi baptizati estis Christum induistis. Alleluja.

DIVISION III.

ORDER OF HOLY BAPTISM OBSERVED IN THE CHURCH OF THE CHALDEANS, NESTORIANS, AND MALABAR CHRISTIANS, FROM THEIR RITUAL.

"Then shall the priest receive the child from the hands of one of its relatives, and he shall proceed to the baptismal waters and shall immerse it, placing one of his hands on its head, and saying, I baptize thee, N., servant of Christ, in the name of the Father. Let them respond, Amen. And of the Son. Let them respond, Amen. And of the Holy Ghost, forever. Let them respond, Amen.

"And let him raise it from the waters," &c.*

DIVISION IV.

OFFICES OF BAPTISM OF THE CHURCH OF ANTIOCH, AND OF THE SYRIANS OF JERUSALEM.

Office I.

(From a Ritual of the Syrians.)

"And he shall let down the child into the baptistery, with its face turned towards the east, and shall place his right hand upon its head, and with his left shall take up water, saying: 'N. is baptized in the name of the Father. Amen. † And of the Son. Amen. † And of the Holy and Life-giving Spirit unto eternal life.' And he shall raise it out of the water.

The following, from this same office, point to immersion. Thus, p. 219: "Nor let the demon of darkness hide himself in these waters, nor let him descend with those who are baptized."

And p. 220: "But do Thou, Lord of all, make these waters . . . waters mystically designated by the death and resurrection of Thy only begotten Son . . . a laver of regeneration."

---

* Caput 5, Ass. Cod. Lit., t. ii, p. 211. Ordo Sancti Baptismi servatus in Ecclesia Chaldæorum, Nestorianorum, ac Malabarum, seu Malebarorum ex Rituali eorundem MS. Nunc primum Chaldaico-Latine evulgatur ex Vaticanis Codicibus.

"Deinde accipit sacerdos puerum de manibus propinqui ejus, et procedit ad aquas baptismatas et mergit eum, imponens manum suam super caput ejus et dicens.

"Ego baptizo te N., serve Christi, in nomine Patris. Respondent, Amen. Et Filii. Respondent, Amen. Et Spiritus Sancti in sæcula. Respondent, Amen.

"Et elevat eum de aquis," &c.

And p. 222: "That those who are planted together in the likeness of Thy Christ by baptism, may be made sharers in His resurrection also."

And on the same page: "Reveal Thyself, oh Lord, above these waters, and grant that those who are baptized *in* them may be changed."*

OFFICE II.

Of the Church of Jerusalem.

"Then shall he let him down into the baptistery,—the face of the person to be baptized being turned towards the east, but the priest's towards the west. And the priest shall place his right hand upon the head of the person to be baptized, and shall take up some of the water, which is in front of the person to be baptized, with his left hand, and shall pour it on his head. In the same manner he shall take up some of the water which is behind the candidate, and shall pour it upon his head. Finally he shall take some of the water from the right and left sides of the candidate, and shall pour it on his head. And he shall wash his whole body. The priest shall not remove his right hand, nor shall he place his left hand on the head of the person to be baptized, as ignorant priests do;

---

* Ordo 1. "Ex Rituali Syrorum, quod MS. servatur in Bibliotheca Collegii Urbani de Propaganda Fide.

"Et demittit puerum (1) in baptisterium, conversa ad orientem facie; dextramque suam capiti ejus qui baptizatur, imponit, et sinistra sua aquas attollit, dicens.

"Baptizatur N., in nomine Patris. Amen. † Et Filii. Amen. † Et Spiritus vivi et Sancti in vitam sæculi sæculorum.

"Et educit eum ex aqua," &c.

"(1) Ter aquam fundunt super caput baptizandi semel præscriptam formulam recitando." Ass. not. in loc.

The following, from the same "Ordo," point to the immersion. Thus p. 219: "Neque delitescat in aquis istis tenebrosus Dæmon. † Neque cum iis, qui baptizantur, descendat."

And p. 220: "Sed tu Domine universorum ostende aquas istas . . . . aquas mystice designatas per mortem et resurrectionem Unigeniti Filii tui . . . † regenerationis lavacrum."

And p. 222: "Ut ii, qui simul plantati sunt in similitudinem mortis Christi tui per Baptismum, ejusdem quoque resurrectionis participes fiant."

And above, on p. 222: "Revelare Domine super aquas istas, et da, ut immutentur ii, qui in ipsis baptizantur."

The immersion in this office is single, and partial only with trine affusion.

but his right hand remaining on the head of the child, he shall take up the water with his left; for it is written, John placed his right hand only on the head of our Lord.

But when the child has been let down into the laver the priest shall say thus: "Such a one is baptized unto holiness and unto salvation, and unto a blameless life, and unto a blessed resurrection from the dead, in the name † of the Father. Amen. And of the Son. † Amen. And of the Holy and Life-giving Spirit † unto life eternal. Amen."

"And when the boy has descended into the laver, let the deacons sing this strophe . . . 'Descend, our brother, and put on our Lord,' &c.

"And when he has ascended out of the laver the deacons shall sing this hymn, &c."*

Office III.

The same Office adapted to the Baptism of Girls, p. 238.

"But, when he lets down the girl to be baptized, into the baptistery, let him say: 'Such a one is baptized,'" &c.

"But when the girl has ascended baptized out of the laver, they shall sing this hymn," &c.

---

* Ordo ii: Ass. Cod. Lit., t. ii, p. 226: Ecclesiæ Hierosolymitanæ e Vaticanis MSS.

"Tum demittet eum in baptisterium, conversa baptizandi, quidem facie ad Orientem, sacerdotis vero ad occidentem. Et imponit sacerdos dexteram suam capiti baptizandi, et accipit manu sinistra aquam, quæ coram baptizando est, funditque eam super caput ejus. Similiter accipit aquam, quæ retro ipsum est, et fundit super caput ejus. Demum accipit aquam, quæ a dextris et sinistris ejus est, funditque super caput ejus. Et abluit totum ipsius corpus. Neque mutat sacerdos dexteram suam, imponitve sinistram capiti baptizandi, ut faciunt sacerdotes imperiti; sed dextera ejus super caput pueri manente, tres sinistra haustus aquæ perficit. Scriptum est enim, Joannem dexteram suam tantum capiti Domini nostri imposuisse.

"*Quum autem puer in craterem demissus fuerit sacerdos sic dicit.*

Baptizatur talis in sanctitatem, et in salutem et in mores irreprehensibiles, et in benedictam resurrectionem a mortuis, in nomine † Patris. Amen.

Et Filii † Amen.

Et Spiritus † Vivi et Sancti in vitam saeculi sæculorum. Amen.

Quumque puer in craterem descenderit, dicunt diaconi hanc stropham. . . . Descende, frater noster et indue Dominum nostrum. . . . Quumque e cratere ascenderit dicunt diaconi hunc cantum," &c.

"At the descent of the girl, let the deacons say: 'Descend, oh daughter, sealed unto Christ, and put on our Lord.'"*

OFFICE IV.

Another Office when many Boys or Girls are to be Baptized, p. 243.

This office gives directions for mixing the warm and cold waters, so that the temperature shall be moderate.

Then the candidate is to be anointed with oil. "Then shall he let down (immerse) the boy into the laver, the boy's face being turned towards the east, &c., as in the baptism of a girl. But when the boy has been let down into the laver let the priest say, thus: Such a one, male or female, is baptized unto holiness," &c.

"And when he lets down, or immerses, the boy in the laver, let the deacons say: 'Descend, my brethren, sealed unto Christ; put on our Lord.'

"And when he has raised him up out of the laver, let the deacons sing this hymn," &c.†

---

* Idem. Ass. Cod. Lit., t. ii, p. 238: In eodem Cod. ita puellis accommodatus legitur.

"*Quum autem baptizandam in baptisterium demittit dicit*, Baptizatur talis, &c. Quumque e cratere baptizata ascenderit, dicunt hunc cantum."

At the descent of the girl: "Diaconi dicunt, descende filia obsignata, et indue Dominum nostrum."

† Item alius Ordo: Ass. Cod. Lit., t. ii, p. 243. Pro pluribus pueris vel puellis ex eodem codice Vaticano.

Id. p. 252: "Sacerdos autem stans ante Baptisterium, aperit craterem vitæ, quem hyeme quidem aqua calida replebit, æstate vero frigida. Sive autem frigida sit, sive calida, nihil refert. Verum quum sacerdos aquam plus nimio calidam viderit, frigidam parum per misceat, ne adurat: id que temperate fiat: manusque contactu experiatur, ne calida nimium aut frigida sit; sed temperata."

And p. 259: "Et effundit chrisma sacrum, scilicet oleum in volam suam, et ungit totum corpus baptizandorum, et inter digitos manuum pedumque eorum, et anteriorem posterioremque partem, nec ullum relinquit in eis locum, quin ungatur. . . . Tum demittit puerum in craterem, conversa baptizandi facie ad orientem, &c. Ut in baptismo puellæ.

"Quum autem puer in craterem demissus fuerit, dicit sacerdos sic.

"Baptizatur talis (mas, vel fœmina) in sanctitatem, &c.

"Quumque puerum in craterem demittit, dicunt diaconi. . . . descendite fratres mei obsignati, induite Dominum nostrum, &c.

"Quumque eum e cratere erexerit, dicunt Diaconi hunc cantum," &c.

Office V.

(From a Syriac Codex in the Vatican.)

At p. 264 : "Thou who wast baptized in the river Jordan, by John, cleanse us," &c.

And on p. 283, are directions for mixing the cold and warm waters, so as to produce a proper temperature.

And p. 297 : "And let him let down (or immerse) him into the laver, and let the face of the person to be baptized be turned towards the east, but the priest's towards the west, and let the priest, placing his right hand on the candidate's head, take up some of the water which is in front of the person to be baptized, and pour it upon his head, saying : 'N. is baptized, that he may become a lamb of Christ's flock, in the name of the Father' And let him take up some of the water which is behind the candidate, and pour it upon his head, saying : 'And of the Son.' And let him take up some of the water which is at the right and at the left of the candidate, and pour it upon his head, saying : 'And of the Holy and Life-giving Spirit unto eternal life.'"

(Severian : "And he shall lead him out from the midst of the waters.") And let him lead out the person baptized, and let the deacons sing this hymn : "Descend, brethren, sealed unto Christ; put on our Lord." And let him raise up the candidate, and let them sing, &c.

In this office, occur in the prayer, the following, p. 269 :

"That we may become spiritual sons of the Father of holiness, through the immersion of this baptism," &c.

P. 283 : "Mix, Lord, these waters, that they may be a spiritual womb, and a source of incorruption, and grant that they may be made to this thy servant who is baptized in them a mantle of incorruption," &c.

P. 291 : "Let not the unclean spirit of darkness descend with this one who is baptized," &c.

P. 293 : "Do thou, Lord, reveal thyself upon these waters, and grant that he who is baptized in them may be changed," &c.*

---

* Ordo iii : Ex Codice Syriaco Vaticano, 31. Ass. Cod. Lit., t. ii, p. 261.

At p. 264 : "Qui in Jordanæ fluvio a Joanne baptizatus es, elue a nobis," &c.

And on p. 283 are directions for mixing the cold and warm waters, so as to produce a proper temperature.

OFFICE VI.

A short Office of Holy Baptism by St. Severus.

(Asseman, Cod. Liturg. t. ii, p. 304.)

"And after the whole body of the candidate has been anointed, let the priest place him in the water with his face towards the east, and let him plunge him in the water three times, placing his right hand on the head of the person to be baptized, and saying : N. is baptized for the remission of sins," &c.

Asseman remarks that "the Syrians use this office or compendium when death is imminent, and when all things prescribed in the office above cannot be performed; but that office was composed by Severus, a Monophysite patriarch of Antioch." He adds, however, that it is extant in Cod. Vatican. Eschellensi, iv.†

And p. 297: "Et demittit eum in craterem, conversa ad orientem quidem baptizandi facie, sacerdotis vero ad occidentem, et dexteram suam capiti ejus imponens, sinistra ex aquis, quæ coram baptizando sunt, attollit, et fundit super caput ejus, dicens.

"Baptizatur N. ut sit agnus in grege Christi in nomine Patris.

"Et ex iis quæ sunt a tergo ejus et fundit super caput ejus, dicens. Et Filii.

"Et accipit ex aqua, quæ est ad dexteram et sinistram ipsius, funditque super caput ejus, dicens.

"Et Spiritus vivi et Sancti in vitam sæculi sæculorum.

"Et educit baptizatum. Diaconi vero canunt hunc hymnum.

"Descendite fratres obsignati, induite Dominum nostrum, &c.

"Et elevat eum, et dicunt. Expande alas," &c.

In this ordo occur in the prayers the following: "Ut Spirituales filii essemus Sancto Patri per mersionem hujus baptismatus," &c. P. 269.

And p. 283: "Misce Domine aquas istas . . . ut sint Spiritualis uterus, et caminus fundens incorruptibilitatem; et servo tuo huic, qui in ipsis baptizatur, concede, ut sint ei vestimentum incorruptibilitatis," &c.

P. 291: "Neque cum hoc qui baptizatur, descendat immundus tenebrarum Spiritus," &c.

P. 293: "Tu Domine revelare super aquas istas . . . et concede, ut immutetur hic, qui in ipsis baptizatur," ut, &c.

* Item alter brevis Ordo Sacri Baptismatis. Ass. Cod. Lit. t. ii p. 300. Auctore Sancto Severo.

P. 304, in id. "Et post quam totum corpus unctum fuerit, demittit eum in baptisterium, conversa ad Orientem facie, et demergit eum in aquas tribus vicibus, imponens dexteram suam sacerdos super caput ejus qui baptizatur, dicens, baptizatur N. in remissionem peccatorum, &c.

Asseman states: "Hoc ordine, seu compendio utuntur Syri cum mors propinqua urget, nec omnia præscripta in superiore ordine peragi possunt. Illud tamen composuit Severus Antiochenus Patriarcha Monophysita. Exstat vero in Cod. Vatican Eschellensi IV."

Office VII.

A very brief Office, to be used for those who are at the point of death, p. 307, ordained by St. Philoxenus.

"Then he is to baptize." No mode stated. The priest is to say: "Thou hast given baptism to thy people, that it might be a spiritual womb," &c.

So far as there is any reference at all, it agrees best with immersion. It should be remembered, however, that it is, as its title implies, an office for clinics.

Asseman adds, that the author of this office was a bishop, and a Monophysite heretic, who was very celebrated at the beginning of the sixth century.*

Office VIII.

(From a Manuscript Ritual of the Syrian Maronites. An Order of Holy Baptism, appointed by St. James of Sarug.)

In the prayers in this office, p. 337, there is this expression, "Christ was baptized in the river Jordan. . . . He dwelt in three mansions, in the womb of flesh, and in the bosom of the baptismal waters, and in places full of the sorrow of the lost."

P. 239 : "Let not the demon of darkness descend into these waters with this person who is to be baptized in them. . . . . Expel all the power of the enemy from him who descends and is baptized in them."

For similar language, v. p. 340, 343, 344.

P. 345, addressing the person to be baptized, the deacon says, "Come, descend; be ye washed, and be ye clean. And ascend."

Same page. "Let the priest place the person to be baptized in the laver, and let him turn the candidate's face to the east and his own to the west, and let him place his right hand on the candidate's head, and with his left hand let him draw up water from the east side of the candidate, and pour it upon his head. Then let him draw up water from the west, and pour it upon his head. Then from the north and from the

---

* Ass. Cod. Lit., t. ii, p. 307. Item Brevissimus Ordo pro iis, qui morti proximi sunt Ordinatus a Sancto Philoxeno.

"Tum baptizat." No mode specified. The priest says, "Baptismum populis dedisti, ut esset uterus spirituales, producens," &c.

south, and let him throw it upon his head, saying, 'I baptize thee,'" &c.

"St. James of Sarug," says Asseman, "was a teacher of the Syrians, and flourished in the fifth century." This saint made a recension of the office of baptism of the Apostles. This office a Maronite patriarch of Antioch, at the beginning of the eighteenth century, "made a new recension of and emended." As it stands now, this office dates from the beginning of the eighteenth century.*

These Maronites were formerly heretics, who broke off from the Catholic Church when it was one and orthodox, but, for some centuries past, have acknowledged the Latin pontiff. The Latinizing tendency of the changes in this ritual will appear the more evident if we compare their present trine affusion with St. Cyril of Jerusalem, as quoted.

---

* Ordo iv. E. MS. Syrorum Maronitarum Rituali. Ordo Sancti Baptismi Institutus, a S. Jacobo Batnarum Sarugi.

On the above, Asseman states: "S. Jacobus Sarugensis Syrorum claruit sæculo 5. . . . Sanctus iste ordinem Baptismi Apostolorum recensuit, ordinavitque ut sequitur, hunc Stephanus Aidoensis Antiochenus Maronitarum Patriarcha, qui doctrina et sanctitate vitæ circa annum quartum hujus sæculi decessit, nova recensione disposuit, ac emendavit." Asseman informs us that his "patruus" Assemanus, tom. i, Bibliothec., cap. 27, defends the "catholicam fidem" of S. Jac. Sarug, against Eusebius Renaudot. (v. Mosheim. Hist., Murdock's ed., vol. iii, p. 127, note 49 and 50.)

In the prayers in this Ordo, p. 337: "Et Filium tuum Unigenitum . . . in Jordane fluvio baptizatus est, &c. . . . Ille . . . . habitavit in tribus mansionibus, in ventre carnis, et in sinu baptismi, atque in mansionibus inferni mœrore plenis."

P. 239: "Neque descendat (demon tenebrosus) in aquas istas cum hoc, qui baptizatur in eis."

P. 239: "Abige ab eo omnem virtutem inimici ab illo, qui descendit et baptizatur in eis." Similar language on pp. 340, 343, 344.

P. 340: "Hoc baptisma, quod est spiritualis venter."

On p. 338: "Hunc ventrem baptismi," without "spiritualis."

P. 345, addressing the persons to be baptized, the deacon says: "Venite, descendite, lavamini, ac mundamini. Et ascendite."

P. 345: "Hæc Rubrica ita legitur in emendatione Aldronensis . . . . Sacerdos . . . aquam manu dextra aut cochleari haurit ter, effunditque super caput ejus. Vel mergit trina mersione, prout fert consuetudo loci: dicens. Sacerdos baptizandum in craterem baptisterii demittit, et illius quidem ad orientem, sua autem facie ad occidentem versa, dexteram suam ejus capiti imponat, ac sinistra ex orientali parte aquas hauriat, et super caput baptizandi effundat. Item ex occidentali, et effundat super caput ejus tum ex septentrionali, et ex australi et proficiat super ejusdem caput dicens. Ego te baptizo," &c. v. Assem. in loc.

LATE LATIN OFFICES.

Another Roman office: Ex Rituali Romano Sanctorii Cardinalis S. Severinæ nuncupati. v. Asseman, Cod. Lit., t. ii, p. 93.

This office directs trine affusion; "but where it is customary to baptize by immersion," the priest "shall baptize by trine immersion, once only invoking the Holy Trinity," &c. But this immersion may be of the whole person, or of the head only, or of a part of the head only. In immediate danger of death, single affusion is allowed.

The church of Milan still venerates, in some degree at least, the ancient mode. The rites used in the administration of baptism of the church of Milan, from the Ambrosian Ritual, put forth, "Jussu Cæsaris-Montii Cardinalis, et Archiepiscopi Mediolanensis," expressly enjoin "trine immersion" in the form of a cross. And again, below, the candidate "must be baptized by immersion, as the rites of the Ambrosian Church demand, where that mode can conveniently be used, but otherwise by pouring."

All three of these rubrics, however, are of late date, as their titles show.

In concluding our examination, it may not be amiss to remark, that the office of Pope Paul the Fifth mentions affusion, immersion, and aspersion, but directs that the two former, as being the more in use, shall be retained, according to the custom of every church. But the affusion and the immersion are both to be trine, and in the form of a cross. Hence the usage of the Latins among Westerns has been trine affusion, since that has been the later Western custom. But in the East, where customs are less easily changed, the Roman pontiff has been induced to *tolerate* the primitive and Catholic custom of trine immersion; though even here, as will be seen by closely scanning the foregoing rubrics of such of the Monophysite or Nestorian heretics as he has induced to acknowledge his usurped and uncanonical authority, he has introduced, instead of the ancient trine immersion, a late custom of placing the child up to the neck in water, and then thrice pouring water upon him. The ancient Fathers, the councils, and the rubrics of the whole Church, East and West, speak of absolute TOTAL IMMERSION. Of this later custom there is no trace for the first thousand years and more.

We have thus traced the statements of the Fathers and the rubrics of the Church regarding the mode. We have seen the early Fathers speaking of the trine immersion as of Divine or Apostolic origin. We find in the oldest rubrics nothing else. But at a late and dark period in the Church's history we find a departure from this, and the use of other modes as this rule, until now scarce any traces remain in the West, except in the disobeyed rubrics of the Church of England, of the early mode.

An epitome of results thus far reached may not be without profit.

THE FATHERS.

All the venerable witnesses for six hundred years testify to the trine immersion as the *rule* where they mention the number of immersions at all. The Church writers, after Gregory the Great, who is enumerated by some as the last of the Fathers, until at least the eleventh century, bear the same testimony.

The following deemed the *trine immersion* of divine origin and of divine obligation, Tertullian, St. Chrysostom, Theodoret, and Pope Pelagius. Canon 50 of the Apostles, seems best to agree with this view. All the earlier, and even all writers for the first thousand or twelve hundred years, seemed, so far as they express any belief at all, that immersion was enjoined by God; but some thought that the *number* of immersions was determined in favor of the trine by tradition. In either case they deemed it obligatory, until Gregory the Great, who first expressed the opinion that, in order to avoid symbolizing with heretics, it was allowable to lay aside the ancient trine for the single. Some in the West followed his notion; but the rubrics, until a late date, enjoined the trine. But it was not universally received in the West, and was reprobated in the whole East as a dangerous novelty, and has never received anything but condemnation from them since. It is a mere unauthorized opinion, with no ecumenical sanction; it lacks the "Quod semper," &c., and the imprimatur of an ecumenical council.

But St. Cyprian's view as to the use of the compends, in case of *necessity*, gained credence and approval so universal as never to be opposed or contradicted; and this, too, when the compends in *such cases* have been used in all parts of the Church, East and West, and are still.

The Ecumenical Councils.

During the period from Nicæa to the Third of Constantinople, no one who would hear an ecumenical tribunal ever advocated the idea that trine immersion should not be used as the rule in ordinary cases, if we except Eunomius and some who were involved in his errors.

By Canon 7 of 1 Constantinople, his followers were to be received as unbaptized. They baptized by "one immersion." This is a mark of distinction given them by the council.

Canon 50 of the Apostles enjoins trine immersion under pain of deposition. Canons 47 of Laodicea and 12 of Neocæsarea, concerning whose ecumenical authority there may be doubt among learned men, but which undoubtedly express the unanimous *practical* assent of the Church, approve the compendious modes *in case of necessity*, or at least are so absolutely worded as not to exclude them.

Of the Provincial Councils.

Greek.

These, while differing as to the validity of the baptisms of Latins and Protestants, nevertheless are uniform in their witness for trine immersion as the regular and primitive mode, and some of them tolerate no other.

Latin.

All these, for more than 1200 years, with the exceptions of the Fourth of Toledo and one of Worms, enjoin trine immersion. The two last the single. Both of these, however, refer to a peculiar and extraordinary case. When the circumstances which, as was thought, authorized this innovation had passed away the old mode again resumed its place and retained it for centuries after.

The Rubrics.

The testimony of these is most important. They exhibit, at the same time, the *law* and the *custom* of provincial and national churches, whose united evidence, added to what has preceded, must remove all reasonable ground for doubt.

Of course, the later rubrics will be of little interest; we shall confine our attention mainly to the more primitive, and to those of orthodox communions.

Ancient Offices, from the Sacramentary of Pope Gelasius.

Office.	What it enjoins.	For whom used.
No. 1.	Trine immersion alone.	For the well.
" 2.	" " "	" "
" 3.	" " "	" "
" 4.	" " "	" "
Of Gregory the Great.	" " "	" "
No. 5.	Mode not mentioned.	For a weak or infirm subject.

Gallican Offices.

Gothic.	Immersion only.	For the well.
Ancient Gallican.	" "	" "
" " No. 2.	" "	" "

Various Western Offices.

Gellone.	Trine immersion alone.	For the well.
" No. 2.	Trine immersion or pouring.	For the weak.
Rheims.	Trine immersion alone.	For the well.
Poictiers.	Immersion.	" "
Paris.	Trine immersion alone.	" "
S. Germain des Pres.	" " "	" "
Mosaic.	" " "	" "
The same.	Immersion.	For the sick.
Gemmit.	Trine immersion alone.	For the well.
Gladbach.	Trine immersion alone, in the form of a cross.	" "
Apam.	Trine immersion alone.	" "
Lodi, in Italy.	" " "	" "
Vienne.	" " "	" "
Limoges.	" " "	" "
"	Trine affusion.	For the sick.
Old Roman altered.	Trine immersion alone.	For the well.
Cadomi.	" " "	" "
Salisbury Use (English).	" " "	" "

Rubrics of the "Orthodox" or "Eastern Catholic Church."

Constantinople, and the four Eastern Patriarchates.	Trine immersion alone.	For the well.
Another office.	Mode not stated.	For the sick.
An Arabic office.	" "	" "
Russian.	Trine immersion.	For the well.

THE RUBRICS.

Eastern Sects.

Office.	What it enjoins.	For whom used.
Copts of Alexandria, and the Ethiopians.	Trine immersion.	For the well.
Same office.	Sprinkling over the whole body.	For the weak.
Armenian Ritual.	Trine immersion.	For the well.
Same office.	" "	" "
Chaldean, Nestorian, and Malabar Ritual.	Immersion. No. of times not specified.	For the well.

Baptismal Offices of the Syrian (Monophysite) Churches of Antioch and Jerusalem.

Office 1.	Partial and single immersion with affusion.	
Office 2.	Not clearly stated.	
Same.	(Altered for girls.) Not clearly stated.	For the well.
Another office.	Not clearly stated.	" "
Office 3.	Immersion, single and partial, with trine affusion.	" "
Ancient office of Saint Severus.	Trine immersion.	For the sick.
Brief office.	No mode stated.	" "
Office 4. Maronite Ritual.	Immersion, partial and single, with trine affusion.	

If we leave out the rubrics of the Monophysites and Nestorians, and those belonging to such of both sects as admit the supremacy of the Roman Pontiff, and consider only those of the Greek and Latin Churches, both which lay claim to Catholicity, the following is the result:

    Whole number of rubrics, . . . 29
    Of which relate to the sick or weak, . . 6

Of these, Gellone, No. 2, enjoins trine immersion or affusion.
    " Moisac, enjoins immersion.
    " Limoges, enjoins trine affusion.
    " The two "Orthodox," or Greek Church rubrics, and the old Roman, No. 5, state no mode.

It should be noted, however, that the first three in every case, except that of weakness or sickness, enjoin absolutely trine immersion.

This was the mode in the ancient Roman Church. It was

the mode in the ancient sees of the "Eastern Catholic communion," and is still. It will be noticed, that even in the case of weak subjects, immersion is mentioned as often as affusion, and that there is no mention at all of sprinkling.

Rubrics which relate to the Well.

Whole number,	25
Of which, enjoin or imply immersion,	25
" " " trine immersion absolutely,	21
" " imply immersion, but do not specify the number of times,	4

It will be seen on scanning the above that Moisac and Limoges are counted twice; once for the part of each which relates to the sick, and once for the part which relates to the well.

It will also be observed:

That in all this last class which relate to the ordinary and regular administration.

a. Positively. That trine immersion, and trine immersion alone, is the mode enjoined.

b. Negatively. That in the four in which it is not enjoined the rubrics are silent as to the number of times, and that in no one of these even, is the *single* immersion ever once clearly mentioned, although the offices themselves most clearly imply immersion as the mode of their administration and no other.

c. That in no one of these is pouring or sprinkling once mentioned.

d. And that, for at least twelve hundred years after Christ, all the rubrics of the Greek and Latin Churches which enjoined any mode at all, enjoined trine immersion, and nothing else, as the *rule* of administration; and that the only case in which there is the slightest trace of a compend being used is that of necessity, *i. e.* weakness or sickness, or in one or two cases, perhaps, to avoid the peril (as they thought) of symbolizing with heretics. Impartial men would not, for the most part, be content with this statement. And, in truth, it must be admitted that all the Greeks, until this hour, practise the trine as the rule, as did some of the Westerns, until the sixteenth century.

If we should adopt the early and Catholic view that the

trine immersion had descended from Christ and His Apostles, we may date the rise of the compendious modes thus:

Mode.	Authors.	How used.	Date.
Single immersion.	Eunomius.	As the rule.	About A.D. 375.
Affusion.	Existing in the Church.	As the exception. Used for clinics alone.	First clearly mentioned by St. Cyprian, about A.D. 250.
Sprinkling.	Existing in the Church.	In necesssity alone, *i. e.* for clinics.	*May* be referred to by Tertullian (De Pœnitent., cap. vi), about A. D. 200.

St. Cyprian seems to include sprinkling as well as pouring in his notion of a divine compend., A.D. 250. His quotations and premises imply this.

In some of the offices of the Monophysite sects, those of the Syrians and Maronites, which have just preceded, it will be seen that we meet with a new mode,—the partial immersion of the candidate and affusion. A glance back at the language of the Fathers and Church writers, as quoted, shows most clearly that for at least the first twelve hundred years the immersion was *total*.

The bodies who use the mode of partial immersion are heretics, condemned by the universal Church in bygone ages.

The Maronite rubric is sufficiently explained by the fact that for several centuries this sect has been connected with the Latin Church, and that it has become much Latinized; many of its leading clergy are educated in Rome; and the effect of her influence in the East, as elsewhere, is to do away with the fuller administration of this sacrament. But we have the clearest evidence from the Maronites themselves that anciently they used trine immersion, and that it was total, and therefore that their rubric is changed. A Maronite synod, held in Mount Lebanon, when J. S. Asseman was legate of the Roman See, in 1736, decreed as follows: "The Holy Synod strictly enjoins that hereafter no one shall use any other form than that which is prescribed in the approved ritual, nor shall any other ceremonies be used in the administration of this sacrament *except those which, established by our ancestors and handed down to us, are preserved in the Oriental Church;*

so that most surely, when the child has been stripped of all his clothing, the priest shall receive it carefully, and *baptize it by trine immersion, by burying the whole of its body*, at the same time invoking the Most Holy Trinity, and saying: 'I baptize thee in the name of the Father;' and let him immerse it once, and lift it up out of the water; 'and of the Son,' and let him immerse it a second time, and lift it out; 'and of the Holy Ghost,' and let him immerse it the third time, and lift it out. And let the deacon at every immersion respond, 'Amen.' But where adults are to be baptized, and especially women, who cherish modesty and honor, we do not permit that they, *according to ancient custom*, shall be stripped of their garments, *and immersed* in a baptistery, as we have above decreed concerning children; but we determine they shall lay bare the head alone, and that the priest shall pour water upon their heads once, saying: I baptize thee in the name of the Father; and again saying: and of the Son; and a third time saying: and of the Holy Ghost. This rite of pouring water upon the head, or even of immersing the head alone in water, the priest may use according to the custom of the place. But he shall use it especially when, were the candidate wholly immersed in the water, his life would be endangered.*

Whether the other offices are used by the Syrians who have joined the Latin communion, or by those who are still Monophysites, is somewhat doubtful. A Greek writer asserts (Orthodoxie et Papisme, p. 87, Paris, 1859, Franck), that trine

---

* "Districte præcipit sancta synodus, ut nemo posthac alia forma utatur, quam quæ in Rituali probato præscripta est, nec ullæ aliæ cœrimoniæ in ejusdem sacramenti administratione usurpentur, præter eas, quæ a majoribus nostris institutæ. nobisque traditæ, in Ecclesia Orientali servantur. Ut nimirum Sacerdos puerum omni veste nudatum accipiat diligenter, et baptizet eum, sub trina immersione totum corpus tegendo, Sanctissimam Trinitatem Semel invocans, ac dicens. Ego te baptizo in nomine Patris, et semel immergat, et ex aqua educat, et Filii, et secundo immergat, et educat, et Spiritus Sancti, et tertio immergat, et educat. Diaconus autem ad singulas immersiones respondeat, Amen. Ubi vero adulti sunt baptizandi, et maxime feminæ, pudori, et honestati consulentes, non permittimus, ut isti juxta antiquum morem vestibus suis nudentur, et in Baptisterium immergantur, ut supra de pueris dictum est; sed volumus, ut illis caput tantum denudantibus, sacerdos super eorum caput effundat aquam semel dicens, Ego te baptizo in nomine Patris, et iterum dicens, et Filii, et tertio dicens, et Spiritus Sancti. Quo ritu effundendi scilicet super caput aquam, vel etiam solum caput in aquam immergendi juxta locorum consuetudinem, sacerdos uti potest; sed tum maxime illo utatur, quando baptizandus vita periclitaretur, Si in aquam totus immergeretur." v. "Synodus Libanensis," ed. Romæ, 1820. See this work, p. 130.

immersion "is still preserved in all the dissenting Oriental communions; and they employ aspersion or ablution only in exceptional cases." By dissenting communions he means the Nestorians and Monophysites, who dissent from the Greek Church, and, of course, he includes the Syrians. This seems to show that the Syrians, whose rubrics these are, must be in communion with Rome.

In stating that the former use *trine* immersion, he teaches that this rubric does not pertain to them; for in the mode of this rubric the child is first let down into the water up to the neck, or to some other part, and then remains partly immersed while the words of baptism, 'I baptize thee,' &c., are said. Of course, therefore, there is but *one* immersion, and but *partial* at that.

But that which renders it most clear that this rubric is a change from the early custom is this, that the Monophysites did not separate themselves from the Church until the last half of the fifth century, prior to which time and at which time trine and total immersion was the universally received custom. The reader will do well to glance at the testimony of Chrysostom, already adduced in confirmation of this remark. Moreover, if any further proof were needed, this mode of partial immersion does not fully express the divine symbolism of the three days' burial in the earth and the resurrection, to which the Scriptures and the early Fathers so often allude. It will be noticed that in all the earlier rubrics there is this very important difference from those which we are considering, that at the invocation of the Trinity, at the naming of every Person, there was an immersion; whereas in these there is none, but affusion is in its place. In some of the later Eastern offices there is indeed an affusion or sprinkling, but this is not the baptism. The words, "I baptize thee," &c., are accompanied by the three immersions.

This mingling of partial immersion and pouring seems to have been a transition from the older mode to the more general use of the compends. It arose, probably, between the beginning of the thirteenth century and the middle of the fifteenth, for in 1439, at the Synod of Florence, Gregory, the monk, says, speaking for the Latins, that "we by no means immerse the whole of the infants' heads," and defends it against the Greeks who, through their champion, Mark of Ephesus, opposed this mode as making two baptisms. This early notice of it is accompanied by a protest. The Greeks were ever more tenacious of the old in rites than the Latins. Indeed, no mistake can be greater than to look to the latter for primitive rites. We have spoken above of the Latins as changing to some extent the baptismal rites of those in the East whom it has drawn within its pale. The reader who is disposed to hear what the Greeks and their opponents say, can consult "Orthodoxie et Papisme," and the work of Gagarin, against which it is written.

We give a few extracts from "Orthodoxie et Papisme," cautioning the reader at the same time, that while much that is said in this work against Western innovations is amply deserved, especially in the matter of rite, yet the Greek Church in the matter of (ikon) image worship and creature worship, and the prevalence of superstition, is nearly as far from primitive truth as the Latin. Nevertheless, in certain points of doctrine in which the Latins have fallen into serious error, but in adherence to primitive rites more especially, they are free from blame and vastly superior.

But the intelligent reader who has studied the peculiarities of differing parts of the Church, has found that no one part monopolizes all the faults or virtues. When the Church is again united in orthodox, scriptural, and primitive truth, we may hope for greater perfection. There never was a period when prayer was so much needed for the erring members of Christ's flock as now, and never, perhaps, such hopes of speedy and blessed answer. But to our purpose.

P. 68: "The papacy having defiled the Roman Church, formerly holy and orthodox, has always known how to find for every one of its innovations injurious words against the universal Church, which it outrages in a manner the most unworthy. It is thus that the notorious apostate Arcudius in blaming the baptism by immersion of the orthodox Church, terms it offensive, indecent, and abominable, and pushes calumny so far as to accuse the Greek priests of infanticide, asserting that they drown infants."

"Can any one push calumny to a more unbridled shamelessness, and cast more blame upon the Divine mode of baptism? And all this is said and done with the consent of the very holy popes and of the holy see, while they protest that 'no one should introduce anything new in the venerable rite of the East, in order that its sanctity may remain unchanged.'"!!!

P. 72: "Let no one do me the injury of supposing that my words are dictated by a desire of converting, or of reforming the Papal Church. No, I propose only to show what iniquitous means the Papacy employs for the purpose of undermining the institutions of the Ecumenical Church. We wish to forewarn the weak against the seductive promise of *nihil innovandum*. We are profoundly convinced that a reform is impossible in that Church so long as she permits herself to be drawn on by an insatiable necessity of innovations in religious matters, which forces her irresistibly to invent new dogmas. What results have been produced by the criticisms and the reproaches directed with so much energy against the illegitimate and unchristian acts of the Papists by the Rinalds, the Lebruns, the Bons, the Calmets, and even by Petaut, all of them Papists so zealous? And who would believe it? The angelical doctor, Thomas (Aquinas) himself, has enounced the opinion that baptism by immersion is the most exact and the most conformable to antiquity? There remains, then, but a single hope of putting an end to the errors of the Roman Church; it is that the initiative will come from the Western Christians themselves, from their own pastors, or even from His Holiness himself, when at some day they shall ask: Why do we not receive and administer baptism by trine immersion, as the Apostles have established the rule, and as it is written in our ritual? Why do we not commune according to the institution of the Lord, as did our fathers? Why is our liturgy no longer the same as that of our predecessors? Why do we no longer confess the symbol of the faith of Nicæa? . . . Why? Why? . . . But, alas! no such voice is raised, and no such voice will ever be raised against the abuses of Popery so long as the holy see of Peter shall be occupied by a progressive Papacy, sustained by the monastic orders of every form, which arrogate to themselves the absolute right of treating arbitrarily dogmas, mysteries, Divine laws and commandments, and which make no scruple of treating as *indecent* and *injurious* all the *sacraments* of the holy Church established during the ages."

P. 80: "The Church of the West has completely altered the ancient doctrine and the ancient discipline. By so doing she has introduced schism into the Christian world. She is obstinate (opinionative) in her dogmatic innovations, which are diametrically opposed to the word of the Lord. She has usurped an authority wholly opposed to all ecumenical laws. She degrades all the ancient rites of the primitive Church into the category of *tolerable* things, for the purpose of destroying or altering them according to her caprices, under the specious pretext, 'justis et gravibus causis.' . . . . Rome has appropriated all the forms of baptism by aspersion. She places them upon the same footing as the true baptism, and attributes to them the same respect and the same virtue. Rome has rejected only that form of baptism which comes to us from the Lord, through the Apostles and the Councils, and which we confess in the symbol of the faith; for the United Greeks she admits the ancient form only as tolerable, and as that which the Papal See suffers only by condescension."

We have given but a small part of what this writer utters on this subject; but enough to show, as indeed the forementioned rubrics do, that the Roman Church has waged as unrelenting war in the East on the ancient mode, and in favor of the compends, as she has in the West on the integrity and perfect administration of the Lord's supper. By educating the clergy of the Eastern errorists, who admit a few tests of her own making, she contrives, as might naturally be expected, to infuse more or less of her peculiar views.

Of course, whatever be deemed the just opinion as to the Syrian rubrics in other respects, it is perfectly clear, from primitive sources, that they are an innovation. St. Cyril of Jerusalem (see above), shows that the mode in Syria was *total* and *trine* immersion in his day, and his testimony is borne out by the other Greeks and Latins of the early ages, and even by the modern Maronites, who have in some measure deserted ancient rite. The later Syrian rubrics then are of little historical worth, though perhaps those *parts* which speak of immersion are to be excepted. It will be noticed that only a part of the Monophysite rubrics are altered, and those in a particular locality, and that a most ancient office of even this locality (that of Severus) enjoins trine immersion.

CHAPTER VII.

OF CHANGES IN THE MODE, AND OF THE CONTESTS BETWEEN THE GREEK AND LATIN CHURCHES.

When Canon 50 of the Apostles was composed, there seem to have been some who baptized by one immersion into the death of Christ. (v. Waterland, vol. ii, p. 187, nn.) Some of the earlier heretics who changed the form, *i. e.* of the words, may have changed also the mode. The passage in Tertullian, Adv. Prax. 26, "non in unum," &c., may refer to such a fact, although it is not so clear as to enable us positively to assert it. At any rate, neither Theodoret nor Sozomen ascribe so early an origin to the single immersion. The evidence, that any before Eunomius practised it, is mainly contained in Canon 50. So little do we hear of those against whom it is directed, in the period between the Apostles and the age of these historians, that, but for the words of the canon, we should be without any clear statement of this mode; and it is not wonderful, therefore, that they should speak of this heresiarch as the father or introducer of it.

But, with the rise of Arianism, came the innovation in a clearer light. Eunomius, an Arian of the most radical kind, a strict Anomæan, not satisfied with the old "form" of baptism into the Father, Son, and Holy Ghost, and the "mode" of trine immersion, because probably they seemed to teach the doctrine of the consubstantiality, and the equality of the three Persons, determined to change both. He therefore baptized by one immersion into the death of Christ. Whether, with respect to these innovations, he was the author, or only a follower of Theophranes and Eutychus, seems uncertain. Sozomen leaned to the opinion that these last were the original propagators. All three were contemporaries, and at one time fellow-workers in the same communion of error. Their innovations in baptism were broached in the beginning or middle of the fourth century. Eunomius, whether from his prominence or zeal, has had his name linked with the change; and the second ecumenical synod, in A. D. 381, expressly condemned his innovations by treating all his followers as unbaptized. The testimony of Theodoret and Sozomen, the two most important witnesses against him, has already been given. The decision of the council seems to have banished the form and mode, which he advocated, from the Church. We find no traces of it, unless we go out of her communion, until the end of the sixth century, two hundred years later. Then for the first time do we see an orthodox bishop favoring it even in the teeth of an ecumenical decision. The circumstances are these, as related by Bingham: "The Arians in Spain, not being of the sect of the Eunomians, continued, for many years, to baptize with three immersions; but then they abused this ceremony to a very perverse end, to patronize their error about the Son and Holy Ghost's being of a different nature or essence from the Father; for they made the three immersions to denote a difference, or degrees of divinity, in the three Divine Persons. To oppose whose wicked doctrine, and that they might not seem to symbolize with them in any practice that might give encouragement to it, *some Catholics began to leave off the trine immersion* as savoring of Arianism, and took up the single immersion in opposition to them. But this was like to prove matter of scandal and schism among the Catholics themselves; and therefore, in the time of Gregory the Great, Leander, Bishop of Sevil, wrote to him for his advice and resolution in this case; to which he returned this answer: Concerning the three immersions in baptism, you have judged very truly already that different rites and customs do not prejudice the holy Church, whilst the unity of faith remains entire. The reason why *we use three immersions at Rome* is to signify the mystery of Christ's three days' burial, that, whilst an infant is thrice lifted up out of the water, the resurrection on the third day may be expressed thereby. But if any one thinks this is rather done in regard to the Holy Trinity, a single immersion in baptism does no way prejudice that; for so long as the unity of substance is preserved in three persons it is no harm whether a child be baptized with one immersion or three; because three immersions may represent the Trinity of persons, and one immersion the unity of the Godhead. But forasmuch as heretics use to baptize their infants with three immersions, I think you ought not to do so; lest this multiplication of immersions be interpreted a division of the Godhead, and give them occasion to glory that their custom has prevailed. *Yet this judgment of Pope Gregory did not satisfy all men in the Spanish Church, for still many kept to the old way of baptizing by three immersions,* notwithstanding this fear of symbolizing with the Arians. Therefore, some time after, about the year 633, the fourth Council of Toledo, which was a general council of all Spain, was forced to make another decree to determine this matter, and settle the peace of the Church. For while some priests baptized with three immersions, and the others but with one, a schism was raised, endangering the unity of the faith; for the contending parties carried the matter so high as to pretend that they who were baptized in a way contrary to their own were not baptized at all. To remedy which evil, the Fathers of this council first repeat the judgment of Pope Gregory, and then immediately conclude upon it that, though both these ways of baptism were just and unblamable in themselves, according to the opinion of that great man, yet, as well to avoid the scandal of schism as the usage of heretics, they decree that only one immersion should be used in baptism, lest if any used three immersions they might seem to approve the opinion of heretics, whilst they followed their practice. And that no one might be dubious about the use of a single immersion, he might consider that the death and resurrection of Christ were represented by it. For the immersion in water was, as it were, the descending into hell, or the grave; and the emersion out of the water was a resurrection. He might also observe the unity of the Deity and the Trinity of persons to be signified by it; the unity by a single immersion, and the Trinity by giving baptism in the name of the Father, Son, and Holy Ghost. Some learned persons find fault with this council for changing this ancient custom upon so slight a reason as that of the Arians using it; *which, if it were any reason, would hold as well against a single immersion;* because the Eunomians, a baser sect of the Arians, were the *first* inventors of that practice; and therefore the exception made by this Spanish council, in the seventh century, cannot prejudice the more ancient and general practice of the Church, which, as Strabo observed, 'still prevailed after this council.'"

This account is impartial and erudite. Alcuin is not so moderate in his condemnation. He did not hesitate to term this decision of Toledo diabolical. Thus, in his 81st epistle, writing to Paulinus, concerning certain Spanish heresies: "From the midst of the thorns of the rural districts of Spain, and from the lurking places of his envenomed perfidy, the old serpent again attempts to lift his head which had been bruised, not by the club of Hercules, but by the power of the Gospel, and, in the cups of his ancient malice, to mingle a new and accursed poison: and like a very freezing blast from the North he has assaulted one side of the solid bulwarks of the Church in his endeavor to change the rule of the holy baptism of Catholic custom, and by introducing the notion that it ought to be administered by invocation of the Holy Trinity, indeed, but with a single immersion only." The learned reader who wishes to find more from his pen, may consult Epis. lxix, ad Fratres Lugdunensis.

Walafrid Strabo expresses a sentiment which men intelligent and dispassionate will approve. (De Offic. Eccles. c. xxvi.) "Which single immersion, although at that time pleasing to the Spaniards who asserted that the trine immersion should be disused because certain heretics, for the purpose of denying the consubstantiality, had dared to propound the dogma that there are dissimilar substances in the Trinity: notwithstanding the more ancient use, and the reason above stated, prevailed. For if we are to desert everything which heretics have perverted, nothing will be left us, since they have erred concerning even God himself, and they have twisted everything which seems to pertain to his worship, and have applied it as though it were peculiarly designed for the support of their errors. But why should I speak farther. Suffice it to say, that the trine immersion prevails everywhere in the world this day, and that it can by no means be changed unless in accordance with a rash desire of novelty, and to the scandal of the weak."

In these testimonials it will be seen:

1. As to the ancient custom; that at that time the custom at Rome, and in Spain, prior to this trouble with the Arians, was trine immersion.

2. That so far is this action from being an approval of sprinkling or pouring, that neither mode is even mentioned.

3. That the adoption of the single immersion is stated to be a change.

4. That its *motive* is to avoid symbolizing with heretics, one of the most silly of all reasons, for a branch of this very sect of the Arians were the first who used this single immersion. Moreover, if, because an errorist perverts a primitive rite from what the early Christians believed to be its intention, the orthodox should lay it aside, what, as Strabo says, will be left us?

5. The authority of Gregory the Great and this synod of the single nation of Spain is not a decision of the whole Church, nor was it meant to apply to the whole Church, but only to a single and small part of it, under certain circumstances, which cannot be said now to exist.

6. Gregory's opinion that single or trine immersion might be used, is expressly contradicted by that of his predecessor, Pope Pelagius, who assures us expressly that it is not a matter of indifference, but that the trine immersion was enjoined by Christ. This was also the opinion of Chrysostom and Theodoret, as we have shown before. Nor was the view of the other Fathers materially different, for they believed it to be apostolic. And if one mode be *the* apostolic one, it is surely not a matter of indifference whether we shall use that or another. Canon 50 of the Apostles being received in the whole Church, sufficiently vindicates it from any sympathy with Gregory or the Spanish synod. So that we may, as did many learned men after Gregory, and in his day, say with certainty that he was the first writer of any note in the ranks of orthodoxy who thought that any other mode than trine immersion should be used where no absolute necessity existed.

7. As to the approval of his opinion, in four patriarchates out of the ancient five it met with no sanction at all. In the West it met with local approval only, and partial at that. Two of the most learned men of a period not long after condemn it in strong terms.

Between the restoration of the trine immersion in Spain, and the first half of the ninth century when Strabo wrote, there seems to have been no important effort to change the mode. In the passage just quoted, he testifies to the universal prevalence of the trine immersion. Of a similar tenor is the witness of Alcuin, Hincmar of Rheims, and the other writers, and the rubrics of the West. And in treating of innovations in the mode, it must be understood that we are speaking only of Western Europe and the Latin communion. The rest of the Church has ever, even until this hour, been zealous for the ancient mode. We are tracing something therefore not ecumenical, nor invested with ecumenical sanction, but a custom which has always been purely local, so far as its use by the orthodox, or by those professing to be orthodox, is concerned. This must not be lost sight of.

The opinion of Gregory and the Toledon Synod, which found no permanent approval in any part of the Church in the seventh century, fared a little better in the ninth. The local Council of Worms, A. D. 868, in its fifth canon is almost word for word the same as Canon 5 of the fourth of Toledo. It also quotes Gregory the Great and favors the single immersion for the same reason, viz., the fear of schism. Yet this decision finds no countenance in any other part of the Church, for the councils of the West, when referring to immersion, never mention any other than the trine. The Council of Worcester in A D. 1240, distinctly orders ("et *trina semper* fiat emersio baptizandi"), that the trine immersion shall *always* be used. In the Council of Nismes, in 1284, we find another trace of the single immersion. It is there ordered, in case of necessity, the trine immersion shall be used, but that if one immersion only has been performed the child is to be considered baptized. And so also if, in the same circumstances, affusion has been resorted to. So far as the councils speak of immersion, up to the period of the Reformation, it is always trine, or the number of times is not stated. The single is never clearly referred to, although the opinion of Gregory must have had some influence in the West, even where the mode was the trine. The councils already cited show clearly that the trine immersion, with the insignificant exception just given, was the *rule* for at least 1200 years after Christ. The first exception that, after diligent search, the author has been able to find, is the local Synod of Ravenna, in the year 1287 or 1311.* Certainly rather a late period for the application of the "quod semper, quod ubique, quod ab omnibus." The case of necessity was not always provided for in the councils. Hence for at least the first 800 years there is no mention of sprinkling or pouring. For when there was no necessity, no one ever thought during all this time of resorting to them. And none of the rubrics

---

* But v. Wall. ii, 393–394. He mentions Angiers, A.D. 1275.

deal with any but ordinary cases. The mode of baptism was a prolific source of discord between the East and the Roman See. The Greeks uniformly resisted any attempt to alter it. Michael Cerularius in the eleventh century brings it as a charge against the Latins, that they baptize by one immersion. The contest seems to have waxed warm between them, for we find Humbert, the Papal legate, complaining that the Greeks, "like the Arians, rebaptize those who had been baptized in the name of the Holy Trinity, and especially the Latins, and that, like the Donatists, they asserted that, with the exception of the Greek Church, the Church of Christ and true sacrifice and baptism had perished from the earth." All the Westerns, however, were not justly liable to the charge of wholly altering the mode, for we know that, long after the disruption, the trine was the rule in some countries, and in England even until the Reformation. After the disruption, the Easterns pursued an inconsistent course, sometimes, but not uniformly, baptizing all Westerns. Some of their synods have affirmed, others have denied the validity of all baptisms not administered by trine immersion.

To return to the West. After the Roman Pontiffs, by their attempted innovations, had succeeded in splitting the Church in two, they could no longer hope for the ecumenical approval of their private opinions, or the opinions of the merely local Western Church, which remained with them. Before, men had regarded an ecumenical council as the only authorized or authoritative *interpreter* of church teaching; until it spoke, there was no final decision. In other words, men were careful not to go *beyond* the Church. But with the rise of the Schoolmen in the West we find a different spirit. Possessed of much subtlety and zeal for their own local views, these men, undoubtedly with good intentions, have wrought irreparable evil, by introducing private opinions, or defending those already introduced as *Church* doctrines. Notions which were either wholly unknown in the early centuries, or if known, were held as the private opinion of some Father, and were without "Catholic consent," and which had never been judged by a general council, these men elaborated into some system, and set up their own "ipse dixit," or their own private interpretation of Scripture and Fathers, where, had they been less subtle, and more reverent, they would have waited until the whole Church spoke. At any rate they were not authorized, nor was the local Church of Western Europe authorized to speak for her; and therefore such a course on their part savored of usurping her office, and blasphemously arrogating her prerogatives to themselves. When one perceives in some of them so much of acumen, even though that acumen be marred by superstition, and (reluctantly it is said) with idolatry, he may find much to interest and to please; but when he finds these men taking upon themselves the office of *the* Church, his feeling must change to sorrow and indignation. The sad results are too visible in all parts of Western Christendom to be lost sight of. The true idea of Church authority was lost, and opinion took its place. Prominent among these stands Thomas Aquinas. He is the first apologist that the author has found for the use of the compends of pouring or sprinkling *as founded in the New Testament*. The difficulty of immersion in the case of the three thousand, &c., are stated by him as serving to show that they might have been used as early as the time of the Apostles. He did not go so far, however, as some have since; for he expressly says that "the figure of Christ's burial is more clearly represented by immersion;" and that, therefore, this mode of baptizing is the *more common*, and the more worthy of praise. To this general practice of immersion in the thirteenth century he expressly testifies in another place, thus: "It is safer to baptize by immersion, because this is the more common use." v. in his Summa ed. Romæ, 1773, tom. viii, p. 3, Quæst. 66, Art. vii, p. 232: "Tutius sit baptizare per modum immersionis, quia hoc habet communior usus." Again, p. 233: "In immersione expressius repræsentatur figura sepulturæ Christi, et ideo hic modus baptizandi est communior, et laudabilior." (v. Thomas Aquinas, Summa, Pars. 3, Quæst. 66, Art. vii and viii, where he concludes: "Quamvis tutius est baptizare per modum immersionis (quia hoc habet communior usus) potest tamen fieri baptismus per modum aspersionis, vel etiam per modum effusionis.") He misrepresents Pope Pelagius. The quotations from him show that Aquinas's attempt to explain them away is a failure. He reasons from the mere opinion or authority of Gregory the Great, and brings proofs which are far from conclusive. He seems not to have examined the ancient Fathers on this point, or he would have come to a different conclusion. The discrepancy of some of his views on this topic with those of the ancient Church, East and West, is worthy of especial notice. Yet, he says, that "significatio Trinitatis est in baptismo per verba formæ, nec est, de necessitate, quod significetur Trinitas per usum materiæ; *sed hoc* fit ad majorem expressionem." Still he seems not to forget the case of necessity, as is evident from his drift.

A learned writer remarks: "Notandum vero ante sanctum Gregorium concilia et Patres locutos esse de trina immersione quasi necessaria et ex Dei institutione quod quidem explicatur a Sancto Thoma. 3 part. Quæst. 66, Art 8. . . . . Ceterum pro unica mersione non videtur sanctus Thomas testimonium ullum afferre ante Conc. Tolet. iv, quod Gregorio Magno posterius fuit. Gussanv. not., p. 498, tom. 3, Greg. Magni Ep. ad Leandrum Episc. Hispal ed. Migne."

All the Fathers and baptismal Offices of the early times witness to immersion as the mode practised in the initiations of the Gospel; and none of them ever expresses a belief in their having been performed in any other mode. Any writer, therefore, who follows Aquinas, must interpret the Scriptures of the new dispensation, not only without the consent of the early Christians, but most clearly against them. He must oppose the clearest "Catholic consent." In other words, he must abandon not only the Church principle of the "quod semper, quod ubique, quod ab omnibus," but every one which is conservative. For any interpretation which ignores and opposes and gives the lie to the immediate successors of the Apostles and to the early Christians, as well as to what on all hands among impartial men is admitted to be the predominant signification of $\beta\alpha\pi\tau\iota\zeta\omega$, must rest on a false basis. It rejects the best means of obtaining a knowledge of the subject, the more especially when, as in this case, their witness is borne, not to some hidden meaning not connected intimately with anything outward, but with a rite whose outward observance and proper administration was always believed to be associated with salvation, and which, for this very reason, would be most carefully observed as it was handed down from inspired men and from Christ. The best answer, therefore, and indeed the only one, if we follow the primitive principle to which we have just adverted, is to ask of every advocate of such an assertion to show that his idea has foundation in Christian and Catholic antiquity; for until this is done it cannot be noticed. "As it *was in the beginning*, is now, and ever shall be, world without end." Not "*as it was in Thomas Aquinas's days*, is now, and ever shall be." Twelve centuries is rather a long stride, altogether too long for the "Quod semper," even were there no testimony during all that time in favor of the immersion. But what shall we say when, so far as being the "regula baptismatis"—"*the rule* of baptism"—there is nothing else during all this long period.

We have already alluded to the action of Ravenna in 1311, and to the fact that Gregory the Monk, at Florence, in 1439, states that the Latin rituals still enjoined trine immersion. Yet, notwithstanding this latter statement, the views of Aquinas and his coadjutors were gradually leavening that body. The rituals seem, until quite a late period, perhaps until the Reformation, to enjoin trine immersion as the rule. The single, however, and the compends were brought in little by little until, at the Reformation, they had become the ordinary modes in certain countries. France, Spain, Italy, Holland, Germany, and perhaps all Latin Continental Europe, seem, for the most part, to have laid the regular administration aside. Milan, and perhaps some other localities on the Continent and England, maintained immersion. Milan, as being the see of St. Ambrose, would be apt to remember his words, and to continue the Apostolic and Catholic practice. The distance of England from Rome, and the attachment of the people to old usages, may account for its retention there.

It is almost useless to follow the Latins since that time. Their present custom is best expressed by Carlo Borromeo and the latest rubrics of that body, as already given.

The Lutheran and Calvinistic communions, especially the latter, have unfortunately been driven by the immersing Antipædobaptists into a position far different from that of the Reformers whose name they bear, and thus have added to their difficulties. Luther and Calvin have already been cited. Because the Baptists made the primitive mode essential in all cases, the later Presbyterians have deemed themselves justified in practically laying it aside altogether. Every effort is put forth to write up the compends and to write down the full form. Just as though such a course were necessary or profitable! or that the originators of the Baptist baptismal succession were not themselves, according to the Baptist theory, unbaptized, and consequently without the power or authority to originate baptism, or to minister it to others.

An ignorant and perverse interpretation has been given to certain passages of Holy Writ, so as to draw support for the present irregularities in using the "compends" in nearly all cases.

This mode is used chiefly by hot headed partisans who, whether from lack of information or passion, make the most frightful blunders, and convey the falsest impressions. This school, instead of calling upon the different Baptist sects to show that the single immersion is not itself a compend, cavil about βαπτίζω, as though anything could be plainer than its use, both in times anterior and posterior to the rise of the Gospel, by finding difficulties in the baptisms of the New Testament so far as the performing of them by immersion is concerned, and by throwing contempt upon the witness of the early Christians. They forget that the disciples of the Apostles could see no unreasonableness of immersion in these texts, that even when, as in the case of Clinics, they searched about them for arguments, the bright idea never struck them that βαπτίζω did not refer to mode, or that multitudes should leave the comfortable neighborhood of cities for deserts where there was "much water" for the sake of having a few drops poured upon them, especially when, according to our present irregularities, any town even the smallest in Palestine, would have furnished water sufficient to baptize all that thronged the Jordan. They did not suppose that any would "go down into" the water and come up out of the water simply for the sake of a mere fillip of it on the head. This might be applied without even going to a river. The water might be brought or might be taken up with the hand. They always speak of immersion and nothing else as the New Testament mode. But all this, the testimony of Scripture, Councils, Fathers, Rubrics, everything, in fine, which bears upon this subject, this school tramples upon. Between them and the Baptists the fight bids fair to be endless. Neither will hear these authorities except where they speak for them. They are all for infant baptism, therefore the Baptist rejects them; they are for trine immersion, and therefore they meet with disapproval from the other party. The great bulk of our own Church writers, together with the Lutherans (German), and the more learned Presbyterians and Latins have been more impartial, though with various degrees of knowledge and with different methods of thinking. With the spread of the tenets of the Baptists has been combined an increased influence among those who have read or thought little on this subject of the views of the most radical and anti-immersion schools. So that now even in our own Church, it is no very rare thing to see men who profess to be Churchmen, who are ever zealous to profess their reverence for Vincent of Lerins and the Quod semper, who actually contradict our older and more learned theologians, and even the teachings of the present rubric of the Mother Church, and indeed the teachings of the whole Church during those early and better centuries which they so much profess to revere. Is it a wonder that when such a man disputes with a Baptist he is confronted with Cranmer and Beveridge and Usher, and his own rubrics? And the worst of it is that in opposing the errors of the Baptists they fall into similar errors. Indeed, the great bulk of works on the mode, issued from the press during the last sixty years, have been written in a spirit of ignorance of the real facts and merits of the question, have been against the English Church rubric, and have been mere rehashes of Aquinas, or of some one who drew his ideas from him. Bishop White, in his Lectures on the Catechism, pleads for the old mode. But such exceptions are rare. Among the great body of the non-episcopal bodies, anything like what their own most learned men have sometimes said would probably receive little or no approbation. To sum up all in a word, the "compends" have driven what Theodoret calls the "Divine baptism" out of use, and have usurped its place.

CHAPTER VIII.

OF THE TRINE IMMERSION.

From the preceding testimony of the Fathers, the Councils, and the Rubrics, it is evident that the trine immersion was the universal *rule* of administration, from which any deviation was *irregular* and *unauthorized*.

On what grounds did the Christians of the first 500 years base this custom? We have already seen from Tertullian, St. Cyprian, Theodoret, St. Chrysostom, Pope Pelagius, and Canon 50 of the Apostles, that trine immersion was derived in the early Church from the immediate command of Christ in his last commission, recorded in St. Matt 28 : 19. And this, it will be seen from some of these, was so understood by them as not only to enjoin this mode, but to forbid all other. Theodoret and Pope Pelagius aim their remarks against single immersion as being a violation of Christ's command. Indeed, the language of all implies the same thing, since they all agree in considering the Divine injunction as modal. They never interpret it as signifying washing or wetting without reference to the mode. This is a late idea. It is true that some thought the number of times determined by tradition, but such tradition was deemed of Divine or Apostolic origin, or at least was deemed so sacred that no man might break it. They do not express the view that the command is not to immerse. Two, and the only two for the first 500 years who ascribe the *number* of immersions to tradition, St. Basil the Great and St. Jerome, present no difficulty. The former states in effect, in a passage already given, that Christ *established* immersion. St. Jerome on Matt. 28 : 19 does not militate against this view. Theodoret and Sozomen regard the trine immersion as of Divine or Apostolic origin. It is clear then :

1. That they all agreed in deeming trine immersion *binding* upon every bishop and presbyter.

2. That most of them derived both the immersion and the number of times of its repetition directly from a Divine command in Holy Writ.

3. That two, while they deemed that *immersion* was of Divine injunction, yet look upon the trine as if not from a traditional *source*, yet from traditional *means;* *i. e.* of transmission. They may have deemed the *source* Divine or Apostolic, as do Theodoret and Sozomen. They say nothing inconsistent with this view.

The general (perhaps the universal) view then was that *trine immersion* is of Apostolic or Divine origin.

2. But is there any ground in Holy Writ for this?

1. The words of the last commission of Christ as interpreted by certain Fathers seem to point clearly to this. "Go ye, therefore, and teach all nations, βαπτίσαντες αὐτοὺς εἰς τὸ ὄνομα τοῦ πατρὸς καὶ τοῦ υἱοῦ καὶ τοῦ ἁγίου πνεύματος." These words they understood thus: "Immersing them in the name of the Father (one immersion), and of the Son (a second immersion), and of the Holy Ghost (the third immersion). The Greek certainly admits this rendering. The early and universal prevalence of the trine immersion is best accounted for by supposing it to have had its origin in these words. If it had been a matter of indifference whether the single or the trine should be used, we should certainly expect to find the former before Eunomius in the fourth century, for it is evidently pleasanter and easier, but we do not.* Between καὶ and τοῦ υἱοῦ, and καὶ and τοῦ ἁγίου πνεύματος, there is an ellipsis of βαπτίσαντες αὐτοὺς, according to common usage. And this fact would seem to point towards the triple rather than the single act. Language is full of such omissions.

The other text which has been adduced in support of this mode is Hebrews 6 : 2, where, among "the principles of the doctrine of Christ, is enumerated the doctrine 'βαπτισμῶν' of immersions." Those who suppose that this plural does not refer to trine immersion are agreed only in rejecting it. They differ endlessly among themselves. The Apostle in the text is not speaking of Jewish washings or proselyte initiation, but of the principles of the doctrine of Christ. Immediately after the reference to baptism is an allusion to the rite of confirmation. What could be more natural than this sequence?

---

* v. Wall. ii, p. 419, and i, pp. 37–38.

Notice the connection of these principles of the doctrine of Christ: 1, "repentance;" 2, "faith;" 3, "baptisms" (*i. e.* "immersions"); 4, the "laying on of hands" (*i. e.* "confirmation"); 5, the "resurrection;" 6, "eternal judgment."

These are all Christian doctrines, some of them exclusively so, which were denied by a large and influential body of the Jewish people.

These statements express the view of the advocates of this rite.

The verbs $\beta\alpha\pi\tau\acute{\iota}\zeta\omega$, $\beta\acute{\alpha}\pi\tau\omega$, both mean ordinarily to immerse. But they differ in form, $\beta\alpha\pi\tau\acute{\iota}\zeta\omega$ being considered a frequentative, while the other expresses the simple meaning only. While perhaps it may not be advanced as an argument, nevertheless it is well to observe that in the New Testament, 1st, $\beta\acute{\alpha}\pi\tau\omega$, with its compound, $\dot{\epsilon}\mu\beta\acute{\alpha}\pi\tau\omega$, is used six times, but never of baptism; 2d, $\beta\alpha\pi\tau\acute{\iota}\zeta\omega$ is used eighty times, in every instance of baptism. Now this circumstance of the uniform use of a frequentative *form* for baptism, in preference to one which expresses the simple meaning to immerse, best agrees with trine immersion. It is true that the difference in meaning between the simple and the frequentative verb is often or even generally overlooked in ordinary discourse; but even were we to admit that this is always the case with $\beta\alpha\pi\tau\acute{\iota}\zeta\omega$, as it appears that it ordinarily is, it would still seem strange that the frequentative is uniformly used, and the simple never, in speaking of baptism. If there were no shade of distinction and of difference in their signification, why should one be used *exclusively* where the immersions of baptism are mentioned? And why, unless the trine immersion be signified, this studied distinction in their use? Can it be mere chance? Let it be remembered that the first Latin who mentions this rite, as well as St. Jerome, translate $\beta\alpha\pi\tau\acute{\iota}\zeta\omega$ at times by mergito. The following, from the pen of one who *did not wholly* agree with the views which he presents, may not be uninteresting:

"It would appear then (he has just shown from Tertullian, De Cor. Mil., c. iii, and from Jerome, Adv. Lucif., as above quoted, that $\beta\alpha\pi\tau\acute{\iota}\zeta\omega$ was early translated by 'mergito') that a feeling existed among some of the Latin Fathers when they rendered $\beta\alpha\pi\tau\acute{\iota}\zeta\omega$ by mergito that $\beta\alpha\pi\tau\acute{\iota}\zeta\omega$ is, in its appropriate sense, what the grammarians and lexicographers call a *frequentative* verb, *i. e.* one which denotes repetition of the action which it indicates. Nor are they alone in this; some of the best Greek scholars of the present and past age have expressed the same opinion in a more definite shape. Buttman lays it down as a principle of the Greek language, that a class of verbs in ζω, formed from other verbs, have the signification of *frequentatives*. Gramm., § 119, 1, 5, 2. Rost lays down the same principles. Gramm., § 94, 2 b. . . . In accordance with this, Stephens and Vossius have given their opinions; and the highest authorities of recent date in lexicography have decided in the same way. Passow, Bretschneider, and Donnegan all affirm that βαπτίζω originally and properly means to *dip, or plunge often or repeatedly.*" Stuart himself, however, does not, *in all respects*, agree with this opinion, or at least with its application to the case of βαπτίζω. (M. Stuart, Prof. of Sac. Lit in the Theol. Sem. at Andover, in Biblical Repository, January, April, 1833, p. 294.)

With the view that βαπτίζω is a frequentative in form agrees Robinson. Liddell and Scott ascribe to it the frequentative meaning as the primary, though they furnish no example.

Is not the existence of the *trine* immersion as the Apostolic and Divine mode, as the early Christians deemed it, rendered the easiest solution of the question of its uniform preference?

Obj. 1. The New Testament, speaking of baptism, simply says he "immersed him," or "baptized" him, without specifying more than a single immersion.

Ans. This they might have done if they had practised the trine. This was the customary phraseology of the early Christians who used it. Whether there be no indications in the New Testament of the trine, let the impartial judge. Who would positively assert the negative? Who can?

Obj. 2. But the passages quoted from Barnabas, Hermas, and Justin Martyr, state only the fact of being immersed or baptized, but do not specify further. We should most naturally understand these testimonies of the single.

Ans. The same modes of expression are common among the early Christians, and yet we know that their universal practice was the trine. These testimonies were understood by them as referring to the latter mode, or they could not have spoken of it as of Divine or of Apostolic origin; for it is hardly supposable that they could have believed that the immediate successors of the Apostles would have departed from their command, if not that of Christ. Indeed the fact that they spoke of the trine as "handed down from the Apostles," and that they deemed certain heretics the first innovators by bringing in single immersion, is in itself the strongest proof that they never supposed these passages to refer to the single; for in that case the Orthodox would have been the first innovators, and not Eunomius. The historians of the early Church, who refer to Eunomius' altering the mode, could find no innovator before him and his followers, and they had probably better means of getting at early Christian records and the rise of heresies than we have, for many of the writings which were extant in their day have been lost.

Obj. 3. But Tertullian says that the trine immersion was derived from tradition.

He says no such thing. Such a representation of his opinions is inaccurate. He expressly asserts, in more than one place, that Christ *commanded* immersion, and that this rite of trine immersion was derived from Him. The learned Waterland says, that the expression in De Corona, cap. iii, beginning "respondentes," &c., refers to the baptismal creed. The view just expressed would make Tertullian contradict himself. See his testimony above, and the reference to Waterland there. It is clear that "respondentes" does not mean "dipping," but answering or pledging, as in Oxf. trans.

Obj. 4. But some writers after Tertullian's time, as St. Basil, St. Jerome, Sozomen, represent it as derived from tradition.

This word derived gives a false idea of their opinion. They believed it to have been derived from Christ or his Apostles, but to have been handed down by tradition. Indeed there is no subject which is so much misunderstood as this of tradition. In later days, for every particular error of the Greek and Latin Churches, even in matters with regard to which they were at swords' points, they both claim tradition, though very unjustly. And this has brought even the term itself into suspicion among many. But it should be remembered that the word means nothing more than "handed down." It is used in the New Testament. St. Paul, in 2 Thess. 2 : 15, uses this language : "Therefore, brethren, stand fast, and hold the *traditions* which ye have been taught, whether by word or by our epistle." He uses similar expressions in 3 : 6 of the same epistle : "Now we command you, brethren, in the name of our Lord Jesus Christ, that ye withdraw yourselves from every brother that walketh disorderly, and not after the *tradition* which he received of us."

And the earliest writers appeal to the fact that a custom or doctrine has been handed down from the Apostles as perfectly conclusive of its truth. But they regard this tradition not itself as the *source*, but as the *means* of the transmission. The tradition had come down from Christ or his Apostles as its *source*, but the means by which it had reached them was by being handed down from one to the other, and witnessed to in the writings of the Fathers; for, when a Father speaks of unwritten tradition, he does not mean unwritten in the Fathers or councils, but unwritten in Scripture. And often, indeed, they use the term tradition of what is contained in Scripture, and such a use is manifestly in accordance with the literal signification of the word. It will follow, then, that *St. Basil and St. Jerome both derived the trine immersion from a Divine or Apostolic source, but believed it to be transmitted by the historical sense and testimony of the early Christians.* They would have spurned it at once if they had believed it to rest on a less basis. Indeed Sozomen expressly calls the trine immersion alone "the divine baptism."

The interpretation which, in its ignorance and self-sufficiency, would reject the HISTORICAL TESTIMONY of the pure eyes of the Church, is like the shifting sands of the desert, or like a ship without anchor or rudder. Many half read persons, who claim to follow *the Scriptures alone*, mean nothing more than that they reject the light which the immediate successors of the Apostles throw upon their writings, and take the Scriptures as they understand them, not as they really teach; hence the crop of Latin, and Greek, and Protestant errors. Every error now existing has come in part from the disregard of right principles. The test by which we are to try every tradition is that of St. Vincent of Lerins, the "quod semper, quod ubique, quod ab omnibus." The aberrations of every part of the Church, from primitive custom or doctrine, all lack this. They have not been held "always, everywhere, and by all." So far as they are noticed at all they are condemned by it. This is patent to every one unprejudiced.

Almost all of every creed admit some *Apostolic* tradition. We admit it in making still more clear the scriptural and primitive Church polity. The Presbyterian admits it when it teaches him the baptism of infants. And the Baptist admits it when it teaches that the first day of the week should be observed as the Christian Sabbath.

Indeed, regard for Apostolic tradition stands opposed not to the written tradition of God's most holy Word, but it is explanatory of it, serving to make clear points which would otherwise be obscure. It is *necessary* to all sound and orthodox interpretation on the subjects of which it treats. It condemns by regarding the Ecumenical or Catholic Church as *the* authoritative interpreter, both of Holy Writ and Apostolic tradition, the Donatistic position of Rome. It most clearly and pointedly condemns the refusal of the cup to the laity, the use and worship of images, the worship of any other being than God, and service in an unknown tongue. But the ignorant often suppose that the traditions of the early Christians and the traditions of that part of the Western Church which is under the usurped dominion of Rome, agree when these last are diametrically opposed to, and subversive of the first.

The *doctrinal* tradition, so far as the only authorized interpreter of it—an ecumenical council—has decided, is embodied in the Nicene creed. No man may without peril usurp its authority and decide further. (v. Can. 7 of Ephesus.) There will probably never be any additions to it by the whole Church, and there never will be peace in Christendom until local Churches learn, that whatever may be their private opinions, whatever in their notion may be the need of adding to or taking from that creed, in favor, as in Pope Pius's creed, of some error or errors of the Latin communion, or as in the Synod of Bethlehem, or in the iconodulic conventicle of Nicæa in 787, in favor of deadly and pestilential innovations, such definition will, after all, be no definition, because without authority. The Anglican communion does not fall under the same censure. At the period of the Reformation she found notions in favor of errors which had never received conciliar (universal) sanction, but were, nevertheless, taught as though they had, and she was obliged to forbid them. In so doing she has not usurped the position of the whole Church, East and West, as have the Greek and Latin communions. She would have encouraged the notion that a part is the whole, had she retained them. In raising a bulwark against their ingress, she acts not only as she had a right, but considering the fatal nature of idolatry as she was bound to do. Until the whole Church is reformed, it may be doubted whether anything but ruin would attend their obliteration, were such a thing possible. She might in that case rue her conduct when the adversary had sowed the tares of heretical opinion among the wheat of sound and authoritative doctrine.

So far as the primitive tradition affects *rites*, it should be remembered that it consists of a few articles, such as to stand praying on Sundays, and from Easter to Whitsuntide, the trine immersion, and a few other *customs*. Some of them fell into disuse in the West, prior to the Reformation, and have not since been restored, although there is no one of them at all inconsistent with the principles or doctrines of the most learned divines of the Anglo-Catholic communion, nor indeed with the most sober of the continental Reformers. If they were restored, primitive tradition would be better understood, and no harm need result to evangelical piety.

CHAPTER IX.

OF ADMITTING THE COMPENDS AS VALID BAPTISM.

The reasons for admitting sprinkling, pouring, or single immersion as valid baptism are as follows:

1. Because necessity admits no law.

Baptism is generally necessary to salvation. But in case of sickness or other necessity the full form is impossible. Hence in such case the question is not whether the full form *or* a compend shall be used,—the choice is between a compend or nothing at all. If the sick man die without baptism he dies without any promise of *covenant* mercy. All admit that baptism is the door to the Church, and to the *covenant* mercies of which it is the sole depository. In such a case the custom of the Church from the days of Cyprian has ever been to act on the principle which the Lord has laid down in speaking of David and his men eating of the show-bread, "which was not lawful for him to eat, neither for them that were with him, but only for the priests," and which, with reference to this very case, he has enunciated in the words, "I will have mercy and not sacrifice." Here was a case in which God had commanded (Levit. 24 : 9), "And it (the show-bread) shall be Aaron's and his sons; and they shall eat it in the holy place; for it is most holy unto him of the offerings of the Lord made by fire by a perpetual statute." Now, this conduct of David is brought by the Redeemer to prove the innocence of the disciples. And it should be noticed that its whole force of application in this particular case depends on its being an instance in which necessity insured guiltlessness, or it would not bear out the conduct of his disciples who, in a similar case of necessity, when they "were an hungered" "began to pluck the ears of corn, and to eat." Here we see a Divine rule regarding a positive institution, in a case of absolute necessity, violated without sin. The case of the clinic is even stronger.

The conditions of salvation, as enunciated by Christ himself, are, " He that believeth *and is baptized* shall be saved." But immersion, in case of danger of death would savor far more of "sacrifice" than of "mercy." Yet the *eternal* life of the clinic is hazarded if he die without the seal of covenant mercy. Whereas, in David's case and the disciples, only the physical was involved. In such a case, although the early Christians believed immersion to be the Divine mode, nevertheless they deemed that Christ, in laying down the principle above mentioned, had provided for the case of necessity, and so came the nearest they could by using the "form" of words, the material—water, and by sprinkling or pouring. And then, that all doubt might be removed, they decreed (Can 47 of Laodicea) that " those who have received baptism in sickness and then have recovered must learn the creed, *and be made to know that they have been vouchsafed the Divine grace.*" No decision of the Church, nor any part of it, has ever deemed such compendious baptism in necessity invalid. The only *individuals* who thought so in the pale of the Church for fifteen centuries were those whom Cyprian mentions only to oppose. After his day we hear nothing of them until the rise of the Baptists in the seventeenth century. During all this time, the view of Cyprian as to their validity was in the Church universally received, or with so little, if any, dissent as not to have come down to us.

2. Because if we deny the validity of the compends we shall have to assume the position that the whole Western Church, including all Latins, and all the Protestants, the English and the American Episcopal Churches, has failed, and consequently that all Western baptism and orders are null and invalid, and that for centuries past no Church has existed in the West.

For three hundred years at least the compends have been the general, almost the universal methods in the western part of continental Europe, wherever the Latins or the Reformed held sway, and in the British Islands for at least two hundred and fifty years. Of course, if any one asserts that they are not valid modes, he must make up his mind to the inevitable consequence,—neither he nor any other Western of any creed is either baptized or ordained.

This is too evident to need proof.

Indeed the compends *in case of necessity* are used and are

admitted as valid by the whole Church, East and West. Even where no necessity compels their administration, they are yet (though irregular) valid—the whole West and four-fifths of the Eastern being witness.

On the Constantinopolitan Rubric, it is observed : "The Greeks generally baptize by pouring thrice a large quantity of warm water (by which according to a canon of a provincial Synod under Germanus, Archbishop of Amathus, the fervor of baptism is signified) upon the head. The child sits in a vessel, or deep laver, up to its shoulders, while they wash it, or, lest it should be overwhelmed by the abundance of the water, or should drink too much, the priest places it lying down, and sustained by the priest's left hand upon its stomach, and then he purifies its head and whole body with the saving waters."*

Now, while it may be doubted whether this remark was true even at the period when made (1749) of the "Orthodox" Greeks in the sense which it conveys, *i. e.* generally (plerumque), nevertheless it is clear that *sometimes* the Greeks, even those of Constantinople and the Patriarchates, who are now much stricter in their requirement of trine immersion of Westerns passing to them than the Russians, did at that time receive such Latins or others who had been baptized only by affusion or aspersion without immersion, and as validly, though it may be irregularly baptized, and they themselves, in case of necessity, and often perhaps, even where none existed, did use the compends, and do even now in that case.

The whole Greek and Russian communion, for a long time, up to 1756, did receive Western baptism as valid. Since then the Greeks have rejected it; but, it should be remembered, that they esteem all not of their own creed as heretics, so that this may have added some little weight with them in their decision, even if a main reason were its lack of trine immersion. Indeed more or less, from the days of Michael Cerularius, in the eleventh century, until 1756, the whole "Orthodox" Church, Greek and Russian, had, at times, admitted Western baptisms performed by the compends and without necessity as valid. At Florence, A.D. 1439, Gregory, the Greek monk, rejoins to Mark of Ephesus, that he (Mark) had never seen Latins baptized by Greeks.

These facts (and the above remark, so far as it applies),

---

* v. Assem. and Goar's Euchologium, notes on this rubric.

shows that, like other parts of the Church, they have not always acted regularly and rubrically.

Since the period when this was written, the rule in favor of trine immersion has been more insisted on in the Patriarchates. In Russia, however, which includes the great bulk of this communion, the baptism of Latins, Lutherans, and Calvinists is admitted.

The conclusion which we have drawn regarding the necessity of admitting the compends in the West, will be found not to be without its application, though not so fully, to the East. There have been irregularities everywhere. With the best discipline there will ever be some. For there will always be much of ignorance, or prejudice, or carelessness in the world. But this does not affect our duty. (On the Eastern views, v. Palmer's Diss. on Orth. Comm.)*

But it must be admitted that the custom of resorting to the compends, except in case of absolute necessity, is wholly irregular and without warrant in the primitive ages. Nevertheless it is only one of many irregularities which prevail to a greater or less extent over the whole Church, and from which not even the purest parts are entirely free. For the reasons stated above it must be regarded as irregular, but yet as valid. "Quod fieri non debet, factum, valet." This maxim has, perhaps, as wide and as frequent application in theology as in law. It *must* be used; for if irregularity be invalidity there is no Church of God on earth, since every part has been more or less irregular. But the Church cannot fail, since Christ has promised that the gates of hell shall not prevail against it. If one part of it has gone astray like Israel, and another like Judah, like Judah and Israel they may reform if they will, and still be God's, with the right to claim his inalienable and sure promise of perpetuity.

In using the compends where no real and unavoidable necessity exists, the American Churchman is *irregular*,—the early Church, the mother Church, and Bishop White being witness. The English Churchman is irregular, both according to the early Church and his present rubric. But it should be remembered that *irregularity* is not necessarily *invalidity*.

The *rule* is that none but a clergyman may baptize. The *custom* in *all* parts of the Church has been from early times to permit this office in necessity to laymen, concerning whose

---

* v. also Blackmore's Doctrine of the Russian Church, p. 209.

commission to minister sacraments we read nothing in Holy Writ. If such baptism be absolutely invalid (as it undoubtedly is irregular, and should be conditionally repeated) much doubt will be thrown upon the orders of some Churches.

The rule in the Church has been that a bishop should "be ordained by two or three bishops."* Yet how many have there been who have been ordained by but one?

Again, the greater part of the Greek and Latin communions have fallen into idolatry,—into the soul-destroying heresy of giving relative worship and honor to painted or sculptured representations of holy things or persons. Besides, they have given *religious* worship, dulia or hyperdulia, to created beings, as the Virgin Theotocos, to saints, and to angels, thereby violating the Divine will, and doing what is essentially the same that intelligent and candid heathen have done; for they would reject with scorn the notion that they give absolute worship to any painted or sculptured representation, or to any of their subordinate deities. In other words, the great bulk of the Church, like the ancient Jewish Church, has added fearful and destructive heresy to the faith. But the Church has ever treated the orders of heretics as invalid, until in some form they had received her imprimatur. Were we to act on that principle we should have to deny the existence of Christ's Church altogether. Indeed, by believing our own orders valid, we assert that the errors in doctrine of the greater part of the Church, and the irregularities in discipline of the West in disregarding, to a very marked extent, the regulations of œcumenical councils, do not constitute invalidity.

Errors are everywhere. No part of the Church is exactly on the primitive foundation. Every part has its own peculiar excellencies and its faults.

The Greek part of the Eastern Church, the main trunk of the whole; the Church whose glory, even at this day, it is to possess all the sees of the Apostles, except Rome; the Church which, in connection with its Sclavonic branches, still observes best the canons and the rites; the Church in whose tongue the New Testament was first given to man; whose is the language of the six œcumenical councils and the Nicene Creed, "the only

---

* Apos. Can. 1. v. Nice, Can. 4; Antioch, Can. 19, 23.

symbol" of the Universal Church;* this Church, with all these grand memories and advantages in its own worship, is, *in practice,* the most thoroughly creature-worshipping part of Christendom; and Rome, which has the Western see of Peter (Antioch is an Eastern),† to which a primacy of honor was once accorded by the Universal Church, has attempted to subvert the œcumenical canons, and seems wholly prone to mingle creature-worship in the universal faith, and has departed from the rites of the Universal Church, and has interpolated and altered the creed simply from its own private fancies and whims; and the Anglican Church, whose sole glory among the Churches claiming an episcopate it is to be perfectly free from the stain of creature-worship, still retains an interpolated and altered creed in the teeth of Canon VII of Ephesus, which, under severe penalties, forbids it, and in laying aside rites and customs belonging to the pure ages of the Church, and in subverting the œcumenical canons, and (so far as the American branch is concerned), in degrading the episcopate, it goes (in some things) even beyond the Roman, and needs RESTORATION, as the Greeks and Latins need RESTORATION AND REFORMATION.

We have mentioned only a few of the irregularities which have been committed. The Church is often in extraordinary positions; or a canon of the Church, or a usage which has primitive and universal consent, is neglected or violated from ignorance or error. In all parts of the Christian world this has been the case. In respect to such irregularities we should pass them by. "Let the dead past bury its dead." The Israelitish Church, after its final reformation, concerned itself no further regarding bygone irregularities and errors than to keep from plunging into them again. We do wisely and well if we do the same. The irregularities which have taken place are numerous. Let any man take a copy of the canons of the early and of the whole Church and study them carefully, and compare their requisitions with the present state of Christendom, and he will not doubt this. We are to do our duty in obeying the rubric. We are not responsible for others. 3. Any

---

* Cyril of Alexandria speaks of it as μόνῳ τῷ Συμβόλῳ τῆς πίστεως, κ. τ. λ. See Mansi, Conc. t. v, col. 348.

† See Hardouin, Conc. t. ii, col. 492, D. This reference is to Chalcedon, act. VII.

theory which would contravene and prove false the promise of Christ to His Church of perpetuity must be rejected. But the notion that irregularity constitutes invalidity would do this, therefore it must be rejected. The rich and precious promises of God to the Jewish Church insured its perpetuity. So similar promises to the Christian insure its continued existence until time ends. The grievous apostasies of the Jews prevent our thinking that infallibility is a sequence from such promises. And the history of Christendom corroborates our disbelief in such error. But the one existed until its mission was accomplished, or it will exist until that time; and the last has the promise that the gates of hell shall never prevail against it. Although for a time it may be weakened by error and rent by schisms, yet reformation and unity shall not be absent forever. St. Jerome testified of a former triumph of error: "The whole world groaned and wondered that it had become Arian."* Yet the right finally triumphed, as it will triumph over creature worship and all error, in God's good time. Till then we are to do our duty and leave results with Him. We need not resort to the impious idea that God's word has failed, or that, because a part of the Church has once erred, it must necessarily remain in error without the right to reform. When a man washes dirt from his face, which had collected there through neglect, he does not remove his face; that remains clearer and purer. So with the different reformed communions. The removal of the incrustations of error was a duty, and therefore Christian doctrine is now more clearly seen and more effective in its results, although they sometimes confounded what is primitive with what is Latin. The Jews when in error were yet in the outer pale of the covenant, but this did not preserve them from the doom of transgressors. So although the unreformed parts of the Church are still possessed of the outward semblance of a Church, this will not be enough to save them if they are guilty of idolatry. No idolater inherits the kingdom of God. The impenitent thief who railed at Christ went from the side of Infinite mercy to perdition. So from the blessings of the covenant many a man has gone to receive the just rewards of his misdeeds. We must not, then, confound a part of the Church with the whole; nor think that the mere existence of orders and sacra-

---

* Hieron. Adv. Lucif. iv, 300. v. note 3 in Edgar's Var., chap. ix, p. 307, for similar witness.

ments is all that is required. Nor, on the other hand, may we form the idea that where these exist there is no Church. The Church may err, it has erred, but it cannot fail. Let it be remembered, too, that the question, whether the Latin Church *or* the Greek Church has erred in a certain point, is not the same as whether the whole Church has erred. Yet a part may err, or even the whole. But if the individual is invited to return to the bosom of his heavenly Father, and if over such a one the angels rejoice, how much more when the one is multiplied to millions, and the voice of a nation, as at the Reformation, calls for light, for pardon, and for the "old paths." If the Church has perished, as the Baptists in effect teach, who may found a new one but God Himself? Can man do this? Where would be his authority? And who would believe such an extraordinary claim without extraordinary signs and miracles, by which God has set His seal to the Mosaic and Christian dispensations?

If the Church and the ministry has failed, if it is no longer in existence, no man can claim to be its minister. He who professes to found the Church anew, inasmuch as he gives the lie to the promise of God in asserting that the gates of hell *have* prevailed against his Church, is guilty of little less than blasphemy. When the Baptists assert the extraordinary claim of possessing that mission which was given to the Church by God Himself, let them make good their claim in the way in which God has always supported His truth and His new revelations. For, by claiming that all baptized in infancy are unbaptized, they really assert that from the Apostles' days the whole Church had utterly perished. They admit that baptism is the door to the Church. They assert that infants baptized before they reach the period of knowledge and faith, are not baptized. And since the rule in Christendom has always been to baptize infants of this character, and since by such infants the orders and the sacraments have been handed down, and since all such Christians were really never in the pale of the visible Church, because never baptized, their acts were in no sense the acts of the Church, but only those of an unbaptized society. The whole Christian world, with its bishops and doctors, the holy Church throughout all the world died outside of the pale of the covenant, and consequently without any claim to *covenant* mercy. And let it be remembered, too, that the first Anabaptists received their baptism from men who had been baptized in infancy, and who could claim no other baptism except it be what they afterwards took up and gave each other. Consequently, the first Anabaptists were on modern Baptist principles themselves unbaptized.

What intelligent man will trace up a succession to the Apostles' age through men, every one of whom was baptized *by immersion* on a profession *of his own faith after coming to adult years, or to such a time of life as he had knowledge, repentance, and faith,* who held to and practised Congregational Church polity, who were Calvinists, who were firmly opposed to a liturgy, and who rejected all aids to the interpretation of the Scriptures from the early Christians' writings and practices. And this the Baptist must find, or he must found a new Church and make Christ's promise a falsity.

We have traced the history of immersion in both modes, and have, besides, touched upon the early testimony in favor of the validity of sprinkling and pouring when used in necessity. The words of Cyprian in his Epistle to Magnus (Ep. 69), refer to both these last-mentioned modes. But the references to baptism of the sick are quite frequent after his time. Such baptism the Church viewed as valid without, so far as I have been able to discover, a single dissentient voice until the seventeenth century. Canon 47 of Laodicea was received and acted upon by the whole Church, as was also the teaching of Cyprian. Clinic baptism is a thing of not unfrequent occurrence now. And so it has been in all ages. A large part of the race die in infancy; and in earlier days many from different motives deferred baptism until death, at which time the Church departed from her usual strictness, and admitted to its blessings even the catechumen who had not fulfilled the period of his instruction and probation. The care regarding the administration of this rite to the sick and dying was a necessary result of the conditions of Holy Writ, that he that believeth *and is baptized* shall be saved. Belief and baptism were with them the indispensable conditions of *covenant* mercy. Many of the baptisms of the sick it is not unlikely were performed by immersion. But instances naturally arose then as now, when the sick man could not receive it. In such a case, pouring or sprinkling was used. Thus it was with St. Lawrence, Novatian, and the Clinics of the third century, whom St. Cyprian mentions. St. Ambrose, on 1 Tim. chap. 3, clearly implies, that to baptize the sick was "an almost daily necessity." ("Etsi non desint, qui prope quotidie baptizentur ægri.") Walafrid Strabo shows that pouring was the usual custom, not only in necessity, properly so called, but even in what is of so mild a type as hardly to deserve that name, viz., in case the font were not large enough for the candidate. The Canon of Laodicea had and still has, in connection with the doctrine of Cyprian, the consent of the Greek Church. It admits sprinkling or pouring *in cases of necessity* in all its parts. In the West, for centuries, these have been the usual modes. We have, then, in favor of clinic baptism the authority of a canon of ecumenical use, whatever may be thought of the authority of that council itself, and the after-claim of its canons to recognition as ecumenical, based upon the first Canon of Chalcedon. (See Hammond, note on Can. 1, Chalc.) Practice, in this case, necessitates the theory. The line of succession is traced in a great part of the Church through this and similar channels. But while all this is true, candor and a due sense of the importance of truth demands the statement of primitive views regarding trine immersion already given; and that the use of any other was based on *necessity* alone.

During the first twelve hundred years no one ever sanctions their use in any other case, unless we except from this category the last case, mentioned by Walafrid Strabo, and by him alone, and that at a comparatively late period. It is best not to put them on any other ground than necessity, if a man would be borne out by the uniform and general custom and opinion of the whole Church. The opinions of those who base the compendious modes on the meaning of $\beta\alpha\pi\tau\iota\zeta\omega$, on the fact that this word is sometimes, like many others, used figuratively, and on the difficulty of obtaining a sufficiency of water for immersion, on the translating of Greek prepositions where the rite is described, and on the supposed proof, drawn from Mark 7 : 2–4 compared with Luke 11 : 38, and Mark 7 : 4–8, that $\beta\alpha\pi\tau\iota\zeta\omega$ means to pour, and that $\beta\alpha\pi\tau\iota\sigma\mu\acute{o}\varsigma$ means, if not pouring, at least washing, are never found, so far, as after the most diligent search the author can judge, during the first 1200 years. Some of them, not until long after even this period. Many of these assumed difficulties run directly counter to the belief and witness of the Church during all this long period. This principle of necessity was applied not only to the mode but even to the minister. For although laymen are nowhere in Holy Writ authorized to baptize, nevertheless their baptism has generally, perhaps almost universally, been deemed valid until a recent period. Those who defend the use of the compends on any other grounds than the whole Church has set forth, ought to take the responsibility upon their own shoulders, ever remembering that Christ has said, "Whosoever, therefore, shall break one of these least commandments, and shall teach men so, he shall be called the least in the kingdom of heaven: but whosoever shall do and teach them, the same shall be called great in the kingdom of heaven." Matt. 5 : 19.* And whether this sacrament do not deserve to be ranked at least as high as "one of these least commandments," let all judge. The argument from necessity is conclusive. This must be admitted unless we would put in doubt all orders, East and West. When one goes beyond this, or at least the private interpretation of Cyprian among the ancients, he should speak cautiously. When he asserts that $\beta\alpha\pi\tau\iota\zeta\omega$ is not expressive of mode, he opposes the quod semper, quod ubique, quod ab omnibus, of primitive testimony, which has interpreted the command of immersion without mention of any other mode. But both the compends and lay baptism were deemed valid, and if, at any period, this last was repeated, yet it was usually when it was doubtful whether some irregularity had not been committed, as a failure to repeat the names of the persons of the Trinity, &c., sufficient to invalidate the administration, or at least to render the person very doubtful and anxious, when, according to the merciful maxim of St. Cyprian (Ep. ad Magnum), the person was to be relieved from his fears by a surer administration. This provision is frequently found in the rubrics regarding lay baptism.

* On the use of the compends in the Ancient Church and its *conditions*, see Bingham, bk. xi, chap. xi, 5, 8, and the index of Wall, under "Sprinkling," "Pouring," "Affusion," "Perfusion."

CHAPTER X.

OF THE MODE IN THE CHURCH OF ENGLAND.

We come now to the Mother Church. We are to scan the history of the mode in the light of—
1. The testimony of historians.
2. The command of her rubrics.
3. And the decisions of her laws.

We shall study these to best advantage by taking them together and in the order of time. Of the ancient British Church little or nothing is left us on this topic. But as all the world, until the period of Augustine's arrival in England, held to the trine immersion as of Divine or Apostolic origin, we may well believe that such was the custom in England. There is not the slightest circumstance to break the chain of probabilities, which becomes, in a case of this kind, a necessary conclusion.

At the period when Augustine landed there seem to have been some slight discrepancies between the ordinary use of Britain and the rest of the Church. For one of his demands was that "the British bishops should administer baptism, by which we are again born to God, according to the custom of the Holy Roman Apostolic Church." As no monuments remain to us as to the precise nature of the differences comprehended in this term "custom," it would of course be idle to speculate or to affirm regarding them.

There is no proof to show that it refers to any difference of mode. It might refer to the times of baptism, or to any one of the many particulars anciently connected with the rite. The presence of British bishops at councils prior to this date, and their signatures to their decrees, plainly show that they were on terms of communion with their brethren, and that their orthodoxy was unquestioned. We have already seen that it was the uncontradicted opinion of the Church, at the period when the Synod of Arles was held, that the mode of baptism, although not necessary in every case, was yet of Divine or Apostolic origin, and that it was trine immersion. If the British bishops had innovated on this and practised any other, it would seem not unlikely to have been remarked, and we should not hear the historians of the Church charging Eunomius, and his followers who flourished after him, with being the corrupters of the "Divine baptism." Indeed *there is not the slightest evidence* of the existence at this period, or at any subsequent time prior to Augustine, of any other than the usual mode. (Against Baptist mistakes, v. Wall, vol. ii, p. 126, and Hodges, p. 402.)

With regard to Augustine's practice we are happily at no loss. He was abbot of St. Andrew's at Rome. And what the Roman custom was, Gregory the Great himself, who sent Augustine on his mission, tells us. In his epistle to Leander he expressly affirms it to have been trine immersion. And as his advice to Leander regarding the dispensing with trine immersion, and the substitution of the single for it, was intended to apply only to Spain, and to Spain only under certain circumstances, which circumstances did not exist in England, there is no ground for supposing that Augustine would change the Roman custom. In the absence of the slightest evidence on the other side we are justified in drawing this conclusion. His demands, and his using the language "according to the custom of the holy Roman Apostolic Church," show his feeling in favor of his own city, whatever be the reference.

Venerable Bede (Eccl. Hist., bk. ii, chap. xiv) relates, concerning the conversion of the Saxons, that "so great was then the fervor of the faith, and the desire of the washing of salvation (desiderium lavacri salutaris), among the nation of the Northumbrians, that Paulinus, coming with the King and Queen to Adgebrin (Yeverin), the royal country seat, stayed there with them thirty-six days, fully occupied in catechizing and baptizing; during which days, from morning till night, he did nothing else but instruct the people resorting from all villages and places, in Christ's saving word; and when instructed, he washed them with the water of absolution in the river Glen, which is close by. . . . . In the province of the Deira also, where he was wont often to be with the King, he baptized in the river Swale (in fluvio Swalua), which runs by the village Catterick; for as yet oratories or fonts could not be made in the early infancy of the Church in those parts."

This was about twenty-two years after Augustine's death.

From this time onward, as all authorities agree, the ordinary custom of trine immersion prevailed in England, as in the rest of the Church. Out of many testimonies which might be gathered, we shall glean such as are most authoritative, and serve to express the general use.

The Penitential of Archbishop Theodore enjoins the early mode, in the words of Canon 50 of the Apostles, as follows:

"If any bishop or presbyter does not perform the one initiation with three immersions, but with giving one immersion only, into the death of the Lord, let him be deposed. For the Lord said not, Baptize into my death, but 'Go, make disciples of all nations, baptizing them in the name of the Father, and of the Son, and of the Holy Ghost.'"*

Venerable Bede uses language in which incidental allusion is made to the mode.

"The person to be baptized is seen to descend into the font; he is seen when he is dipped in the waters; he is seen to ascend from the waters; but what effect the washing of regeneration works in him can be least seen. This, the piety of the faithful alone knows, that the candidate descends into the font a sinner, but ascends purified from guilt. He descends a son of death, but ascends a son of the resurrection; he descends a son of apostasy, he ascends a son of reconciliation; he descends a son of wrath, he ascends a son of mercy; he descends a son of the Devil, he ascends a son of God."†

Alcuin, whose strong testimony has been already cited, was an Englishman, and was educated in the Episcopal School of York; and we have found him, in the eighth century, contending for the trine immersion as of Divine origin, and stigmatizing the single, even when the proper words were used, as one of the contrivances of the Devil.

---

* v. Maskells Mon. Rit. Eccl. Anglic., vol. i, p. 203. v. Lib. Poenit. xlviii, 20, and Thorpe, vol. ii, p. 58.

† Beda, Hom. in Dom. i, post. Epiph.: "Nam videtur quidem baptizandus in fontem descendere, videtur aquis intingi, videtur de aquis ascendere; quod autem in illo lavacrum regenerationis egerit, minime potest videri. Sola hoc fidelium novit pietas, quia peccator in fontem descendit. Sed purificatus ascendit; filius mortis descendit, sed filius resurrectionis ascendit; filius prævaricationis descendit, sed filius reconciliationis ascendit; filius iræ descendit, sed filius misericordiæ ascendit; filius diaboli descendit, sed filius Dei ascendit."

In A.D. 816, shortly after Alcuin's death, a synod assembled at Cealichyth. Wulfred, the Archbishop of Canterbury, presided. Canon 11 determines as follows:

"And let the presbyters know that, when they administer holy baptism, they may not pour water upon the heads of the infants, but the infants must always be immersed in the laver, for the Son of God furnished an example in His own person for every believer when He was thrice dipped in the waves of the Jordan.

"Therefore it is necessary that baptism be retained and observed according to the rule."*

Missal Leofric.

"Let the presbyter receive them (*i.e.* the children), and let him baptize them; first the males, then the females, by trine immersion; once only invoking the Holy Trinity, and saying thus," &c.†

Use of Salisbury.
(Compiled by Osmund, about A. D. 1067–1099.)

"Then let the priest take the child by its sides in his hands, and having asked its name, let him dip it thrice, invoking the Holy Trinity thus: 'N., I baptize thee in the name of the Father,' and let him dip it once with its face towards the north and its head towards the east; 'and of the Son,' and let him dip it a second time with its face towards the south; 'and of the Holy Ghost: Amen,' and let him dip it the third time with its face towards the water." (v. Fallow's Order of Bapt. pp. 19–122.)‡ Yet this use allows lay baptism by pour-

---

* Synodus apud Cealichyth, Anno Domini 816. Præsidente Wulfredo, Archiepiscopo Cantuar. Kenulph was at the time King of the Mercii (Mercians). Canon 11: "Sciant etiam presbyteri quando sacrum baptismum ministrant, ut non effundant aquam sanctam super capita infantium, sed semper mergantur in lavacro, sicut exemplum præbuit per semetipsum Dei Filius omni credenti, quando esset ter mersus in undis Jordanis. Ita necesse est secundum ordinem servari et haberi."

† Mon. Rit. Eccl. Anglic., p. 23: "Et accipiet presbyter eos a parentibus eorum, et baptizantur primi masculi deinde feminæ, sub trina mersione, Sanctam Trinitatem semel invocando, ita dicendo." Missal. Leofric.

‡ v. Fallow's "Order of Baptism," p. 19. Use of Salisbury: "Deinde accipiat sacerdos infantem per latera in manibus suis, et interrogato

ing, or single immersion, *but only in case of necessity.* (v. Fallow, Ord. of Bapt. pp. 21, 135, 137.)

The importance and authority of this rubric may be judged from Palmer's statement.

"The Church of Rome, strange to relate, had no uniform ritual until after the era of the English Reformation. . . . Hence it was that different rituals were at that time in use in different dioceses of this kingdom. 'Some followed Salisbury use, some Hereford use, some the use of Bangor, some of York, some of Lincoln.' v. 'Concerning the Service of the Church,' prefixed to the Book of Common Prayer. The most celebrated of these, 'the Use of Salisbury,' was generally followed throughout England, Wales, and Ireland. It is ascribed to Osmund, bishop of Sarum, who died in the year 1099. The baptismal office copies very closely the Sacramentary of Gregory the Great." v. Palmer, Orig. Lit. vol. i, p. 187.

From the evidence which has preceded, it is evident that so far as the trine immersion in baptism is concerned, Osmund did no more than set forth the old mode in the new "Use."

This rubric will serve to bind all the individual testimonies, in times posterior to its compilation, until the Reformation, in one irrefragable chain.

Indeed, the baptismal rubric in the first book of Edward VI, is almost a verbal translation from this.

The Council of Cashel.
(Held in Ireland, A. D. 1172.)

This synod is worthy of note as representing the voice of all the archbishops and bishops in Ireland. It was attended also, by direction of Henry II of England, by two of his own clergy. The design of the synod was to procure conformity, ecclesiastical as well as secular, between England and Ireland.

It decreed, Can. 1, "That children shall be brought to the church, and shall there be baptized in pure water by trine immersion, in the name of the Father, and of the Son, and of

---

nomine ejus, baptizet eum trina immersione, sanctam Trinitatem invocando, ita dicens.

"N., et ego baptizo te in nomine Patris (*et mergat eum semel versa facie ad aquilonem, et capite versus orientem*), et Filii (*iterum mergat semel versa facie ad meridiem*), et Spiritus Sancti. Amen. (*Et mergat tertio recta facie versus aquam.*)"

the Holy Ghost. And let this be done by the priests, unless in imminent danger of death it behoove that it be administered by another person and in any other place, and then let it be performed by any one, without distinction of sex or rank."*

The Council of London.

("Held A. D. 1200, by Hubert, Archbishop of Canterbury, for the Reformation of the Church of England.")

The third decree of Hubert, after giving directions regarding baptism and confirmation, and forbidding a deacon to baptize, except in extraordinary cases, adds:

"But if, in necessity, a child be baptized by a layman, which can be done by the father or mother, and without prejudice to the bond of matrimony, let the parts of the baptismal office which follow, but not those which precede the *immersion*, be filled up by the priest."†

This language evidently implies immersion as the ordinary mode.

Synod of Worcester.

(A. D. 1240.)

"We enjoin that, in every church where baptism is performed, there shall be a font of stone, of sufficient size and

---

* "Concilium Cassiliense. In Hibernia habitum, A. D. 1172."
Hardouin, Conc. tom. vi, parte ii, sub finem, p. 1628, after giving the names of the Irish archbishops and bishops, and the Irish kings, and after stating that the Irish clergy, archiepiscopi, episcopi et abbates titius Hiberniæ, received Henry, King of England. "in regem et dominum Hiberniæ, jurantes ei et hæredibus suis fidelitatem," &c., and that "exemplo autem clericorum reges prædicti" did the same. He states: "Rex Angliæ misit Nicolaum capellanum, Radulphum archidiaconum de Landaff, clericos suos, una cum archiepiscopis et episcopis Hiberniæ ad Cassiliensem civitatem ad celebrandum concilium de statutis ecclesiæ. In concilio autem illo statutum est."

"Ut pueri deferuntur ad ecclesiam, et ibi baptizarentur in aqua munda, sub trina mersione, in nomine Patris, Filii, et Spiritus Sancti. Et hoc a sacerdotibus fiat, nisi metu mortis impediente, ab alio et alias oportuerit fieri: et tunc a quolibet fiat, sine exceptione sexus et ordinis."

† Concilium Londoniense. (v. Hardouin Conc. t. vi, parte ii, subfinem, p. 1958.) Apud Westmonasterium . . . pro reformatione Ecclesiæ Anglicanæ per Hubertum Cantuariensem Archiepiscopum celebratum, A. D. 1200, tempore Innocentii Papæ III.

"Si vero in necessitate puer baptizetur a laico, quod fieri potest a patre vel a matre absque matrimonii præjudicio, sequentia immersionem, non præcedentia, per sacerdotem expleantur."

depth for the baptizing of children, and that it shall be decently covered. . . . And let the candidate for baptism ALWAYS be thrice immersed."

This is the rule, and this council further decrees that " Children baptized in case of *necessity*, if they recover, must be brought to the church, that those things which are wanting may be supplied; namely, those things which follow the immersion in baptism."*

SYNOD OF EXETER.

(A. D. 1287.)

This council decreed as follows:

" We strictly enjoin it upon the priests to whom pertains the care of souls, that they shall instruct their parishioners more frequently in the vulgar tongue concerning the *form* of baptism. And this they shall do as follows: They shall teach them that they shall have water ready whenever a child is born, in which, if it be necessary, the parishioners may immerse the child, saying : ' I baptize thee in the name of the Father, and of the Son, and of the Holy Ghost.' . . . When, therefore, it shall happen, on account of danger of death, that a child has been baptized at home, if it shall recover, let it be brought to church, so that if it be not rightly baptized, the parts of the rite which follow *the immersion*, but not those which precede it, nor *the immersion* itself, may, as is fitting, be supplied by the priest. But let the vessel in which a child has been baptized at home be burned, or reserved for church use; and let the water in which the child has been *immersed*, be poured out in the baptistery, or at least let it be cast into the fire for the sake of the reverence due the sacrament."†

This immersion, let it be remembered, was even in a case of

---

* Synodus Wigorniensis, A. D. 1240, Hardouin, Conc. t. vii, p. 332.
" Præcipimus, quod in qualibet ecclesia baptismali, sit fons lapideus, decentis amplitudinis et profunditatis; decenter etiam coopertus, in quo parvuli baptizentur." . . . " Et trina semper fiat emersio baptizandi." . . . " Pueri autem *in necessitate* baptizati, si forte convaluerint, ad ecclesiam deferantur; ut quæ defuerant, suppleantur: ea scilicet quæ baptismalem immersionem consequi dignoscuntur."

† Synodus Exoniensis, A. D. 1287. v. Hardouin, Conc. t. vii, p. 1075.
" Sacerdotibus, quibus cura animarum incumbit, districte præcipimus, quod formam baptizandi parochianis suis exponant sæpius in vulgari : videlicet, quod tempore partus aquam habeant promptam; in quam, si oportuerit baptizandum immergant, dicentes: Ego baptizo te in nomine

necessity. Could a stronger testimony be given to the value of the *mode?* Even in "danger of death," the council enjoins not a compend, but the full administration.

Incidental allusions still remain in the monuments of this period to immersion as the usual custom.*

Lyndwood in his "Provinciale," in commenting upon an order of Edmund, who became Archbishop of Canterbury in 1234, bears witness to the mode prevalent at that time, and in his own day, in the first half of the fifteenth century.

"Lyndwood," says Fallow, "remarks upon the order that the font must be of stone, or of any other proper material, ('lapideum vel aliud competens.') '*Competens* sic quod baptizandus possit in eo mergi.' From this last gloss it seems evident that even though a child, through necessity, was baptized at home, yet the vessel was to be of sufficient size to immerse the infant: as Lyndwood expressly says in the gloss which immediately precedes, '*Vas illud* sc. in quo puer baptizatus est. Et hæc litera, ut videtur, innuit, quod baptismus debet fieri in aliquo vase, sic quod in aqua mergi possit baptizandus. Et talis immersio debet esse trina, nisi consuetudo habeat ut sit unica tantum.'"†

Patris, et Filii, et Spiritus Sancti. . . . Cum igitur contigerit parvulum domi propter mortis periculum baptizari, si postea convaluerit, ad ecclesiam deferatur, ut si rite fuerit baptizatus, non ipsa submersio, nec ipsa præcedentia, sed subsequentia dumtaxat per sacerdotem, ut convenit, suppleantur. Vas vero in quo puer domi fuerit baptizatus, comburatur, vel ad usus ecclesiæ reservetur : ac aqua, in qua puer immersus fuerit, in baptisterium effundatur, vel saltem projiciatur in ignem ob reverentiam sacramenti." . . . "In levatione pueri de fonte sacro . . . præcipimus, ut in levatione maris, duo mares et una femina; in feminæ vero levatione, unus mas et duæ feminæ adhibeantur.

* Spelman's Concilia, p. 142, Constitutiones Ricardi Poore Sarum Episcopi. De Baptisterio.

"Baptisterium habeatur in qualibet ecclesiâ baptismali, lapideum vel aliquod competens, quod decenter cooperiatur, et reverentur conservetur, et in alios usus non convertatar: aqua vero in quâ puer fuerit baptizatus ultra septem dies in baptisterio non servetur."

This same constitution is repeated word for word in the "Constitutiones Richardi Episcopi Dunelmensis." Durham, A. D. 1220. v. in Spelman's Concilia, p. 167.

The Synodal Constitutions of Winchester. (Synodus Wintoniensis, A. D. 1308.) This body allowed a laic to baptize at home in case of "inevitable necessity," and adds, "Puer autem domi, forma qua præmissimus, baptizatus, si forte convaleat, ad ecclesiam deferatur, ut per sacerdotem omissis immersione, et præcedentibus, ipsam immersionem sequentia suppleantur." v. in Spelman's Concilia, p. 445.

† v. Lyndwood's Provinciale, lib. iii, tit. 24, 25.

Lyndwood discusses the question "whether immersion should be trine or single, and whether aspersion will suffice." He concludes, that "it is safer to baptize by immersion of the whole body;" but he says in another place that "single immersion may be used, as I have said in the beginning, but the habit of trine immersion is the more commendable, because it symbolizes the belief in the Trinity, and the three days' burial of Christ."

The importance of this testimony will be seen the more clearly if we remember that Lyndwood was a doctor, a chancellor of the Archbishopric of Canterbury, and Bishop of St. David's, and that his work comprehends the provincial constitutions of Archbishops of Canterbury from Stephen Langton, A. D. 1207, to Henry Chicheley, A. D. 1414, inclusive, and that he wrote at the request of this last prelate. (v. Robinson's Hist. p. 132, Am. ed.) No change, it will be perceived, was made in the *laws* of the Church, or the rubrics which enjoined trine immersion as the rule, though it is evident that individuals had, at this time, adopted the opinion of Gregory the Great, that the single, though not preferable, was yet allowable.

From this time until the Reformation, an instance or two will suffice.

In A. D. 1486, Prince Arthur, son of Henry VII, was baptized by immersion, as was also the Princess Margaret, afterwards Queen of Scotland, three years afterwards. They were both "put into the font." King Edward VI and Queen Elizabeth were both baptized by trine immersion. (v. References in Robinson's Hist., chap. xviii, "On Baptismal Fonts.")

The "Use of Salisbury" was in general use at the Reformation.

The authoritative documents of the Reformed Church of England all favor immersion.

Book of Edward VI.

"Then shall the priest take the child in his hands, and ask the name; and naming the child, *shall dip* it in the water THRICE; first dipping the right side, secondly the left side, the third time dipping the face toward the font; so it be discreetly and warily done, saying, 'N, I baptize thee,'" &c.

"And if the child be weak, it shall *suffice* to pour water upon it, saying the aforesaid words, 'I baptize thee,'" &c.

This is a translation of the ancient Salisbury Use, which, in respect to trine immersion, agrees with all the oldest rubrics, and with Cyril of Jerusalem and Tertullian.

The whole office should have been retained, for the ceremonies which it commanded are Catholic, not Latin. But we must not wonder if all the early customs of this office are not now binding. They had been abused in the Western Church, and perhaps in the Eastern also, to purposes of superstition, and it was deemed advisable to remove them. It should also be remembered that the Reformers had all been educated in the private opinions of the West, and that they sometimes confounded these with what was Catholic. Witness their course regarding the retention of the "filioque" in the creed of Nicæa without the assent of a council of the whole Church. Of course, we do not now speak of the truth of that doctrine, but only of the principle involved in the interpolations and changes in that creed—the principle that a part of the Church should or could speak for the whole: a thing manifestly wrong, and which produced the division into East and West. (v. Pearson on the Creed, p. 486, n ed. N. Y., 1853.) So the mere opinion of Gregory I, though never meant to apply to ordinary cases, was nevertheless so understood, so that in the second book of Edward VI the trine immersion was for the first time in the history of the English Church no longer specified as the normal mode in the rubrics.

BOOK OF EDWARD VI, 1552.

"Then the priest shall take the child in his hands, and ask the name; and, naming the child, *shall dip* it in the water, so it be discreetly and warily done, saying, 'N., I baptize thee in the name of the Father, and of the Son, and of the Holy Ghost. Amen.'"

"And if the child be weak it shall *suffice* to pour water upon it, saying the aforesaid words, 'I baptize thee,'" &c.

"The *Latin* books of Elizabeth read, both here and in private baptism, 'immerget infantem,' except an office in the Bodleian, 1560, which has tinget." v. Bulley's Off. of Ch. of England.

The Scotch Liturgy of 1637 is exactly like the second book

of Edward VI as to the mode of baptism. While these last offices cannot be said absolutely to forbid dipping three times, yet they fail to specify, and so leave it indefinite. Becon, Cranmer's chaplain, speaks of the trine immersion as a custom of the ancient Church, both Greek and Latin, and refers in proof to "Tertullian, Damasus, Cyril, Austin, Ambrose, Basil, and Theophylact." Nevertheless it is clear that those who changed the rubric were willing to leave the number of immersions to the administrator.

How much importance the people attached to the mode at the beginning of the Reformation will be seen from the language of Tyndale (Doctrinal Treatises, p. 277).

"Behold how narrowly the people look on the ceremony. If aught be left out, or if the child be not altogether dipped in the water, or if, because the child is sick, the priest dare not plunge him into the water, but pour water on his head, how tremble they! how quake they! 'How say ye, Sir John' (the priests were styled sir), say they, 'is this child christened enough? Hath it his full christendom?' They believe verily that the child is not christened."

In Cranmer's Catechism, A.D. 1548, this question is asked: "What greater shame can there be than a man to professe himselfe a Christen man because he is baptized, and yet he knoweth not what baptisme is, nor what strength the same hath, nor what the dyppynge in water doth betoken?"*

Dipping, as the rule for every healthy infant, is still the rule of the Church. It has never been omitted from the rubric, but notwithstanding this even as the *rule* it has been generally laid aside.

It is worthy of note, as serving to show the strong preference of the English Church for immersion, that in the office for the private baptism of infants, which is to be used only in "great cause and necessity," pouring is commanded. But when the child is afterwards brought into the church, that is on his recovery, and it is uncertain whether he has been baptized or not, and conditional baptism is used, dipping alone is mentioned. The American rubric contains the same idea.

The learned Wall remarks: "One would have thought that the cold countries should have been the first that should have changed the custom from dipping to affusion. . . . . But by history, it appears that the cold climates held the custom of

---

* v. pp. 48, 49, above.

dipping as long as any; for England, which is one of the coldest, was one of the latest that admitted this alteration of the ordinary way. Erasmus says: 'Perfunduntur apud nos, merguntur apud Anglos,' with us (the Dutch) they have the water poured on them; in England they are dipped."

"The offices or liturgies for public baptism in the Church of England did all along, so far as I can learn, enjoin dipping without any mention of pouring or sprinkling."

"In Queen Mary's time the custom of dipping seems to have continued." In 1558, "Watson, the Popish Bishop of Lincoln, asserts, 'though the old and ancient tradition of the Church hath been from the beginning to dip the child three times, &c., yet that is not of such necessity, but that if he be but once dipped in the water it is sufficient. Yea, and in time of great peril and necessity, if the water be but poured upon his head, it will suffice.' A sign that pouring was not in Queen Mary's time used but in case of necessity."

"But there are apparent reasons why that custom should alter during Queen Elizabeth's reign. The latitude given in the Liturgy, which could have had but little effect in the short time of King Edward's reign, might, during the long reign of this Queen, produce an alteration proportionably greater. It being allowed to weak children (though strong enough to be brought to church) to be baptized by affusion, many fond ladies and gentlewomen first, and then by degrees the common people, would obtain the favor of the priest to have their children pass for weak children, too tender to endure dipping in the water," especially (as Mr. Walker observes) "if some instance really were, or were but fancied and framed, of some child's taking cold, or being otherwise prejudiced by its being dipped. And another thing that had a greater influence than this was, that many of our English divines and other people had, during Queen Mary's bloody reign, fled into Germany, Switzerland, &c.; and coming back in Queen Elizabeth's time, they brought with them a great love to the customs of those Protestant churches wherein they had sojourned; and especially the authority of Calvin, and the rules which he had established at Geneva, had a mighty influence on a great number of our own people at the time."

"Calvin had not only given his dictate in his 'Institutions,' that 'the difference is of no moment whether he that is baptized be dipped all over, and if so, whether thrice or once; or whether he be only wetted with the water poured on him;' but he had also drawn up, for the use of his Church at Geneva, and afterwards published to the world, a form of administering the sacraments; where, when he comes to order the act of baptizing, he words it thus: 'Then the minister of baptism *pours* water upon the infant, saying: "I baptize thee," and so on.' There had been some synods, in some dioceses of France, that had spoken of affusion without mentioning immersion at all, that being the common practice; but for an office or liturgy of any Church, this is, I believe, the first in the world that prescribes aspersion (affusion?) absolutely, ... and for sprinkling, properly called, it seems it was, at sixteen hundred and forty-five, just then beginning, and used by very few. It must have begun in the disorderly times after forty-one."

"Mr. Blake, who wrote, in 1645, a pamphlet, entitled 'Infant's Baptism freed from Antichristianism,' says: 'I have been an eye-witness of many infants dipped, and know it to have been the constant practice of many ministers for years together.'"* Thus far Wall.

Rev. Dr. Featley, whose "Clavis Mystica" was published in A.D. 1636, speaks thus: "Our font is always open, or ready to be opened, and the minister attends to receive the children of the faithful, and to dip them in that sacred laver."

"Upon the review of the Common Prayer Book at the Restoration," says Wall, "the Church of England did not think, however prevalent the custom of sprinkling was, to forego their maxim, that it is most fitting to dip children that are well able to endure it."

So it stands now, although sadly neglected. The English clergy are zealous for the other rubrics. In time to come let us hope that the voice of Christ and his Apostles, with the testimony of the whole early Church, which speaks to them in their present rubric, will be heard and obeyed, and the anomalous and irregular customs of the present be done away forever.

Against the present irregularity and departure from the primitive practice the most learned divines of the Church of England have constantly witnessed. And this they have done, 1st. By clear statements of what the primitive mode was, and that the compendious modes were resorted to only in necessity. 2d. By stating that immersion is the normal mode of

---

* v. Wall, Pt. ii, chap. ix. His account is full.

the English Church. 3d. And by pleading for its restoration in practice.

But notwithstanding the irregularities have continued, individual instances of the strictest fidelity to the rubrics have not been wanting; but ignorance regarding the baptismal customs of the primitive Church, the prevalence of popular prejudice, the lack of baptisteries, and, more than all, the later notion of the indifference of the mode, not only for validity, but also for regularity, which remained with most of the reformers, after they had emancipated themselves from Roman error, have overborne all the efforts of learning and clerical fidelity. Indeed the most radical views, views unheard of for six hundred years after Christ, have become so fearfully prevalent, that it is to be feared that the English rubric, the last stronghold of Apostolic and primitive practice, may itself be merged in the general ruin, and suffer the same changes as has the American. Up to this period it has been the silent witness against irregularity. Amid the war of later opinions it points us back to the ages when men believed that one particular mode, and one alone, had descended from the Apostles, or that was commanded by Christ himself, and which they denominated "the Divine baptism," and from which they suffered no departure, except in absolute necessity.

CHAPTER XI.

ANGLICAN THEOLOGIANS WHO FAVOR THE PRIMITIVE MODE, OR ITS RESTORATION IN PRACTICE.

In the preceding part of this work we have referred to many of our own divines whose interpretation of those passages in the New Testament which speak of baptism accords with the belief and practice of the primitive Church. Our great divines have ever stated the facts.

The references already given are but a part of the whole. A volume might be filled with similar passages and the supply would still continue. Indeed their number was surprising to the author. He has found himself at a loss only as to what he should choose.

All the writers whose views are expressed below will be found to witness to immersion as the *rule* of the Church of England, or as the usual mode in primitive times, or as the fittest mode of administration; in other words, their views bear upon the question of its greater fitness or obligation. It will be noticed that the statements regarding the ancient use of the compends have reference to the case of necessity. Of course no Churchman deems the mode invariably essential to validity, although many have preferred it for regularity and fitness.

See Bishop Trower, "On the Epistle for the Sixth Sunday after Trinity;" and Dr. Whitby, on Rom. 6:3, 5, given above.

Mede, A.D. 1586–1638: "I add, because, perhaps, some men's fancies are corrupted therewith, that there was no such thing as sprinkling, or $\beta\alpha\nu\tau\iota\sigma\mu\acute{o}\varsigma$, used in baptism in the Apostles' time, nor many ages after them." ("Works of the pious and profoundly learned Joseph Mede," ed. London, 1772, p. 63.)

ARCHBISHOP USHER: "Some there are that stand strictly for the particular action of diving or dipping the baptized under the water, as the only action which the institution of the sacrament will bear; and our Church allows no other, except in case of the child's weakness; and there is expressed in our Saviour's baptism both the descending into the water and the rising up." (Sum and Substance of the Christian Religion, p. 413, edit. 6th.)

SELDEN, who was born in A.D. 1584, and died 1654, witnesses to the change which had occurred when he wrote his "Table Talk," and his own opinion of it. Thus on p. 2008, vol. iii, of that work: "In England, of late years, I ever thought the parson baptized his own fingers, rather than the child."

BISHOP JEREMY TAYLOR: "Ductor Dubitantium, or Rule of Conscience." Bk. iii, chap. iv, Rule xv, 12, 14: "A custom in the administration of a sacrament, introduced against the analogy and mystery, the purpose and signification of it, ought not to be complied with. I instanced before, in a custom of the Church of England, of sprinkling water upon infants in their baptism, and I promised to consider it again. 'Baptizabant enim veteres, non manibus suis aquam baptizando aspergentes, sed trinâ immersione hoc evangelii sequentes, ascendit ex aqua, ergo descenderat. Ecce immersio, non aspersio,' said Jeremy, Patriarch of Constantinople. 'Straightway Jesus went up out of the water (saith the Gospel); He came up, therefore He went down. Behold an immersion, not an aspersion.' And the ancient churches, following this of the Gospel, did not, in their baptisms, sprinkle water with their hands, but immerged the catechumen or the infant; and therefore we find in the records of the Church that the persons to be baptized were quite naked, as is to be seen in many places. . . . . All which are a perfect conviction that the custom of the ancient Churches was not sprinkling, but IMMERSION, IN PURSUANCE OF THE SENSE OF THE WORD IN THE COMMANDMENT, AND THE EXAMPLE OF OUR BLESSED SAVIOUR. Now this was of so sacred account in their esteem that they did not account it lawful to receive him into the clergy who had been only sprinkled in his baptism, as we learn from the epistle of Cornelius to Fabius of Antioch (apud

Euseb., lib. 6, cap. 43). *Μὴ ἐξὸν ἦν τὸν ἐν κλίνῃ διὰ νόσον περιχυθέντα ὥσπερ καὶ οὗτος εἰς κλῆρόν τινα γενέσθαι.* 'It is not lawful that he, who was sprinkled in his bed by reason of sickness, should be admitted into holy orders.' Nay, it went further than this: they were not sure that they were rightly christened, yea or no, who were only sprinkled, as appears in the same epistle of Cornelius in Eusebius, *εἴγε χρὴ λέγειν τὸν τοιοῦτον εἰληφέναι*, which Nicephorus thus renders: 'If at least such a sprinkling may be called baptism,' and this was not only spoken in diminution of Novatus and indignation, for it was a formal and a solemn question made by Magnus (Epist. 76), to St. Cyprian: 'An habendi sint Christiani legitimi, eo quod aqua salutari non loti sunt sed perfusi;' 'whether they are to be esteemed right Christians who were only sprinkled with water, and not washed or dipped.' He answers, that the baptism was good when it was done. 'Necessitate cogente, et Deo indulgentiam largiente.' 'In the case of necessity God pardoning, and necessity compelling.' *And this is the sense and law of the Church of England; not that it be indifferent, but that all infants be dipped, except in the case of sickness,* and then sprinkling is permitted. And of this sprinkling, besides what is implied in the former testimonies, there was some little use in the primitive Church. 'Quis enim tibi tam infidæ pœnitentiæ viro aspergincm unam cujuslibet aquæ commodabit?' says Tertullian (De Pœnit., cap. 6), speaking to an impenitent person: 'Who will afford thee so much as one single sprinkling of water?' meaning for his baptism. And Surius, in his Life of St. Lawrence, tells, that, as he was going to his martyrdom, one Romanus, a soldier, brought to him a pitcher of water, that he might be baptized of him as he went; which, in that case, must have been done by pouring water upon him. 'Fudit aquam super caput ejus:' so did St. Lawrence also to Lucillus; 'he poured water upon his head.' And Walafridus Strabo (De Rebus Eccl., cap. 26), from these very examples, concludes that, in cases of *necessity,* it is lawful to use sprinkling. He adds, also, that it is lawful to do it when there is a great multitude of persons at once to be baptized: and Aquinas supposes the Apostles did so when the three thousand and when the five thousand were at once converted and baptized. *But this is but a conjecture, and hath no tradition, and no record to warrant it;* and therefore, although in cases of need and charity the Church of England does not want some good examples in the best times to countenance that permission, yet we are to follow her command, because that command is not only according to the *meaning and intent of the word βαπτίζετε in the commandment*, but agrees with the mystery of the sacrament itself: 'for we are buried with Him in baptism,' saith the Apostle. 'In aqua tanquam in sepulchro, caput immergentibus, vetus homo sepelitur et submergitur; deinde nobis emergentibus, novus resurgit inde.' So St. Chrysostom (In illud., 3 Johan. Nisi quis renatus): 'The old man is buried and drowned in the immersion under water; and when the baptized person is lifted up from the water, it represents the resurrection of the new man to newness of life.' In this case, therefore, the contrary custom not only being against an ecclesiastical law, but against the analogy and mysterious signification of the sacrament, is not to be complied with, unless in such cases that can be of themselves sufficient to justify a liberty in a ritual and ceremony; that is, a case of necessity.

"And of the same consideration it is, that the baptism be performed with a *trine* immersion, and not with one only. In England, we have a custom of sprinkling, and that but once. To the sprinkling I have already spoken; but as to the number, though the Church of England hath no law, and, therefore, the custom of doing it once is the more indifferent and at liberty; yet if the trine immersion be agreeable to the analogy of the mystery, and the other be not, the custom ought not to prevail, and is not to be complied with, if the case be evident or declared. Now, in this particular, the sense of antiquity is clear."

Then, after quoting many passages, which we have given elsewhere, to prove that the ancient Church both practised and deemed *trine* immersion binding, he adds: "Now, in these particulars, it is evident that the ancient churches did otherwise than we do: but that is not sufficient to force us to break the ecclesiastical custom, which is of long abode with us. But when they say these things are to be done by Divine precepts, we are to consider that upon its own account: and though some of the fathers did say so, yet it can never be proved to be so; and it were strange that there should be a Divine commandment, of which there is no mention made in the four Gospels, nor in the Acts or Epistles of the Apostles. But then that there is in dipping, and in the repetition of it, more correspondency to the analogy and mystery of the sacrament, is evident; the one being a sacrament of the death and burial of Christ, the other a confession of, and an admission to the faith and profession of God in the most holy Trinity: and therefore I say, it is sufficient warrant that every single person break that custom of sprinkling, which is against the ecclesiastical law; and it is also a sufficient reason to move the Church to introduce a contrary custom to the other of single immersion, concerning which as yet there is no law. But because there is, even in sprinkling, something of the analogy of the mystery, as is rightly observed by Aquinas and Dominicus a Soto; and because it is not certain that the best representation and the most expressive ceremony are required; therefore the Church, upon *great* cause, may lawfully do either: but because it is better to use dipping, and it is more agreeable to the mystery to use it three times, and that so the ancient Church understood it, therefore these things are a sufficient warrant to acquit us from the obligation of the contrary custom; because a custom against which there is so much probability, and in which there is no necessity and no advantage, is to be presumed unreasonable."

REV. DR. HAMMOND, A. D. 1605–1660, in his "Practical Catechism," p. 348: "Whosoever should be thus received into His family should be received with this ceremony of water, *therein to be dipped* (i. e. *according to the primitive ancient custom, to be put under water*) *three times*, or instead of that, to be sprinkled with it," &c.

REV. DR. CAVE, A. D. 1637–1713, in his "Primitive Christianity," p. 155: "The party to be baptized was wholly immerged, or put under water, which was the almost constant and universal custom of those times, *whereby they did more notably and significantly express the three great ends and effects of baptism;* for, as in immersion there are, in a manner, three several acts, the putting the person into water, his abiding there for a little time, and his rising up again, so by these were represented Christ's death, burial, and resurrection, and in conformity thereunto, our dying unto sin, the destruction of its power, and our resurrection to a new course of life: by the persons being put into water was lively represented the putting off the body of the sins of the flesh, and being washed from the filth and pollution of them; by his abode under it, which was a kind of burial in the water, his entering into a state of death or mortification, like as Christ remained for some time under the state or power of death; therefore 'as many as are baptized into Christ,' are said 'to be baptized into his death, and to be buried with him by baptism into death, that the old man being crucified with him, the body of sin might be destroyed, that henceforth he might not serve sin, for that he that is dead is freed from sin,' as the Apostle clearly explains the meaning of this rite: and then by his emersion, or rising up out of the water, was signified his entering upon a new course of life, differing from that which he lived before; 'that like as Christ was raised up from the dead by the glory of the Father, even so we also should walk in newness of life.' But though by reason of the more eminent significancy of these things, immersion was the common practice in those days, and therefore they earnestly urged it and pleaded for it, yet did they not hold sprinkling to be unlawful, especially in cases of necessity, as of weakness, danger of death, or where conveniency of immerging could not be had; *in these, and such like* cases, Cyprian does not only allow, but plead for it, and that in a discourse on purpose, when the question concerning it was put to him." . . . .

"This immersion was performed *thrice*, the person baptized being three several times put under water."

DEAN COMBER, "On the Common Prayer," London, 1688, p. 197: "Because the way of immersion was the most ancient, our Church doth first *prescribe* that, and only *permits* the other, where it is certified the child is weak, although custom has now prevailed to the laying the first wholly aside;" then he expresses the opinion that sprinkling is sufficient.

SIR NORTON KNATCHBULL: "With leave be it spoken, I am still of opinion, that it would be more for the honor of the Church, and for the security of religion, if the old custom (*i. e.* immersion) could be conveniently restored." (Annot. on 1 Peter 3 : 20, 21; v, also id. p. 300, ed. Camb. 1693.)

BINGHAM, A. D. 1668—1723: Every clergyman who would go beyond the crude and ignorant treatises now so common to the fountain-head of knowledge should attentively read the whole of chap. xi, book xi, of Bingham's Antiquities, and a part of chap. v, book xiii, of the same. It is difficult to find anything so thorough.

It will suffice to say that he bears witness to the *trine* immersion as the primitive and Catholic custom, and that he testifies to this as the Church mode, except in cases of necessity. Some Baptists have given a false impression by quoting a part of what he asserts so as to make it appear that he witnesses to the *single* immersion as in universal use in the early Church. If they had taken the trouble to look at what he says of Eunomius, they would never have made such a mistake. v. as above.

BISHOP BEVERIDGE, A. D. 1638—1708, one of the most learned men that the Church of England has ever produced, defends the trine immersion against Daille. He says in one place, speaking of this mode, "That this was in some way handed down from the Apostles we dare not deny." ("Aliquo tamen modo id ab apostolis traditum, negare non ausi sumus.") v. Codex Can. Eccl. Prim. Vindic. cap. vi, pp. 247, 248.

In his Works, vol. viii, Oxford ed., 1846, speaking of Baptism "in the name of all the three Persons" of the Trinity, he says: "Which the primitive Christians were so strict in the observance of, that it was *enjoined* that all persons to be baptized should be *plunged three times* into the water, first at the 'name of the Father,' and then at the 'name of the Son,' and lastly, at the 'name of the Holy Ghost;' that so every Person might be distinctly nominated, and so our Saviour's institution exactly observed in the administration of this sacrament."

ROGERS and WALKER (quoted by Wall, vol. ii, p. 410) were in favor of the restoration of immersion. The latter even says, "If I may speak my thoughts, I believe the ministers of the nation would be heartily glad if the people would desire, or be but willing, to have their infants dipped, after the ancient manner, both in this and in other churches." This was in 1678.

REV. DR. TOWERSON, "On the Sacraments," London, 1686, p. 20. "One other particular there is, wherein I have said the water of baptism to have been intended as a sign, and that is in respect of that *manner* of application, which was sometime used, I mean the *dipping* or *plunging* the person baptized in it. A signification which St. Paul will not suffer those to forget who have been acquainted with his Epistles. For, with reference to that manner of baptizing, we find him affirming (Rom. 6:4) that we are 'buried with Christ by baptism into death; that like as Christ was raised up from the dead by the glory of the Father, even so we also should walk in newness of life.' And again (Rom. 6:5), that 'if we have been planted together in the likeness of his death, we shall be also in the likeness of his resurrection.' To the same purpose, or rather yet more clearly, doth the Apostle discourse where he tells us (Col. 2:12), that as we are 'buried with Christ in baptism, so we do therein rise also with him through the faith of the operation of God who hath raised him from the dead.' For what is this but to say, that as the design of baptism was to oblige men to conform to Christ's death and resurrection as to die unto sin and live again unto righteousness, so it was performed by the ceremony of immersion, that the person immersed might by that very ceremony, which was no obscure image of a sepulture, be minded of the precedent death, as in like manner by his coming again out of the water, of his rising from that death to life, after the example of the Institutor thereof; for which cause, as hath been elsewhere observed, the ancient Church added to the rite of immersion the dipping of the party three several times, to represent the three days Christ continued in the grave (for that we find to have been the intention of some), and made the eve of Easter one of the solemn times of the administration of it.

"The third thing to be inquired concerning the outward visible sign of baptism is, how it ought to be applied; where again these two things would be considered, first, whether it ought to be applied by an immersion, or an aspersion or effusion. Secondly. Whether it ought to be applied by a threefold immersion or aspersion, answerably to the names into which we are baptized, or either by that or a single one.

"The former of these is, it may be, a more material question than it is commonly deemed by us who have been accustomed to baptize by a bare effusion or sprinkling of water upon the party. For in things which depend for their force upon the mere will and pleasure of him who instituted them, there ought, no doubt, great regard to be had to the commands of him who did so; as without which there is no reason to presume we shall receive the benefit of that ceremony to which he hath been pleased to annex it.

"Now, what the command of Christ was in this particular, cannot well be doubted of by those who shall consider first the words of Christ (Matt. 28 : 19) concerning it, and the practice of those times, whether in the baptism of John or of our Saviour. For the words of Christ are, that they should BAPTIZE or DIP those whom they made disciples to him (*for as, no doubt, the word βαπτίζειν* PROPERLY *signifies*), and which is more and not without its weight, that they should baptize them *into* the name of the Father, and of the Son, and of the Holy Ghost; thereby intimating such a washing as should receive the party baptized within the very body of that water which they were to baptize him with. Though if there could be any doubt concerning the signification of the words in themselves, yet would that doubt be removed by considering the practice of those times, whether in the baptism of John or of our Saviour. For such as was the practice of those times in baptizing, such in reason are we to think our Saviour's command to have been concerning it, especially when the words themselves incline that way, there being not otherwise any means either for those or future times to discover his intentions concerning it.

"Now what the practice of those times was as to this particular, will need no other proof than their resorting to rivers and such like receptacles of waters for the performance of that ceremony, as that too because there was 'much water' there. For so the Scripture doth not only affirm concerning the baptism of John (Matt. 3 : 9; 6 : 13; John 3 : 23), but both intimate concerning that which our Saviour administered in Judea (because making John's baptism and his to be so far forth of the same sort, John 3 : 22, 23), and expressly affirm concerning the baptism of the eunuch, which is the only Christian baptism the Scripture is anything particular in the description of; the words of St. Luke (Acts 8 : 38) being, that both Philip and the eunuch went down into a certain water which they met with on their journey, in order to the baptizing of the latter. For what need would there have been either of the Baptist's resorting to great confluxes of water, or of Philip and the eunuch's going down into this, were it not that the baptism, both of the one and the other, was to be performed by an immersion? A very little water, as we know it doth with us, sufficing for an effusion or sprinkling. But besides the words of our blessed Saviour, and the concurrent practice of those times wherein this sacrament was instituted, it is in my opinion of no less consideration, that the thing signified by the sacrament of baptism cannot otherwise be well represented than by an immersion, or at least by some more general way of purification than that of effusion or sprinkling. For though the pouring or sprinkling of a little water upon the face may suffice to represent an internal washing, which seems to be the general end of Christ's making use of the sacrament of baptism, yet can it not be thought to represent such an *entire* washing as that of new-born infants was, and as baptism may seem to have been intended for, because represented as the '*laver* (Tit. 3 : 5) *of our regeneration;*' that though it do [not?] require an immersion, yet requiring such a *general* washing at least as may extend to the whole body, as other than which cannot answer its type, nor yet that general, though internal purgation which baptism was intended to represent. The same is to be said yet more upon the account of our conforming to the death and resurrection of Christ, which we learn from St. Paul to have been the design of baptism to signify. For though that might and was well enough represented by the baptized person's being buried in baptism, and then rising out of it, yet can it not be said to be so, or at least but very imperfectly, by the bare pouring out or sprinkling the baptismal water on him. But, therefore, as there is so much the more reason to represent the rite of immersion as *the only legitimate rite of baptism, because the only one that can answer the ends of its institution, and those things which were to be signified by it,* so especially if (as is well known, and undoubtedly of great force) the general practice of the primitive Church was agreeable thereto, and the practice of the Greek Church to this very day. For who can think either the one or the other would have been so tenacious of so troublesome a rite, were it not that they were well assured, *as they of the primitive Church might very well be, of its being the* ONLY *instituted and legitimate one.*"

On p. 24 in id. he remarks, that "Our forefathers" were "strangely tenacious of that rite," and that "both they and their posterity" were "not without a venerable opinion of it."

He continues, "Our Church hath acquitted itself from all blame, because manifestly licensing the sprinkling of infants, with respect to the *weakness of their state*, and I have the more carefully noted both that and the ground of our practice, the better to defend ourselves from a retort of the Romanists, when we charge them with sacrilege in the matter of the eucharist, for taking away the cup from the laity. For why not (as they sometimes answer) as well as change the rite of immersion in baptism into that of sprinkling? especially when a great part of the symbolicalness of that sacrament lies in the manner of the application of its sign: which answer of theirs were not, in my opinion, easy to be repelled, were it not that we have that necessity to justify our practice, which they cannot pretend for their own." (v. also on the Catechism.)

William Wall, D. D., A. D. 1645 or 1646 to 172⅜. This learned man, whose immortal history of infant baptism forms the strongest bulwark against modern error, and attests his own laborious and impartial investigation, has left incidentally on record his thoughts on the mode. He, indeed, states that with the mode he had "meddled as little as possible" (vol. iv, p. 105), but yet the author has found little more reliable; for it is a subject which is too apt to be passed over in a few remarks. What he says, with his quotations and references, are too voluminous to be here given. We can only epitomize and refer to the work.

1. He states that dipping was the general mode in the Apostles' days, and interprets certain passages of Scripture of it. Pp. 152, 153, vol. iv.

2. That in the ages succeeding the Apostolic times, immersion was the general usage. P. 153, vol. iv.

3. That the Church of England still enjoins dipping for every healthy infant, and that it should be obeyed. P. 404, vol. ii; pp. 460, 461, vol. iv.

4. That the mode is not indifferent, but that dipping *should* be used, except in weakness, necessity, or urgent cause, and that a clergyman is "bound in conscience," and by his ordination vows "before God and the bishop," to dip healthy children. Vol. iv, pp. 150, 162.

5. That the Antipædobaptist schism in England never made much headway until "abuses" in the mode and manner of administration had come in, and he thinks if these were

remedied, the schism might be curtailed or healed. Vol. iv, pp. 172, 457–463.

6. That the schism was not made on account of dislike of infant baptism. P. 458, vol. iv.

7. That dipping is the more fitting mode. Vol. iv, p. 106.

He states, iv, 106, that in his work he had employed himself in "pleading," as well as he could, "for the retrieving of the use of it (immersion), according to the rubric of the Church." Pt. ii, chap. ix, and the Defence, pp. 151–173, 458–483, are especially valuable. He refutes the common, foolish, and insufficient reasons for not dipping, and gives excellent and most judicious advice to the clergy as to their intercourse with the different sects or kinds of Antipædobaptists.

His opinion as to the origin of the schism, or at least its success, having arisen not to opposition to the subjects so much as to the modes, is undoubtedly the correct one.

DEAN WATERLAND, A. D. 1683–1740. "I shall begin with what comes first in order, and which chiefly belongs to *fathers* and *mothers*, *godfathers* and *godmothers*,—the bringing children to the font to be publicly baptized, according to the rules and orders of the Church of England, formed exactly upon the *primitive* model, saving only as to the allowing and dispensing with the *pouring* on of water upon the child instead of *immersion*, which allowance has at length, by custom, took place of the rule, and unhappily excluded it, perhaps, beyond recovery, though many good and pious men have hinted their desires or wishes for restoring the primitive practice, which had constantly obtained in England, from the first planting of Christianity till within less than two hundred years ago, and has not been entirely laid aside above a century and a half at most." Works, vol. v, p. 370, 371.

REV. THOMAS STACKHOUSE, A. D. 1680–1752. "New History of the Holy Bible," London, 1744, vol. ii, p. 1284. "The observation of the Greek Church in relation to this matter is this, that he who ascended out of the water must first descend down into it, and consequently, that baptism is to be performed not by sprinkling but by washing the body; and indeed, he must be strangely ignorant of the Jewish rites of baptism who seems to doubt of this, since to the due performance of it, they required the immersion of the whole body to such a degree of nicety, that if any dirt was upon it, that hindered the water from coming to that part, they thought the ceremony not rightly done. The Christians, no doubt, took this rite from the Jews, and followed them in their manner of performing it. Accordingly, several authors have shown that we read nowhere in Scripture of any one's being baptized but by immersion, and from the acts of councils and ancient rituals, have proved that this manner of immersion continued (as much as possible) to be used for thirteen hundred years after Christ. But it is much to be questioned whether the prevalence of custom and the over fondness of parents will, in these cold climates especially, ever suffer it to be restored."

WHEATLEY: "And it must be allowed that by dipping, the ends and effects of baptism are more significantly expressed; for as in immersion there are three several acts, viz., the putting the person under the water, his abiding there for some time, and his rising up again; so by these were represented Christ's death, burial, and resurrection, and in conformity thereunto (as the Apostle plainly shows, Rom. 6: 3, 4) our dying unto sin, the destruction of its power, and our resurrection to newness of life." See "On the Common Prayer," p. 348, Bohn's ed.

BISHOP A. P. FORBES, of Brechin: "Baptism was originally generally administered by way of immersion; the catechumen was dipped three times. But, although our Church still *prescribes* immersion where the child can bear it, she is satisfied to administer it by affusion or aspersion. This has been permitted from the earliest times in the baptism of clinics; and, although these afterwards were ineligible to offices in the Church, it was not from any doubt of the validity of their baptism, but because it was such a bad sign in a man putting off the responsibilities of the Christian state till late in life, that such persons were prejudged not to have a vocation for the Christian ministry. Since the thirteenth century, affusion has been the universal custom of the Western Church, except in the Diocese of Milan, and many early monuments of the Church show the existence of the practice; and affusion should be trine, but this is not of necessity to the validity of the ordinance. It is, however, highly to be recommended, both as giving greater security for the ablution, and also as symbolizing that adorable Trinity into whom the child is baptized." Explan. of the Nicene Creed, xvii, on the Remission of Sin, p. 299.

BISHOP WILSON, of Calcutta, in his Lectures on Colossians, lect. xviii, p. 175, ed. N. Y., 1846, says: "The expression *buried with him in baptism*, alludes to the ancient form of administering that sacred ordinance, *still directed in our own Church, except when health permits*, of the immersion or burial, so to speak, of the whole person in the water, after the example of the burial of the entire body of our Lord in the grave."

CONYBEARE AND HOWSON, in "Life of St Paul," i, 471: "It is needless to add that baptism was (unless in exceptional cases) administered by immersion, the convert being plunged beneath the surface of the water, to represent his death to the life of sin, and then raised from this momentary burial, to represent his resurrection to the life of righteousness. It must be a subject of regret that the general discontinuance of this original form of baptism (though perhaps necessary in our northern climates) has rendered obscure to popular apprehension some very important passages of Scripture." P. Schaff, D.D., in his History of the Apostolic Church, p. 570, after quoting the above, continues: "With this we entirely concur. It is well known that the reformers, Luther and Calvin, and several old Protestant liturgies, gave the preference to immersion; and this is undoubtedly far better suited than sprinkling to symbolize the idea of baptism, the entire purifying of the inward man, the being buried, and the rising again with Christ."

REV. H. NEWLAND, in "Confirmation and First Communion," p. 363, London, 1854, addressing "the Anabaptists of Emsworth," says: "But you say that dipping is the more proper way of baptizing; so do I, and so does the Church. Do read your own Prayer Book before you find fault with the Church, and see whether the Church does not tell you to do that very thing which you find fault with her for not doing. See whether the fault does not lie in you, and not in the Church. This is what the Church says: 'And then naming it after them (if they shall certify him that the child may well endure it) he shall DIP it in the water discreetly and warily, but if they certify that the child is weak, it *shall suffice* to pour water upon it.'

"Now, then, if rhantizing, as you call it, is practised with your children instead of dipping, whose fault is it? Try; demand of your parish priest, after due notice given, that he baptize your child by dipping, and see if he dares refuse to do it. . . .

"You see then that in fact two-thirds of your supposed difference from the Church is no difference at all; that it is a mistake of your own, arising simply from your not having read your Prayer Book. While the only real difference between us, viz., that *besides* baptizing grown persons, we suffer little children *also* to come to Christ, arises from your not having read the Bible with sufficient attention."

WILLIAM PALMER, Deacon; Essays on the "Orthodox Communion," London, 1853; Diss. viii, sect. iii, p 112. "It is undeniable that if baptism is unnecessarily administered otherwise than by trine immersion, some of those lesser mysteries which it contains are no longer visibly exhibited in each particular case of its administration. Neither the three persons of the Trinity (so far as the act of baptism is concerned), nor the three days and nights of Christ's lying in the grave, nor our being buried with Christ (by being submerged under the water), and rising again with him (by rising out of the water) to newness of life, are expressed as they were formerly expressed by the Catholic and Apostolic ritual. And the greater or more powerful any part of the Church which disregards these lesser mysteries of baptism, the greater also will be the danger that the remaining portions of the Church may become infected by the same irreverence, and so the full type of the sacrament be lost altogether. In principle, therefore, it might seem reasonable to deny the right of an individual Pope, or even of the whole Western Church, to change the ecumenical form of baptism, and to insist upon the correction of this abuse as an indispensable preliminary to reunion. And we may hope that in an united ecumenical council there would be no difficulty in obtaining such a correction."

He states, p. 179: "The *rule* of the Anglican Church is to baptize children by *immersion*, unless it be certified that the child is too weak to bear it, in which case *affusion* is allowed. But the common practice is not even to ask for any such certificate, but to baptize by affusion, or rather by *sprinkling*."

. . . . . . "Now to say nothing of the omission of other important ceremonies, adjuncts of baptism, from the Anglican ritual, the writer is aware that there is a deep sense both in the immersion (*signified by the very word baptism*), and in the threefold repetition of that immersion, once at the name of each person of the Blessed Trinity. He is aware that to dispense with either the one or the other of these things without any real necessity, is contrary to the custom of the whole Catholic Church for many ages; so that baptism so administered must be irregular and uncanonical, and any individual so administering it, worthy of canonical punishments. And although St. Gregory the Great, also called 'Dialogus,' may have thought the Spaniards justifiable in using baptism with one immersion only (they using it in an orthodox sense, not to symbolize any heresy, but to oppose the heresy of some who drew a perverse argument, for three separate substances in the three Persons of the Trinity, from the three immersions in baptism), still he cannot see that either the Spaniards or Pope Gregory could rightly, without a council, authorize any departure from the universal custom and tradition of the Church in such a matter."

REV. ISAAC WILLIAMS, late Fellow of Trinity College, Oxford, in "Plain Sermons on the Catechism," London, 1851, p 194. "But in speaking of this, the outward element, of 'water wherein the person is baptized' as of so much importance, it is necessary to speak of a custom which now prevails, of sprinkling with water rather than immersion. For *baptism more properly signifies washing or dipping*, i. e. immersion in water. The reasons given for this change are, that in the countries we read of in Scripture, from the warmth of the climate, bathing in water is commonly practised, and there is not the slightest danger or risk; but in our colder countries, all that is intended by this outward sign is equally shown by the pouring of water. . . . . Now this and more to the same effect may be said for 'the pouring of water,' rather than 'dipping in water,' sufficient to satisfy any scrupulous mind, where mercy or charity requires it; *but where they do not,* IT IS BETTER TO ADHERE TO THE PRIMITIVE CUSTOM, both because it was the ancient and general practice, and because it more fully bears out the fulness of the sign of washing. Moreover, immersion in water has always been considered to imply the death unto sin, the being buried with Christ, as the Apostle says in baptism (Rom. 6 : 4; Col. 2 : 12), as set forth also in those figures of old, when they seemed, as it were, overwhelmed and buried in the midst of the waves of the Red Sea; or when the Ark of Noah was in the midst of waters above, below, and on every side, the windows of heaven pouring down the flood, and the fountains of the great deep opened below. In Naaman, also, there was immersion, even sevenfold in the sacred stream. For these reasons, THIS OUGHT TO BE THE RULE IN BAPTIZING, AND THE SPRINKLING OR POURING OF WATER OUGHT TO BE THE EXCEPTION TO THE RULE. So you will find it in the Prayer Book, in the rules given for baptism. And every clergyman, it is to be hoped, will be glad to abide by these rules, wherever he has an opportunity of doing so."

These constitute but a part of the passages from Church of England authors, in favor of the meaning of the rubric, or the restoration of the ancient dipping.

We may well, therefore, appreciate the truth of Dr. Wall's remark: "Since the times that dipping of infants has been generally left off, many learned men in several countries have endeavored to retrieve the use of it, but more in England than anywhere else in proportion." Hist. of Inf. Bapt., p. 406, vol. ii.

CHAPTER XII.

THE AMERICAN RUBRICS.

As during the colonial existence of the republic, the American Church formed a part of the English Church, as the colonies themselves were a part of the British Empire, in describing the opinions of the great Anglican divines, we have given those of the American Church.

But after the great struggle, certain alterations were made in the Prayer Book, one of which was the change of the rubrics in the office for the "Public Baptism of Infants." The two rubrics of the English office are combined in one.

The difference will be best seen by a comparison.

The English rubric reads: "And then naming it after them (if they shall certify him that the child may well endure it), he shall dip it in the water discreetly and warily, saying,

"N. I baptize thee," &c.

"But if they certify that the child is weak, it shall suffice to pour water upon it, saying the aforesaid words."

The American directs: "And then, naming it after them, he shall dip it in the water discreetly, or shall pour water upon it, saying:

"N., I baptize thee," &c.

It will be seen at once that the American rubric differs from that of the parent Church,

1. In not *requiring* dipping for healthy infants.
2. In not specifying that pouring shall be used only when "they certify that the child is weak."

We have traced in the first book of Edward VI the primitive mode of trine immersion, its change in the second book into the single, and the still further modification of it in the present English rubric. But this rubric of the American Church makes the mode more indefinite still. The immersion is placed first; that is all.

The language of the preface compared with that of Bishop White would seem to point towards at least one cause of the alteration. "This Church," are its words, "is far from intending to depart from the Church of England in any essential point of doctrine, discipline, or worship; *or farther than local circumstances require.*"

Why, with such strong views in favor of immersion as Bishops Seabury and White held, they should, when they alone sat in the Upper House, have agreed to the change in the rubric, which makes it more indefinite than the English, it is somewhat difficult to discover. Bishop White (see below) deemed that, after the alteration, "the standard" of the American rubric is dipping. While the placing it first and the language of the office itself are in consonance with this, the enjoining of immersion is not so clearly expressed in the rubric. Yet on the former points he was right.

The following *may* serve to point out the cause of the alteration in the rubric.

It will be found in the "General Convention Journals with notes, 1785 to 1853," vol. i, p. 560.

Rev. Dr. Smith to Rev. Dr. White.

CHESTER, 9th April, 1786.

DEAR SIR:
* * * * * *

"We had a *considerable* majority of all our clergy (not many of the laity) at our Convention, and have agreed to receive and recommend to public use the new book, as far as the power of our State Church may be supposed to extend in our present *unorganized* state. A few alterations are proposed, to be offered to the next *convention*. The Nicene Creed, to follow the Apostles', with an 'or this,' a little alteration or rather discretionary power in the administration of baptism, *where the minister may have great numbers to baptize together.*"

With reference to these alterations, Rev. Dr. White, afterwards Bishop, writes to Dr. Smith in reply, "I think y[e] proposed alterations of your convention will render our service more compleat." See the above work, p. 561.

This is all the clue which we have been able to find.

In the lack of any other means of arriving at the sense of those who made or concurred in the alteration of this rubric, we may turn to the writings of the only three bishops who were consecrated in 1789, the date of the alteration, in General Convention. These three were Seabury, White, and Provost.

Bishop Provost was not present at the Convention of 1789. The author has not found anything of his on the subject of the mode of baptism.

But with regard to the other two, we are better able to state their views.

BISHOP SEABURY, A.D. 1728–1796. This prelate thought that "strong" "probabilities" exist that the jailor and his household (Acts 16) were baptized by *affusion* and not by *immersion;* and again, that "baptism being a figure of inward purity, or of cleansing the soul from sin, it cannot be supposed that the quantity of water adds to the *validity* or *efficacy* of the sacrament." Whether he would deem the *regularity* of the administration at all affected by the lack of the primitive custom, he does not say. Yet he states just above the passages quoted, "The fair induction is, that the original mode of administering Christian baptism was the same that had obtained among the Jews in the baptizing of proselytes; that is, by washing or immersing the whole body in water. This, too, seems most congruous to the general expressions of holy Scripture; and, I presume, it will, upon examination, appear to have been the general practice of the primitive Church. The subject is too long to be here considered; I shall therefore only observe, that though immersion was the general practice, yet in cases of sickness baptism was administered by pouring water on the head; and this baptism was never repeated, but, upon recovery, confirmation followed. They probably received it from the Apostles, that at least in cases of necessity, baptism might be so administered; on any other ground it will be hard to give an account how the practice obtained in the Church at all.

"Though I have supposed that the Apostles administered baptism by immersion of the whole body, and have said that such a supposition is most agreeable to the general scope of the New Testament, still I am ready to own that from the circumstances related in the account of the jailor's baptism, it seems improbable that immersion was practised in that instance." "Sermons," vol. i, Discourse iii, pp. 94, 95.

BISHOP WM. WHITE, of the American Church, in his "Lectures on the Catechism," Philadelphia ed., 1813, p. 362. "On the question between immersion and affusion, it is not designed to add much to what was delivered in the lecture. John's baptizing in a place where water abounded, the description of our Lord as coming up out of the water, and many other circumstances in addition to the general sense of the Greek words expressive of baptism and the act of administering it, strongly mark the original practice to have been generally by *immersion. That it continued to be so during the best ages of the Church is evident*, among other monuments, from their baptisteries."

Then after contending against the *absolute necessity* of immersion, he adds, p. 363, id.

"*The result, in the estimation of him who now writes, is, that* THE PRESENT GENERAL PRACTICE IS A DEVIATION FROM WHAT IT WAS ORIGINALLY, *which it is* DESIRABLE *to restore to the standard of the rubrics as they were framed in the Church of England, and as they continue to this day in the liturgy of that and of the American Church, although fallen by universal custom into neglect.*"

These utterances of opinion best coincide with a preference for immersion. Indeed, the language of Bishop White shows this very markedly. Let it be remembered, too, that these two were the only ones present, and that they alone constituted the Upper House, and we see how strongly their testimony bears for immersion as the primitive rule in all cases except those of sick persons. It is clear that both bishops thought that immersion was the primitive mode so far as ordinary practice was concerned. One of them expressly brands the present general practice as a deviation from what it was originally, and in the same sentence expresses a desire for the restoration of immersion in practice. It is to be remarked, too, that Bishop White deemed the present rubric even of the

American Church to be favorable to immersion. This is evident from the last sentence of the quotation. It is observable then that of these both deemed immersion the primitive mode, and that Bishop White thought that with this mode as the preferred one, *the American* no less than the English rubric agrees. They are mentioned by Bishop White as of the same purport. Nevertheless, it is to be regretted that our own Church had not imitated the conservative character of the English Church at the Restoration in refusing to make further alterations. In lowering the standard of primitive requirement, we always run the risk of going too far.

Since the Revolution, and even long before, the greatest negligence, and in too many cases be it said to our shame, the greatest ignorance, has prevailed with regard to the mode.

The same anti-Catholic and anti-primitive notions which originated with Eunomius, and which were afterwards favored with additions by some Latins, and in more modern times by the adherents of Calvin, have found extensive credence even in the American Church. One thing which has materially contributed to this has been the aggressive character of the numerous Baptist sects. These have been among the most earnest foes of the Church. It is no wonder then that many of our people have in the heat of controversy run into an extreme contrary to that which they favored. This is but natural. History is full of it. In this we have fought at a disadvantage. Instead of remedying our own irregular practice in making pouring, or even sprinkling the rule, and attacking the many weak points of their system, we have often met them on the only topic, that of the mode, in which they possess any real strength, and sometimes almost ignored all others. As a natural consequence we have lost fearfully. The different Baptist sects outnumber us in the United States ten to one in the number of communicants. It is perhaps not too much to say that at least half the Baptists are descendants of Church of England or American Church families. Had the English rubric been better observed, this would not have been so. For the denial of infant baptism can coexist only with ignorance of right principles of interpretation; all history shows plainly that even among the ancient errorists who wandered in almost every direction from the truth of God, none were so wild as to suppose that Christ had made no *covenant* provision for infants. The few sects who opposed the baptism of infants in the middle ages and in modern times have been among the most ignorant and fanatical of all who have ever professed the Christian name. Within the last century or two they have produced some men well educated in the languages and sciences, but as theological learning increases they must lose many of those who are disposed fairly to examine the testimony of the Scriptures as interpreted by the practice of the immediate successors of the Apostles.

CHAPTER XIII.

THE REMEDY.

When the present irregularities in using the compends instead of the fuller administration is considered, two widely different cases must be considered:
1. That of the Church of England.
2. That of the American Church.

In the case of the English and Colonial Churches, the remedy is very easy. It is simply to obey their rubric in the office for the public baptism of infants. The immersion may be trine or single. The case of the American Church is much more difficult.

The obstacles are mainly three:
1. The change in rubric so that the primitive rite receives no other preference than in being placed before pouring, and the language of the office itself.
2. The prevalent ignorance and carelessness as to the mode so highly prized in the early Church, and in the English Church in other days, among our own clergy and people.
3. The danger which would arise from the Baptist sects if we should return to the primitive custom. Now let us glance at these in their order.

I. Although the rubric has been changed, nevertheless immersion is not laid aside. All that can be said is, that it is no longer absolutely enjoined for every healthy infant as in the English rubric. It is the first mentioned of the two modes mentioned in the rubric.

For its restoration in practice these things plead:
1. The general meaning of $\beta\alpha\pi\tau i\zeta\omega$.
2. The usage of the Apostles and their coadjutors in the apostolic age, as that usage is testified to during the first six hundred years by all Catholic testimony.
3. The uniform custom as the *rule* in all ordinary cases for the first twelve centuries of our era.

4. All the rubrics of the whole Church, East and West, for the same period.

5. The custom of our own Church until the Reformation, and for some time after.

6. The general "consensus" of our own most learned divines from the Reformation, that it was the *general* mode of administration in apostolic and primitive days.

7. The very words of the Catechism and the offices for baptism, which have in a great measure remained unchanged since the days when immersion was the ordinary use, and which best agree with that mode.

Let us glance at the language which the Church puts into the mouth of her clergy.

"By the baptism of thy well-beloved Son, Jesus Christ, *in the river Jordan*," &c., "Office for the Public Baptism of Infants," and "Office for the Baptism of those of Riper Years."

"Almighty, ever living God, . . . sanctify this water to the mystical washing away of sin, and grant that this child, now to be baptized THEREIN," &c. "Office for the Baptism of Infants," and "Office for the Baptism of those of Riper Years," except that this last "these persons" occurs in place of "this child." Compare also the 1st and 2d Books Edw. VI in loc., and Scotch Liturg. of 1637.

All this occurs in solemn address to God. What could be stronger? Comment is unnecessary.

In the Catechism occurs the question, "What is the outward visible sign or form in baptism?" and the Church still teaches the child this answer: "Water, WHEREIN the person is baptized," &c.

In the first of these, the minister who uses the prayer must believe that Christ was baptized in the river Jordan, and in the last two, immersion is referred to as the general mode of administration.

II. Undoubtedly there is much ignorance and carelessness, both among clergy and people. Many men who have entered our ministry were originally Congregationalists or Presbyterians. They have, in some cases, brought with them the radicalism and contempt of early authority, and ignorance of the real facts now, unfortunately, so prevalent among our dissenting brethren. Yet the greater part of this large class already hold the view, that Scripture should be interpreted in accordance with the historical testimony of the early Christians, where that exists. They hold then the principle which would lead them to conformity with the early mode, though some have never taken the trouble to examine this subject, and hence, are ignorant. But a careful study of Bingham, Wall, and the primitive authorities to whom they refer, will do away with indifference in all impartial minds. Another class are, perhaps, more affected in some few things by *opinions* which originated with some one isolated individual in the Church, and have been taught as doctrines or as prevalent opinions in the Latin communion. In other words, they are in some things Latinized, in those points in which Latinism has gone either *against* or *beyond* the Church decisions in the six ecumenical councils. But even here a more enlarged and impartial scholarship will, in time, teach them to distinguish between what is Latin and what is Catholic; between what is Western and what is ecumenical; between what is local and what is universal; between what is mere opinion and what is Church doctrine, pronounced such by the sole authority, an ecumenical council.

Our own most learned men, whatever might be their own opinions, have told the facts. Besides this, these facts are known to our more learned clergy. The constant agitation of the baptismal controversy has induced many to glance back to the earlier administration.

III. As to the danger to be apprehended from the Baptist sects, little need be said. It is evident,

1. That if we restore immersion, we only restore what has ever been our theory, so far back as the history of the Anglican Church extends. We correct only a late and not primitive practice.

2. Should we restore the trine immersion as the general practice, we shall have good reason to lay claim to the only mode which, so far as we can judge from all the testimony which the early Church affords, can lay historically attested claim to being the normal mode of the Apostles.

While, perhaps, we may not say absolutely that single immersion was never resorted to in the Apostolic times, yet all the facts of the ages immediately subsequent are against the view that it is anything more than a compend, and it is clear that for 500 years after Christ, all orthodox Christians deemed the trine immersion itself *the* Divine or Apostolic institution, which some thought commanded in Scripture, and others thought had been handed down in the practice and teaching of the Church, from the Apostles or Christ, as its source.

The rubric does not specify the number of immersions. It may be single or trine. But the latter is far preferable, since it is admitted as valid baptism by all, even by the Baptists, while the whole Eastern Church brands the single as the Eunomian mode, or as a departure from the form of all Christian antiquity.

For the sake of following the primitive mode, or that which the whole early Church deemed so, as well as because it is the only mode whose general use can restore peace as to the mode to the Church, we should practise trine immersion as the rule, admitting the compends only, where St. Cyprian and the custom of the whole Church are agreed in authorizing a departure from it, viz., in necessity. "In sacramentis salutaribus, necessitate cogente, et Deo indulgentiam suam largiente, totum credentibus conferunt divina compendia." Cypr. Ep. ad magnum.

Among others these things are desirable.

1. The restoration of the office for the public baptism of infants in the first book of Edward VI, and *every* primitive rite.

2. The injunction of the immersion as the general mode by the General and Diocesan Conventions.

3. Its general observance by the clergy, and their influence for its restoration.

The bishops and the clerical and lay delegates would do the Church a great service, and be the means of drawing multitudes into our communion, were they to restore even the rubrics in the First Book of Edward VI.

But even with the present rubric, zeal combined with prudence would bring into general and ordinary use the mode of the ancient Church and her Apostolic founders. If every one were to do his duty, all would be well.

One other and a most important topic remains, with reference to the ordinary meaning of βαπτίζω. We have seen that the whole early Church, and indeed, the whole Church for at least the first eight hundred years after Christ, speak of the command of Christ as enjoining not mere washing, but immersion. Nothing can be clearer than this. The Eastern communion still holds this view. In the West, it has been the received opinion until a few centuries past. And the history of the mode amply demonstrates this truth, that where the primitive idea of its meaning in the command (St. Matt. 28 : 19) has been preserved, trine immersion has been retained, and where the people have been made to believe that it is synonymous with καθαρίζω, to purify, or λούω, to wash, the compends have become not the exceptional but the ordinary administration. It is not difficult to see why this should be so. The ancient mode, although it possesses a divinely ordained symbolism, although whenever administered it sets forth, as God designed it, the types of the death and resurrection of the believer with his Lord, although it is embalmed in the pages and practice of the Apostles and Doctors, and of the Holy Church throughout all the world, is notwithstanding a more troublesome rite than pouring or sprinkling, or even the single immersion. If in Christ's command it be not enjoined, if it be not modal, anxious parents will be ever ready to plead the tenderness of infants, and the greater ease of administration of the first two, and the primitive rite will be thrust aside. These motives are prevalent and powerful. The only way in which they have ever been effectually resisted has been by instilling the early belief.

There has been no lack, in the Church of England, and in all parts of Christendom who admit the compends in ordinary use, of true knowledge of the facts, and strong pleas for the restitution of ancient custom. The great evil has been, that in order to oppose Antipædobaptist error, and without diligent search of the grounds upon which the primitive Church placed its mode, and in direct hostility to it, the word βαπτίζω has been explained of ablution or washing. The early Church position was,

Christ said, "Go ye therefore and teach all nations, IMMERSING them in the name of the Father, and of the Son, and of the Holy Ghost."

The position of many later writers has been,

Christ said, "Go ye therefore and teach all nations, WASHING them in the name," &c. Mr. Beecher would substitute *purifying* in place of washing.

Now, although many, like Wall, who held the view of its meaning washing, still preferred and pleaded for immersion, yet he and they have failed; so has Bishop White, and wholly because men were taught that the command is not modal.

This will ever be the result. Suppose, under the Old Testament, the injunction to circumcise had been interpreted by the later Jewish doctors of some rite not one-tenth the trouble of circumcision, who believes, even although they assured the people that circumcision was the original, and in earlier times the universally received rite, that anxious parents would not plead the weakness of infancy, its liability to injury, and the bloody nature of the ordinance itself, and chiefest of all, the indifference of the rite, as compared with some abbreviation of it, in favor of the latter?

Of course we do not plead against the view of St. Cyprian, that in *necessity* divine compends may confer the full blessing; all we ask is, that he be not perverted to favor such compends where no necessity exists.

The view that Christ enjoined immersion has been held in our own communion by Palmer, Dr. Towerson, and Bishop Jeremy Taylor. But it is undoubtedly true that Wall, and many, if not most of our divines have leaned to or expressed the views that $\beta\alpha\pi\tau i\zeta\omega$ means in the command to wash, or that its signification is doubtful, or not modal. But the whole is matter of opinion. The Anglican communion, though enjoining immersion except in the case of necessity, states no ground for such injunction. Her authority therefore cannot be pleaded on either side. It is clear, however, that if her rubric ever be obeyed and restored, it will be by men who believe with Dr. Towerson, St. Chrysostom, Pope Pelagius, and the whole early Church. The trine immersion has never existed and never can exist where the idea is prevalent that the mode is not enjoined by God.

We do not propose to ourselves the task of refuting that interpretation which threatens to whelm the rubrics, as it has whelmed their injunctions, in ruin and silence.

Let one thing be cleared away forever, that on all rational grounds the Baptist sects and their position have nothing to do with this question. Their baptism is invalid.

There is no need, therefore, of resorting to the idea and the interpretation, if it deserves the name, that Christ went down into the river Jordan, or that he even wetted the soles of his feet to have a fillip of it on his head, or to cavil learnedly regarding the *possible* meaning of $\dot{\epsilon}\nu\ \tau\tilde{\omega}\ \ddot{\upsilon}\delta\alpha\tau\iota$, as though it were not sufficient that "in the water" is the only interpretation heard of for 1200 years after Christ, and that the other is the product of the crude and ignorant brain of some one within the few last centuries, or to prove that there was not water enough at Jerusalem to baptize the 3000 or the 5000, or that time would be lacking, as though immersion cannot be performed as quickly as sprinkling, or any other of the silly notions and, considered in the light of primitive interpretation, perversions of Holy Writ, which have abounded among a certain class of our dissenting brethren.

Suppose these interpreters to be brought front to front with the bishops and teachers of the early Church, and to ventilate their notions before them, can any man doubt their astonishment at being informed of what this late learning, which rests wholly upon suppositions and unproved possibilities, not upon facts, has seen fit to put forth? Poor creatures that these primitive Christians were, they never even heard these wise interpretations. Only think of Dr. Miller, of Princeton, teaching St. Chrysostom, and rebuking his ignorance of the proper meaning of $\beta\alpha\pi\tau i\zeta\omega$, in supposing it modal. Why the Doctor would have convinced the saint in no time that he was an ignoramus, and the testimony of Justin Martyr, Tertullian, and Cyril of Jerusalem, would have fared no better. But it might be said that they would be backed by the whole primitive Church. So much the worse for the primitive Church. Dr. Miller would have sacked them all as easily as Father Tom Maguire did the Pope, or as Dr. Carson, or Mr. Robinson show that the whole primitive Church, where it was so unfortunate as to differ from them as to infant baptism, were errorists and ignoramuses.

What our most learned divines have thought of Christ's baptism, and the general administration in the apostolic and in the primitive Church, is seen elsewhere.

CHAPTER XIV.

BAPTISTERIES. ANCIENT BAPTISMAL RITES.

These are intimately connected with the subject of the mode. But they have already been described by the masterly Bingham. The reader will do well to look at such parts of his Antiquities as relate to this subject. They may be found under "Baptisteries" in the index of his work. The late custom of placing the font in the church instead of in the baptistery began with the Latins, and is now almost universal in the whole West. Our rubrics do not require it to be in the church. It would certainly be more in conformity with the general custom of the Church, for the first thousand years of our era, to baptize in baptisteries. Indeed, the Catholic mode of administration would *require* this. The church is not the most suitable place for immersion. "The first ages," says Bingham, "all agreed in this, that whether they had baptisteries or not, the place of baptism was always *without* the church." Bk. viii, chap. vii. This he has substantiated by proofs from the Fathers. There is no reason why the act must be made so public as the Baptist sects amongst us make it. The rabble who often congregate at the water side are very different from the spectators at the baptisms of St. John the Baptist, and of the Apostles and their disciples.

Besides, there is a proverb about "casting pearls," &c. Of course where there is every probability that everything shall be done decently and in order, where the crowd is not great, or, if so, is composed of those who will treat the sacrament with reverence, it will be well to go "to the water," as they did in the days of Justin Martyr and Tertullian. The place of baptism is a question of order and of convenience, both which ends experience teaches will be best attained by following the primitive customs.

For an account of the ancient rites of baptism, see Wall,

Hist. of Inf. Bap., part ii, chap. ix; Bingham, books xi and xii; and especially Cyril of Jerusalem, Lectures to Catechumens, Oxf. trans., or original.

The student who wishes to see descriptions of the ancient baptisteries and their symbolism, may consult with profit Migne's Cursus Completus of the Fathers, passim.*

---

* On the size, form, &c., of the ancient and later baptisteries, see most fully in Ileck's Iconographic Encyclopædia, N. Y., 1851, vol. iv, pp. 127, 137, of the part on "Architecture," with the plates there referred to. v. in "Plates," vol. ii, plate 27, fig. 21–29, of the same work. Some modern works on architecture are defective on these points. They describe only the fonts in modern use, omitting wholly the baptisteries. On the Pisan baptistery, see Pictorial Gallery of Arts, London. 1847, vol. ii, p. 67, and fig. 381, p. 97. See on that of Florence, id. p. 97, fig. 379, and id. p. 55, as to the position of the baptistery of St. Sophia at Constantinople. See also Appendix G.

CHAPTER XV.

OF THE TESTIMONY OF THE GREEK CHURCH.

The witness of the Eastern communion, so far as respects Catholic tradition, is far more important than that of the Latin Church, and for the following reasons:

1. It has been more tenacious of ancient rites than the Latin Church.
2. It represents four out of the five ancient patriarchates, in which four the six ecumenical councils were held.
3. It contains every apostolic see mentioned in the New Testament except Rome, and it includes the mother Church of Jerusalem.
4. It has followed more closely than any other portion of the Church the *canons* of ecumenical councils.

By acknowledging the image-worshipping council of the wretched Irene as ecumenical, and by receiving its decrees regarding idolatry, she has put herself in the same position as the Jewish Church did when it added to the true faith a relative worship of images and other beings at the same time that they worshipped the true God. The Eastern Church has also its relative worship of images, and in practice at least it gives the Christian saints nearly such a position, so far as worship and intercession is concerned, as was given by the ancient Greek to the subordinate deities of his mythology, with this exception, that while the fact of the honor and worship paid is the same, the Oriental Church never calls the Virgin or the saints θεοί: in *name* then there is a slight difference, but not in *fact*. See Faber's Difficulties of Romanism, bk. ii, chap. vi. The idolatry is the same; and as the idolatry of the Jews brought down upon them the heavy judgment of God in the form of enemies who were allowed to subvert for a season their venerable polity, and to quench the flame upon their altar; so it has been with the Eastern Church. Saracen and Tartar and Turk have been the instruments of heaven in scourging her for her sins, until in ancient cities which saw the blessed Apostles, where Christianity was known from its very dawn, and where idolatry-hating martyrs and noble bishops have preferred the rack and torture to apostasy, the apostates and their descendants are counted by millions, and the Christians by handfuls. And yet amid all its errors the Greek admits no Latin purgatory nor Roman supremacy; and in the matter of rite, he has clung to old Christian usages with true unchanging Oriental pertinacity; and in this matter of the mode, his testimony is especially valuable, since, as we have shown before, his own writers from the earliest period in the history of the Church have always witnessed to the mode as one and uniform and well-defined, and of Divine obligation.

What the testimony of the Greek Fathers is, what the testimony of the ecumenical councils, we have before shown. We have also adverted to the facts that the "filioque"* and the single immersion were the things most complained of by the Greeks against the Latins.

We purpose here to state what is their present belief and practice.

The only authority which the Eastern Church regards as final, is an ecumenical council. By examining, as we have already done, the testimony of the seventh canon of the second ecumenical council, and Canon 50 of the Apostles, we have already seen what she *now recognizes as authority.*

But we will go farther, and descend to a later period.

The Confession below quoted is assented to by both the Greek and Slavonic branches, which constitute the whole Eastern communion. It is the Oriental Church that speaks, not one individual in her pale. It is the voice of all.

"Orthodox Confession of the Catholic and Apostolic Eastern

---

* We speak not of the doctrine, but of the mode of its attempted enactment; that is, by a part of the Church wrongly arrogating to itself the authority which God gave to the whole. Bishop Pearson has some judicious remarks on this; v. On the Creed, p. 488, n., ed. N. Y. 1853. "Thus did the Oriental Church accuse the Occidental for adding *filioque* to the Creed, contrary to a general council which had prohibited all additions, and that without the least pretence of the authority of another council; and so the schism between the Latin and the Greek Church began and was continued, never to be ended until those words καὶ ἐκ τοῦ Υἱοῦ or *filioque*, are *taken out* of the Creed." v. the whole.

Church," Part 1, Question 102. "What is the first mystery, —the sacrament of Baptism?"

"Answer. Baptism is a washing away of, and a removal of original sin, by means of the trine immersion in the water, the priest saying these words: In the name of the Father, Amen, and of the Son, Amen, and of the Holy Ghost, Amen."

The following, from the "Doctrine of the Russian Church," is of the same tenor. The translation is that of Blackmore, an Anglican clergyman.

The Primer, p. 8. "I came up clean and sinless from the water."

Shorter Catechism, p. 21. "In what consists baptism?"

"Answer. In this, that the believer is dipped thrice in water, in the name of the Father, and of the Son, and of the Holy Ghost."

Longer Catechism, p. 84. "What is baptism?"

"Answer. Baptism is a sacrament, in which a man who believes, having his body thrice plunged in water, in the name of the Father, the Son, and the Holy Ghost, dies to the carnal life of sin."

"What is most essential in the administration of baptism.

"Answer. Trine immersion in water, in the name of the Father, and of the Son, and of the Holy Ghost."

Two distinguished members of the Russian part of the Orthodox Church will serve to dissipate whatever errors have prevailed, regarding the views of their communion.

The first is Alexander de Stourdza, the Imperial counsellor, who published against the attacks of the Latins, his work entitled "Considérations sur le Doctrine et l'Esprit de l'Eglise Orthodoxe." Stuttg. 1816.

The second is Macarius, a doctor in Divinity, Bishop of Vinnitza, and Rector of the Ecclesiastical Academy of St. Petersburg, in the work, in two volumes, "Théologie Dogmatique Orthodoxe," Paris, 1860.

ALEXANDER DE STOURDZA, "Considérations sur le Doctrine et l'Esprit de l'Eglise Orthodoxe, par Alexander de Stourdza."
—"It is painful to say it. The attacks carried on by the Western Church against the integrity of the sacraments of baptism and the eucharist, are of a more serious nature than is supposed, in that they establish a tyrannical restriction on the blessings of Jesus Christ, and put obstacles in the way of unity of communion among the faithful." Page 94.

"Let us sum up what has been said above. 1st. That the Western Church had separated herself from the Primitive Church, her cradle, by causes inherent to the state of error into which she was plunged. 2d. That this was a cutting off of the diseased part, and not a separation of two parts equally healthy. 3d. That the state of decay and dissolution of the Western Empire, powerfully contributed to distort this portion of Christianity. 4th. That the authority of the See of Rome, the principal means of this separation, has been able to increase only by means of trouble, of ignorance, and of anarchy. 5th. That a crowd of secular causes and of germs of enmity between Greece and Italy, have concurred to produce schism, which existed in fact before it was openly declared. 6th. That the ambition of sundry pontiffs encouraged on both sides these germs of discord. 7th. That Divine Providence wished to try the Orthodox Church, and to preserve it from all share in subsequent heresies, in delivering it to the iron rule of the Ottomans." Page 169.

"The institution of Baptism, then, is not an indifferent or arbitrary thing. It presents entire harmony between the laws of nature and those of revelation, as does all which has been founded by the Divine Mediator. 'Go and teach all nations,' said the Son of Man, 'and baptize them in the name of the Father, and of the Son, and of the Holy Ghost;' which is equal to saying in other words, 'Go and spread abroad the word of God, the Saviour for all races, which have fallen by the sins of their forefathers; *plunge* (plongez) *them* in living water, a symbol of the primitive state of their affections and of their passions, rebellious after the fall, and by the invocation of the threefold essence of the Divinity, work in the inner man the miracle of eternal alliance between the Creator and the creature.' In His quality of representative of human nature, Jesus Christ subjected Himself to the office of baptism in the waters of Jordan.

"So let us contemplate with gratitude our Divine Redeemer, when He received from the hands of a passive instrument of His adorable will, the baptism of regeneration and life. This sight will suffice to convince us that the Orthodox Church is the only one which has remained faithful to the example of its Divine Master, and which administers this sacrament in all its primitive purity. The Lord is in the desert, for man is alone in the midst of creation when he is not with God.

He is plunged in the torrent of living water, the emblem of a transitory existence, and of the tumult of the passions. He is buried beneath the waves, to typify the shipwreck of the human race, and goes out of this agitated tomb in order to be raised in the air, the type of the region of intelligence, which reveals to us the necessity of traversing the storms of the passions, before we are exalted to a heaven without storms. The Holy Spirit, under the form of a dove, the symbol of the primitive purity regained by baptism, overshadows the Son of Man, and as soon as the silence of creation is broken, the wilderness, until then dumb with grief, repeats a thousand times the accents of that Divine expression: 'This is my beloved Son, in whom I am well pleased;' the stains are effaced, the adoption is accomplished, and the vivifying forces of regeneration penetrate all the depths of space.

"Yes, Lord, it is for this that we cry to Thee 'out of the depths,' as says the kingly prophet, and that we affirm with confidence, that 'he who believes and is baptized, shall be saved.'

"The distinctive character of the institution of baptism is then *immersion*, βάπτισμα, *which cannot be omitted without destroying the mysterious sense of the sacrament, and without contradicting at the same time the etymological signification of the word which serves to designate it.*

"The Church of the West has then departed from the example of Jesus Christ; she has caused to disappear all the sublimity of the outward sign; in fine she commits an abuse of words and of ideas in practising *baptism by aspersion*, the mere statement of which is in itself a ridiculous contradiction. In effect the verb βαπτίζω, immergo, has only one acceptation. *It* SIGNIFIES, LITERALLY *and* ALWAYS (plongez), TO PLUNGE.* Baptism and immersion are then identical, and to speak of *baptism by aspersion*, is as if we said *immersion by aspersion*, or any other contradiction of the same kind. Who would, after this statement, refuse his assent, or hesitate to pay homage to the wise fidelity of our Church, always immovably attached to the dogmatic tradition and ritual of primitive Christianity. She alone has preserved the profound sense as well as the imposing forms of the initiatory sacrament, and we have only to

---

* See all the lexicographers, the fables of Æsop, the more modern writers, the Fathers of the Church. (De Stourdza's note.)

read in the annals of the first centuries, the description of baptismal ceremonies through which the catechumens passed, in order to be struck with their perfect identity with our present rites.

"So simple and clear an agreement has surely not escaped the doctors and writers of the Roman Church. But they, perhaps, believe that it suffices to turn away the eyes from evidence in order to destroy its effect. We will only quote here in passing the celebrated author of the 'Génie du Christianisme,' who, in speaking of baptism, enlarges greatly on the practices of the primitive Church in the administration of this sacrament. Now these practices are exactly the same as those which are now observed by the Orthodox Church. Nevertheless, the apologist for the beauties of religion takes care to make no remark on this for the instruction of his readers. He even pushes his ill faith (for we cannot suppose it ignorance) so far as to appear to admire at a distance these beautiful and ancient forms of baptism as having fallen into disuse. He speaks of them only as if these were obsolete practices, and he affects to doubt whether they are still in force. Can we suppose with any probability that M. de Chateaubriand could be ignorant of the truth? And if he were informed of it, is his reserve pardonable? Was he right in concealing from his readers that, at the present hour, nearly sixty millions of Christians yet administer baptism in imitation of that of Jesus Christ, of the Apostles, and according to the institutions of the primitive Church? Let any impartial man judge after that if these people merit any confidence, who, directed by a sectarian spirit, despise all the gifts of the Spirit of peace, of concord, and of truth." Page 85.

MACARIUS, in his "Theologie Dogmatique Orthodoxe," vol. ii, p. 376. "By the word baptism is understood the sacrament by which sinful man, born with the taint of hereditary corruption from his first parents, is 'born again of water and the Holy Ghost' (John 3 : 5), or, to speak more particularly, in which the sinner, instructed in the Christian faith, immersed thrice in the water (immergé par trois fois dans l'eau), in the name of the Father, and of the Son, and of the Holy Ghost, is purified by divine grace from all sin, and becomes a new man, justified and sanctified. (Conf. Orth., p. 1, ans. 102.)"

Again, p. 385, he continues: "Baptism ought to be administered by plunging the candidate three times in the water: three times according to the Apostolic Canon (Canon 50) and the doctrine of the ancient doctors of the Church, in the name of the three persons of the holy Trinity, as a memorial of the death, burial, and resurrection of the Lord Jesus; besides, the Church has decided that the baptism of Eunomians and of other heretics, which was administered by one immersion, is invalid.

"Immersion, that is the plunging of the catechumen in the water, is *necessary*,

"1. Because Christ was thus baptized by the Baptist (Matt. 3 : 16; cf. Mark 1 : 5; John 3 : 23).

"2. Because the holy Apostles thus baptized (Acts 8 : 37, 38).

"3. Because baptism is represented in Scripture as being an exact likeness of the universal deluge, 'the like figure (ἀντίτυπον), whereunto even baptism,' says the Apostle St. Peter (1 Pet. 3 : 19–21), as 'the washing of water,' by which the Saviour 'cleanses' us (Eph. 5 : 26; Tit. 3 : 5), and as a grave in which we are buried with Christ into death (Rom. 6 : 4; cf. Col. 2 : 12). All these are expressions to which the sacrament will correspond only when it is administered by immersion.

"4. Finally, because by the avowal even of the heterodox, the ancient Church thus administered this sacrament, as Saint Dionysius the Areopagite, Tertullian, Saint Basil the Great, Saint Gregory Nyssen, and others, indisputably attest.

"As to aspersion, the form in which the Church of the West at this day ordinarily administers baptism, it should be observed that it was admitted anciently only as an exception to the rule, in cases of *absolute necessity*, and most of all for bedridden invalids (called *clinics*, from κλίνη, a bed), who were unable to be baptized by immersion; and it is to be noted that even in the third century this form of baptism was, among some, still a subject for dispute, to a certain class of whom St. Cyprian deemed it his duty to write, in order to remove their uneasiness, that the sacrament of baptism lost nothing of its force from being thus administered. So the Orthodox Church to this day, in acknowledging that aspersion in the administration of baptism diminishes nothing of the force or virtue of the sacrament, nevertheless admits this form only in cases of urgent need, and solely as an *exception* to the general rule."

See also the citations in his notes for learned and able references, which amply bear out all the above.

The Easterns, while thus agreeing in the requirement of trine immersion in ordinary cases, and as the rule, yet, as Macarius says, admit sprinkling in cases of necessity, and practise it themselves.

And so far does this principle of necessity apply, that Metrophanes Critopoulos, Patriarch of Alexandria, in his "Confession of the Catholic and Apostolic Church in the East," cap. vii, ad fin., teaches that "when necessity urges, the child is baptized immediately after its birth. And if a presbyter be not present, the midwife performs the baptism, and repeats the divinely enjoined words. And if the child gets well, it shall rest content with this baptism." And again, cap. xxii, id., he testifies that in such case every ceremony is not essential, but may be dispensed with. And a Greek (not a Russian) testifies that the compends are allowed in cases of necessity, although he strongly opposes them in any other case. And this, too, while himself expressing a doubt of such baptism. "These last forms (sprinkling or washing) are not, properly speaking, baptism; but, as Saint Cyprian says, they are a species of abbreviation of the one and only baptism in which we believe, and which, as Saint Thomas Aquinas attests in terming it *tutum*, is alone authentic. Exceptional baptism is not true baptism, unless by faith it is placed in relation to its prototype, whence it derives all its sanctifying virtue; and it is admitted only in case of inevitable urgency, and even then the efficacy of such baptism is doubtful." (v. "Orthodoxie et Papisme," p. 87.)

The above language occurs in controversy with a Latin, and may be taken as a type of the most violent feeling and thinking on this subject in the Patriarchates. It should be remembered, however, that it is condemned by the great bulk of the Easterns. The formularies of the Russians differ, as will be perceived, very widely from this extreme view. So far as the point of the efficacy of a compend is concerned, it may well be doubted whether it would be approved, even among the more impartial of the Greek clergy of Constantinople. At any rate, it is condemned by four-fifths of the whole communion to which the writer belongs. Even he admits its *use* in necessity. Were every case of compendious baptism which has occurred in the Eastern Church, deemed without efficacy, what countless myriads, whose number has been accumulating among whole nations since the early ages, would be cut off from covenant mercy. Such a principle in any part of the Church is, in a greater or less degree, suicidal. This opinion of the author is a private one. It is not expressed in the formularies of even the Greek part of the Oriental Church. And Palmer states positively, that even among them it is "the fact, that the Church allows clinic baptism without immersion on the ground of necessity, but forbids so to baptize in cases where she sees no necessity." And indeed for hundreds of years (v. above, pp. 97, 98), even the Greeks in the Patriarchates admitted persons baptized by the compends as validly baptized, and used the compends to some extent themselves, as they do even now. (v. p. 164, 165, above.)

It should be remembered, too, that while the *Greeks* reject Latin baptism on account of the lack of trine immersion, nevertheless, this is not the only reason. The Constitution of 1756 expressly styles them heretics. On this account alone, even were such baptism rightly performed, they would regard it as null.

Indeed, Macaire, as already quoted, testifies to the fact, that the "Orthodox" Church (he does not limit the expression), receives the compends as valid baptism.

The Russians, as will be seen, admit the baptism of Westerns, even when the compends have been used. On p. 209 of the "Doctrine of the Russian Church," occurs the following "On the Duty of Parish Priests:"

"There are some ignorant men among the clergy, who would rebaptize Romans as well as Lutherans and Calvinists, when they come over to the Eastern Church, while the schismatics among ourselves are not ashamed even to rebaptize those of their people who fall away from the Church in order to go over to their errors. But the seventh canon of the second ecumenical council sufficiently condemns both the ignorance of the first and the blindness of the last; for that holy council, in the canon cited, forbids to rebaptize not only such as the Romans, Lutherans, and Calvinists (who all clearly confess the Holy Trinity, and admit the work of our salvation accomplished by the incarnation of the Son of God), but even the Arians themselves, and the Macedonians or Pneumatomachi, with other heretics named in the same canon, and orders that they should only be made to renounce and anathematize both their own and all other heresies, and so be received by unction with the Holy Chrism." This was put forth in 1833. v. id. p. 144.

This is the *present law* of the Russian Church, which comprises about four-fifths of the whole Eastern Catholic communion.

But the same Church, or rather the remaining fifth of it, included in the Patriarchates of Constantinople, Alexandria, Antioch, and Jerusalem, looks upon Latin baptism and Latin ordination also as invalid.

On this whole subject, the work of Palmer the deacon (Diss on Orth. Comm.) is perhaps the best thing. At times he may lean more than he ought to the Latins, and certainly he sometimes fails to give the ancient doctrines against Latin or Greek error, or both, their relative importance. Yet he brought to his subject much erudition, and this he had improved by personally visiting the East. The reader who is curious in such matters may find an account of Greek baptism in "Baird's Modern Greece," p. 98. Some of the statements are warped by his prejudices, while others show an ignorance of the fact, that some of the rites of which he so irreverently speaks, have been used from the days of Justin Martyr or the Apostles. The work is a *popular* one, but it contains, nevertheless, one of the best accounts that we possess of Modern Greece and its Church. Palmer in some parts of his work shows his Latinized tendencies.

He is to be distinguished from his illustrious namesake.

We have thus given in the words of the Easterns themselves, their own tenets and differences. There are so many misstatements current, that this seemed the best course. Of course, the single immersion of the Baptists, the Greeks would treat as defective. They require trine immersion. Some Baptist writers (unintentionally or ignorantly it is to be hoped), have given a false impression as to the views of the Easterns. They are as strenuous for trine immersion as for immersion itself. Indeed, the dispute between them and the Latins, at the time of the separation, was concerning the number of immersions, rather than concerning the general or ordinary use of sprinkling or pouring; for the Latins were not guilty of this fault until later. While on the other hand it is certain that in Spain the Latins, at the end of the sixth century, had, for a time at least, changed the old mode, and brought the single immersion into ordinary use, and although even in Spain the trine was restored, yet in the eleventh century it is plain, from the remonstrances of the Greeks, that some of the Latins, swayed perhaps by the mere opinion of Gregory the Great, were disposed to treat the number of immersions as a matter of indifference, and some went even so far as to baptize by the single immersion.

It will be noticed, 1. That all the Easterns are agreed in requiring trine immersion as the rule, and in ordinary cases.

2. But that in necessity they all agree in admitting it as a substitute.

3. That they require trine, not single immersion, and that this last they regard as an infraction of the rule of divine baptism.

4. But that in the case of Westerns baptized by a compend, where no absolute necessity exists, although all agree in considering such baptism irregular, four-fifths admit it as valid baptism, while one-fifth reject it, and looking as they do upon the Latins as schismatics and heretics, they reject it from lack of trine immersion, *and* from its being administered by a heretic.

CHAPTER XVI.

WRITERS OF THE LATIN COMMUNION.

To some of these we have already referred. The learned reader will find the following quotations and references apposite.

PAUL MARIA PACIAUDI.—Robinson states that "this great man published by authority, at Rome, in the year 1755, dedicated to Pope Benedict XIV, a beautiful volume of Christian antiquities. His Holiness being fond of antiquities, admitted him to his presence, and took pleasure in examining his compilations. In the fourth chapter of the second dissertation, he speaks of the two baptisteries at Ravenna, and finds fault with the artist for pouring water on the head of Jesus. 'Nothing,' exclaims he, 'can be more monstrous than these emblems! Was our Lord Christ baptized by aspersion? This is so far from being true that nothing can be more opposite to truth, and it is to be attributed to the ignorance and rashness of workmen.'"

The following is a fuller translation:
"The Baptist pours water from a small vessel upon Christ's head. . . . But what monstrous notions do such representations convey! Was Christ the Lord baptized by aspersion? So far is this from the truth that nothing can be more contrary to it. This thing ought to be attributed to the error and ignorance of the painters, who, either because they are often ignorant of history, or because they deem themselves at liberty to be presumptuous in any respect they please, sometimes wonderfully misrepresent what they depict. . . . One follows the example of another, and the latter shuns not by proper correction the mistakes of the former."

"Praecursor vasculo aquam in caput Christi effundit. At quæ monstra nuntiant ejusmodi emblemata! Numquid Christus Dominus *adspersione* baptizatus? Tantum abest a vero, ut nihil magis vero possit esse contrarium : sed errori et inscientiae pictorum tribuendum, qui quum historiarum sæpe sint ignari, vel quia quid libet audendi potestatem sibi factam credunt, res, quas effingunt, mirifice aliquando depravant. . . . . alter ex altero exemplum sumat, nec prioris errata posterior apta correctione devitet."

JOSEPH DE VICECOMES, in his work on the Ceremonies of Baptism, lib. iv, cap. vi, as quoted by Robinson : "' I will never cease to profess and teach that only immersion in water, except in cases of necessity, is lawful baptism in the Church. I will refute that false notion that baptism was administered in the primitive Church by pouring or sprinkling.' He proceeds through the whole chapter to prove, and particularly refutes, the objection taken from the baptism of three thousand in one day by the Apostles, by observing . . . that it was a long summer day, . . . that the words pronounced in baptism were as long in the mode of sprinkling as in that of dipping, . . . that dipping might be performed as quick as sprinkling, . . . that many ceremonies now in use were not practised then, . . . and that even since several ceremonies had been added, many fathers at Easter and Whitsuntide had been known to baptize great numbers in a day by dipping.'"

DÖLLINGER, "History of the Church," translated by Cox, vol. ii (ed. Dolman, London), p. 294, speaking of "the first ages :" "Baptism was administered by an entire immersion in water; this immersion was three times repeated, as expressive of the faith in the Trinity, a custom which was ascribed to an apostolical ordinance, or to a command of Christ. In the East, . . . Eunomius, who referred his baptism only to the death of Christ, was the first who introduced the single immersion; so that there the Church, as we see in the 50th of the Apostolical canons, forbade this kind of baptism under pain of deposition. Baptism by immersion continued to be the prevailing practice of the Church as late as the fourteenth century."

CARDINAL BELLARMINE, in his "Disputationes," ed. Ingolstadii, A.D. 1601, tom. iii, p. 279.—"Significat autem βάπτισμα proprie immersionem. Ordinarie enim baptismus fit per mersionem, idque ad Christi sepulturam representandam, juxta illud, Colos. 2. 'Consepulti ei per baptismum.'"

CABASSUTIUS, in his "Notitia Ecclesiastica," Lugduni, 1690, p. 28. "Ritus baptizandi antiquissimus et communis erat per trinam immersionem, quam indicat apostolus, Rom. 6. 'Consepulti enim sumus cum Christo per baptismum in mortem, ut quomodo Christus surrexit a mortuis per gloriam Patris, ita et nos in novitate vitæ ambulemus. Si enim complantati facti sumus similitudine mortis ejus, simul et resurrectionis erimus.' Eadem fere repetit, et commemorat, Colos. 3. Quamvis ergo immersio plus haberet incommodi, et pudoris, quia tamen plus habebat mysterii ob Dominicæ mortis, sepulturæ, et resurrectionis conformitatem, ac similitudinem majorem, erat in ordinario Ecclesiæ primitivæ usu ; neque adhibebatur infusionis ritus nisi erga periculose ægrotantes; nunc vero major habetur incommodorum corporis, atque pudoris ratio, simulque amovendarum tentationis illecebrarum, adeo ut ritus immersionis jam ubique propemodum exoleverit."

See also of similar purport,
THOMAS AQUINAS, Summa ed. Romæ, 1773, tom. viii, p. 3 ; Quaest. lxvi, art. vii, p. 232 and 233.
MURATORI, Antiquitates Italicæ, t. iv, diss. lvii, p. 843, ed. Mediolan., 1741.
MARTENE, "De antiquis Ecclesiæ Ritibus, Rotomagi," A.D. 1700, tom. i, pp. 127, 129.

CHAPTER XVII.

WRITERS OF THE LUTHERAN AND REFORMED CHURCHES.

Of these we select a few. The more learned writers of these communions have uniformly, or at least generally interpreted Scripture in accordance with the idea of the general prevalence of immersion in the Apostolic age. They have not, however, deemed the mode essential. The reader who is curious to see many of their views grouped into a brief space, may consult " Booth's Pædobaptism Examined," pt. i. Of course it should be remembered that Booth's motive was to favor his sect, and that while he quotes such parts of their works as favor the primitive method, he does not always give those in which they differ from him. Nevertheless, it is evident that the older and more learned writers of these communions differed from their American brethren, in admitting immersion as the general mode in apostolic and primitive times, and in so interpreting Scripture.

CALVIN (Instit. Rel. Chr. lib. iv, c. xv, § 19.)—" Et ipsum baptizandi verbum mergere significat, et mergendi ritum veteri ecclesiæ observatum fuisse constat."

LUTHER'S opinions on Baptism. v. as quoted above, p. 39, and opera ed. 1551, vol. ii, p. 76.

GERHARD, in his Loci Theol., t. ix, p. 147.—" In primitiva ecclesia trina immersio usitata fuit."

GEORGE CHRISTIAN KNAPP, D. D., Professor of Theology in the University of Halle, in his Lectures on Christian Theology, trans. by L. Woods, Jr., D. D., N. Y., 1850, p. 486.—" Immersion is peculiarly agreeable to the institution of Christ, and to the practice of the Apostolical Church, and so even John baptized, and immersion remained common for a long time after, except that in the third century, or perhaps earlier, the baptism of the sick (baptisma clinicorum) was performed by sprinkling or affusion. Still some would not acknowledge this to be true baptism, ... and controversy arose concerning it, so unheard of was it at that time to baptize by simple affusion. Cyprian first defended baptism by sprinkling when necessity called for it, but cautiously and with much limitation. By degrees, however, this mode of baptism became more customary, probably because it was found more convenient. Especially was this the case after the seventh century and in the Western Church, but it did not become universal until the commencement of the fourteenth century. Yet Thomas Aquinas had approved and promoted this innovation more than a hundred years before. In the Greek and Eastern Church, they still held to immersion. It would have been better to have adhered generally to the ancient practices, as even Luther and Calvin allowed. vide Storr. Doct. Christ. Pars Theoret., p. 291.

PHILIP SCHAFF, D. D., in his History of the Apostolic Church, N. Y., 1856, p. 568.—"Finally as to the outward *mode* of administering this ordinance, immersion and not sprinkling was unquestionably the original normal form. This is shown by the very meaning of the Greek βαπτίζω, βάπτισμα, βαπτισμός, used to designate the rite. Then again, by the analogy of the baptism of John, which was performed *in* the Jordan (ἐν, Matt. 3 : 6, compare 16; also εἰς τὸν Ἰορδάνην, Mark 1 : 9). Furthermore by the New Testament comparisons of baptism with the passage through the Red Sea (1 Cor. 10 : 2), with the flood (1 Pet. 3 : 21), with a bath (Eph. 5 : 26; Tit. 3 : 5), with a burial and resurrection (Rom. 6 : 4 ; Col. 2 : 12). Finally, by the general usage of ecclesiastical antiquity, which was always immersion (as it is this day in the Oriental, and also the Græco-Russian Churches), pouring and sprinkling being substituted only in cases of urgent necessity, such as sickness and approaching death." See also Liber Christianæ Concordiæ ed Lipsiæ, A.D. 1700, p. 329, v. in id. Catechismus Major, Pars iv, de Bapt., p. 548, and Catech. Minor, Sacram. Bapt. iv.

Some of the most distinguished Lutherans and Reformed

have expressed their regret that the ancient mode was discontinued, and have wished its restoration.

Duncan's Hist. of the Baptists has given quotations from many of them. (See pp. 206–211; Conant on Baptizein, p. 102, 103; Booth's Pædobaptism Exam. and Baptismal Tracts for the Times, p. 49–51.)

The two of most importance are Hagenbach's "Christian Church of the First Three Centuries," chapter xix, p. 324; and Matthies's "Baptismatis Expositio," p. 116.

Both refer to the change from the ancient rite as for the worse, and as tending to obscure the signification of the rite. "Lamented, indeed," says Matthies, "is it to be, that this rite has been changed."

CHAPTER XVIII.

THE ANTIPÆDOBAPTIST SECTS AND THEIR WEAK POINTS.

The history of the mode will be hardly complete, without a reference to those sects which have departed from the Church for various causes connected with baptism. Robinson (Hist. of Baptism, ed. Boston, 1817, p. 412), divides them into six classes. "There are," he says, "in general, six sorts of Christians, who have been called Anabaptists, *as different from one another as can well be imagined.* The first placed the essence of baptism in the virtue of the person baptized; the second placed it in the form of words pronounced in the administration; the third in the virtue of the administrator; the fourth in the consent of the person baptized; the fifth in dipping, and the sixth in both a profession of faith and an immersion."

The different sects of English and American Baptists, Regular and Freewill, Campbellite and Seventh Day, are reckoned by him in the sixth class; the Mennonites in the fourth. The impartial will do well to consult Robinson in this place, and Wall's account of the Antipædobaptist sects. The American Antipædobaptists deny all connection with the first five classes. Their principles, that dipping on personal profession after repentance and faith is necessary, force them to this. The first, second, third, and fifth classes admitted infant baptism, therefore, say the Baptists, such baptism is no baptism. The fourth use sprinkling or pouring, therefore it is no baptism. Of course since, even on the Baptist theory, baptism is the door into the visible Church, and since these classes do not enter it, they were never of it; they died without it.

Robinson's distinctions are sometimes forgotten. Benedict states clearly the marked antagonism between the Mennonites and the American Baptists, for he avers, "We can have *no fellowship* with their present mode of administering baptism, for with every true Baptist, pouring as well as sprinkling is *null and void."* It would tend much to lucid and just views, if these very necessary distinctions were borne in mind.

The burden of our remarks will be of the sixth class, since they constitute, with the trifling exception of the Mennonites, the great bulk, if not the whole of the Antipædobaptist sects in America.

A radical weakness of this system is that it necessarily rests upon these bases :

1. The visible Church had perished from the days of the Apostles until John Smith, at the beginning of the seventeenth century. The gates of hell had prevailed against the Church, and Christ's promise is made a falsity. He could not be with the visible Church, for there was none to be with.

2. After the visible Church perished, John Smith, in Holland, and Ezekiel Holeman in America, neither of whom on the Baptist theory were baptized, and hence not of the visible Church, nor sent of God to administer ordinances, had power and authority to found the Church and to establish a ministry, and such church would be Christ's Church, and such ministry would be Christ's ministry. Both these conclusions rest upon facts in accordance with this principle, common to the Baptists and to the Orthodox, viz. : Baptism is the door into the visible Church, and where it is lacking there is no visible Church.

For baptism is, as they say, a necessary rite in order to entrance into the visible Church. And they add further that the candidate must himself know and believe, or the baptism is null and invalid ; in other words, that infant baptism is no baptism, and that baptism must invariably be performed by immersion. Now from these premises they must prove a succession from the Apostles of churches of *baptized believers,* as they say, or else Christ's Church has failed. If the links in this chain be broken even for a single century, if the succession be traced even for a time through those baptized in infancy, or otherwise than by immersion, the whole chain is worthless to prove a succession. The chain is not only broken ; it wants links which are absolutely necessary to the Antipædobaptist system. If the Church has failed, the ministry has failed also. And who may claim to institute all these anew? Such a claim being extraordinary, would need extraordinary proofs. It could else lay no claim upon us to abrogate the old and to receive the new.

The immersing Antipædobaptists, or Baptists, first arose in Holland, in A.D. 1607. At least this is the earliest date that can be assigned.*

The mode prior to that period was not insisted on by the few ignorant fanatics who rejected the orthodox view as to the subjects. Indeed, no such question could have arisen in England until the end of the sixteenth or the beginning of the seventeenth century, and not in other parts of Europe for the first 1200 years or more. It should be remembered then that the Baptists differ from the other Antipædobaptists in making the mode *essential* and an article of faith.

The following, from an anonymous pamphlet, published by Burnett & Blodget, Providence, 1843, will serve to make more plain the points stated above.

"An Enigma for the People.

"According to Indian mythology, the earth stands on the back of an elephant, the elephant on the back of a huge tortoise. *But what does the tortoise stand on?* It was not for being a *Baptist* that he (Roger Williams) was expelled (from Massachusetts), for he *was not* one at that time, nor did he become one until after having left the colony, but for his peculiar opinions and tenets touching other matters; opinions and doctrines dangerous to the safety and welfare of the community. He publicly preached against and denounced the *King's Patent*, under which the colony held its lands; denied the right of the magistrates to punish for any offences except those against the *second* table of the law; reprobated the calling of *natural* or unconverted men to office, and the official oath, and sternly denounced and refused to commune with the churches of the colony, *his own* not excepted, because they had in England communed with the Established Church, and would not now publicly repent of that sin; with various other tenets and doctrines equally at variance with the public sentiment of the community, and subversive of the principles on which the colony was founded. He came over to this country strongly tinctured with fanaticism, and under the tuition of

---

* But see Appendix I—N.

Mrs. Hutchinson, the first *female lecturer* in the colony, his radicalism rapidly developed itself, until the civil arm was provoked to interfere, and he was ordered to leave the jurisdiction; whether justly or unjustly, we do not say, but only that *it was not* for being a Baptist. It was not until *four years after leaving the colony* that he embraced the peculiar views of that sect."—Haven's Discourses on Baptism, p. 47, note.

Who Baptized Roger Williams? Baptizing in a Circle.

"The wife of one Scott being infected with Anabaptistry, and going the last year to live at Providence, Mr. Williams was emboldened by her to make open profession thereof, and accordingly was rebaptized by one Holeman (the name of Roger Williams's immerser is sometimes spelled Holeman, sometimes Holliman), a mean fellow, that went from about Salem; then Mr. Williams rebaptized him, and some ten more."—Mass. Hist. Coll., vol. vi, p. 338.

The following is an extract from the history of the Baptist Church at Providence:

"Being settled in this place, which, from the kindness of God to them, they called Providence, Mr. Williams and those with him considered the importance of Gospel union, and were desirous of forming themselves into a church, but met with considerable obstruction. They were convinced of the nature and design of believers' baptism by immersion, but, from a variety of circumstances, had hitherto been prevented from submersion. To obtain a suitable administrator was a matter of consequence. At length the candidates for communion nominated and appointed Ezekiel Holliman, a man of gifts and piety, to baptize Mr. Williams, and who in return baptized Mr. Holliman and the other ten."

Upon this baptism, the Rev. Mr. Chapman, in his sermons, p. 262, remarks: "According to the doctrine of our Baptist friends, the only right mode of initiation into the Church is by the actual submerging of the whole body, in the name of the Father, and of the Son, and of the Holy Ghost. But of the twelve persons above referred to, not a single one had so passed beneath the waters. Upon their own principles they were consequently aliens from the visible Church, being neither ministers nor members thereof. And yet notwithstanding this, notwithstanding the difficulty lying heavy upon their own minds, occasioned by the absence of an authorized administrator, these individuals at length determined to surmount an *insurmountable* obstacle, and posterity are invited to survey them in the most puerile of all puerile attitudes. One of their number, not a member of the Church, undertakes to admit a second by immersion into the sacred inclosure, and then this second very kindly admits the one who had admitted him, with ten of his associates, to the same high privilege. Certainly, brethren, a more extraordinary spectacle was never exhibited by men having the smallest pretension to either reason or religion. Here is a baptism more invalid than lay, for like reasoning in a circle, it is baptizing in a circle, commencing with the unbaptized. I hazard nothing in saying that there is not a Baptist Church in the country which would *now* tolerate a ceremonial so utterly absurd and inefficacious. It would be denounced by all as freely as was the Otis plebeian ordination." Thus, in March, 1639, *originated* the first Baptist Church in the United States.

But as the Baptists, when urged with the invalidity of immersion originating in the lay immersion of Roger Williams by Holliman, do sometimes intimate that the Roger Williams' church is not the mother of all the close communion churches in this country, a few historical facts will be added to show their origin in England.

"The first regular congregation of English Baptists appears to have originated from certain English Puritans who returned from Holland after the death of their pastor, Rev. John Smith, who died in 1610." Mosheim vol. iii, p. 472; ed. N. Y. of Murdock, note (10); and id. p. 219, note 35.

In Young's Chronicles of the Pilgrims, p. 450 and 451, we read that "he (Mr. John Smith) first fell into some errors about the Scriptures, but afterwards was drawn away by some of the Dutch Anabaptists, who finding him to be a good scholar unsettled, they easily misled the most of his people, and others of them scattered away. Being at a loss for a proper administrator of the ordinance of baptism, *he plunged himself*, and then performed the ceremony upon others."

But to return to Roger Williams. Morton, in his Memorial of New England, published in 1669, says Mr. Williams and others, who first settled in Providence, "had not been long together, but from rigid separation, they fell to Anabaptistry, renouncing the baptism which they had received in infancy, and taking up another baptism, and so began a church in that way; but Mr. Williams stopped not *there long*, for after some time, he told the people that followed him and joined with him in a new baptism, *that he was out of the way himself*, AND HAD MISLED THEM, for he did not find that there was any upon earth that could administer baptism, and therefore their *last baptism* was a NULLITY as well as their first, and therefore they must lay down all, and wait for the coming of the Apostles."

In the Mass. Hist. Coll., vol. vi, p. 338, after stating that Holeman rebaptized Mr. Williams, the history continues: "Then Mr. Williams rebaptized him and some ten more. But soon after, one of their company, of the like capricious brain, started *this* objection, which none of them could answer, viz.: if they renounced their former baptism because it was antichristian in its administration, then what right had Mr. Holeman to baptize Roger Williams? *which so gravelled* them all, both baptizers and baptized, that they turned Seekers, and so continued ever after." Allen in his Biographical Dict. says, in the later periods of his life "his (Roger Williams's) mind was so shrouded in doubt and uncertainty, that he lived in neglect of the ordinances of the Gospel. He did not contend like the Quaker that they were superseded, but found himself incapable of determining to what Church it was his duty to unite himself."

"It is a singular fact," says Haven, p. 48, "that Mr. Williams himself, perceiving the inconsistency of his principles with his practice, very shortly renounced all faith in his baptism, and told his people that they were not baptized, and never could be until some one could be found divinely commissioned to administer the rite, or who could trace back his baptism to Apostolic times; in other words, there was no such thing as proper baptism or a *proper* church on earth. So he lived, and in this belief he died. If all immersers (he should have said Baptists) were equally consistent, would they not do the same?

"It follows then, that they who deny the validity of infant baptism (and of all other modes except immersion), not only unchurch all other denominations, but they unchurch themselves; they nullify all baptism, consequently, upon their principles, none of any denomination are now properly baptized, and none can be properly baptized, till Jehovah shall favor our race with a new dispensation from heaven." Fowler, p. 100. Yet in view of all this, do not the Baptists *virtually* maintain that they are the only true Church of Christ, and that their ministry is the only Christian ministry? With them as with all others, no unbaptized person can be a member of the Church, consequently, they unchurch professors of all denominations; they unchurch all churches not baptized by immersion, and with the same "jaw bone," they prostrate the ministry of all others from the ministry of Christ. For how can a man be a *minister* of the Church of Christ, who is not even a *member* of the Church of Christ? So with them, to be consistent with their principles, every immersed person not only can not be a minister of the Church of Christ, but can not even be a member of his Church. Such have been the wonders wrought by the lay immersion of Roger Williams, and the self-plunging of John Smith. Truly the earth stands upon the back of an elephant, and the elephant stands upon the back of a huge tortoise, but the question is, What does the tortoise stand on?"

Strictly speaking on the Baptist theory, such baptism as was that of Smith or Williams is not lay baptism, for neither of them, nor those who dipped them, were members of the visible Church.

Crosby, Ivimey, and later Baptist writers assert, that Smith did not baptize himself, but they suppose that some one who had not been immersed dipped him, and that then he dipped them in return. How this mends matters it is difficult to see, for they are all agreed that whoever among Smith's party commenced the operation of dipping others, had not himself been baptized, so that whether their supposition be admitted or not, it comes to the same thing, viz., baptism had been lost, and it was restored in 1607, by one man unbaptized (on the Baptist theory), baptizing another unbaptized man.

The case is thus stated by Crosby, Ivimey, and Brown, all Baptists.

The last, after stating that Smith had been a clergyman of the Church of England, but became a Brownist, and that he had left England for Holland, adds that during his stay at Amsterdam, he "became convinced that he must discard infant baptism. Consistency in separation from the Church of

England also demanded this; for if she were no true Church of Christ, her baptism could not be true baptism. Most of his brethren, including two ministers, Thomas Helwisse and John Morton, shared the same conviction. But where were they to find true baptism? Not perfectly satisfied with the Mennonites, they concluded that in a case of necessity, it was lawful to restore baptism among themselves. . . . . Accordingly, *Mr. Smith baptized Mr. Helwisse, and he in turn baptized Mr. Smith, who then baptized Mr. Morton and the rest.*" Baptist Family Magazine, May, 1860, p. 143. See also Crosby and Ivimey to the same effect.

We have then Baptist testimony as to this sacrilegious farce or travesty on the Divine baptism, as though the *administrator* were not as divinely appointed as the *mode*, and as though Christ in promising to be with His Church, made a promise which was falsified!! as though the Son of God were a liar!!! For there was no Church to be with, since there was no baptism, which is the door to it.

But yet miserable as is the plea in favor of Smith's not having baptized himself, it rests upon nothing but the merest supposition of Crosby and Ivimey, which the later Baptists, and Brown among them, too often receive, without inquiry, as facts.

The basis for this view, strange as it may seem to impartial minds, is drawn from the following words of Smith, in his work entitled "The Character of the Beast," &c., printed in Holland, A. D. 1609, p. 59.

Smith is arguing against Clifton, a Puritan, from whom he had separated on account of infant baptism.

"The Anabaptists, as you call them, do not set up a new Covenant and Gospel, though *they set up a new or Apostolic baptism*, which Antichrist had overthrown, and whereas, you say they have no warrant to baptize themselves, I say, as much as you have to set up a new church, yea, fully as much. For if a true church may be erected, which is the most noble ordinance of the New Testament, then much more baptism, and if a true Church cannot be erected without baptism, for baptism is the visible sign of the Church, as disciples are the matter; then seeing you confess that a true church may be erected, you cannot deny (though you do deny it in opposing the *truth*), that baptism may be also recovered, and seeing when *all Christ's visible ordinances are lost*, either men must recover them again, or must let them alone; if they let them alone till extraordinary men come with miracles and tongues, as the Apostles did, then men are Familists (for that is their opinion), or if they must recover them, men must begin so to do, and then two men joining together can make a church as you say. Why might they not then baptize, seeing they cannot conjoin into Christ without baptism? (Matt. 28 : 19; 18 : 10; Gal. 3 : 27.) But it is evident that all Christ's commandments must be obeyed, ergo, this commandment of having and using the communion of the Church, ministry, worship, and government, those holy means which the Lord in his mercy has given us in his covenant, and commanded us to use. And if all the commandments of God must be obeyed, then this of baptism and this warrant is sufficient for assuming baptism. Now for *baptizing a man's self*, there is as good warrant as for a man's churching himself; for two men singly are no church, jointly they are a church, and *they both of them put a church upon themselves*, for as both of these persons unchurched, yet have power to assume the church, each of them for himself and others in communion, so *each of them unbaptized hath power to assume baptism for himself and others in communion.*" See Ivimey, ed. London, 1811, vol. i, p. 117.

Now upon these words, Ivimey concludes strangely enough and in sufficiently positive language.

"The seceders (from the Puritans, *i. e.* Smith and his party) *must* first have formed themselves into a church, and then the church must have appointed two of its ministers to restore the ordinance by baptizing each other, and after that, to baptize the rest of the church."

That is, while he frankly admits the statement that unbaptized men *baptized each other*, and that such an act was meant to *restore* the ordinance, thus admitting that Smith claimed no succession, he yet thinks it desirable to assert that he was not guilty of self-baptism. And for this assertion he finds nothing more than these words; from these he draws the inference. Rather a strong conclusion from very narrow premises, or rather from no premises at all.

For the view that he baptized himself, we have the plain testimony of Clifton and Robinson, his acquaintances, and prior to his separation from them, his co-workers and associates. They resided with him in the same city, Amsterdam, at about the time when he "assumed" baptism.

They must, therefore, have known the facts in the case, and as they were Puritan ministers, who although mistaken, were yet so conscientious as to give up home and friends for what they deemed right, we can hardly suppose them to have iterated and reiterated a wilful falsehood. We have then,

1. In these *two* witnesses,* *knowledge* and *conscientiousness*, the most reliable traits in all testimony.

2. The fact that Smith, although repeatedly pressed upon this point, never denied the story, although he notices it.

3. The fact that he *justified fully* such an act, in the passage which Ivimey quotes. Both he and Clifton were separatists from the Church of England; they admitted and acted on the view that in setting up another communion, they were doing rightly, and yet, with reference to this very thing, he tells Clifton that "the Anabaptists" (himself and company) had "*as much*" warrant "to baptize themselves," "as you have to set up a new church, yea, fully as much." And this he repeats again. And indeed *his* language best agrees with the view that he dipped himself first, and the rest afterwards, after they had joined themselves together, perhaps, for that purpose. "Each of them unbaptized hath power to *assume baptism for himself* and others in communion."

Even the Baptist Orchard, Hist. of Eng. Bapt., p. 248, states, with reference to the charge of self-baptism against Smith: "We acknowledge that the point has never been satisfactorily cleared by his adherents." Crosby's work, which attempts on the mere supposition thus mentioned to clear away this charge, was not published until A. D. 1728, 118 years after Smith's death. Ivimey is even later. At the time when Crosby first published the story "said" to be by Kiffin, that person had been dead about thirty-five years —This fact does not strengthen the authenticity of the hearsay. The whole attempt, therefore, to clear him of this charge, which were it untrue he might have denied during his lifetime, is dictated by mere partisan feeling, and is wholly without just data. All the testimony involved emphatically condemns it.†

A word in conclusion of this poor erring founder of the immersing Antipædobaptist sects. Surely, few or none who hold his opinions as to the propriety of running without being

---

* Crosby adds "Mr. Ainsworth, Mr. Jessup, and some others do indeed charge him (*i. e.* Smith) with it," *i. e.* baptizing himself.
† See Appendix K.

sent, of making schisms on the subject of baptism, will indorse all his visionary novelties.

Wilson (Dissenting Churches, vol i, p. 28), states of him: "He entertained some absurd and enthusiastic notions, such as the unlawfulness of reading the Scriptures in public worship, that no translation of the Bible was the word of God," &c., "that the new creature needed not the support of creatures and ordinances, but was above them; that perfection is attainable in this present life." He further states, that Crosby fails to vindicate him from the charge of sebaptism.

Let the reader compare what is said of the heretic Eunomius in Socrates and Sozomen with what contemporaries say of this wretched heresiarch, Smith, and he will find, that in many respects, the faults of the former innovator were reproduced in the personal traits of the latter.

Even the Baptists, who are so hard pushed to find anything of their heresy in the ancient Church, or until Peter de Bruis, that they are ever ready to lay claim to any one, even though he smack strongly of Manicheism, do not altogether commend Smith.

Brown (Bapt. Fam. Mag., May, 1860, p. 144) states, that he was "not always sound in his opinions." Orchard thinks that "it is probable," that Smith's views "allowed persons of Arian views to communion." v. Hist. of Eng. Bapt., p. 249, n. His contemporaries speak not so gently. They speak of Smith as a "brute beast, a man of a wolfish nature," as "one whom God hath struck with blindness." v. Bapt. Fam. Mag., May, 1860, p. 143. Those who would see more should consult the writers mentioned above, and the references to his friends and opponents, in vol. iii, Murdock's Mosheim, notes on pp. 218, 219, and 472, and Neal.

His followers under Helwisse passed over into England after his death, and then commenced on English soil the work of schism and ruin.

Neal indeed, states, that his congregation perished with him, but the Baptists assert the contrary. v. Brown as above, and Orchard, Eng. Bapt., p. 247.

At any rate, these are the only immersing Antipædobaptists who make any figure in English history until A. D. 1633.* This last body constitute a different sect from the former. They are Calvinists. Its origin we shall give in the words of

* See Appendix X.

the Baptist Orchard (Hist. of Eng. Bapt., p. 249. v. also Crosby and Ivimey.)

"A congregation of Protestant dissenters of the Independent persuasion was gathered and formed in London, in 1616 (Neal, ii, 92), of which Mr. Henry Jacob was the first pastor; after him succeeded Mr. John Lathrop, who presided as minister in 1633. In this society, several persons finding that the congregation kept not its first principles of separation, and being also convinced that baptism was not to be administered to infants," and since they "believed that baptism was not rightly administered to infants, so they looked upon the baptism they had received at that age as invalid. They accordingly separated from the Independents, and set up a new body, with Mr. John Spilsbury for their minister, at Wapping."

As to the late account of Blount's being sent over into Holland to get baptism for this sect, Ivimey states, that it was not for Mr. John Spilsbury's congregation, which was the first Calvinistic Baptist Church in England, vol i, p. 145. From his account of the sending of Blount, the whole manner of his being sent at all may well be doubted Edward Hutchinson, who first mentions the circumstance, does not do so until 1676, and speaks indefinitely. He says, that when the Baptist sect arose in England, "the great objection was the want of an administrator, which *I have heard*, was removed, by sending certain messengers to Holland, whence they were supplied." v. in Ivimey, p. 142, vol. i.

Here it will be seen there is nothing said as to Mr. Spilsbury's congregation, and therefore, besides being mere *hearsay*, it is not to the purpose.*

Nothing is here said as to time or place, yet our author proceeds with as much confidence as though these were all certain.

---

* No date is stated, but if we adopt, as the Baptist Orchard wishes, the *mere supposition* that it is as early as 1633, one thing might favor the idea that Smith's followers, on their return to England, laid aside their views of immersion being essential (if they ever held it), and that there were no immersing Antipædobaptists in England at the date of the manuscript *said* to have been written by Mr. Kiffin. The expression is found in that document.

He states, that the persons who belonged to dissenting congregations about London, and who had become "convinced that believers were the only proper subjects of baptism, and that it ought to be administered by immersion, or dipping the whole body into water, . . . could not be satisfied about any administrator in England to begin this practice, because, though some in this nation rejected the baptism of infants, *yet they had not, as they knew of, revived the ancient practice of immersion.*"

"Crosby," continues Ivimey, says that "this agrees with an account given of the matter in an old manuscript, *said* to be written by Mr. William Kiffin." v. Ivimey, vol. i, p. 142. Then follows the account of sending over Blount.

Now Hutchinson's account may have been derived from the story of Smith, and the other story is at least not perfectly certain as to authorship or reliability. Indeed, nothing is clearer than that Ivimey did not believe that the bulk of the Baptists had received their dipping through the Mennonites, but that they invented it themselves. Thus he says, vol. i, p. 159: "It must be admitted that there is some obscurity, respecting the manner in which the ancient immersion of adults, which appears to have been discontinued, was restored, when, after the long night of Antichristian apostasy, persons were at first baptized on a profession of faith." Page 143, he quotes the following from Crosby: "But the *greatest* number of the English Baptists, and the more judicious, esteemed all this but needless trouble (that is, sending Blount over into Holland for baptism). . . . They affirmed, therefore, and *practised* accordingly, that after a general corruption of baptism, an unbaptized person might warrantably baptize, and so begin a reformation." Again, p. 146, he concludes, regarding sending out of England to Holland for baptism : " But as we are told that the greater number of Baptists, and the more judicious of them, considered all this to be needless trouble, it is highly probable that this *account refers to a few people*, rather than to the Baptists in general."

Again, p 146 : "These observations are made for the purpose of explaining and reconciling matters of fact, which have been generally misstated, and not as an apology for the conduct of our predecessors, since the Baptists of the present day unite with the greater part, and the more judicious of that time, in

---

This would give us 1633 for the date of the first Baptist congregation that ever existed. And since there is no proof that Blount had any connection with Spilsbury's congregation, and since this is denied by Ivimey, and since both Crosby and Ivimey assure us that most of the first Antipædobaptists immersed each other, when all were unbaptized on their notion and express assertion, it is clear that this must have been the case with Spilsbury and the founders of the sect in 1633. Their baptism, then, was reciprocal, like that of Holliman and Williams, six years after, in Providence. Indeed there is no proof that Spilsbury or his sect made the mode *essential* until A.D. 1644. Nothing of the kind occurs in the account above.

See Appendix L., M.

maintaining that after a general corruption of baptism, an unbaptized person may warrantably baptize, and so begin a reformation."

Collins, another Baptist quoted by Ivimey, proves nothing beyond the bare assertion, that he did not believe that *all* the Baptists received their baptism through Smith. From the Baptist accounts, Helwisse and the congregation which Smith founded, passed over into England, and "increased greatly in their number." Some of them, then, derived their baptism from his self-dipping, for it would be profane to call such an act baptism. It is very likely that Collins's remark may have been true in part, at least, so far as the great bulk of the sect were concerned, for they, as Crosby and Ivimey teach, acted on the principle (from what part of Holy Scripture it is drawn he does not inform us), that "an unbaptized man may warrantably baptize," and so when on their own theory they were unbaptized, baptized or rather dipped each other. But if they baptized each other, what does this advantage the Baptist position? The origin of the rite among them is human, not divine. The act itself was unauthorized. They usurped a mission which God never gave to any but the Apostles and their successors. If it be said, as it is sometimes, that Smith was a clergyman of the Church of England, and that some others of these people may have been at one time members, yet it should be remembered that Smith and the first Baptists assigned as a reason of their repeating baptism, that the sacrament in the Church of England was invalid, because received by them in infancy, and that true baptism and the true Church had ceased from the earth. If it was valid, why repeat it? if invalid, where did they get their authority to restore it? for unless they show this, we must believe that practise their single and Eunomian immersion as often as they please, it is not divinely appointed baptism.

Finally, as to the sending of Blount, we have seen on what a slender base rests this whole story. In addition, these difficulties lie in the way:

1. There is no clear proof that any body of the Mennonites deemed immersion *essential* when this sending is said to have taken place.*

2. It is clear that in A. D. 1607 there was no such sect,

---

* See Appendix I., J.

for one of Smith's reasons assigned for self-baptism is, that "all Christ's visible ordinances *are* lost." But if the Mennonites *immersed* adults invariably, or if any sect of them did so, this would have been untrue. Unless, indeed, he deemed their baptism as "assumed" like his own after it had been lost, an idea as fatal to baptismal succession through Blount. This was the charge against Smith, that finding no one on earth who had been *immersed* on a profession of his faith, he dipped himself.

But even if the Baptists could prove every part of this story, it would not avail them. They must have a line of administrators, immersed on profession of their faith, from the Apostles, or else their baptism is not Apostolic; it is human.*

The insuperable obstacles in addition to those just stated are:

1. The first deniers of infant baptism arose in the twelfth century. This is the difficulty as to the subjects.

2. There is no proof that De Bruis or any of the Antipædobaptists, from the date above-mentioned until John Smith, A. D. 1607, made the mode essential. This is the difficulty regarding the mode.

3. There is no clear proof of any well-maintained succession being kept up in the ministry of the Antipædobaptists before Menno. Those whom the Baptists claim as such were widely different, and sometimes bitterly hostile to each other. Some of them entertained the wildest notions, and erred on prime articles of faith. This with the foregoing affects their succession.

In much of the above, we have given the Baptist statements, even where they might be disputed, and were disputed or told in a modified form by their Puritan adversaries. We have corrected some statements of their later writers by those of the Baptist historians and others, who lived nearest the times of the events in question.

Smith and the first Baptists then founded new bodies which lacked

1. A ministry divinely appointed.
2. Administrators who derived their authority from the commission.
3. Baptism of divine appointment in the same commission.

In other words, they lacked what was absolutely essential

---

* See Appendix N., O., P.

to the very existence of the visible Church. Of course, authority derived from them is not divine authority. It is the plainest and simplest intrusion into divine offices. This is the necessary sequence of Mennonite and Baptist views.

Smith and Holliman, the author of the Baptist commission! an unbaptized man the author of a commission to the baptized! a man (on the Baptist theory) not a member of the visible Church, the founder of the visible Church!! a man without ministerial commission, the giver of a divinely appointed ministerial commission!!! And yet such are the views of men who profess to feel much for the attributes and prerogatives of Christ. Alas! that their intentions are marred by such fearful error and presumption!

On his own principles, the Baptist will be forced, if he will but divest himself of prejudices, to confess himself unbaptized, and without the right to administer it. Such an act on his part is a profanation of the sacrament. The words of Christ in his last communion are addressed to the eleven, and so far as we know, to them alone. THE ADMINISTRATOR IS AS DIVINELY APPOINTED AS THE MODE. The regular administration is by a divinely appointed ministry. Let him suffer a Churchman to be as strict in the interpretation of this part of our Lord's words, as he is in respect to the rest of the commission. Or if not, let him prove from these words of Christ that the ministry of the sacraments is given to the unbaptized, such as on the Baptist theory were the fathers of their error.

It will follow then, that the Baptist sects commenced with man, not with Christ; that their baptism and their orders being of human not of divine institution, are invalid, and that whatever may have been the early mode of baptism, they neither possess it themselves, or have authority to give it to others. Every such assumption is fearfully sinful.

In this we speak not with any feeling, but from a sense of duty. If we have spoken earnestly, it is because as God's messengers and witnesses to dying men, we cannot speak otherwise. We would gladly separate the error from the errorist. We cheerfully grant what must be conceded to all sincerity and good intentions. Alas! that these are so often joined with usurpation of divinely appointed offices, and even of the mission of the Church itself, and with a deification of their own unsupported private opinions, and with such radical and demoralizing notions, which, if successful, would overthrow the solid bulwarks of Christian doctrine, and rend the Church of Christ into a thousand hostile sects, and thus render the very name of Christian, already too heavily burdened, a hissing, a shame and contempt among Jews, Mohammedans, and Heathen.

Thus much has been said, because it is desirable at the start to disabuse the minds of those who have connected obedience to the rubrics with Antipædobaptist errors.

3. Another is their ignorant or careless misstatement of historical facts, and their perversion of the expresssions of orthodox divines.

Their later writers copy the ideas and often the words of the Antitrinitarian Robinson, whose reading, extensive in certain branches, was marred by gross ignorance or malign misrepresentation in others. Bitterness and scurrility mark his tone. To show how this scoffer blundered, let us take one instance out of many. The error is repeated servilely by the equally unreliable but more Christian-spirited Hinton. It is in relation to the testimony of Tertullian in De Baptismo, cap. xviii.

Hinton says, that "nothing can be more evident from the passage itself (De Bapt, cap. xviii), than that the error Tertullian is combating, is that of baptizing young children, not babes," and this he supports by Robinson's mistranslation of "norint petere salutem, ut petenti dedisse videaris." This he translates "They just know how to ask for salvation."

Below he boldly begs a question which he ought to prove, by stating that sponsors were not used as early as Tertullian's day for infants. There is no foundation for his assertion, in the original records of the early Church. Now for the facts: The word used is "parvulus," a diminutive from "parvus." If it does not mean infants, there is no word in the language which does.

The true rendering of the whole passage is, "Let them learn to seek salvation, so that you may seem to have given to one who asked." He does not say that "they just know how to ask." He contemplates their learning and their asking in the future. At present, they are "parvulos;" "norint" is not the present tense, and "just" is an addition. He admits that "most of the German critics receive" this passage "as evidence that *infant* baptism was then coming in." He adds, "After the most mature reflection, I apprehend the idea of

Robinson to be the correct one, and that in which all critics on further investigation will agree, that it was the baptism of young children, and not of babes, that Tertullian alludes to;" a clear evidence that the baptism of babes was not then practised, because children having been baptized when a few days old, the question of baptizing them "when they are just able to ask for it" cannot arise. Now whatever "mature reflection" Mr. Hinton may have devoted to this subject, it is evident that either he had not examined the original, or did not know how to translate it, or he would not have blindly followed Robinson's mistake.

Tertullian's isolated opinion on the subject is of little importance. It was not approved by the Church, and it is to be noted that he does not speak of infant baptism as "coming in." He combats an *established* custom. He nowhere censures it as a novelty. The whole of this part of De Baptismo is not directed against the *lawfulness* of infant baptism, but to show the *expediency* of delay, not only in the case of infants, but also in that of adults. The whole works of Robinson, Hinton, Orchard, and Benedict are full of such mistakes when they touch upon the *subjects* of baptism. Indeed, it would be very difficult to find anything like the same amount of mistake and misrepresentation among writers of any other communion. The fearful responsibilities of the Christian historian should prompt every future writer in the Antipædobaptist sects to remember that ignorance or misrepresentation should be studiously avoided.

The copious mistakes of the different Baptist historians, if, indeed, this term can be applied to works so full of misrepresentation, are abundantly met, even their later productions, in the exhaustive work of Wall, and in an abridged form in the excellent work of Hodges on Infant Baptism, to which the reader is referred for a true view of the Baptist mistakes, in attempting to prove that any held their views until Peter de Bruis. In conclusion, it is worthy of remark that the American and English Antipædobaptists must look in some other direction than the Mennonites to prove their baptism. For the Mennonites use pouring, as Brown, in the Encyclopædia of Religious Knowledge, witnesses.

4. Another point of weakness is found in their rejection of and abuse of the testimony of the immediate successors of the Apostles. Mr. Hinton (p. 204 of his History), in effect says,

that if this primitive testimony does not decide in favor of the Bible *as he* understands it, he will not receive it. His phraseology is different, but this is the idea. But when he rejects the testimony of the early disciples, he substitutes for them his own opinion!! Did Roman pontiff ever go farther? Did Roman pontiff ever dare to vilify the primitive writers, bishops, and martyrs, as do Robinson and Hinton? Now with regard to infant baptism, we admit this principle, that the Bible is the source of doctrine. But we contend that infants as well as adults are included in the commission to baptize.

Mr. Hinton says not. There is a difference. Who shall decide? God's Word, says Mr. Hinton. Agreed, say we. But, says Mr. Hinton, the *only means* of getting at the meaning of the New Testament, which I will admit, is *my own opinion*. We say let us see how the disciples of the Apostles, and their more immediate successors, understood it. Mr. Hinton and the Baptists say the Bible alone, as we, with our novel opinions, understand it. We say the Bible alone as it was understood by the earliest and best ages of the Church, when the spirit and the precepts of the Apostles were yet fresh, before error had entered. Which position is the stronger and the more reasonable, we leave the impartial to judge. There is not a Baptist who would profess that his own opinion regarding an historical passage in Cicero should override the consent of contemporary and immediately subsequent writers. It is only when warped by prejudice or religious matters that men are so unreasonable. A man *must* interpret the Scriptures by *some* criteria. If it is not the early testimony and the ecumenical councils, it will be the private opinion of some synod not universal, or the private opinion of the Roman bishop, or the private opinion of the person himself. This testimony, as it condemns all the novelties and departure from truth of the Baptists, so does it also those of Rome and Constantinople, so far as each has erred, as learned men have shown.

A favorite way seems to be to search some of the modern German authors until they find an *opinion* against the authenticity or genuineness of the writings of some father, and then to take this as final. And the German whom they quote will reason in this way, in effect at least: The New Testament seems to me to teach Presbyterianism or Congregationalism, but Ignatius teaches otherwise; therefore Ignatius, in those places in which he differs from what I would expect he ought to write, must be interpolated. If we reply that the most searching investigation fails to verify this view, but on the contrary abundantly refutes it, we are presented with these opinions nevertheless, as though in view of well-attested facts such opinions were worth a straw.

The truth is, that every sect in Christendom is ever anxious to bring out the full force of any early testimony which bears in their favor, but, in case they cannot make the primitive witnesses testify for them, they forthwith begin to rail at them as did the heathen populace of old. And the blessed martyrs who witnessed for Christ at the tribunal of the Roman magistrate, and whose warm blood soaked the sands of the arena because they would not deny their Master, are reviled as ignoramuses, or as men who did not understand the Gospel, although they had sat at the Apostles' feet. Or if they escape this worse than pagan usage, their writings are brought into discredit. They are stigmatized often without the slightest reason, as interpolated, but nearly always, be it remembered, only or mainly in those portions which are so unfortunate as to conflict with and to condemn the errors of the vilifiers.

Indeed, it would be well if the abuse had gone no further. The Holy Scriptures have been attacked. The same school from whom the Baptists are supplied have assaulted either the genuineness or authenticity of nearly every book of the Bible.

5. Another is the *source* from which they draw the support for their views.

Incapable of proving their cause from the primitive Church, rebuked and condemned for their awful error, they leave the original authorities and betake themselves to the Anti-trinitarian Robinson and the German writers of the naturalistic or rationalistic schools. But opinions prove nothing against facts. The original sources are the only authority. As an example of the worth of these opinions which contradict primitive testimony, let us take a single case.

Gesenius, who is quoted, page 223 of Hinton's History, against Infant Baptism, kindly takes Moses and the writers of the Old Testament in hand, and corrects what he conceives to be the mistakes of the inspired record. This man made no secret of his cherished unbelief. Even the Encyclopædia of Religious Knowledge, edited by Brown, a Baptist, after speaking highly of his learning, speaks of him thus: " His version of Isaiah, with a commentary, is one of the ablest critical works that have ever appeared; but, unfortunately, the neological views of the author have deeply tinged many parts of his exposition, especially such as relate to the prophecies respecting the Messiah. The last twenty-six chapters of the book he considers to have been written, not by Isaiah, but by some later author." Below the fact is stated: "He and Wegscheider take the lead of the naturalist party." And he is spoken of as "the speculating, unbelieving philologist." Yet the testimony of such a man is adduced against that of the early Christians!

It should be remembered, too, by the Baptists that the very same class of men whose mere and unsupported opinions against infant baptism are thought so much of, testify not only against it, but even against the Sunday as a divine institution, the inspiration, the authenticity, and the canon of God's Word, and even against the divinity of Christ, and the doctrine of the Trinity.

The learning of Robinson we have already commented on.

From really orthodox sources, the Antipædobaptists receive no countenance. And if they would but be more impartial and examine in full the writings even of Robinson and the Germans who favor them, they would find that sceptical tendencies regarding infant baptism are in almost every instance conjoined with sceptical tendencies upon the PRIME articles of faith. These Germans still hold to and practise infant baptism. Even those who are cited by the Baptists do not contend against it, but only against *some* of the grounds upon which it is placed, not against *all*. They deem that sufficient reasons exist for its practice.

The Baptists and all others who profitably investigate Ecclesiastical History can do it only in one way, *i. e.*, by patient and impartial investigation of the ORIGINAL SOURCES. It is impossible to write history without an animus. A man's education or prejudices are ever apt to warp his judgment. And this is as true of a German neologist as of any other. For the unbelief of such a man must appear when he leaves the region of facts and enters upon that of judgment. When he tells us not what was in the estimation of the early Christians, but what he thinks or does not think. It may be safely asserted that all the foreign divines who have deemed infant baptism *opposed* to the Bible and Christianity were infected with scepticism or disregard of early Christian testimony.

There is a day coming when men who write history from their own "inner consciousness," and who do not regard the historical testimony of the men who sat at the feet of the Apostles, will pass not for historians but for givers of their own opinions. Mosheim or Neander assure us that their own system of church polity is found in the writings of the Apostles. They mean that such is their opinion. But Ignatius, who was a companion of the Apostles, teaches the doctrine of the three orders. And this is the uniform testimony of all the early Christians. Even the Syriac recension of the Ignatian epistles retains some of the strongest passages in favor of the Episcopal office and power. Yet our non-Episcopal brethren follow the *opinions* of Neander, and reject the plain witness of Ignatius.

We judge from the Scripture account that Timothy possessed the office and powers of a bishop. It suits our brethren to make him only a presbyter.

Who shall decide between us? Who can so well as the immediate successors of the Apostles. There is surely nothing unreasonable in this. The Church in their day was pure.

Apply these same principles to infant baptism. We read the New Testament, and we find that an Apostle declares that "the promise is unto you and to your children." We find other passages of a similar tenor. Indeed, all the *covenanted* mercy of which the New Testament speaks is to the baptized. Now, from all these passages, we deem the baptism of infants scriptural.

But the Antipædobaptist reading the same passages draws a different and opposite conclusion. Has God appointed no judge in this case.

It is hardly to be supposed that any one, whatever be his prejudices, can fail to find in the New Testament passages which bind us to "hear the Church," and which speak of it as the pillar and ground of the truth. Do not start at this dreadful word "Church." It was used by our Saviour and his Apostles. It is not the Greek Church or the Latin Church, or the English Church, or the Lutheran Church which we are to hear, but τὴν ἐκκλησίαν, *the* Church, not a part of it. Now what has the whole Catholic Church of Christ set forth in her six universal synods as matter of faith?

Why, chiefly the Nicene Creed, without the Western additions, and one of the articles of this creed is, "I acknowledge one baptism for the remission of sins;" that is, as the council understood it, baptism for all—infants as well as adults. It was their doctrine that baptism is necessary to salvation. They found this one of the conditions which Christ had imposed, and they were not so liberal as to unsay it. They feared to alter what He had rendered by His omnipotent fiat unalterable.

But it may be that some whose minds have been abused by the common misrepresentations which claim for almost everything—error as well as truth—the variable and mediæval minutiæ of the Latin schoolmen, as well as the great doctrines, few in number, which alone have ecumenical sanction, may refuse to hear the Church. They may ignorantly and in simplicity fear that if they hear *the* Church, they must hear and obey all the private notions of each particular church.

If *the* Church teaches the use of a liturgy as the usual form, if in its canons it teaches the superiority of bishops to presbyters, if it condemns all image worship and creature worship, in fine all the errors which have crept into this or that part of the Church, they will not yet be satisfied. They still retain an undefined dread of the very word "Church."

But in that case let us follow the method of Wall. Let us find what is said on the subject of the baptism of infants by the writers of the centuries immediately succeeding the Apostles. They surely would be the best judges, we do not say of every passage of Holy Writ, but of what was the doctrine and practice of the Apostles in this matter, unless we suppose that the whole world went to bed some night stiff Antipædobaptists, and awoke shortly after so stiffly in favor of infant baptism that they actually deemed it essential to salvation.

The Christian literature of the second and third centuries, although not so voluminous as we could desire, still speaks clearly in favor of infant baptism, not as an addition, or as a "development," but as of Divine origin. There is nothing in all this period which is inconsistent with the idea of its general observance; all that remains plainly favors it, as Wall has shown.

And let it be remembered that the "onus probandi," the burden of proof, rests on those who dispute this rite. If the early Christians who, as Tertullian testifies, practised it were wrong, will not the Antipædobaptists tell us, by way of getting rid of the burden of proof, when it began, and who was its author, and how comes it that such a stupendous and radical change, as on the Baptist theory this would be, occurred with so little noise or struggle.

The value of the consent of the early Christians is by no means despised even among the more intelligent of the Baptists in other matters where that testimony favors them. Their writers are not slow to claim the suffrage of the Fathers in favor of immersion, and of the observance of Sunday as the Christian day of rest. On these points we are at agreement. On these points we practically say, the Scriptures as interpreted by those who had the best means of knowing the teaching and the customs of the Apostles. And this argument puts the Seventh day Baptist to rout. But let any Baptist impartially and candidly examine the question of the Sabbath on the principle that primitive testimony is to be despised or ignored, and he will find himself bound either to give up the principle or become a Seventh-day Baptist or an Antisabbatarian.

Indeed he might not be able to rest there. For as the "Bible alone" would, in that case, mean not the Bible alone as interpreted by apostolic men, but the Bible alone as interpreted by twenty or thirty jarring theories, not one of which was known for hundreds of years after the Apostles, he might be caught up by the next newfangled notion which comes along. There are but two principles upon which the Bible can be interpreted: one which, acting upon the common-sense maxim upon which we all act in ascertaining the meaning of an expression in an ancient literary production, or in legal works; or, to use an example which is familiar to all, in the Declaration of Independence. What should we think of a man who should reason against the *fact* of the existence of slavery in the country at the period when that instrument was drawn up from the expression: "We hold these truths to be self-evident, that all men are created equal; that they are endowed by their Creator with certain inalienable rights; that among these, are life, LIBERTY, and the pursuit of happiness."

In judging of the meaning of this expression, we uniformly consider the facts, the contemporary circumstances.

This reference to the facts and the interpretation founded on this reference, is designated in theology as the "Quod semper, quod ubique, quod ab omnibus," and we mark any doctrine or practice approved by it as being witnessed to "always, everywhere, and by all."

The other principle that this assent is unnecessary, that every man, so long as he chooses, may invent whatever doctrines or practices he pleases, even where they contradict this assent, has done more to distract and divide and to corrupt Christ's flock, to tear to pieces his seamless robe, to defeat his last prayer "that they all may be one," than any other. Those who most heartily indorse it suffer the most from it. This and the kindred idea of going beyond the few articles which *the whole* Church has approved have been the prolific source of evils which no man can number. The Greek and Latin communions, and the various more radical sects in their endless disputes and in their deplorable schisms, furnish the fearful commentary upon its adoption.

6. Another and a cardinal weakness in the theory and practice of the Baptists is their use of single instead of trine immersion. It has already been seen that no clear case of this mode occurs before the time of Eunomius in the fourth century. And that when, in the writings of Tertullian, the trine is first mentioned, it is as the established and usual custom. The words "Nam nec semel, sed ter, ad singula nomina in personas singulas tinguimur" (Lib. adv. Prax. cap. xxvii), "We are dipped not once but thrice, at the naming of every person of the Trinity," show not only that the trine immersion was the rule at the end of the second century and the beginning of the third, but also that the single immersion was not. The words seem to imply from his using it against Praxeas that even the heretical sect to which he belonged used the trine as well as the orthodox Church. The use of this custom in a controversy to establish a doctrine points clearly to its general reception, and these words above quoted occurring in the connection in which they stand show clearly that Tertullian believed it the mode commanded by Christ. "For," says he, "Christ gave it as his last commandment that they should immerse into the Father, and the Son, and the Holy Ghost, not into one. For we are dipped not once but thrice at the naming of every person of the Trinity," *i. e.*, we are thrice immersed *because* Christ commanded it. The "for" which begins the last sentence is plainly causative.

Of course it will be asserted at once that single immersion

was the original mode. But if we come to this conclusion it hardly seems in consonance with the preference exhibited throughout the New Testament for the frequentative βαπτίζω, and the fact that βάπτω is never used of the ordinance of baptism. But βαπτίζω is uniformly.

Another difficulty lies here. There were, in all probability, aged Christians in the Church in Tertullian's day whose memories, allowing some of them to have been seventy or eighty years of age, would have spanned (especially if we consider what they might have gleaned from their predecessors) nearly the whole period from Tertullian back to St. John. Now had any change in the administration of a rite which was deemed necessary to saltation been made, they would have known it. And it surely would have been reported to one who, like Tertullian, was a presbyter, and who took, as his works evince, the deepest interest in every custom which the Church held. By connecting the memory of aged people with that of their fathers, we can even now reach over nearly a century. Justin Martyr mentions that "there are many persons among us, of both sexes, of sixty and seventy years of age, who were made disciples to Christ from their childhood." As Carthage and North Africa were in close and frequent communication with Rome and the East, there is every reason to suppose that the Church was established there at a very early day. So that had any change been made, it seems remarkable that here and elsewhere not the slightest trace of it can be discerned. And it seems still more perplexing to find the presbyter Tertullian asserting that Christ gave the trine immersion in the commission to baptize.

Whether one agree with the early interpretation or not, since all admit trine immersion as baptism, it can be put forward as the only mode which can insure agreement among Christians, and as the surest and safest.

7. Still another and a very prominent error in their system is, that they hand all infants over to the *uncovenanted* mercies of God. Observe, we do not say that they deem them lost, but that they assert that Gospel mercy, that is, the only covenant mercy, has nothing to do with them. Their great authority, Carson, is thus reviewed by Dr. Schaff, on this very sequence from their views.

P. SCHAFF on CARSON. v. Schaff's Hist. Apos. Ch., p. 572, note 1. "And yet this is the inevitable consequence, nay, in fact the principle of the Baptist theory. Dr. Alexander Carson, its most learned advocate, openly declares (Baptism in its Mode and Subjects, p. 173), that children cannot be saved by the Gospel nor by faith. '*The Gospel has nothing to do with infants*, nor have Gospel ordinances any respect to them. The Gospel has to do with those who hear it. It is good news, but to infants it is no news at all. They know nothing of it. The salvation of the Gospel is as much confined to believers as the baptism of the Gospel is. None can ever be saved by the Gospel who do not believe it, consequently, *by the Gospel no infant can be saved*. When, however, the Baptists suppose, as they commonly do, that infants are saved, and saved without baptism, without faith, without the Gospel, they reject the fundamental principle of the Gospel, that out of Christ there is no salvation; that faith in Him alone can save.

"'Infants who enter heaven,' says Carson, l. c., 'must be regenerated, but not by the Gospel. Infants must be sanctified for heaven, but not through the truth as revealed to man.' (Is there, then, says Schaff, another truth besides the revealed, and could this be anything else than an untruth; and can such an extra and anti-evangelical truth save?) 'We know nothing of the means by which God receives infants, nor have we any business with it.' Fine consolation for Christian parents, especially at the grave of their beloved child!" The controversy between the Pædobaptist and the Antipædobaptist involves more than the mere baptism. The great question is, is there *covenant mercy* for infants? The Pædobaptist asserts the affirmative, and therefore admits them into the covenant by what both agree is the door. The Antipædobaptist holds the negative, and if like Carson consistent, maintains that " by the Gospel no infant can be saved."

If there be no ground in the New Testament for infant baptism this sequence is necessary: there is no ground in the New Testament for covenant mercy to infants, and Carson is right. If infant baptism is not included in the commission to baptize, then infant salvation by the Gospel is not. Only let every Antipædobaptist manfully like Carson teach this inference, and we have no quarrel.

As to the exclusion of a part of our race from the blessings of the covenant on account of age, v. Schaff's Hist. Apos. Ch., p. 572 et seq. His discussion is very valuable.

8. Another point of weakness is their departure from primitive doctrines.

a. The Apostolic ministry is disregarded.

b. The laying on of hands is forgotten.

c. The doctrine of the Trinity is openly denied by some of these sects.

d. Schisms have already separated them into no less than eight sects in the United States alone, excluding from the number the Mennonites.

e. Radical views with regard to the manner of worship obtain among them.

f. Various doctrines, as Calvinism, a rejection of the Trinity, &c., are made essential to Church membership by some.

Can any lover of Christ and His Gospel look with other than feelings of dismay and horror upon the destructive and demoralizing opinions which have produced results such as these within so short a space of time. Is schism no sin? Is there nothing in the New Testament against it? Are we never commanded to cultivate unity, and to mark those who cause division?

Already the Baptist body has disintegrated, and their disorganizing principles will make more and smaller fragments of them as time wears on. Some even deny the divinity of the Son of God. Well-meaning and pious men among them, who were sound upon this doctrine, have labored zealously and gathered congregations, which have since fallen into heterodoxy, even denying the Lord who bought them.

This has been a necessary fruit of their system. The principle of despising the *historical* testimony of the early Christians, and furnishing nothing conservative in its stead, is the first point of weakness in their system. Will not the more reflecting among their ministers and people see that they are frittering away their strength for no result; that their system is so radical and so opposed to early Christianity, that the first blast of heretical violence often dissipates the results of the labors of a lifetime. The people whom they have gathered, acting on the principles which their preachers have taught them, are led away now by Campbellism, and now by the errors of the so-called "Christians." And the end of these sects is not yet. It was an unwise and evil day when the Baptists left the sure grounds of Gospel truth and Apostolic order, in the Church of England and in the American Church.

CHAPTER XIX.

CONCLUSION.

In concluding we would call attention to the fact that Antipædobaptist sects have never arisen where the ancient trine immersion has been faithfully observed. Instances have indeed existed of heretical sects who have denied all water baptism. But these have nothing to do with the Baptists. In the pale of the great Eastern Catholic or "Orthodox" communion we find no evidence of Antipædobaptism.

And in the West we shall find that this error had no existence until ideas were somewhat loosened on the subject of the mode from the primitive strictness, and that even then it had comparatively little hold. But after the ancient mode was practically laid aside, we find it increasing in strength.

In England particularly we find few and faint traces of it. The earlier Antipædobaptists seem not to use the abandonment of the mode as a weapon; indeed, as they were Dutch, it is not unlikely that they symbolized with the Mennonites on the point of the indifference of the mode. The first *clear* case of the existence of a congregation which condemned as *invalid* the prevalent mode of sprinkling or pouring, as well as infant baptism, is ascribed to the year A D. 1607 or 1633.* At this time it is probable that the rubric in the Prayer Book which requires immersion, had come to be practically disregarded in the general practice. And since this period dates their greatest increase.

So thoroughly convinced of this was Wall, that he advocated the restoration of the primitive mode with the intention of taking away this strong point from them, and thus checking the spread of the contagion. Indeed, a Baptist (Orchard's

---

* See Appendix N.

History of English Baptists, p. 258, 259) states, in reference to the year 1632, that "The change now partially adopted in the administration of baptism from dipping to pouring awakened the attention of the thinking pious to investigate the grounds of Pædobaptism altogether."

This is preceded by the statement that "the sentiments of the Baptists about this time became diffused," which amounts to this, that many of the poor, ignorant people, foolishly connecting that disregard for the mode which came in with Puritanism with infant baptism, finally fell into schism, and some of them into a denial of Christ's divinity. And this process, owing to our sinful encouraging of late notions in preference to the clear meaning of the word and the belief of the early Church and our most learned divines, goes on still, to the rending of the Church, and the spread of heresy and schism. What account shall we render to Christ at the last day for the souls of those who have strayed away from truth and unity? Nothing will so much mitigate (I do not say excuse) the guilt of the schismatic, and nothing will so much weigh with condemnation upon Christ's ministers, the chosen guardians and depositaries of the sacraments, as unfaithfulness to their trust.

Peter de Bruis and his followers, who first started the heresy, did not insist on immersion alone. Their point of divergence seems to have been the subject, not the mode. And the general disappearance of these sects is a striking proof of the weakness of this position alone. But when, through the increase of unprimitive teaching, the ancient mode fell into disuse, these two points of the mode and subjects being combined, many who would otherwise have remained in the Church being convinced that the general use as to mode was wrong, were by this entrapped, and fell into schism and heresy. The great masses of men are ever prone in considering a question to take a part and not the whole. Thus many a man has given up Apostolic order, "the laying on of hands," the whole primitive constitution of the Church, and even in some cases the doctrine of the Trinity itself, for the sake of the mode alone. They reject nine truths for what they deem one truth, and still the process goes on. The Antipædobaptist sects, although disorganizing and splitting, have yet increased rapidly; and that too, let it be remembered, from Pædobaptist bodies, and not a few of their converts have been less educated members of the Church. Restore the mode, and this is stopped. The

English and American Baptists draw their chief vitality from the present irregularities.

It is useless to deny that the progress of intelligence has opened to them the abundant witness of the primitive Church, the English Church, and the present rubric, and that they will make use of these with much force against us so long as weak and modern views are preferred to those of the ancient Church. But the Church should rid herself of every such weight. Even with our present rubric much may be done for the restoration of the primitive practice. It is needless, and it would be going against the Church in all ages, to say that the trine immersion is *invariably* essential. Nevertheless, it ought to be the mode for every healthy child. The General Convention, by restoring the English rubric in the first book of Edward VI, would do more by this single act to make the Church the great body, the bulk of the people, than by any other, and that, too, without giving up a single principle which she has ever held. She would be acting in consonance with the constant and strong preference of all her abler theologians for the primitive mode, and their appeals for its restoration in practice. But whether this ever be done or not the clergy can do no better than to follow the advice of Bishop White, already quoted. As things are now, we are slowly but surely drifting away from *the preference* even which the Anglo-Catholic communion enjoins for the Apostolic mode. Many have become accustomed to look upon the whole question of the mode as one of *indifference;* and some in practice at least assume the position that sprinkling, which is not even mentioned in the rubric, and pouring, which is mentioned as the *exceptional* mode in the English book, should be the *rule* (*i. e.*, the preference) in ordinary administration.

They thus foster constantly increasing crowds of Antipædobaptist schismatics, and hinder the fullest development of the Church. For experience teaches that the slightest amount of truth, such as they contend for as to the mode, will serve as the salt of a dozen errors, and furnish cohesive power sufficient to keep such sects, amid all their jarrings, from total disintegration. The prophecy may well be hazarded, that if the Church, clergy, and people but do their duty, these sects will mainly disappear within the next half century.

The policy of crying down the teaching of the rubric, of opposing primitive testimony, has been tried long and stoutly, and the result is a perfect swarm of schisms and errors. The use of the ancient and divinely enjoined mode never produced such evils, and never will.

The mode of baptism is a subject which interests every one. Many a man who thinks little of the question of Orders or of the Church, thinks much of this, because on its proper administration and reception depend his hopes of covenant mercy. To neglect the primitive rite, therefore, is to spurn a great advantage in favor of unity and truth; to commit an unpardonable folly and sin.

Even were there nothing in the meaning of Βαπτίζω, in the baptisms of the New Testament, in the belief of the primitive Church, in the rubrics of the whole Church, and in the rubrics of the Anglican part of the whole Church, to favor immersion as the rule, yet would it be better and wiser to follow it as the rule, when such a course will surely promote truth and dissipate schism.

But when all these combine, no man should wish to break this commandment, with its divinely ordained and venerable symbolism, or to teach men so to do.

A word in conclusion. If in any part of the American Church anything be not as we could wish; if imperfections still cling to it, or to its clergy or people, let us remember that by these very things will the Church militant ever be distinguished from the Church triumphant. The Church on earth will never be perfect, because its affairs and interests are managed by imperfect men. But let it be remembered that this furnishes no excuse for causeless schism. If anything is wrong, let it be corrected by the Church and *in* the Church, not out of it. Schism generally ends in attempting to correct one error, and in falling into many and greater.

It is almost a peculiarity of the English-speaking races, that with a Church unequalled for doctrinal purity, which fosters enlightened piety, and allows sufficient freedom for anything except heresy, they should be constantly creating new schisms without curing the older ones.

All the threats and warning of Holy Writ seem to read in favor of those who create divisions among the household of Christ, so that in a small village which can hardly well support one church, we generally or often have two or three sects, and as many congregations. The energies of the followers of Christ are wasted in discords and dissensions about petty matters, and this goes on century after century, with Christ's pleas for unity, and the dread warnings of the Holy Ghost against schism, sounding in our ears. Now let us in this learn the lesson of reforming abuses and negligence, not by rending the Church afresh, but in witnessing against what is wrong in either. If our own opinions in favor of Calvinism or some other idea, do not become prevalent, let us reflect that there is a bare possibility, that in refusing to cram this doctrine down every man's throat, the Church may be right and we wrong. If what is advocated be true, and in accordance with our formularies (and they allow more liberty than any body of schismatics in the world), it will receive attention; if not, otherwise. It is wrong to suppose that because the views of Augustine are not made, wickedly made, a condition of Church communion, therefore such doctrines will utterly die out. Far from it. The Church of England and the American Church have always contained many who sympathized with the private opinions of the Bishop of Hippo on predestination and election, and so long as the human mind is constituted as it is, probably ever will. All the rest of us ask is, that as these have never been sanctioned by the whole Church, and as they are not in the creed, we may not be forced to indorse them. The whole question is one of opinion, not of doctrine. Were the opinion even true, the fact that it is a distinctive tenet of a *schism* would prejudice many against it. Such has been the effect on the whole Anglican and American Churches, so that probably not one favors this now, where ten did in the days of Hooker and Bishop Andrews.

And this train of remark is true of all schism. Had the multitudes who have left the Church from the mode alone to add to the rout of Antipædobaptist sects remained, and insisted on a faithful observance of the rubric, immersion would still be the rule. By leaving the Church, they gave up all for nothing and gave their efforts to the spread of the unscriptural and pestilential idea, that God's covenant of mercy has nothing to do with infants.

The author fervently prays, that nothing in these pages shall be construed in favor of the compends, except in case of *absolute* necessity, and then they are compends only. And on the other, that no man will pervert what has been adduced, in support of the preference expressed by the rubric, into justifying or even excusing Antipædobaptist schism. His object has been to knit more firmly the hearts of all, in closer bonds of unity to Christ and his Church, to illustrate and to vindicate from primitive and orthodox sources the wisdom and obligation of the preference for immersion in the rubrics of the English and American Churches, and to refute the late and opposing notions now so sadly current, and by removing from its hands its most effective weapon, to check the progress of Antipædobaptist error, and to draw back into the fold the sheep, who in their simplicity have been allured from its green pastures and still waters, to ever shifting sands. The task has not been a pleasant one. The author well knew at the start that even with the rubric and the great doctors of the Church on his side, he was undertaking a task which would run counter to popular ignorance and prejudice, and be esteemed accordingly by many, and that Antipædobaptist writers might *pervert* his words to their purposes of error and of sin. To call attention to the existence of a criminal carelessness, and indeed disobedience as to the injunctions of a rubric is never a pleasant task, and least of all when the grounds of the injunctions have been among the mass forgotten and in some cases even opposed. The author has even met a clergyman who did not know that the rubrics of the Church of England express a preference for dipping! He craves not for his own views but for the belief of the early Christians, as well as for the despised and neglected rubric, a fair and impartial hearing, satisfied as he is, that if the present carelessness and disobedience continue, the noblest monument of primitive practice in the whole West will have disappeared, a last stronghold of catholic belief will have succumbed forever, and that the Church in her future history may discern its lack, in the rapid and fearful spread of countless errors. These have been his motives. To the learning and candor of all pious men he commits it. That no one will ever be warped into false doctrine, schism, and heresy through him, he ventures to hope; if any pervert his words to their own hurt, it will be a cause to him of sorrow in life and in death. He has presented only God's truth, as interpreted by the primitive doctors and fathers of the Church. It was in the beginning, it is now, and it will be evermore.

It is the only right way to deal with this question, because the only truthful way.

Let it be remembered that while baptism is not all of religion, it holds by the awful sanction of God a place, which, even though it be a positive rite, we may not rashly trifle with, and that God will not acquit him as guiltless who does. Even if it be a "least commandment," yet Christ has said, "Whosoever therefore shall break one of these least commandments, and shall teach men so, he shall be called the least in the kingdom of heaven, but whosoever shall do and teach them, the same shall be called great in the kingdom of heaven."

APPENDIX.

A.

PASSAGES OF HOLY WRIT RELATING TO BAPTISM DISPUTED AMONG LATE AUTHORS.

The following gives in brief some of the best statements and arguments on passages which in late years have begun to be adduced against the view that βαπτίζω is modal and that it enjoins immersion which the author has seen. The authors are Profs. Robinson and Ripley. The remarks of the former which the latter combats, are to be found in his "Lexicon of the New Testament" under βαπτίζω.

Both belong to the school which represents its own opinions, rather than the practice of the primitive Church, as the standard by which to interpret the baptismal passages of the Bible. But so far as immersion is concerned, the latter stands not fully and clearly upon, but yet much nearer to the line of primitive Christian practice than the other. The Christian who interprets Holy Writ in accordance with that usage, and who believes that those who lived nearest the Apostolic age ought to know as much of Apostolic practice as some late disciples of Calvin and John Smith, and who thinks that because they were so very unfortunate as to differ from the former as to the mode and the latter as to the subjects, having been born in an age of the world when these great luminaries had not arisen, they should not, therefore, be branded as ignoramuses, or as men who did not know the Gospel which they taught, will not need the arguments of either. The principle of Vincent of Lerins, to which Bishop Ridley appealed in a former age, will be enough. Early testimony admits no doubt in these passages.

Without committing ourselves in favor of all, therefore, that may be said by either of these authors, we give them; what Ripley has said against infant baptism we omit, trusting that he and all like him who causelessly promote schism, will see their error and return. He is speaking of what Robinson says of βαπτίζω.

"After presenting a just view of its use among classic Greek writers, he proceeds to its use in the New Testament, and states as the first meaning, *to wash, to lave, to cleanse by washing.* As an authority for, or illustration of, this indefinite signification, he produces Luke 11 : 38, in which ἐβαπτίσθη ebaptisthe occurs, and compares it with Mark 7 : 2–3, where νίψωνται nipsōntai occurs, the circumstances in the two cases being represented by Dr. Robinson as alike. Mark 7 : 4, in which βαπτίσωνται baptisōntai occurs, is also referred to. The author's judgment, apparently, is that the words in these instances are used alike, and that νίπτω nipto, *wash*, serves to explain βαπτίζω baptizo, *baptize.*

"This judgment is certainly incorrect. A careful examination of the verses cited from Mark shows that two quite diverse cases are there spoken of, one requiring a comparatively slight washing (νίψωνται), and the other a copious ablution (βαπτίσωνται). With this latter case corresponds the one mentioned in Luke 11 : 38 (ἐβαπτίσθη). The very candid view taken of Mark 7 : 2–4, by Dr. George Campbell, in the notes to his translation of the Four Gospels, is worthy of careful consideration. He translates the passage in the following manner: 'For the Pharisees . . . eat not until they have washed their hands by pouring a little water upon them; and if they be come from the market, by dipping them.' In his note, he says: 'For illustrating this passage, let it be observed that the two verbs rendered *wash* in the English translation are different in the original. The first is νίψωνται nipsōntai, properly translated *wash;* the second is βαπτίσωνται baptisontai, which limits us to a particular mode of washing; for βαπτίζω baptizo denotes *to plunge, to dip.* . . By this interpretation the words, which, as rendered in the common version are unmeaning, appear both significant and emphatical; and the contrast in the Greek is preserved in the translation.'

"More modern writers, of the first ability, also differ from the author of this Lexicon. Olshausen, on Mark 7 : 2, 3, after saying that the Evangelist felt it necessary to explain to readers who were not Jews the Jewish custom of washing the hands before meals, thus proceeds: 'Mark passes on from the custom of washing hands to similar customs, for washings of every sort were customary among the Jews; he ends, however, with the washing relative to provisions. Βαπτίζεσθαι baptizesthai differs from νίπτεσθαι niptesthai. The former is here the immersing and cleaning off of provisions that had been purchased, in order to remove every possible impurity which might have been on them. Νίπτεσθαι niptesthai embraces also a rubbing off, since such an act occurs in every form of washing.'

"C. F. A. Fritzsche, in his Commentary on Mark, after a very copious discussion of the passage, presents the following views. 'Verse 4. And when they have come from the market, that is, from business in the market, they do not eat unless they have washed their body. Thus Beza and Grotius explain this passage most rightly.' In alluding to a possible charge of tautology in this interpretation, he remarks: 'So far from there being tautology in this method, the writer advances to a still stronger case. The Pharisees,

APPENDIX A. 275

says Mark, according to traditional precepts, do not eat bread unless after having carefully washed their hands. And when they have come from the market they do even more; namely, they do not take food *unless they have washed their body*. The Pharisees judged it necessary to wash their bodies on returning from the market, because there was ground for fear lest in a public concourse they should, even through imprudence, have contracted some serious defilement, as they might have either ignorantly fallen in with an unclean man, or incautiously touched some very impure thing.' In reference to Kuinoel's remark that antiquity bears no testimony to the practice among the Pharisees of washing their persons before meals, after returning from the market, he says, ' the testimony of antiquity which Kuinoel required is in the New Testament itself, in Luke 11 : 37, 38.'

"De Wette, after assenting to the insertion for explaining the Evangelist's idea of the clause *when they have returned* before the clause *from the market*, adds: ' This explanation receives a better sense when, with Beza, Grotius, Fritzsche, we understand βαπτίζεσθαι baptizesthai of the whole body, than with Lightfoot and Wetstein merely of the hands.'

"H. A. W. Meyer, in his Manual on the Gospels of Mark and Luke, has the following note: ' The expression in Mark 7 : 4 (ἐὰν μὴ βαπτίσωνται) is not to be understood of the *washing of the hands* (as interpreted by Lightfoot and Wetstein), but of the *immersing* which the word always means in the Classics and the New Testament; that is, here, according to the context, *the taking of a bath*. So likewise Luke 11 : 38. Having come from the market, where among a crowd of men they might have come in contact with unclean persons. they eat not without having first bathed themselves. The representation proceeds after the manner of a climax; before eating they *always* observe the washing of hands, but [employ] the *bath* when they come *from the market* and wish to take food.'

"It is no part of my object here to determine whether βαπτίσωνται baptisōntai relates to the persons spoken of, or, as Olshausen and others suppose, to provisions which had been purchased in the market; nor even whether it relates to the entire body or only to the hands. This is wholly unnecessary, so far as the meaning of the word is concerned; since, in either case, the difference between this word and νίπτεσθαι niptesthai is perfectly obvious. My purpose has been to show that Dr. Robinson's judgment in regard to Mark 7 : 2, 3, as employing νίπτω nipto and βαπτίζω baptizo in the same sense, opposes leading authorities of the present age. So far as βαπτίζω baptizo is concerned, his Lexicon cannot be regarded as a ' memorial of the progress and condition of the Interpretation and Lexicography of the New Testament at the close of the first half of the nineteenth century.'

"Dr. Robinson produces in this connection the two Hebrew words טָבַל and רָחַץ, apparently as illustrating the resemblance between βαπτίζω baptizo and νίπτω nipto. The comparison fails, however; for the relation between the two Hebrew words, as is evident from the very passages he quotes, 2 Kings 5 : 14 compared with 10, is not the same as between βαπτίζω baptizo and νίπτω nipto, but the same as between βαπτίζω baptizo and λούω louo; the two words, both in Hebrew and Greek, being so related that when the prophet Elisha directed Naaman to go and *wash* (וְרָחַצְתָּ, λούσαι lousai, properly *bathe*) in the Jordan, Naaman went and *dipped* (וַיִּטְבֹּל, ἐβαπτίσατο ebaptizato) himself. Now, while λούω louo and βαπτίζω baptizo are thus kindred in idea, λούω louo and νίπτω nipto are distinct from each other, as appears from the Gospel of John 13 : 10. In this passage it is said that a person who has been *bathed*, λελουμένος, needs after that copious use of water only *to wash*, νίψασθαι nipsasthai, his feet. The distinction between νίπτω nipto and λούω louo is here obvious. Equally obvious is the distinction between νίπτω nipto and βαπτίζω baptizo. The cases in John 13 : 10, and Mark 7 : 2, 3, are remarkably similar as to the relation of these several verbs, and amply show how uncritical it is to regard βαπτίζω baptizo and νίπτω nipto as interchangeable and as indiscriminately employed.

"Two passages are also produced from the Apocrypha as confirming the statement that βαπτίζω baptizo bears the general signification of *washing*. In these passages, however, the cases referred to are such that a very *copious* use of water is intended to be expressed, and not *washing* merely, without necessary reference to the idea of copiousness.

"Appended to the article we have been considering is a note, designed to support the opinion that 'in Hellenistic usage, and especially in reference to the rite of baptism, βαπτίζω baptizo would seem to have expressed not always simply *immersion* but the more general idea of *ablution* or *affusion*.' It ingeniously acknowledges that 'in Greek writers, from Plato onward, βαπτίζω baptizo is everywhere *to sink, to immerse, to overwhelm*, either wholly or *partially*.' The opinion above stated the author, however, labors to confirm by the following considerations:

"1. 'The circumstances narrated in Luke 11 : 37, 38, compared with those in Mark 7 : 2–4.' These passages have been already sufficiently examined. A word or two more may seem requisite in regard to βαπτισμούς baptismous in the fourth verse of the passage in Mark, as applied to cups, pots, brazen vessels, and tables. No valid objection against the specific meaning of the word can arise from its use in this connection, since all these articles, even the more bulky ones, were capable of immersion part by part, if not the whole at once; and the more bulky articles were expressly required by later Jewish regulations to be actually covered with water in order to be cleansed. In regard to the smaller articles, we find in Lev. 11 : 32 the direction that any vessel on which the dead body of an unclean animal had fallen,—and Jewish scrupulosity would, doubtless, in subsequent times, extend the rule to all cases of defilement, real or presumed,—'whatsoever vessel it be wherein any work is done' (except only earthen vessels which, when polluted, were to be broken in pieces, Lev. 11 : 33), 'it must be *put into water*' in order to be cleansed. Meyer, also, whom we have already quoted, says of βαπτισμούς baptismous in this verse, 'It is to be understood of the cleaning off by *dipping in.*'

"2. Another consideration adduced to sustain the indefinite signification of the word in question is, that in Acts 2 : 41, three thousand persons are said to have been baptized at Jerusalem apparently in one day at the season of Pentecost in June; and in Acts 4 : 4, the same rite is necessarily implied in respect to five thousand more. Against the idea of full *immersion* in these cases, there lies a difficulty, apparently insuperable, in the scarcity of water. There is in summer no running stream in the vicinity of Jerusalem except the mere rill of Siloam, a few rods in length, and the city is and was supplied with water from its cisterns and public reservoirs. From neither of these sources could a supply have been well obtained for the immersion of eight thousand persons.

"We will repress levity, and in seriousness ask, if three thousand persons were baptized on one day and five thousand were subsequently baptized, whether on one day or at several different times, how does this furnish a ground for objecting that there was not water enough for immersing eight thousand persons? So far as the number is concerned, the entire statement of the sacred record is met by the opinion generally received that, in Acts 4 : 4, not a fresh addition of five thousand persons to the Christian company is meant, but that the company had increased to five thousand; and this increase was not, so far as it appears, simultaneous, but gradual. Then as to the water itself, without starting the inquiry which the author's statement certainly suggests, How much water is consumed in baptizing a person? or how many persons will any considerable mass of water allow to be baptized without being exhausted or rendered unsuitable for the purpose? Without starting these inquiries, but limiting our view to the sufficiency of water in the city, we may, in the absence of precise testimony from ancient times, well believe that so populous a city as Jerusalem was not destitute of adequate supplies of water for the purpose, but that, as the ancient geographer Strabo testifies, it was 'well watered;' especially as, by the prescriptions of their religion, all the adult males of the nation were required to repair to Jerusalem three times every year; and one of those times was the very festival which was occurring when the three thousand embraced the Christian religion. The burden of proof that Jerusalem was destitute of sufficient water and conveniences, in face of the acknowledged meaning of the word as commonly used, and in face of divinely appointed customs which required large quantities of water both for religious purposes and for personal cleanliness, lies on those who raise the suspicion that Jerusalem was not able to furnish an adequate supply of water. This proof has never been given, and the subject is far enough from such a state as would authorize a departure, in sense, from the ordinary meaning of a word which a sacred writer has employed. Should researches continue to be made, we have a right to presume that, as has happened on other subjects and on other questions pertaining to baptism, the increasing light of science will confirm the plain, unsophisticated declarations of the Holy Scriptures.

"Desirable as it is to oppose facts to doubts, we must sometimes be content to oppose probabilities to improbabilities, and wait for additional light. That additional light in regard to the present subject may never be obtained, because the question relates to the ancient city, which has been so sadly devastated, and has undergone so many changes. And yet, so far as explorations have been made which might create or warrant a general impression on the subject, a perusal of Dr. Robinson's Researches in Palestine (vol. i, section vii, art. ix, on the Supply of Water in Jerusalem), and of the additions to the Researches grounded on communications from Messrs. Smith and Walcott, can hardly fail to produce conviction that a city, so wonderful for the labor and skill expended in securing immense quantities of water for both public and private use, could not have been destitute of places in which baptism, immersion we mean, could have been administered to an indefinite number of persons. When we read of remains of ancient reservoirs, in length 316 feet, in breadth from 200 to 218 feet and 18 feet in depth; also, in length 592 feet, in breadth from 245 to 275 feet, and in depth from 35 to 42 feet, and when various notices of aqueducts and other means of supply pass before our minds, showing great ampleness of accommodations for water, and a most remarkable attention to the safety and comfort of the city in every vicissitude of circumstances, it does seem utterly unreasonable to cast suspicion on the meaning of the word *baptize* by the suggestion that the city could not supply a sufficient quantity of water for immersing so many as the inspired account may warrant us in saying were baptized. A more particular reference to the interesting facts presented in the works above named is unnecessary.[*] Future years may bring to light other and still more definite facts, for the researches thus far made give stimulating promise of yet more wonderful disclosures to reward the enterprise of explorers, and to confirm the sacred records. In the meantime, the general impression from researches hitherto prosecuted is by no means adverse to the belief that the baptism in Jerusalem, on the occasions referred to, was, in accordance with the meaning of the word, a veritable immersion.

"3. Another consideration produced by Dr. Robinson as adverse to the idea of immersion being involved in baptism is, that 'in the earliest Latin versions of the New Testament, as, for example, the *Itala*, which Augustine regarded as the best of all, and which goes

---

[*] See Samson's letter on "The sufficiency of water for baptizing at Jerusalem and elsewhere in Palestine, etc."—Author.

APPENDIX A. 279

back apparently to the second century, and to usage connected with the Apostolic age, the Greek verb βαπτίζω is uniformly given in the Latin form *baptizo*, and is never translated by *immergo*, or any like word; showing that there was something in the rite of baptism to which the latter did not correspond.'

"Without entering into the doubtful, and, for the present purpose, unnecessary inquiry, how far any existing Latin renderings belong to the genuine Itala, a satisfactory account can be given of the transfer of the Greek βαπτίζω baptizo into the early Latin versions in preference to a real translation of that word. There is no necessity for supposing such a flexibility, or comprehensiveness, of meaning in the Greek word as would not allow any existing Latin word to be its representative. The supposition has been made that the earliest Latin versions, unless we may except the Itala, had their origin in Africa, where the Latin was generally used, but was not spoken or written in purity; and where, of course, a word not of the genuine language, yet well understood, would without repugnance be adopted. Whatever may be in this, the expressing of the Greek word in a Latin form proves only that, at the very early period when Latin versions commenced, the word βαπτίζω baptizo had come to be so associated with the sacred observance, and had become so familiar among the people for whom the versions were made, that it was naturally transferred, instead of being translated. It is by no means surprising, then, that, even among those Christians in the Roman empire who used mostly the Latin language, a classical or a colloquial Latin word was not employed in Latin translations instead of that to which, in sacred matters, they had become accustomed, and which was by usage as well understood as the corresponding genuine Latin word.

"4. The remaining consideration presented in the Note is drawn from 'the baptismal fonts still found among the ruins of the most ancient Greek churches in Palestine, as at Tekoa and Gophna, and going back apparently to very early times,' which 'are not large enough to admit of the baptism of adult persons by immersion, and were obviously never intended for that use.'

"How ancient were these fonts? A question of essential importance to the purpose for which the Lexicon mentions them; namely, showing how a certain word was understood in the Apostolic age."
"They 'were obviously never intended for the baptism of adult persons by immersion.' For what use were they intended? Will any one inform us, and thus enable us to conjecture whether they oppose the idea of immersion as belonging to baptism? If any one says they were designed, not for the immersion of adults, but for some other mode of using water at the baptism of adults, let him prove this; else he begs the question. But if they were designed, according to the practice of Greek churches elsewhere, for the baptism of infants, then they do not oppose the ordinary meaning of the word: they rather favor it; for why was a font 'four feet in diameter

on the inside and three feet nine inches deep'* employed for the baptism of infants, unless the baptism was an immersion?"

"Having examined, as was meet, the several grounds on which the acknowledged classical signification of this word is withholden from it when used in reference to the rite of baptism, I may be allowed to say, that any word which is descriptive of an act might easily become shrouded in darkness, if the same license were practised in regard to it as has fallen to the lot of this much abused word. And as an offset to the irrelevant considerations which are so often produced to disprove its retaining in the New Testament its confessedly classical signification, I beg to ask how can it be fairly accounted for that, in the earliest Christian writers after the Apostolic era, whenever the mention of the rite of baptism is associated with descriptive circumstances, or when descriptive terms are employed instead of the words *baptize* and *baptism*, the descriptive terms or circumstances invariably point to immersion as the act of baptism?"

A word further on the four main points last mentioned. They are often heard. They constitute the main reliance of the opposition to the modal signification of the baptismal terms.

The first consideration which Robinson urges is drawn from "the circumstances narrated, Luke 11:38, compared with those in Mark 7:2-4, where νίπτω is employed, implying, according to Oriental custom, a pouring of water on the hands." Of this enough has been said.

The force of this argument lies in this, that βαπτίζω in the first passage is used to describe the same act meant by νίπτω in the second. But this cannot be clearly proved from the Greek. The English version translates both Greek words by "wash." And this indefiniteness may have given rise to the error. While it may be true that the idea of washing is contained in both, it does not follow that the kind and mode of the washing is the same. And until this is proved the onus probandi must rest with those who oppose the view of the early Church, that βαπτίζω in the New Testament is expressive of mode. Some think that the washing of the hands in Mark 7:2, 3, cannot be the same as that in verse 4 of the same chapter unless it be a repetition. Dr. Bloomfield (Gr. Test. in loc.), thinks that ἐὰν μὴ βαπτ, "is best explained 'unless they wash their bodies,' in opposition to the washing of the hands before mentioned."

Dr. Hammond in loc. thinks that "the word here used βαπτίζεσθαι (as it differs from νίπτεσθαι, verse 3), signifies not only the washing of the whole body (as when it is said of Eupolis, that being taken and thrown into the sea, ἐβαπτίζετο, he was immersed all over, and so the baptisms of cups, &c., in the end of this verse, is putting into the water all over, rinsing them), but washing any part, as the hands here, by way of immersion in water, as that is opposed to affusion

---

* Robinson's Biblical Researches in Palestine, vol. i, p. 78; vol. ii, p. 182.

or pouring water on them." But Dr. Bloomfield does not think that immersion is implied. Kuinoel has a note which is worthy of attention. He states three views of the words καὶ ἀπὸ ἀγορᾶς, ἐὰν μὴ βαπτίσωνται κτλ.

1. And when they come from the market except they wash *their hands* they eat not. This he condemns.
2. When they return from market they immerse the body in water before they eat.
3. They eat nothing which has been sold in market until *it* has been washed and purified in or by water. This is Kuinoel's view. All these views have learned advocates. The first view favors Dr. Robinson. The second opposes him. And the washing in the third was not by pouring or sprinkling.

2. He thinks that the scarcity of water presents a difficulty, apparently insuperable, against the idea of full immersion in Acts 2 : 41 and Acts 4 : 4.

But this difficulty never appeared such to the early Christians. It dates from a period comparatively late. As the seasons of baptism in the early Church were mainly two, Easter and Whitsuntide, the number of candidates must have been large, especially when infants and adults are added. Yet Cyril of Jerusalem, at a period in the history of his city, when water privileges were much less than at the founding of the Church, uniformly speaks of the trine immersion as the mode, and addresses all his hearers as thrice immersed. And yet the same objections very nearly would lie *a priori* against this mode in his days, as against its use by the Apostles and their disciples in this case. Besides, the Apostles in that extraordinary era of the Church, were not restricted to ordinary laws as to the administrators. The primitive Church were not; and trine immersion takes but little more, if any, time than pouring. Instances are mentioned when this was the custom, of thousands being baptized in one day.

3. The statement of Dr. Robinson as to the Itala, is coupled with the idea that among the early Christians there was a belief that there was something in the rite of baptism, to which neither immergo or any like word corresponded. In other words, he seems to think that the early Christians did not deem βαπτίζω modal.

But facts are against him. See above, pp. 38.

1. TERTULLIAN, who lived in the second century quotes St. Matt. 28 : 19: βαπτίζω, in this passage, is rendered in his version, or that from which he quotes, by a word (tinguo), signifying to immerse. So does St. Cyprian in the third century. He uses tingo in the same passage. (v. more in Conant's work on baptizein, sec. vii.)

CLEMENT of Alexandria, in the third century, uses βαπτίζω in the sense of immersion or overwhelming. v. Bishop Kaye's Clem. of Alex. p. 441, and examples under note there.

TERTULLIAN as already quoted uses mergito. (See also St. Jerome above.)

The universal use at the end of the second century, of the troublesome rite of trine immersion is, in itself, a strong proof that the early Christians understood the command as enjoining this mode, or they would not have gone to this unnecessary trouble, when pouring or sprinkling would have been just as regular.

But that which effectually settles this whole question is, that always and without a single dissentient voice the whole Church, for at least eight hundred years, held, taught, and practised immersion, as expressly enjoined by God in Holy Writ.

4. As to the baptismal fonts at Tekoa and Gophna, enough has been said already. We close with the wish that soon we may have in all our churches, fonts like them, "four feet in diameter on the inside and nine inches deep." We shall have no excuse then for breaking the rubric; every infant may be dipped.

METAPHORICAL USE OF BAPTISMAL TERMS.

JESUS COMPARES HIS OWN SUFFERINGS TO A BAPTISM.

Some in later days find much difficulty in these passages. The main objection is, that here βαπτίζω and βάπτισμα cannot mean immersion. But even if they do not, do they mean sprinkling or pouring? Should the passage read, I have a sprinkling to be sprinkled with, or a pouring to be poured with, or a washing to be washed with?

The general drift of comment is, that the allusion is figurative.

The question as to what βαπτίζω may mean in an exceptional case or two, does not invalidate its general and prevalent meaning, so that, even should it be admitted that it here means to sprinkle or to pour, nothing would be gained.

But the author has seen no one who expounds it of either.

The metaphorical sense is borne out by

BLOOMFIELD on St. Matt. 20 : 22. "This metaphor of *immersion* in water, as expressive of being overwhelmed in affliction, is frequent, both in the scriptural and classical writers, with this difference, that in the latter there is usually added some word expressive of the evil of affliction." v. also id. on Luke 12 : 50, which he explains of suffering.

KUINOEL, on St. Matt. 20 : 22, explains it of immersion, *i. e.* of being overwhelmed by evils v. also id. on St. Luke, 12 : 50.

It is explained of suffering by Dr. S. Clarke, Dean Stanhope, and Bishop Trower, on the same text. v. the former quoted in Bishop Brownell, on the Prayer Book on the Gospel for St James's day, and the latter on the same feast, in his work on the Gospels. Kuinoel's note is valuable.

POOLE'S SYNOPSIS, on St. Matt. 20 : 23. "I refer the noun 'baptism' to that metaphor by which afflictions are compared in Holy Scripture to abysses of waters in which those who are harassed by calamities are as if submerged. Besides, the baptisms of the Jews in their purifications were bitter trials; for the whole of their bodies were immersed in the waters, even while these excited shuddering by frost and snow: so that not unfitly, partly on account of the submersion, partly on account of the cold, is the meaning of a most painful death thence derived." "*Baptismi* autem nomen refero ad metaphoram illam, quâ afflictiones in S. S. saepe comparantur gurgititibus aquarum, quibus veluti submerguntur qui calamitatibus vexantur. Tum acerba res erant Judaeorum Baptismi in purificationibus suis, in quibus toto corpore immergebantur in aquis, etiam gelu et nivibus horrentes, ut non immerito inde, partim ob submersionem, partim ob frigus, desumeretur significatio asperrimae mortis."

CORNELIUS A LAPIDE (a Latin), on St. Luke 12 : 50. " I have a baptism to be baptized with."

"He calls his death and passion a baptism, because in it he was immersed and overwhelmed according to Ps. 69 : 2. I sink in deep mire where there is no standing, I am come into deep waters where the floods overflow me."

Comment. in S. Lucam 12 : 50. "Baptismo autem habeo baptizari."

"'Baptismum' vocat suam mortem et passionem, quia in eam plane immersus et demersus fuit, juxta illud, Psal. 68 : 2." " Infixus sum in limo profundi, et non est substantia. Veni in altitudinem maris, et tempestas demersit me."

See Maldonatus on Matt. 20 : 22. He explains similarly, and adds, "In Greek to be baptized is the same as to be submerged."

Kuinoel in loc. says: " To be baptized ($\beta\alpha\pi\tau\iota\sigma\theta\tilde{\eta}\nu\alpha\iota$) is to be oppressed with ills, with distresses, or to be immersed in evils."

Whitby on this text (cf. with Luke 12 : 49), has an excellent note with references. It is too long to be here given.

On " baptizing with the Holy Ghost and with fire ($\dot{\epsilon}\nu$ $\pi\nu\epsilon\dot{\nu}\mu\alpha\tau\iota$ $\dot{\alpha}\gamma\dot{\iota}\omega$ $\kappa\alpha\dot{\iota}$ $\pi\nu\rho\dot{\iota}$), CHRYSOSTOM, in Aurea Catena, on St. Matt. 3 : 11, 12, says, He does not say shall give you the Holy Ghost, but *shall baptize you in the Holy Ghost*, showing in metaphor the abundance of the grace."

In Aurea Catena, on St. Luke 3 : 15-17. "And having said that his own baptism was only with water, he next shows the excellency of that baptism which was bought by Christ, adding, He shall baptize you with the Holy Spirit and fire, signifying by the very metaphor which he uses the abundance of grace ; for he says not ' He shall give you the Holy Spirit,' but He shall *baptize you*."

It will be observed that the early Christians translate the "$\dot{\epsilon}\nu$" in both these texts by the Latin preposition " in," thus, "in Spiritu Sancto."

Such expressions as $\dot{\epsilon}\nu$ $\tau\tilde{\omega}$ $\ddot{\upsilon}\delta\alpha\tau\iota$, $\dot{\epsilon}\nu$ $\pi\nu\epsilon\dot{\nu}\mu\alpha\tau\iota$ $\dot{\alpha}\gamma\dot{\iota}\omega$, whatever may be their *possible* meaning grammatically considered alone, are placed beyond all doubt by the belief and practice of the early Church, and by the fact that the style of interpretation which would found arguments against immersion from them, is of very recent date.*

* See Turney on Baptism, pp. 30-35, for patristic comment.

CHRISTIAN BAPTISM SPOKEN OF WITH REFERENCE TO EVENTS IN THE OLD TESTAMENT.

1 Cor. 10 : 1. "Moreover, brethren, I would not that ye should be ignorant, how that all our fathers were under the cloud, and all passed through the sea. 2. And were all baptized unto Moses in the cloud and in the sea."

WHITBY, on 1 Cor. 10 : 2. "They were *covered with the sea on both sides*, Exod. 14 : 22, so that both the cloud and the sea had some resemblance to our being covered with water in baptism. Their going into the sea resembled the ancient rite of going into the water, and their coming out of it, their rising up out of the water."

DEAN STANHOPE. "This covering of the cloud and safe conduct through the sea, as they resembled the ceremonies of Christian baptism, the being put under and rising out of the water, so did they answer the same end too. For upon this miraculous deliverance they entered into covenant with, and professed their faith in God." Quoted in D'Oyly and Mant. on 1 Cor. 10 : 2.

1 Pet. 3 : 20. "The long suffering of God waited in the days of Noah, while the ark was a preparing, wherein few, that is, eight souls, were saved by water. 31. The like figure whereunto *even* baptism doth also now save us." v. Macaire, as given above.

We might, had we been so disposed, have much increased these quotations and references, but our aim has been only to show from reliable or generally recognized authorities, both in our own communion and elsewhere, that the perverse spirit of quibbling which some late authors exhibit, is opposed to older and more learned criticism. We wish to show that whoever adopts their theories, adopts them in the face of the unanimous interpretation of the first twelve hundred years, and of the great bulk of authorities.

We have noticed them, not because of any intrinsic weight which they possess, but because within the last century, and more especially within the last half, they have gained such fearful and destructive currency, as finally to threaten the integrity of the letter, as they have long since destroyed the practice of the rubrics themselves.

One class of passages we have omitted to speak of; those relating, as is thought by many learned men, to the case of baptism in necessity, such, for instance, as the baptism of the jailor.

This we have done, not only because of the difficulty which exists of reasoning with absolute certainty where so few facts are given, but also because, in common with St. Cyprian and the whole Church, we deem it necessary to admit the compends in such cases, as it is clear that unless this be done, no part of Christendom can be sure of its orders or baptism.

Whatever may be thought of some of these passages, Tertullian believed that *all* the baptisms of the New Testament were performed by immersion. (v. as quoted above.)

The Fathers and the whole Church, for the first 800 years after Christ, believed that in St. Matt. 28 : 19, He enjoined this mode, and nearly all that the *trine* immersion is enjoined, in the same words. Unless, therefore, they thought that the Apostles and the early disciples disobeyed, they must have believed that, unless in the case of absolute impossibility, the command was obeyed, and the early converts were all thrice immersed.

B.

TOTAL IMMERSION IN BAPTISM.

Some within the last few years have doubted whether the immersion was total, and have attempted to identify the single, partial immersion combined with affusion, with the primitive trine immersion. This opinion is a novelty, and is opposed to the consent of antiquity. This will appear by a careful perusal of the quotations from Dionysius, the Areopagite, p. 59, above; Hippolytus, p. 62; Athanasius, p. 69; Cyril of Jerusalem, p 70, 71; Gregory Nyssen, p. 76; Chrysostom, p. 76; Maximus of Turin (see the Latin), p. 79; Atto, bp. of Vercelli, p. 85; Hildebert of le Mans, p. 86.

Besides:

1. The rite is constantly spoken of among the early writers as a type of burial and resurrection, which the late mode above mentioned does not fully express.

2. The rubrical direction is always absolute, not limited to a part of the body.

3. In no ancient description of the rite is the immersion spoken of as partial, nor is affusion used with the words, "I baptize thee," &c.

4. This mode is never heard of until the thirteenth century, and then only as an innovation. See above, pp. 137–142.

C.

THE APOSTOLICAL CONSTITUTIONS.

These writings possess a high antiquity, and are not without their weight in historical inquiry.

The rites of baptism, including the immersion and their symbolism, are amply treated of. As there is a translation, we deem it necessary to give only the references. These are bk. iii, 15, 16, 17; vii, 22, 29–45.

D.

COUNCIL OF NICE.

DESCENDIT quidem is qui baptizatur peccatis obnoxius et servititutis corruptione detentus; ascendit autem ab ea servitute et peccatis liber, factus filius Dei, et hæres, gratia ipsius factus cohæres autem Christi, indutus ipsum Christum sicut scriptum est, "Quicunque in Christum baptizati estis Christum induistis." Concil Nic. de S. baptismo apud Gelas Cyzian. lib. iii, c. xxxi. [p. 173.]

And the Council of Nice: "He that is baptized descends, indeed, obnoxious to sins, and held with the corruption of slavery, but he ascends free from that slavery and sins, the Son of God, heir, yea, coheir with Christ, having put on Christ, as it is written, " If ye be baptized into Christ, ye have put on Christ " v. in Bishop Beveridge, on 39 Art., Art. 27, note. The whole of Beveridge's remarks on this article are valuable.

E.

CANON VII OF THE SECOND ECUMENICAL COUNCIL. I. CONSTANTINOPLE.

BALSAMON.—" Note that by this canon all who have been baptized by one immersion only are to be rebaptized."

ZONARAS —" These, therefore (the Montanists, &c.), and all other heretics, the holy fathers have decreed shall be baptized. For either they have received no baptism at all, or at least one which is alien from that of the orthodox Church. Therefore, as having always been unbaptized, baptism is to be administered to them, which is indicated in these words: 'we receive them as heathen.' Afterwards the canon decides what they are to do; first, that they are to be initiated, then to be instructed according to our rites in the divine mystery, and then to be baptized."

To the same purport Aristenus in loc.

F.

ANCIENT PICTURES OF BAPTISM.

In Taylor's "Apostolic Baptism," pp. 187–218, may be found remarks upon certain engravings there given, which are said to represent the ancient customs of baptism.

But they all lack *certain* date. The assertions of the author without proofs go for nothing. The use of such representations is to illustrate. They ought not to be taken for productions of the early ages, much less as expressing either the belief or the normal practice of the early Christians against their express and abundant testimony.

Mr. Taylor's assertions as to their age are wholly without proof. If we could find any clear statement other than his unsupported statement, we should endeavor to show his mistake, but by neglecting to bring the data upon which he bases his statement he acquits us of any such obligation.

But yet we have deemed it but just to notice a few of the difficulties in his theory as to their expressing the ancient belief.

The engravings represent Christ as baptized by affusion or by partial immersion and affusion.

Objection 1 This is *opposed* to the belief of the whole Christian world for the first 1200 years. See p. 62 above, Hippolytus, and pp. 42–45. These state positively that he was immersed

2. The mode of affusion with one partial immersion does not appear in history until the thirteenth century, nor affusion until the third, and then only as a compend and as such and such alone it was used during 1200 years. The early Christians if they had believed Christ baptized by any other mode than immersion, must have believed him baptized by a compend. It is needless to add that not a trace of such an idea appears during the whole period last named.

3. The engravings do not state the same mode. In engraving i, Christ is not in the water. In the others He is partly immersed. The last speak a local custom of centuries 13, 14, and 15. The former, if it refer to Christ at all, is of late date. Still another represents not pouring but immersion. Do these pictures then prove that He was baptized in *three* ways? Did the primitive Christians believe that Christ was baptized by what they deemed a compend, and that without necessity?

Engraving xii is an exception. It differs from the rest. This represents not affusion but immersion, for John the Baptist stands with his right hand upon the Saviour's head ready to plunge Him beneath the waters. The others represent him as pouring something from a vessel.

Engraving viii represents baptism by "a man in a military

habit," and therefore is, in all probability, a case of baptism by a layman, a thing never allowed in the Church except in necessity. (As to Taylor's statements, see Murdock's Mosheim, i. 384, 385.)

Engraving viii seems also, from the dress of the officiator, to represent a case of lay baptism, and hence one of necessity.

Engraving ix, the author assures us, is by "Greek artists in the ninth or tenth century." Rather a late period for proving the *apostolicity* of a rite. But we are at no loss for an answer here. In the preceding pages and the writings, the rubrics and the law of that period, the Greek mode was trine immersion as the rule. The compends were resorted to in necessity only.

With engravings x and xi we have no quarrel. They represent, as is well known, baptism in necessity, at which time the Church departed from the more full administration and used what were deemed divine compends.

But it is clear from Church law, rubrics, and historical witness, that so far as the normal mode of administration is concerned, it was during twelve centuries three total immersions. These are the "incorrupta monumenta," the incorrupt monuments of her teaching, and do not lie.

All of these pictures which stand opposed to them are late or at least historically untrue. The true reason why events are so represented will be found in the words of Paciaudi, p. 231, above. They are to be attributed to the ignorance and rashness of painters, whose representations of scripture scenes and characters, as well as the events of early Christian history, are often amusing or painful.

Even the Last Supper, a production of Da Vinci, exhibits Christ and his Apostles as sitting about a table in modern style!!

The only one (xii) *of all these representations which professes to come from the Catacombs is for total immersion.*

As an instance of how little reliance is to be placed upon the rest let us take No. 1. Notice, 1. That it is an ornament on a door of a church. Now this circumstance, if it had been regarded as ancient, seems queer. How long has the great church of Pisa been built? How long has the door upon which this stands stood there? Finally, when was it placed upon the door? After these questions are answered, we may be able to tell somewhere near its age. It surely seems a strange place to put antiquities.

2. As to "the tradition current among the Pisans," that "it was brought from Jerusalem by the Crusaders, about the commencement of the twelfth century," who will give us historical basis for it? The more especially when it is understood, that it actually opposes the Greek belief of that period. Mr. Taylor's reasonings and statements concerning infant baptism are good, but he is visionary when he speaks of mode.

G.

FONTS.

The primitive font must not be confounded with that which in late days, though much altered, still bears the name. The word "font" is from the Latin "fons," a fountain. This term plainly points us to the ancient mode. See Wheatley, Comm. Prayer, "On the Ministration of Pub. Bapt. to Inf.," pp. 336, 337.

Both Wheatley and Hart state that the fonts were adapted for immersion. The latter says, "The basin was always large enough to admit of the immersion of the infant, its interior averaging one foot in depth by about two feet in diameter, comparing strangely with the pigmy scoops that now *adorn* the chancel arch of so many of our churches, and which prevent the possibility of complying with the rubric or the parent's wish, when total immersion is desired." Parish Churches, p. 44.

"The font should be sufficiently capacious to admit of the total immersion of an infant, a practice which has become nearly obsolete, but this injunction of our Church is occasionally required to be observed, and provision ought always to be made for its due performance." Bart's Anglican Ch. Architecture, Oxford, 1843, p. 52. See as to the requirements of the Church of England in regard to the font, Wheatley, p. 337, n. 52.

But the circumstances which surround the Church in our day resemble more, so far as baptism is concerned, those of the first ages. For like them, we baptize adults as well as infants, and therefore, need what they had,—baptisteries capable of answering the design of total immersion in case of both. Wheatley, as above quoted, describes them. See also as to form. Hart as above, and best of all, Bingham, under "Baptisteries," in the index to his Antiquities.

The service of baptism in the ancient Church was not thrown open to the public in all its parts, in the case of adults, at least so it may be inferred from the candidates being naked. Infants are still immersed naked among the Greeks. v. Baird's Modern Greece, p. 99.

"*A Series of Ancient Baptismal Fonts,* Chronologically arranged, drawn by F. Simpson, Jr., and engraved by R. Roberts, London, Septimus Prowett, 1828, fol.," contains engravings of fonts intended for immersing infants.

H.

INTRUSION INTO OTHER MEN'S DIOCESES.

(Note to page 168.)

We have no disposition to add to present disputes, but while we are so often unjustly attacked for following the authority of the whole Church in preference to that of a part only of the Western Church, we may, at least, call the attention of those who blame us, to the decisions of the ecumenical councils. The British bishops at the Reformation did only what, in accordance with ecumenical law, pertained to their powers, and after that event (and, indeed, before), the Patriarch of Constantinople or the Patriarch of Jerusalem had as much right to violate the above-mentioned canons as the Bishop of Rome, and the British Church has now as much right, and considering the doctrine involved, tenfold more right, to appoint a Bishop of Rome, than he had a few years since, and at other periods, to introduce schism and heresy into the British Islands. Those who left the British Churches at those times were misguided, though sincere. No learned Anglican is indisposed to give Rome the place assigned her by the ecumenical councils, although the reason alleged in the twenty-eighth canon of Chalcedon no longer holds, if she would repent and go neither *against* nor *beyond* the ecumenical decisions. The *primacy* which the councils gave her, and the reasons for it are one thing; the *supremacy* which she claims, and the reasons upon which she bases it, another and widely different thing. Why should any one for the sake of this last, which rests not upon the decision of an ecumenical council but upon private Western opinion, leave his own bishop, whose power and authority are guaranteed by the laws of the whole Church, and embrace the cause of schism, and what after all is idolatry, for the arguments of its devotees are simply those of the intelligent heathen? For they are not such fools as to give anything more than relative worship and honor to those who among them hold the same position that the Virgin and saints do in Rome; they look upon images in the same way, and defend them by as subtle arguments. In judging Rome lightly, we often think wrongly of the ancient and modern heathen, and this, too, against the testimony of those who know them best. They worship now, as did their ancestors, not the image itself absolutely, but "per simulachra," through the image.

The Anglican communion did, at the Reformation, restore to the bishops their canonical rights, of which they had been deprived by the Pontiff of the Western communion. It restored to the people the Holy Scriptures. It drove away all idolatry, as did the primitive Church, by teaching men to worship God alone. Like the primitive Church, its liturgy was to be read in the tongue of the people, so that they might offer God an intelligent and acceptable worship, and the rich and abundant blessing of heaven has attended the Anglo-Catholic communion ever since. Because in these things she has been true to God, no weapon formed against her has prospered. In proportion as England has stood firmly by primitive truth has she advanced; in proportion as she has wavered has she lost. Her history for the past three hundred years is a striking proof of the truths of Holy Writ: "Righteousness exalteth a nation, but sin is a reproach to any people." "Godliness is profitable unto all things, having promise of the life that now is, and of that which is to come."

Because some abuse the Scriptures, shall we forbid their use? Because men confound the primitive position of the right and duty of reading them, and of profiting by their teaching and examples, with the later notions common to Latins and Puritans, that a part of the Church or an individual, may usurp the position of the whole Church, in ecumenical council assembled, and convert private opinion into Church doctrine, shall we desert the primitive position? Besides, if the Roman Pontiff has a right to appoint bishops in England, in the face of decisions of the whole Church, 1500 years old, and trample under foot ecumenical laws, what guarantee have we that anything sacred is safe? In this case, infallible power is placed in the hands of a bishop, whose predecessor stands to this hour condemned, not only as fallible but as absolutely heretical, and condemned, too, by an ecumenical council. So that the Church has decided in the case of Honorius, not only that a Pontiff may err, but that he has erred. A man then who admits the Latin notion, opposes the whole Church acting with the promised aid of the Holy Ghost. Whether in this case, the whole Church or a part is most likely to be right, and whether it is safe to follow a part against the whole, the individual must decide. Of one thing we may be sure, that the Roman theory lacks authority, and that it has never been universally received, and never will, and that, moreover, the British bishops at the Reformation, so far as they obey the ancient councils, so far as they adopted and acted upon the principle that they should not go against, not beyond the decisions of the whole Church, did only what was their solemn duty as keepers of God's heritage.

And if, in some things, defects may be pointed out, and we frankly admit, as have many of her most learned men and as she herself does in her commination office, that in some things she might be more perfect, yet it should be remembered that she is free from all heresy, from all idolatry, and is now in doctrine the purest part of the whole Church. If faults exist, going to Rome, to Constantinople, or to Geneva, will not heal them. Schism is not God's way. This is no remedy for lack of perfection. Indeed, the Church's teachings if carried out would leave less cause to complain. And the Church in her best state has had many imperfections,—imperfect men, imperfect obedience to her teachings, and often, indeed, opposition. While we strive for perfection (and this is our duty), let us not fail to remember that to be harassed by imperfections is often the lot, indeed we had almost said, a mark of the militant Church.

Let every one remember then that if, in some few things, defects may be pointed out, rending asunder the body of Christ is not a way to remedy them. Indeed, nothing would so much add to the Catholic and Apostolic character of the Anglican communion as for the Latins to cease the work of drawing off some inexperienced person here and there. Rome has enough to do to care for her own fearful errors. Yet she will not learn. For 800 years she has been endeavoring, right in the face of the decisions of that Church which she confesses in the Nicene creed, to stir up schism in the Eastern Catholic communion. But her gains in the Patriarchates have been in a great measure from Monophysite and Nestorian sects alone, and the events of 1839 in Russia show how slight is her hold upon those of the "Orthodox" whom in Europe she has drawn within her pale, when the secular pressure is removed. In the British Islands she has been more successful, but mainly from political or national causes. And she has herself lost many. So that her uncanonical efforts to distract and divide have chiefly resulted in producing, wherever it has been tried, a feeling of disgust and abhorrence. History teaches us the lesson that no one part of the Church can usurp the mission of the whole. Such claims never find universal recognition. And one not of the least evils is, that whatever of truth is held by Rome is often confounded to its prejudice with her error. We do not say that any part of the Church is what it ought to be in every respect, but if there is a defect let it be remedied by the proper, the canonical, authorities, not by a foreign and intruding body of schismatics who have no purity to spare. And in doing our best to reform others let us remember the same. One great difficulty in the way of union is the harassing and proselytizing attempts of the Latin part of the Western Church. And there never will be union so long as it continues. Its natural result is alienation and hostility between all concerned. The canons of the Church recognize the *duty* of every Christian's continuing in communion with his own, not a foreign, bishop. It seems doubtful whether, unless for urgent cause as heresy, *defined as such by the whole Church*, he severs himself from him, he does not also sever himself from Catholic communion or rather from the Catholic Church. The language of the canons in favor of the bishops' rights and against outside interference is very strong. The safest way is to guard the SACRED LIBERALISM of the Church, to distinguish between *mere opinion* and *ecumenical doctrine*, to recite the creed as the Church made it, to carry out all the ecumenical canons so far as they can be, and to observe all the ancient rites, where it may be done without prejudice to the weak, and perhaps this may always be.

APPENDIX II.

The Greeks in cursing the Latins and all Westerns, the Latins in cursing the Greeks and all Protestants, must curse many whom God hath not cursed, and curse them, too, for holding some doctrines dear to the primitive Church and which no council of the whole Church has ever condemned. All do well to avoid this sin, and the kindred one of raising in a diocese an altar against an altar without ecumenical authority. Of course we do not condemn altogether the position of Luther. The bishops of the Latin communion are bishops, but, so far as independent synodical action is concerned, in name only, and may be set up or removed, not by the canonical authority, but by Rome, for whose right to do these things the conciliar decisions furnish no pretext. While, therefore, the Continental Reformers had many faults and did some things which we cannot approve, and held some opinions which we do not, yet it must be remembered that in the main their movement was for the restoration of primitive doctrine and against not the whole Church but a part; and if they acted against the bishops, yet the bishops acted in obtaining their office and in failing to discharge its duties against the whole Church. All controversialists are too narrow. The truth is there are more or less of faults in every quarter. No part is perfect; nor do the narrow limits of any part contain all the elect. It may have been so ordered by God that all might see the necessity of unity, and that finally schism might be done away by the voluntary union of all.

Conciliation, the taking of such steps as shall pave the way to union among all Christian people, the removal of all just grounds of objection, combined with firmness against idolatry and everything unauthorized, will be sure of reward with God, and be beneficial to the Church, by enabling it to turn in other channels the mighty energies which, for 800 years, it has been wasting in intestine discords. If the pure are blessed, no less blessed are the peacemakers. On page 164 we have spoken of Latin orders conferred in dioceses not Latin as invalid. We do not mean, however, that the British and Oriental Churches may not receive them as valid. On the contrary, since this rule, if applied with strict impartiality, would condemn many irregularities and defects in both, and since in all parts irregularities have prevailed, the consequence is, that if irregularity be invalidity no Church will be left. The English Church then does prudently and in accordance with some ancient precedent. When she observes the canons fully herself, she may with less inconsistency rebuke others. The case of the American Church and its reception of Latin orders is not precisely similar to the English. The case is one of some difficulty, even so far as the British Churches are concerned, there being arguments for and against receiving any as ordained, except those who derive their succession through the legitimate Anglican Bishops. The whole subject may be left with them.

I.

MENNO ON THE MODE.

It is sometimes stated that Menno held to immersion as essential to baptism, but such a notion is without warrant. He does, indeed, speak of immersion in his Instruction (v. Concerning Baptism, p. 32), but he refers to the custom of those who immersed infants, not his own. The Reformers, who deemed pouring valid, use much stronger language. Calvin and Luther have been already quoted. Melancthon and Zuingle may be added. Melancthon even states, " Baptism is the entire action, that is to say, the mersion and the pronunciation of the words, I baptize thee in the name of the Father, and of the Son, and of the Holy Ghost." Loci Comm., quoted by Bishop Whittingham, on Baptismal Regeneration. The Mennonites plead the authority of Menno for the use of pouring or sprinkling as baptism. (v. Brown Encyc. of Relig. Knowl., art. " Mennonites.")

But Morgan Edwards, in his materials towards a " Hist. of the American Baptists," p. 92, Philada., 1770, states as follows:

" The Mennonists in Pennsylvania, and in other parts of the world, have somewhat deviated from Menno in matters both of faith and practice, particularly in that of baptism. He (in his *Declaration concerning Christian Baptism in Water*, printed in 1539, page 24), expressly saith : ' After we have searched ever so diligently, we shall find no other baptism besides dipping in water, which is acceptable to God and maintained in his word ;' after which he adds, p. 39 : ' Let who will oppose, this is the only mode of baptism that Christ Jesus instituted, and the Apostles taught and practised.' Accordingly, Menno was dipped, and did dip others. His successors did the same, except when they made proselytes in prisons, or were hindered from going to rivers, and this they excused from the consideration of *necessity*, just as Cyprian in his 60th epistle, excuses the usage of *sprinkling* or *pouring* instead of *dipping*, because the subjects were confined to their beds, which made it to be called *clinical baptism*."

According to Mr. Edwards then, the early Mennonite view was like that of the primitive Church, so far as the *immersion* is concerned (though he does not state whether it was trine or single), that is, it was the rule, but the compends were used in necessity. In other words, the mode was not *in all cases* essential.

Upon seeing the statement of Mr. Edwards, the author put himself in connection with Rev. Amos Herr and his brother, who are both Mennonite ministers, and who reside near Lancaster, Pa., and he was positively informed by them, that Mr. Edwards must have made some mistake ; that Menno nowhere made the mode essential ;

APPENDIX I.

that on that point he had said but little, and that the little uttered by him seemed to show that his use was not immersion. Their testimony is corroborated by that of other Mennonites, whose views have met the author's cognizance.

Knowing that men who are well intentioned may, in the heat of party spirit, be led beyond the truth, and not possessing the original of Menno's works, the author wrote to a Baptist, second to none of his brethren in learning, and the following is the reply.

"When Menno, in his explanation of Christian baptism, makes the statement to which you call my attention, he is replying to the representation of some, 'that Christ and his holy Apostles *have taught two different baptisms in the water*,'* one of believers, and the other of unconscious infants. And he takes occasion to say, 'How diligently soever we seek, night and day, yet we find not more than one baptism in the water that is pleasing to God, expressed and contained in God's word, namely, this baptism upon faith, commanded by Christ, taught and practised by his holy Apostles, which is administered and received unto the forgiveness and remission of sins, with such measure or limitation as we have very amply set forth above in the first words of Peter, Acts 2 : 38. *But this other baptism, namely, of little children, we never find.*'†

"Mr. Edwards, I doubt not, misunderstood the words which he quoted. Had he been familiar with the Dutch language, and had he examined what precedes and what follows those words, he would not have quoted them for the purpose for which he brought them forward. It would be entirely wrong to suspect him of any intention to deceive his readers. I can see how the mistake here was very easily made, and this naturally led to a similar mistake in regard to the Latin passage. By the phrase *modus baptizandi*, I suppose that Menno there referred, not to what with us is commonly understood of the *mode* of baptizing, but to such a baptism as he had been advocating, namely, the baptism of believers. He had prefixed to his treatise, an address in Latin to his learned readers, and at the close of the treatise, he subjoined for their benefit a kind of peroration as follows:

"Gaudeat Sponsa Christi: Hic habes, piissime lector, debitum in ecclesia Dei baptizandi modum, qui longissima temporum obliteratione perierat, largissimo Dei dono ab integro restitutum. Obsistant ergo principes ut velint. Obsistant Docti ingenii sui acumine ut norint. Obsistant universi qui sub coelo sunt omnibus modis quibus possunt, hic est unicus ille baptizandi modus, quem Christus Jesus ipse instituit, et apostoli docuerunt, celebraruntque. Invicta semper manebit veritas, quamvis a multis oppugnatur fortissime. Qui vero legit Christiano judicio, et bene intelligit, coelestem hanc

---

* Twee verscheyden Doopselen in den water geleert hebben, p. 766.

† Maer dit andere Doopsel, namelijck, der onmondiger kinderen, en vinden wy ymmers niet, p. 767.

veritatum Christi tam multis seculis deperditam jam jam ita repertam gratulabitur, quod non immerito, pro suo erga nos favore. Deo optimo maximoque immensas gratias agat. Vale, humiliare, lege, cape, crede, vive, et Dominus erit tecum."*

The statement of a Reformed Mennonite minister verifies the above. It occurs in a letter to a Baptist friend who has kindly allowed me to glance at it. We have heard similar statements from the lips of Old School Mennonite ministers. The work of Rev. John Newton Brown on the "Life and Times of Menno," contains the statement of Edwards, and the Mennonite alludes to it throughout.

"Dear Friend:

"Your favor of the 11th is received; also the 'Life and Times of Menno,' in English and German, for which please accept my sincere thanks. . . . .

"The usual mode of administering baptism in our Church is by once pouring water on the head of the candidate, in the kneeling posture, accompanied by the laying on of the hands of the officiating bishop, who pronounces the benediction. This is the mode in all the Churches which we know of that are recognized by us as brethren.

"You assert that 'such of the works of Menno as you have seen, show that he believed and practised baptism by *immersion*,' and wish to know 'why immersion (the Apostolic mode) was *given up*, and upon what grounds pouring is practised.'

"To answer this question fully would require more space than the limits of a letter will admit of. It also seems to me that before you require me to show why we have departed from the Apostolic mode, you should prove that immersion really was the only mode the Apostles practised. I am not acquainted with the Greek language; and amongst those who are acquainted with it I believe there is a difference of opinion about the signification of the word you rely upon as authority for your assumption. Command, you have none from the Apostles, and cannot show that they ever dipped a single person under the water.

"I have read and re-read all the works of Menno I have seen,

---

* "Let the bride of Christ rejoice.

"Here thou hast, most pious reader, the due custom of baptizing in God's Church, which had been forgotten for a very long period, and had perished, but by the most ample gift of God has been restored anew. Let, then, princes oppose as they may. Let the learned oppose with all their acumen. Let all under the heavens oppose in every way they are able; this custom is the only one which Christ Jesus Himself instituted, and which the Apostles taught and practised. Truth will ever remain unconquered, however strongly it may be attacked by many. But he who reads with a Christian's judgment and has a good understanding, will wish well to this celestial truth of Christ, which, during so many ages, was lost but is now discovered, and with good cause will he return great thanks to God, the best and greatest for his favor towards us."

especially those sent by you, and am at a loss to know how you arrived at the conclusion that he 'believed and practised baptism by immersion.' I have never seen the words quoted in note No. 1 of the appendix to the 'Life and Times of Menno,' and for reasons which I will give, *doubt very much* whether Menno ever *uttered* them.

"In the times of Menno baptism was almost universally administered by pouring or sprinkling. At least this was the mode practised by the Catholics, Lutherans, Zuinglians, and Calvinists (if I am not mistaken). There was a warm controversy kept up between Menno and all these different persuasions about infant baptism, and also about the qualifications of adult candidates, and in his writings he speaks much of their abuse of the ordinance by administering it to carnal persons and infants, but we do not find any reference to the mode, which is unaccountable if he held the views imputed to him by you and the author referred to. The Mennonites were very much persecuted and cruelly maltreated on account of their opposition to infant baptism, but no severity could deter them from protesting against what they viewed as a perversion of a Gospel ordinance. They also zealously protested against and opposed all the wicked and ungodly practices of all perverted sects and denominations of professing Christians, and every perversion of the doctrine and ordinances of Christ and his Apostles. But, so far as I have seen, I cannot find one word with regard to their mode of administering baptism being a perversion.

"If Menno and his brethren of his day held the views of the present 'Baptists' with regard to the mode of administering this ordinance, I am at a loss to account for their silence on this one subject whilst they are so bold and free on all others.

"Whilst I do not know of a single sentence in the works of Menno which can *fairly* be construed into the *idea* that he held that there 'is no other mode of baptism besides dipping in water which is acceptable to God and maintained in his word,' there is at least one sentence which affords strongly presumptive evidence of a contrary view. In his 'Admonition addressed to the scorners of the word and baptism,' speaking of the weighty commands of Christ in regard to confessing Christ, loving our enemies, serving our neighbors, and suffering for our brethren, he says: 'We think that these and the like commands were more powerful and weightier to perverse flesh, which is naturally prone to follow its own way, than to have a *hand full of water applied.*'

"In the second part of the 'Martyr's Mirror,' embracing a period from 1524 to 1660, wherein the chief part of the sufferers were Mennonites, and a great many controversies about the subject of baptism are recorded, so far as I know, we do not find a single instance where either party charged the other with a departure from the true mode of administering the rite. All the departures of the Mennonites from the established mode of worship by the Papists, were charged against them to establish the charges of sedition and heresy. On the other hand, the Mennonites urged the irregular lives and immoralities of the Catholics against them, as well as their 'idolatrous *infant baptism*, sacrament, confessions, indulgences, mass, vespers, &c., &c.,' proving their inconsistency by the Scriptures. But never a word about *baptism* by *immersion!* Is not this strong presumptive evidence that the *Mennonites did not consider* the mode of pouring unscriptural, or that the Mennonites did not employ a different mode of administering the ordinance from what the Papists did?

"Besides this we find that they were often closely interrogated in regard to things connected with their worship; where they held their meetings, who was present, what minister served them, where they were baptized, who was present, and by whom the ordinance was administered, and how many were baptized, &c. But never do we find a question with regard to the stream or fountain wherein they were dipped! But we do find that some of those who did give answers to these questions, mention that they were baptized in such and such a *house*. These *houses* were not Churches, and consequently not likely to have fountains in them. I think I remember to have noticed this repeatedly in the 'Martyr's Mirror,' but cannot now mention many of the places where it occurs, but on page 479 we find one informing his interrogators that he was baptized in a *small new house*, and another instance occurs on page 967, where it is expressly said the ordinance was administered in a *house*.

"These were Menno's brethren, with whom he associated, and with whom he communed; and whilst he was so strict in requiring a unity of the Spirit, and that believers should be of one mind, is it not strange that he should be silent on so important a subject as this would be, if he held the sentiments imputed to him by the Baptists of the present day? Is there a *Baptist* production in the world, of half the size of Menno's works, where the sentiments of the author, in respect to baptism, are not clearly expressed?

"The author of the 'Life and Times of Menno' says the Mennonites have degenerated. This we admit, of the old Mennonite Church, and it has been the case with the body of other Churches before them. But we find that where such degeneracy takes place, there are usually some faithful persons, or conservative spirits, who protest against such degeneracy. Especially is this the case where some of the important rules or ordinances of the Church are to be changed. There were still some faithful members and ministers in the Church, when this degeneracy commenced, who were moved by the spirit which animated Menno, and these protested stoutly against changes and innovations. But, so far as I know, we have no account or history of the time, manner, or means, when, where, or how this change was made; or a single voice of warning raised against this great departure, if Menno ever *taught* or *practised dipping*.

"Now I think the above good and sufficient reason why I should doubt whether Menno ever having held the sentiments attributed to him in the note referred to, or that the Mennonites ever did '*give up*' immersion. . . . .

"In the little book you sent me, I find nothing new about Menno (as I expected to do), but the author's attempt to show that he held immersion as the only true Apostolic mode of baptism; and his endeavors to associate him and his brethren with the present Baptist society. If he could even prove the first, it would no more establish the latter than the opposition to infant baptism was ground to confound the Mennonites and Munster sect, or the dipping does the Baptists and Mormons.

"There are not many of what we are used to call Baptists in our vicinity, and I have never had much intercourse with them, but from what I have read of them, and heard of them, as well as considerable conversation I have had with several members, I think there is a very wide difference between their profession and his, and a still wider one between them in principle. Menno insisted upon a good evidence of conversion and a change of life in applicants for reception into the Church, protested against swearing, against all self-defence, either in civil law or by force of arms, against holding office in government, or in any way connecting ourselves with the administration of justice. He maintained an entire separation of the kingdom of Christ from the kingdom of this world, and also an entire separation of the Church of Christ, or children of God, from all idolatrous worship. He held that all worship which was not in accordance with the doctrine of Christ and his Apostles is idolatry, and it is the duty of every child of God to protest against it by refusing to associate with them in worship, and that if they did so, they thereby made themselves partakers of their sins and evil deeds. They also held we must withdraw ourselves from every brother that walks disorderly, and have no company with them (read his articles Sending and Conduct of Preachers, Counter Arguments of Babylon, and of its Builders, with their Replications, and that on Excommunication), that they may be ashamed. All this (I think) your society reject, unless it is the first, and that (if I am not very much misinformed and my own observation deceives me), they reject practically in many places. The author of the book says 'comparisons are odious,' but I think if he admires Menno as much as he professes, he might profitably compare the body of which he is a member with Menno's precepts and example. At least if he were disposed to follow the side which had the advantage in the comparison."

If any one doubts the belief of Menno's followers, and supposes the statement on p. 48 of the American Baptist Almanac for 1860, which is reiterated on p. 48 of the same Almanac for 1861, by which the Mennonites are included with Antimission Baptists, Freewill Baptists, Six Principle Baptists, Seventh-day Baptists, Winebrennarians, Disciples or Campbellites, and Tunkers, as "denominations that practise immersion," is true, he had better visit a Mennonite community, or consult the following of their works. Mennonite Confession of Faith, with Burkholder's Reflections, Winchester, 1837, p. 405–417, and Conversation on Saving Faith, Lancaster, Pa., 1857, pp. 229–238, and 248–250. All these will most clearly evince the truth that they are among the most earnest opponents of total dipping. Indeed, Rev. Amos Herr, one of their ministers, stated to the author that they *never* use it. They sometimes use, however, baptism "in water with water" (see last ref. p. 249, 250). The person to be baptized kneels in the water and the administrator then pours water upon him. But see Brown, Encyclopædia of Relig. Knowl., art. "Mennonites," for their ordinary practice.

J.

WHENCE DID MENNO AND THE MENNONITES DERIVE THEIR BAPTISM?

We have already had occasion to refer to the mistakes of some writers who, perhaps, led astray by the fact that the term Anabaptist is now generally confined to Antipædobaptists, suppose that these terms are synonymous. Anabaptist simply means rebaptizer, and the great bulk of those who have been charged with it, have been strenuous supporters of infant baptism. Even in the present day, the Greeks of the Patriarchates rebaptize Latins. The Latins give conditional baptism to some who join them, and many clergymen of the English and American Churches rebaptize dissenters. All these are in this respect deemed Anabaptists by their opponents. Robinson is one of the few Baptists who avoided this error in the use of terms. (See his History of Baptism, pp. 412–420, Am. ed.) He states, that four of the six classes whom he there denominates Anabaptists, based rebaptism on other grounds than opposition to infant baptism. Up to the twelfth century, the term is ever used of Pædobaptists. All or nearly all after De Bruis, who bore it, were also Pædobaptists. Since Menno and the pouring Antipædobaptists and the English immersing Antipædobaptists, it has been, in common usage in England, applied only to them.

When Menno arose, it is not clear that there were any Antipædobaptist societies in existence. We know not who baptized him, or whether, indeed, he received any besides what was given him in infancy, though it is probable either that he baptized himself, or was baptized by some one who had received no other baptism than what was received in infancy. We have been able to find no facts on any of these points. But his own language places it beyond all doubt, that he did not make the slightest pretension to a baptismal succession even by pouring.*

His own words are,

"Here thou hast, most pious reader, the due custom of baptizing in God's Church, which had been *obliterated for a very long period*, and HAD PERISHED, but by the most ample gift of God has been *restored* ANEW. . . . . He who reads with Christian judgment, and understands well, will wish well to this celestial truth of Christ, which, *during so many ages, was lost*, but is now *discovered*, and, with good cause will he return great thanks to God, the best and greatest, for his favor towards us." See the original, p. 295, above.

The Latin is fully as strong as this English, so that it is evident,

1. That Menno believed that true baptism had been lost during *many ages*,

2. And hence, that for ages, no sect had existed from which he could obtain it.

3. That it was *discovered*, restored *anew* at the time when he wrote,

4. Consequently, he must have been self-baptized, or like Roger Williams and the English Baptists, he and his followers must have reinstituted a Divine ordinance by baptizing each other.†

The first Antipædobaptists with whom Menno connected himself

---

* John Smith, the founder of the English Antipædobaptists, lived among the Mennonites in Amsterdam, and it is worthy of note that, with all his prejudices against infant baptism and in favor of the Mennonite view, he yet deemed their claim to a baptismal succession so worthless, as to include their baptism in his assertion, that "all Christ's visible ordinances are lost." Indeed, Menno, in the passages cited above, is so far from making any such claim, that he frankly confesses that he had commenced adult baptism *anew* after it had been "*lost*" for "many ages."

† As to Menno's view on Modes, see Appendix I. As to the ancient Anabaptists, like the Novatians and Donatists, they were, as Wall (see references in index to his works to "Novatians, Donatists," &c.) has shown, and as even Robinson, in his classification above referred to, seems to confess, not rebaptizers on account of infant baptism, which they received and practised. The same is true of the Anabaptist sects of the middle ages, with the exception of De Bruis, and possibly a few others, who were, however, exceptions to the rule. The Munster fanatics seem to have been Antipædobaptist Anabaptists, but their baptism must have begun with themselves, as the followers of De Bruis's opinion on the subjects. His error on infant baptism disappeared almost at the time that was broached. A remark of Mosheim, which is perverted in almost every Antipædobaptist historical writer, as well as the perfectly unfounded claim of an Antipædobaptist succession through the Waldenses, will be found explained in Murdock's Mosheim, vol. iii, p. 200, n. 4. See also Faber's Vallenses and Albigenses. The Antipædobaptist writers, with the exception of Robinson, and perhaps, a few others, are perpetually confounding all the Anabaptists with the Antipædobaptists, although Wall has made such ignorance inexcusable. Let any one at all conver-

were *all*, so far as he has given us any account of them, originally not Antipædobaptist Waldenses, as some without warrant falsely assert, but Pædobaptists, and hence baptized in infancy. Compare "Menno Simon's Instructions," Rupp's translation, pp. 2–6, with the "Martyr's Mirror," Rupp's ed. 1837, preface p. 15, note, and id. p. 378, "Sicke Snyder."

K

RISE OF THE BAPTISTS IN ENGLAND.

By Baptists, we mean the immersing Antipædobaptists, as distinguished from such Antipædobaptists as the Mennonites, who do not make the mode essential. Let this be kept in mind, for it is a cardinal distinction. On the Baptist principles as to mode, the Mennonite is unbaptized and out of the visible Church. Dr. Cutting, in a work lately published (Historical Vindications), has attempted to clear up in favor of his brethren, the story of Smith's sebaptism. But at most he proves, that according to Smith and his companions, they instituted baptism among themselves, when all of them, administrators and candidates, were unbaptized. He brings the confession of Smith and his associates to prove this, so that it may be considered as admitted on all sides, that the Baptist denomination commenced in the early part of the 17th century, and that its baptism and ministry depend for their validity on the acts of men who were, on the Baptist theory, unbaptized. But Dr. Cutting does not touch the plain testimony of Robinson which he quotes, viz., "Mr. Smith, Mr. Helwisse, and the rest, having utterly dissolved and disclaimed their former Church, state, and ministry, came together to erect a new church by baptism, unto which they also ascribed so great virtue, as that they would not so much as pray together before they had it. And after some straining of courtesy who should begin, and that of John Baptist (Matt. 3 : 14) misalleged, Mr. Smith baptized first himself, and next Mr. Helwisse, and so the

sant with the facts, glance at Orchard, and he will find it an instance throughout of most wicked and continuous misrepresentation, in which the facts are the exceptions and the lies the rule. His fault may have been ignorance, but considering the fearful amount of harm his works have done and are doing to mislead, his account must be a fearful one at God's judgment bar.

rest, making their particular confessions." Robinson's Works, vol. iii, p. 168.*

As to the source of this information, Robinson has left us in no doubt. He says, "As I have heard from *themselves.*" v. id.

As to the speculations of the Baptist historians, Crosby and Ivimey, Dr. Cutting ingenuously remarks, that they "are hardly a reply to the express testimony of Robinson." But he starts this question, "Did he (Robinson) misinterpret *instituting baptism among themselves* by supposing it to mean *self-baptism?*" But Robinson, in the part quoted by Dr. Cutting, uses neither of these italicised expressions. His words are, "Lastly, if the Church be gathered by baptism, then will Mr. Helwisse's church appear to all men to be built upon the sand, considering the baptism it had and hath, which was, as *I have heard from themselves, on this manner.*" He witnesses, on the authority of these first Baptists, to the *specific fact, that Smith did begin that body by baptizing himself.*

Dr. Cutting states as a reason why this statement was not denied, that Smith was dead and Helwisse in England. But has he not shown that some of Smith's followers remained in Holland, and joined the Mennonites in that very city of Amsterdam? They still sympathized with Smith's Antipædobaptist views. Why did not they deny it? But Helwisse did, after his return to England and after Smith's death, find time to write. v. Crosby, vol. i, pp. 271, 272. Crosby, indeed, although he attempts as much as possible to clear Smith from this charge, yet says, on pp. 268, 269, that Smith

---

* The reference in full is as follows: (See Robinson's Works, iii, p. 168.) "Lastly, if the Church be gathered by baptism, then will Mr. Helwisse's appear to all men to be built upon the sand, considering the baptism it had and hath, which was, as I have heard from themselves, on this manner: Mr. Smith, Mr. Helwisse, and the rest, having utterly dissolved and disclaimed their former Church, state, and ministry, came together to erect a new Church by baptism, unto which they also ascribed so great virtue, as that they would not so much as pray together before they had it. And after some straining of courtesy who should begin, and that of John Baptist, Matt. 3 : 15 misalleged, Mr. Smith baptized first himself, and next Mr. Helwisse, and so the rest, making their particular confessions. Now to let pass his not sanctifying a public action by public prayer, 1 Tim. 4 : 4, 5; his taking unto himself that honor which was not given him, either immediately from Christ or by the Church, Heb. 5 : 4; his baptizing himself, which was more than Christ himself did, Matt. 3 : 14, I demand into what Church he entered by baptism, or entering by baptism into no Church, how his baptism could be true by their own doctrine? Or Mr. Smith's baptism not being true, nor he by it entering into any Church, how Mr. Helwisse's baptism could be true, or into what Church he entered by it? These things thus being, all wise men will think that he had small cause either to be so much enamoured of his own baptism, or so highly to despise other men's, for the unorderly or otherwise unlawful administration of it." v. note which follows, on p. 169, id. Ashton's ed., Boston, 1851.

baptized two ministers, Helwisse and Morton, which agrees, so far as it goes, with Robinson's account.

Besides, it should be remembered that these facts are narrated, not by Robinson alone, but by at least three or four others who had all the means of knowing, and who lived at that era, and Crosby does not so much deny as doubt them, and even this doubt is not expressed until more than a hundred years after Robinson gave this statement, although it was constantly reiterated.

If a mere doubt, with no foundation, can overbalance the open and uncontradicted witness of four or five individuals, most of whom were ministers, and all of whom were so conscientious as to follow what they deemed truth, at the cost of suffering and exile, and who were possessed of all the means for knowing the facts, what testimony need we believe? Of what fact of history can we be assured?

Dr. Cutting states, indeed, that the notion that they could institute baptism among themselves, was renounced by Smith and some of his company. But the words of Smith imply more. He and his companions renounced "the sentiment that they may, *se ipsos baptizare*, baptize themselves, as contrary to the order of Christ." Now if Smith and his fellows had wished to abjure the notion that, as Dr. Cutting surmises, baptism might be originated *among themselves*, the Latin language is surely sufficiently copious to express this idea without the slightest ambiguity. But their choice of the expression above, which Dr Cutting rightly translates, puts their intention out of dispute. The facts as stated then by Dr. Cutting, so far from militating against Robinson's statement, tend to confirm it. For why, unless Smith had baptized himself and the baptism of his followers were received from him, should they renounce the view that they could baptize themselves?

Such mere *suppositions* and "*speculations*" amount to nothing against the plain statement of *contemporary*, *competent*, and *conscientious witnesses*.

But Smith's renunciation of the principle of self-baptism does not affect the English Baptists. Helwisse, who carried the sect into England, is not among the number of those whose names were affixed to this renunciation. Nor can it be shown that any who may have accompanied him had any other adult baptism than what, on Baptist principles, derived its divine authority and validity from the self-baptism of John Smith. The position, then, of the English Baptists amounts to this: their present baptism is derived from the self-baptism of an unbaptized man, which self-baptism he afterwards renounced as contrary to the order of Christ. This conclusion is based upon the *facts* in the case.

Their position, as stated by the Baptists themselves, is that unbaptized men dipped each other and called that baptism, but the chief man among them afterwards renounced such dipping.

This is founded upon the mere conjecture of Baptist writers, not one of whom lived for at least a century after the statement of the facts by Robinson and others.

Whichever view is adopted it comes to this: the first administrator and the first candidate were both unbaptized, and consequently out of the visible Church and without any claim to valid ordination.

Of course such baptism and all derived from it, like that of the modern Baptists, are equally without validity on the Baptist hypothesis.

But such an absurdity is admitted among the Baptists in regard to their own baptism, though few of them, probably, if placed 250 years back, would have looked upon Smith's act as being other than wild and unauthorized, as did the Mennonites.

Yet who of them can prove that his own baptism is not derived from him?

Such was the "Rev. John Smith, founder of the *first English Baptist Church*," as he is termed by a late Baptist writer (J. Newton Brown, in Bapt. Fam. Magazine, May, 1860, p. 142), and such the origin of the first congregation of immersing Antipædobaptists in the world.*

L.

BLOUNT'S MISSION.

(See pp. 248–249.)

Of Richard Blount and Samuel Blacklock little is known.

Was John Batte the individual whose bad conduct is reported in Ivimey, vol. ii, p. 389? (v. also id. p. 159), and whose name is spelt John Batty?

Some of Smith's followers joined the Mennonites when he did, and with him renounced their self-baptism. Some of them *may have* remained until 1643, the date of Batty's dispute at Tarling against

---

* On the whole subject of Smith's views and conduct, see Robinson's works, ed. Boston, 1851, index "Smith," "Baptism," and "Immersion." From all these references it is concluded that there is no proof in the original documents of the time that Smith was an *immersing* Antipædobaptist, although strongly opposed to infant baptism. That nothing occurs in the disputes between him and his opponents to show that he made the mode essential. Indeed, it is stated (v. id. vol. iii, p. 461), that "incidental allusions there are in their own works (Smith and Helwisse), and in the replies of Robinson, that the baptism which Mr. Smith performed on himself must have been rather by affusion or pouring. Nor is this supposition improbable from the fact that the Dutch Baptists, by whom they were surrounded, uniformly administered baptism by affusion." If this be so, we must date the rise of the societies of immersing Antipædobaptists about 20 or 30 years later. But this language is not specific, and is opposed to the general belief.

infant baptism, v. Ivimey, vol. ii, p. 159. As Puritans were constantly passing over, to avoid penal liabilities, and as they were zealous for the Bible alone as interpreted by their own heated fancies against primitive consent, it is easy to see that many *might* have connected themselves with these English Mennonites, and, perhaps, more than fill up the gaps made by death or return to England.

Batty may have been one of these converts, unless we suppose him to have been of the original number of Smith's dupes. If so, his baptism was given by Smith after he had plunged himself. In any event, whether he was baptized by Mennonites or by Smith, his baptism on the Baptist theory came through unbaptized men. For the Mennonite baptismal succession no man can be sure of. Who will tell us who baptized Menno, and demonstrate, not from unfounded supposition but from facts, a succession of those baptized before him after coming to adult age? As to the connection between Smith's followers and the Mennonites in Amsterdam, we know but little. But it is not unlikely that Baptist notions as to mode made some progress between Smith's day and 1705, the date when Dr. Wall wrote. For he states (vol. ii, p. 303), that "their general humor is to divide into several Churches on the least difference of opinions. . . . Some of them allow of no baptism but by immersion, or putting the baptized person into the water; but the most part of them admit of baptism by affusion of water. In short, every congregation of them almost does espouse some particular tenets, only they do all of them renounce infant baptism." The authority cited by him I have not seen, but from his known accuracy presume it reliable.

A reliable authority states, that Dr. Starck (Geschichte der Taufe, p. 348), "speaking of a strict party which arose in Friezland and its vicinity, some time after the beginning of the seventeenth century, says, some of them have again *introduced among themselves* even entire immersion, and on this account they have been called the immersers by other congregations. Still with the most, only the pouring of water upon the head has been introduced." This probably explains the origin of the kind of them, to whom Dr. Wall refers as dipping. It will be observed that Blount is said to have received his baptism not in Friezland but in Amsterdam. Whether, if sent at all, he was sent before or after their rise, from the lack of date in the manuscript, we cannot tell. At any rate, the circumstances are not in favor of his having been baptized by the Friezlanders. Who the first administrator among them was is not known, but from the words italicized above, what his baptism was may be inferred. As an instance does occur among the first Antipædobaptists in the sixteenth century, it is probable that like those among whom they dwelt, they used all modes alike. The language of Zuingle seems to imply, that immersion was still the ordinary custom in Switzerland. It is here that the case occurs, viz., the baptism of the pastor of St. Gall, Wolfgang, in the river Rhine. But this does not prove that this mode was deemed invariably essential. They baptized also by pouring. Their practice varied like that of the Latins and Reformers. From these last we have stronger proofs of regard for immersion than from the bulk of the Mennonites.

A prominent Antipædobaptist states, that "In the Confession first edited, probably about the year 1580, which was inserted by Schyn in his Latin history of the Mennonites, early in the eighteenth century, there is no definite statement respecting what is usually called the mode of baptism, nor is there any in the four Confessions (those of 1600, 1627, 1630, and 1632), that are found in the work of Van Braght."

Why this silence if they held to immersion? The Dutch Protestants and the Latins of that period generally used affusion. There must have been antagonism if the Mennonites held to immersion as *essential*, but of this there is no mention.

The date of the rise of the Particular Baptist congregation of Spilsbury, to which, with so much boldness and so little authority, Orchard assigns Blount's sending, is 1633. Now of "the leading articles of the Christian faith of the churches of the United Flemish, *Friesland* and other Mennonites, and those in America, adopted A. D. 1632," article 7 is the only one which treats of baptism. It pointedly forbids infant baptism, but says not a word of the necessity of immersion; indeed, the only allusion is that contained in the expression " baptized with water." The conclusion is, " Done and finished in our United Churches, in the city of Dordrecht, 21st April, A. D. 1632. Subscribed, ... Amsterdam, Tobias Govertson, Peter Jahnsen Moyer, Abraham Dirkson, David ter Haer, Peter Jahnsen van Singel." Here then we find no proof that the Amsterdam Mennonites from whom Blount received baptism made the mode *essential*.

We have devoted so much space to this manuscript without date, or anything more than hearsay authority, not because it could claim serious consideration, but because of the stress laid upon it by later Baptist writers.

M.

THE BAPTISM OF THE FIRST IMMERSING ANTI-PÆDOBAPTIST CONGREGATION IN ENGLAND.

WE have already alluded to the manuscript, "*said* to be written by Mr. William Kiffin." Crosby, vol. i, p. 101.

This lacks the bases necessary for all sure historical conclusions, viz.: 1. Date. 2. And certainty as to the authority. The expression *said* shows this.

But Crosby and Ivimey seem to place some reliance upon it. And Orchard, with his characteristic disregard of facts and unauthorized statement, states positively that the account in the manuscript refers to Mr. Spilsbury's congregation. (Hist. of Eng. Bapt., p. 262.) But Ivimey states that it "does *not* relate to the people who left Mr. Lathrop's church in 1633, and who settled at Wapping under the care of Mr. Spilsbury," and this he repeats on the same page. (Vol. i, p. 145.)

Orchard afterwards modifies his assertion so far as to say, that "it is *natural* to conclude he (Kiffin) gave a statement of the rise of his own community."

The reason which he assigns as justifying this conclusion is somewhat remarkable. "As Mr. Kiffin joined the church at Wapping, it is *natural* to conclude he gave a statement of the rise of his own community." But is this a *necessary* conclusion from the premises? Why may not the account have been written by some one besides Kiffin? What proof is there except mere hearsay or supposition, that he ever penned a line of it? And even were this proved, a thing which is not even attempted, why *may not* the account relate to some Baptist congregation, organized some time after Spilsbury's, if it should be deemed sufficiently authentic to base any conclusion upon?

Crosby and Ivimey state, that most of the English Baptists immersed each other for baptism, and that the account which *is said* to have been Kiffin's, pertains to a few only. Even if it should be admitted, therefore it would not prove, for the great bulk of the Baptists, that their baptism or dipping does not come through unbaptized men.

What proof is there that any of them possess any other than we have given? But in addition to the difficulties which we have mentioned in admitting this manuscript as Kiffin's, or as referring to Spilsbury's congregation, it should be remembered that Spilsbury has left us something which bears upon this subject, and will serve to make clear the mode in which this first Particular Baptist congregation, as Crosby admits, first obtained baptism. We give it from Crosby, vol. i, p. 103. It is taken from Spilsbury's Treatise of Baptism, pp. 63, 65, 66. "And because some make it such an error, and, so far from any rule or example, for a man to baptize others *who is himself unbaptized*, and so think thereby to shut up the *ordinance* of God in such a strait that *none can come by it but through the authority of the Popedom of Rome;* let the reader consider who baptized John the Baptist before he baptized others. And if no man did, then whether he did not baptize others, he himself being unbaptized. *We are taught by this what to do upon like occasions.*"

He continues: "Further, I fear men put more than is of right due to it, that so prefer it above the Church, and all other *ordinances* besides; for they can assume and erect a church, take in and cast out members, elect and ordain officers, and administer the supper; and all anew, without any looking after succession any further than the Scriptures. But as for baptism, they must have that sucessively from the Apostles, though it comes through the hands of Pope Joan. What is the cause of this, that men can do all from the Word but only baptism?"

We can only add with Crosby, who quotes this: "Now is it probable that this man should go over the sea to find an administrator of baptism?"

From Spilsbury's own words, then, it is evident, 1. That he believed that all baptism had perished; and, 2. That it is perfectly right for unbaptized men to begin it; 3. That unbaptized men had so acted.

Let the reader consider what he says of baptism being shut up in the Church of Rome, unless it were to be recovered by unbaptized men dipping each other, and his reasoning from this as a fixed fact, and his adducing the case of St. John the Baptist as apposite to the position of the first Baptists. See also his way of speaking of those who opposed the view which he advocates; that is, that unbaptized men may originate baptism, and how he places the acts to "take in and cast out members, elect and ordain officers, and administer the supper," in the same category with the right to reinstitute a divine ordinance by reciprocal immersion. His point is, that for all these acts, his opponents looked for no "succession," and that succession as to baptism was as unessential.

There is in all this no claim to a succession through the Dutch Antipædobaptists, nor anything to imply that he thought this essential; on the contrary, he seems to have no doubt as to the perfect validity both of his reciprocal baptism and reasoning. The alternatives with him are, either go to Rome and Pope Joan for baptism, or begin it yourself, not between the former and the Mennonites.

And it is a noticeable feature in the writings of Spilsbury and the earlier Baptists, that they never adduce any claims to any baptism but their own. They frankly state the principle upon which they acted to be that unbaptized men may baptize. They state that all baptism had perished. They never except the Dutch Antipædobaptists. They never deny the charge, constantly reiterated by their opponents, that they had established a new baptism and a new church, but, on the contrary, they fully indorse these acts.*

At a later period we do indeed find one making the statement on mere hearsay that they had received baptism from Holland; but, setting aside the fact that there is no proof that the Mennonites at that time were themselves immersed, much less that they could prove a succession of immersed adults through all ages, there is this fact to be considered, viz., that such an event is never mentioned by

---

* See Tracts on Liberty of Conscience, Hanserd Knolly's Society's ed. London, 1846, pp. 86, 164, 167. Compare Brown Bapt. Family Magazine, March, 1859.

Spilsbury, the first pastor of a Calvinistic Baptist congregation, although he touches upon the origin of their baptism, nor by any other who lived in the period of their rise and acted with them. When such a report does arise, it is founded upon no certain documents, but upon mere hearsay, without mention even of an author for the story. Spilsbury, by implying that they had their baptism from unbaptized men, shows that whoever the first administrators were, they had not been themselves immersed on their own profession of faith, else he would have deemed them baptized.

This most effectually disposes of all the hearsay of the Mennonites or others being the administrators, even if we should admit what no man can prove, that there was an immersing Mennonite in the world at the time. Whoever they were, Spilsbury and all the earliest Baptists imply as clearly as words will make it, that they were unbaptized,—and they should know best.

Let any Baptist read Crosby, in this place, and he will find little ground to believe that Spilsbury's baptism or his own began with the Apostles. All goes to show that unbaptized men began it; else, why should Spilsbury defend himself and his brethren and justify such dipping as valid baptism. It would have been sufficient to deny it if he believed the charge false. But on the contrary his whole tenor implies its truth. So Crosby, who cites this, understood him. Crosby does not stop here: he quotes from two other Baptists, Tombes and Lawrence, to prove that the baptism administered by an unbaptized person is valid. Both presuppose what Crosby confesses, that the founders of the Baptist sects when on their own theory unbaptized dipped each other. To these the Baptist reader will do well to refer. Crosby, p. 106, vol. i, adds with reference to this mode of what he terms (p. 104) "restoring the true baptism," as follows: "It was a point much disputed for some years. The Baptists were not a little uneasy about it at first; and the Pædobaptists thought to render all the baptizings among them invalid, for want of a proper administrator to begin their practice; but by the excellent reasonings of these and other learned men, we see their beginning was well defended, upon the same principles on which all other Protestants built their reformation !!!"*

Did the Protestants then *found* a new Church,—did they not profess merely to *reform* the old as the Jews did after their apostasy? The Baptist theory is a founding anew of the Church—the Protestant is that of a reformation, the essence of the Church still remaining, only those things which were foreign to this being cast aside. The Baptist view is that a rite essential to the being of the visible Church had utterly perished, *i.e.*, true baptism, and consequently the visible Church itself; a conclusion which makes Christ a liar.

---

* Crosby, vol. i, pp. 147–148, frankly states that Spilsbury's Calvinistic Baptist congregation, which broke off from the Independents in 1633, was the first of that faith in England.

N.

DATE OF THE ADOPTION AMONG ENGLISH ANTIPÆDOBAPTISTS OF THE IDEA THAT IMMERSION IS ESSENTIAL.

THAT the mode among the Mennonites was not uniform or essential, a late Baptist writer of learning and acumen plainly states. After remarking that the English Brownists became converts to the Mennonite view of the subjects, he adds: "They parted from the Dutch (Antipædobaptists) where the Dutch parted from Christ and his Apostles. . . . . The mode of baptism, unsettled and various on the continent, became with them the fixed mode of immersion, with the greater facility, perhaps, because dipping had been preserved to about this time in the Church of England, but especially for the reason that a voluntary profession of personal faith must be in exact accordance with the statutes of the great Lawgiver himself.

"The English mind thus dropped off at once the leading eccentricities of the continent." v. Dr. Cutting, Hist. Vindic. pp. 38–39.

Yet some Baptists, unlike Robinson and Cutting, forget this point of the difference of mode so far as to attempt to trace a succession through these same Dutch Anabaptists. All the Anabaptists, Antipædobaptists, or Mennonites, who figure in English history prior to Smith, seem to have made the subjects the great point. The author has failed to find any clear evidence of any Antipædobaptist confession in which immersion is made essential until 1644. Article 40 of the London Confession of that date is clearly in favor not only of the primitive character of immersion, but also of its necessity to baptism. From Dr. Featley's statement it is evident that their custom was to immerse.

Three Baptist productions, "Confessions of Faith," "Broadmead Records," and "Tracts on Liberty of Conscience," contain quite full notices of the first English Antipædobaptists, but it is a striking fact, that up to 1644 there seems no clear evidence that any of them made the mode *essential*. All modes seem to have been used among the earlier Antipædobaptists of the continent indifferently. But the ordinary practice, so far as any notice exists, was pouring or sprinkling.

If we attach any value to the account upon which Orchard places so much reliance, it is clear that at the date when Blount is said to have been sent over to Holland to get baptism, the English Antipædobaptists had not revived the ancient custom of immersion.* See p. 248 above, note.

---

* Even as late as Fox's day there seem to have been no Englishmen of Antipædobaptist views. For he says, "There is great reason to give God thanks on this account, that I hear not of any Englishman that is inclined to this madness." See Wall, vol. ii, pt. ii, chap. viii, 6, p. 315. See this whole section.

It is somewhat doubtful, whether, if Smith's claims be rejected, Roger Williams has not the best claim to the name of father of the immersing Antipædobaptists. From the early records of the English branch of the society, it does not appear that any clear statement exists that they made immersion *essential* until 1644, five years after Williams and his companions started the notion. Spilsbury's move in 1633 was based on opposition to infant baptism. Nothing is said concerning mode. Between this date and 1644 it made its appearance, and was received by those who signed the London Confession. Hanserd Knollys, one of the most prominent Antipædobaptists of the seventeenth century, spent from 1633 until 1642 in America (see article upon him in Brown's Encyc. Relig. Knowl.). During all this period, he was, says Brown, a Baptist, that is, he was an opponent of infant baptism. He was in New Hampshire, Massachusetts, and Long Island, and may have learned something of Williams, particularly as Williams was well known, and Knollys may have adopted his ideas as to mode. His name is attached to the second edition of the London Confession. At any rate, Williams is one of the first, if not the first Antipædobaptist whom history mentions as making immersion *essential*.

O.

BAPTISMAL SUCCESSION AMONG THE TUNKERS OR DUNKERS.

The following account is from a Baptist minister, Morgan Edwards, who favors them.

After stating that two parties of them came to America, the former in A.D. 1719, and the latter in 1729, he continues: "These two companies had been members of one and the same church, which originated at Schwardzenau, in the year 1708. The first constituents were Alexander Mack and wife, John Kipin and wife, George Grevy, Andreas Rhoney, Lucas Fetter, and Joanna Nethigheim. These had been bred Presbyterians, except Kipin, who was a Lutheran, and being neighbors, they consorted together to read the Bible, and edify one another in the way they had been brought up, for as yet they did not know that there were any Baptists in the world. However, believer's baptism, and a congregational church soon gained upon them, insomuch that they were determined to obey the Gospel in these matters. They desired Alexander Mack to baptize them, but he, deeming himself in reality unbaptized, refused, upon which they cast lots to find who should be administrator.

On whom the lot fell hath been carefully concealed. However, baptized they were in the river Eder by Schwardzenau, and then formed themselves into a Church, choosing Alexander Mack to be their minister. They increased fast, and began to spread their branches to Merienborn and Epstein,* having John Naass and Christian Levy to be their ministers in those places. But persecution quickly drove them thence, some to Holland and some to Creyfelt. Soon after, the *mother Church* removed voluntarily from Schwardzenau to Serustervin, in Frizland, and from thence, migrated towards America in 1719. And in 1719, those of Creyfelt and Holland followed their brethren. Thus we see that all the Tunker churches in America sprang from the Church of Schwardzenau in Germany; that that Church began in 1708 with only seven souls, and that in a place where no Baptists had been, in the memory of man, nor any now are." See Morgan Edwards' Materials towards a History of the American Baptists, pp. 65, 66.

Here we have Roger Williams's reciprocal immersion by men who, on their own views, were unbaptized. If baptism administered by the mode then common be no baptism, where do they get the right to baptize? Is the immersing of an unbaptized man by another unbaptized man God's divinely appointed baptism, and is it written in Scripture that such possess authority to baptize, and if so, where?

P.

WHENCE THE ANTIPÆDOBAPTISTS DERIVE THEIR BAPTISM.

The three sources from which the American Antipædobaptists claim baptismal and ministerial succession have thus been treated of. They are the English and American source, from which are derived the Regular or Calvinistic Baptists, the Freewill Baptists, the Campbellites, the Six Principle, the Seventh Day, and the Antimission Baptists. The German or Schwardzenau source, from which the Tunkers come. The Dutch source, from which have sprung the Mennonites. Between Roger Williams and Spilsbury's congregations, there is but a difference of six years in origin. Some from the English source in after years came over and connected themselves with the American Baptists, or founded new congregations, so that these sources may be considered as one. Their streams are so commingled that no man can separate them.

The two former sources symbolize so far as their views of the in-

---

* This word is blurred in the original.

validity of infant baptism and the necessity of immersion is concerned. But the last wholly dissents from this last position.

The baptism possessed by all the sects above enumerated under source i, is derived from Smith, Spilsbury, and Williams; and unless their self-dipping, or reciprocal immersion, was valid baptism, all these sects on their own principles are without it.

The Mennonites are in the same strait, for they are unable to prove a succession of baptized adults beyond Menno or the fanatics of Munster. Like pretty much every sect in Christendom which has started novelties, it falls back upon some of the Waldenses, though without any documentary proof to back their claim. Indeed, it has now become common for any body in want of ecclesiastical paternity for its ideas, to claim the poor Waldenses. Of all their persecutions this is the worst, for they must have been very fecund to produce such a perfect host of wild and contradictory notions as are attributed to them, not to say very wild and contradictory themselves. In justice to them it should be said that they prefer to be held responsible only for the opinions which they hold or held, and that beyond mere assertion there are no facts to substantiate the view that they can justly be made to father Menno's or Smith's notions as to infant baptism. And the same statement is true of many other errors with which they are charged. Those who charge them with such notions slander them.

But the learned are now generally agreed, that the origin of the Waldenses must be ascribed to the twelfth century, so that a succession through them would amount to nothing; they, themselves, being an offshoot from the Latin communion, and having no other succession than what is derived through this channel. On this whole subject, see most fully and impartially in Murdock's Mosheim, vol. ii, p. 270–273, with the notes, and especially note 21.

INDEX.

Aix, synod of, on mode, 108.

Alcuin, strict for the trine immersion and condemned every other mode, 82, 146, 176.

Alexandrian (Coptic) rubric, 121.

Ambrose, St., on mode, 71; on the frequency of cases of clinic baptism, 171.

Anabaptists, six sorts of, 237; all of them often confounded together as Antipædobaptists, 237, 300.

Ancyra, synod of, 96.

Anselm, bishop of Lucca, his testimony as to mode, 85.

Antioch, 96.

Antipædobaptists, would be drawn back into the English and American Churches if the rubric as to mode were observed, 28; their false views, 170, 171; their baptism on their own theory invalid, 216; they are included in the term Anabaptists, but are only a part of that class, 237, 238; weak points of their system, 238–264; origin of the immersing Antipædobaptists, 239; Roger Williams and the sects founded in America by him, 240; their baptism given and received by the unbaptized, 240; this their own confession, 243, 244; Smith the founder of the English Antipædobaptist congregations, 241; his baptism and character, 241, 243–247; the Calvinistic Antipædobaptists, their rise, 247, Appendix K.; their baptismal succession, Appendix I.-P.; what all the Antipædobaptist sects lack, 251; their misrepresentations, 253; their rejections of primitive testimony, 254; sources on which they rely, 256; they do not use the Gospel mode, 261; they hand over all infants to the uncovenanted mercies of God, 262; their departure from primitive doctrines and rites, 264; their future, 264; their strength lies not in the point of the subjects, but the mode, 265–268.

Apamea, rubric of, 115.

Apostolical Constitutions, their language on mode, 285.

Apollinarians, 94.

Apostasy in the Church, 105, 168, 169.

Arians, 94.

Arianism, 169.

Aristeri, 94.

Armenian rubric in baptism, 122.

INDEX.

Asseman (or Assemani), J. A., 108, 130, n.
Asseman (or Assemani), J. S., 130, n. 137
Athanasius, St., on mode, 69, 75.
Atto, bishop of Vercelli, 85.
Augustine, St., bishop of Hippo, on mode, 40, 43, 74.
Augustine, archbishop of Canterbury, nature of his demand of the British bishops, 174; his practice, 175, 176.

Baptism (see Compends, Modes, Dipping), rubrics in baptismal offices for infants, 26; infant, 27, 29; mode, 28; clergyman's vows how connected with mode, 29, 30; proselyte, was by total immersion, 31, 32; baptismal rites, see Rites; departure from the ancient mode a cause of schism, 28, 29, 53; of clinics valid, 97; but St. Cyprian thought might be repeated where doubt exists, 65; Christ's, 42–45.
Βαπτίζω, 37; its signification, 37, 151–158, 173, 224; other terms relating to baptism, 38–52, see also versions; late views of, not found in the first 1200 years, 172; trine immersion cannot exist as the general rule unless it be thought modal, 214; this view has been held by some Anglican divines, 216.
Βάπτισμα, its meaning, 172; see Errata.
Βαπτισμός, 156, 172.
Baptisteries, 218, 219; ancient baptismal rites, 218, 219.
Baptists, see Antipædobaptists.
Βάπτω, 157.
Barnabas, 57, 58.
Barrow, 40.
Basil, St., 71; on mode, 71.
Becon, on trine immersion, 184.
Bede, his witness, 176.
Beecher, on baptism, 38.
Bellarmine, on mode, 39, 232.
Beveridge, bishop, on mode, 44, 154, 194.
Bingham, 38, 173, n. 193.
Blake, 176.
Bloomfield, 45.
Blount, his mission, 248, 248–251; Appendix L., M.
Borromeo, Carlo, his view of baptism, 99, 108.
Bourges, council of, on mode, 108.
British Churches, see Church of England.
Bruno, bishop of Segni, 86.

Cabassutins, 233.
Canon L of the Apostles, its teaching and authority, 89, 90, 143, 155, 176.

Canon VII of 1 Constantinople, 94–96, 286.
Calvin, 39, 40, 46, 185, 234.
Carthage, council of, its decision, 99.
Cashel, council of, 178.
Cathari, 94.
Catholic Church (see Councils), 33–94.
Cave, Dr., 192.
Cealichyth, synod of, 177.
Chaldean rubric, 123.
Changes of mode, see Mode.
Christ's baptism.
Chrysostom, St., 76, 77, 91, 155.
Church of England, on mode, 26, 29, 154, 174–187, 265–271; importance of obeying its rubric, id.; her most learned divines in favor of dipping, 188–204.
Church, American, 26, 27, 154; how its rubric differs from that of the English, 205, 206; causes of the change, 205, 206; bishops White and Seabury, on mode, 207, 208; its present position, importance of a due observance of the rubrical preference for dipping, 265–271.
Church of Christ cannot perish, 168–171; error may pervert many within it, 168–171.
Clermont, council of, its decision, 103.
Clinic baptism (see Baptism, Immersion, Trine Immersion, Affusion, Sprinkling, Compends), the rubrics enjoin dipping as often as pouring even in this case, 136; St. Ambrose's statement, 171; on this whole subject see 163–173.
Cologne, council of, on mode, 103.
Comber, Dr., on mode, 193.
Compends, 28; generally approved in necessity, 132–136; date of their rise or first mention, 137; the rubrics which enjoin partial and single immersion with trine affusion, 137–139; see Pouring, Sprinkling, Rubrics, their use, 154; reasons for admitting them as valid baptism, 163–173; used in the Church from ancient times in cases of necessity, 163–173; best grounds upon which to rest their use, 172; a noteworthy preference for immersion in the Prayer Book, 184.
Constantinople, council of, A. D. 381, on mode, 94, 286.
Constantinople, synod of, A. D. 1484, admits the compends, 98.
Controversy, 28.
Conybeare and Howson, 201.
Coptic rubric, in baptism, 120.
Councils, ecumenical, 33–35, 88–97, 133; the only tribunal of the whole Church, 88.
Council, provincial or not ecumenical, 97–108, 133.

318 INDEX.

Cranmer's Catechism, 48, 184.
Creed, Nicæno-Constantinopolitan, the sole creed of the whole Church, 33, 34.
Cyprian, St., on mode, 63–69.
Cyril, St., of Jerusalem, on mode, 69, 108.

De Vicecomes on mode, 185, 232.
Dionysius, the Areopagite, 59, 75.
Dip, exceptions to its general meaning, 37.
Dipping, favored especially by learned Anglicans, 204; difficulties in restoring it, and the remedy for irregularities, 211; favored by the language of the Prayer Book, 184, 211; Greek view in favor of, 220.
De Stourdza, on mode, and against the Latins, 222; preference of the rubric for it, disobeyed in the English Church, 186, 187.
Döllinger, on mode, 232.
Dutch the, their custom in Century XVI, pouring.

Edward VI, catechism of, 49; was dipped, 182; Book I of, 182; Book II of, 183.
Elizabeth, Queen, Latin Prayer Books of, enjoin dipping, 183; but the compends were used, 185.
Error, its triumph always only temporary, 169.
Ethiopic rubric, 121.
Eunuch, the, his baptism, 45.
Eunomians, 94, 95, 159.
Exeter, synod of, on mode, 180.

Fathers, 25–28; value of their historical witness, 33, 34; this different from their opinions, 33, 34, 57–87; for the first 600 years show that trine immersion was the rule, 32; some of it of divine origin and obligation, 32; all deemed immersion a divine command, 32; single immersion approved by Pope Gregory I, but not favored by the rest, 32.
Featley, Dr., on mode, 200.
Filioque, the, 221.
Florence, synod of, 105.
Fonts, 289.
Forbes, bishop, on mode, 200.

Gallican rubrics, 110.
Gangra, synod of, 96.
Gellone, rubric of, 111, 135.
Gennadius of Marseilles, his views, 79.
Gerhard, on mode, 234.
Germanus, Patriarch of Constantinople, 82.

Gothic rubric, 110.
Gladbach, rubric of, 115.
Gratus, synod under, 99.
Greek Church, 26–28; what canons it receives, 90, n. 95, n. 221; provincial synods or synods not ecumenical, 97, 98; its virtues and defects, 105, 140, 220; its rubrics in baptism, 119, 120, 165; on mode against the Latins, 149–221; it received the compends as valid, 165, 166; its idolatry, 167; why its testimony is valuable, 220; on mode, 221, 222; admits the compends in case of necessity, 226–228; the Greeks proper differ from the Russians as to receiving the compends administered by Westerns, 227, 228; regards the single immersion as a compend, 229; see Russo-Greek Church.
Gregory I, bishop of Rome, his views on mode, 81–89; not universally received, 145; condemned by his predecessor Pope Pelagius, and others, 147.
Gregory, a monk, on mode, 105, 106.
Gregory Nyssen, 76.
Gregory, presbyter of Antioch, 80.
Grotius, views of, 38.

Hammond, Dr., on mode, 192.
Haymo, bishop of Halberstadt, 84.
Hermas, 57, 58.
Hildebert of Le Mans, 86.
Hincmar of Rheims, 84, 101.
Hippolytus, 62.
History, ecclesiastical, its teaching as to the compends, 26.
Howson, on mode, 192.
Hugo of St. Victor, 86.
Hymn, ancient baptismal, 113, n.

Ikon or picture worship of the Greeks, 140 (see Greek Church).
Immersion, the rule in the British Churches now, 29, id.; grounds of its preference, chap. IV; was total in the primitive Church, Appendix B.
Immersion, single, not traceable for the first three hundred years, 96; Eunomius its reputed author (see Sozomen, Theodoret), 96; summing up regarding it, 136.
Immersion, trine, 26, 28; was the ordinary use in England, 174, 187; when changed, id., and chap. VII; grounds upon which it rests (see Theodoret, Sozomen, Pelagius, Chrysostom), 89, 96, 155–162, 261, 262; in century XV, 106; ignorance of facts as to mode, 29, 53; symbolism of, 99 and passim; the rule of baptizing, 136; how a later custom differs from it, 139; Greeks in favor of, 220–229; summary of their opinions, id. (see Dipping).

Infant baptism (see Baptism).
Irregularity not always invalidity, 167, 168, Appendix II.
Ivo, bishop of Chartres, 85.

Jeremiah III, Patriarch of Constantinople, admitted affusion as valid, 98.
Jerome, St., 72, 169.
John III, 23, 46.
John Damascene, 81.
John, the Deacon, 84.
Justin Martyr, 59.

Knapp, 234.
Knatchbull, 49, 193.
Kuinoel, 45.

Lanfranc, archbishop of Canterbury, 85.
Laodicea, synod of, its authority, 89, 96; canon 47 of, in favor of the validity of clinic baptism, 97.
Lapide, Cornelius à, 46.
Latins, offices of late date, 131.
    Their writers referred to, 141.
Latin communion on mode, 139–142, 149–151; its learned men testify in favor of trine immersion, 231, &c.
Lawrence, St., 171.
Leo I, bishop of Rome, 79, 99.
Leidrad, bishop of Lyons, 83.
Lightfoot, Dr., 30, 44.
Limoges, rubric of, 116; remarks on it, 117, 135.
Lodi, rubric of, 115.
London, synod of, on mode, 179.
Luther, 39, 234.
Lutheran views of mode, 152–154, 234–236.
Lyndwood, on mode, 181.

Macarius, bishop of Vinnitza, 225.
Macedonians, 94.
Macknight, 45.
Maimonides, 32.
Malabar rubric, 123.
Maldonatus, 39.
Mark, of Ephesus, charges the Latins with error as to mode, 106.
Maronite baptismal office, 129; remarks on, 130; the ancient use was trine immersion, 137.
Martene, 233.

Matthew, St., 18 : 19 ; ancient interpretation of, 91–94 (see Chrysostom, Pelagius, Theodoret).
Maximus of Turin, 79.
Mede, 188.
Menno, on mode, Appendix I.; his baptism, Appendix J., P.
Metrophanes, Critopulus, 227.
Michael Cerularius, 97.
Missal Leofric, 177.
Modern notions of mode contradict the ancient, 99.
Moisac, rubric of, 114, 135.
Moscow, synod of, its decrees, 98.
Muratori, 233.
Mode, changes in, by early heretics; by Eunomius; trine immersion altered to the single in Spain, 144; Bingham's account, 144, 145; the single immersion, according to some, first introduced by Euromians, id.; remarks upon the change in Spain, 146, 147; mode of trine immersion, the use after Pope Gregory I. 147; changes in the mode a local peculiarity, 147, 148; when it ceased to be the rule in one place, 148; a source of discord between the East and the West, 149; false views of, 151–154; trine immersion, grounds for its observance, 155–162 (see all words relating to baptism in index, Compends, Clinics, Immersion, Trine Immersion); in the Church of England, 174–204; Anglican divines in favor of dipping as the general practice, 174–204.

Neocaesarea, synod of, its authority, 89–96; canon 12 of, respecting clinic baptism, 97.
Nestorian rubric, 123.
Newland on mode, 201.
Nice, council of, on mode, 286, Appendix D.
Nismes, council of, 104, 149.
Northumbrians, baptized in the river Glen, 175.
Novatian, baptism of, 171.
Novatians, 94.

Offices, baptismal, 28, 47
Opinions (see Fathers).
Origen, 43.
Orthodox Church (see Greek Church).
Orthodoxie et Papisme, 138.
Osmund, 177, 178; set forth the Use of Salisbury, 177, 178.

Paciaudi, 231.
Palmer, W., 202, 228.

Paris, rubric of, 113.
Paschasius Radbert, 84.
Patriarchates, the four Greek have not approved the opinion of Gregory I, bishop of Rome, 147–149.
Paul, St., 47.
Paul V., pope, office of, 131.
Paulinus, baptizes in England, how, 175.
Pelagius, bishop of Rome, 80, 91, 99, 147, 155.
Peter Chrysologus, 79.
Peter Lombard, 87.
Philaret Niketich, synod held under him decreed the rebaptizing of Latins, 98.
Philoxenus, baptismal office of, 129.
Pictures representing baptism (see Paciaudi, and Appendix F.).
Poictiers, rubric of, 112.
Poole M., 40, 43, 46.
Pouring, 26 (see sprinkling); combined with single, partial immersion, 106.
Prejudices as to mode, 28.
Presbyterians, on mode, 152–154, 234–236.
Proselyte (see Baptism).
Provincial synods (see Councils).
Pulleyn or Pullus, Robert, 86.

Quartodecimans, 94.
Quod Semper, &c., 34 (see Vincent of Lerins).

Rabanus Maurus, 43, 83.
Ravenna, council of, on mode, 104; of local authority only, 105.
Reformed, on mode, 234–236 (see Presbyterians).
Regino, abbot of Prum, 84.
Remigius, 112.
Rigaltius, 38.
Rites of baptism, 51; restoration of all the ancient rites, 52 n.
Rogers, 194.
Roman missal altered, 118.
Romans VI, 3–5, 47.
Rome, trine immersion the custom of, in Century VI, 100; ancient rubrics of, 109, 110, 118.
Rubrics, 25; of Church of England, 26, 185; of the whole Church given, 108 *et seq.*; the law and custom of the whole Church, 133; summing up of their teaching, 134–142; sometimes enjoin immersion for clinics, 134; Syrian and Maronite rubrics, 137; how they differ from the ancient use, 137–142.
Russo-Greek Church, rubrics of, 120 (see Greek Church)

Sabbatians, 94.
Salisbury, Use of, 177; its importance, 178.
Schaff, 235.
Schism, 290, Appendix II., and 168.
Scotch Liturgy of 1637, 183.
Scripture, 28; the source of doctrine, 33; its interpretation, 33, 36, 216; misinterpretations of passages relating to mode, 216; interpretation of, 36-56, and Appendix A.
Seabury, bishop, on mode, 27, 207, 208.
Selden, 189.
Severus, baptismal office of, 128.
Smith, John, founder of the English Antipædobaptists sects, 241; his baptism, 241; his character, 241, 246, 247; baptized himself, 244-246 (see Appendix K.); his confession of this fact, 244-246, Appendix K.
St. Germain des Pres, rubric of, 113.
Sozomen, 78, 95.
Spain (see Toledo, Alcuin, Walafrid Strabo, Gregory I).
Sprinkling (see Pouring), 37.
Stackhouse, 199.
Stephen II, pope, admitted pouring in necessity, 101.
Stuart, Prof., on $\beta\alpha\pi\tau i\zeta\omega$, 157, 158.
Symbols (see Types).
Synods, Latin provincial, 99; their historical testimony, 99; their authority, 99.
Syrian rubrics, 123-129, 138-142.

Taylor, Bishop Jeremy, on $\beta\alpha\pi\tau i\zeta\omega$, 189, 191; on modes, 39, 44, 189.
Terms expressive of baptism, 38.
Tertullian, 60-62, 108, 155.
Tetradites, 94.
Theodore, archbishop of Canterbury, enjoined trine immersion, 176.
Theodoret, 78, 91, 95, 155.
Theodulphus, 83.
Thomas Aquinas, on baptism, 141, 150, 151, 233.
Toledo, Council IV of, 81, 89, 100, 148.
Towerson, Dr., on $\beta\alpha\pi\tau i\zeta\omega$, 39; on mode, 194.
Tradition, how the term was used in the early Church, 159-162.
Trent, synod of, 107; catechism of, on baptism, 107; opposed to the primitive Church belief.
Tribur, council of, 102.
Trine immersion (see Immersion), grounded by the early Church upon Holy Writ, 155, 156; examination of their belief, 155-162.
Trower, bishop, 50, 155.

Tunkers, their baptism began by one man, unbaptized on their own theory, dipping another unbaptized man, Appendix O., P.
Tyndale, his statement as to the mode in England in Century XVI, 184.
Types of baptism, mistakes concerning, 87.

Usher, archbishop; 154, 189.

Versions, ancient, 54–56.
Vienne, rubric of, 116.
Vincent of Lerins, 154.

Walafrid Strabo, 146, 172.
Walker, 194.
Wall, Dr., 27 n., 40, 173 n., 184–186, 198.
Waterland, 199.
West, the, retained for a long time the ancient mode.
Wheatley, Dr., 200.
Whitby, Dr., 51; favored dipping as the rule, 51.
White, bishop, on mode, 27, 154, 206, 208.
Williams, Rev. Isaac, 203.
Williams, Roger, his views, 239; Mrs. Scott's influence upon him, 239; his baptism, 240; its absurdity, 241; his own frank confession of its nullity, 242; his belief as to baptism, 242.
Wilson, bishop, 201.
Worcester, synod of, orders trine immersion always, 148, 179.
Worms, a council of, orders single immersion, 102, 148; why, 102, 148.
Wulfred, archbishop of Canterbury, presided in a synod which enjoined trine immersion, 177.

Zacharias, pope, 100.
Zeno, bishop of Verona, 76.

www.ingramcontent.com/pod-product-compliance
Lightning Source LLC
Chambersburg PA
CBHW031903220426
43663CB00006B/745